CORRECTION SYMBOLS

Ab	17	Improper abbreviation
Ad	4	Improper use of adjective or adverb
Agr	8	Error in agreement
Appr	42	Inappropriate level of diction
Awk	14	Awkward construction
Ca	2	Faulty pronoun case
CF	7	Comma fault
Comp	13	Faulty or incomplete comparison
CS	7	Comma splice
Dgl	12	Dangling construction
Dir	41	Indirectness, redundancy, weakening repetition
Emp	36	Lack of needed emphasis
End P	19	Faulty end punctuation
Ex	40	Inexact word
Frag	6	Unacceptance sentence fragment
FS	7	Fused (run-together) sentence
Glos	43	Check glossary
Gr	1-5	Faulty grammar
Int P	20-25	Faulty internal punctuation
K	14	Awkward construction
Log	37	Faulty logic
Mis Pt	11	Misplaced part
Mix	10	Mixed construction

MS	15	Improper manuscript form
Nos	16	Error in use of numbers
Obsc	14	Obscure construction
Om	13	Careless omission, incomplete construction
P	19-30	Error in punctuation
¶ Coh	32c-d	Paragraph lacks coherence
¶ Con	32h	Paragraph lacks consistent tone
¶ Dev	32e-g	Paragraph is poorly or inadequately developed
¶ Un	32a-b	Paragraph lacks unity
‖	35	Faulty parallelism
Plan	31	Paper is poorly planned
PV	10	Shift in point of view
Q	26	Faulty punctuation of quoted material
Ref	9	Faulty pronoun reference
S	6-14	Poor sentence structure
Sp	44	Error in spelling
Sub	33	Poor subordination
Syl	18	Improper division of word
T	3	Wrong tense of verb
Var	34	Sentence structure lacks variety
Word P	27-30	Faulty word punctuation
X		Obvious error
?		Is this right? Do you mean this?

PROOFREADERS' MARKS

℘	Delete	
(℘)	Delete and close up	
⌒	Close up	
#	Insert space	
stet	Let it stand (i.e., the ~~crossed out~~ material above the dots)	
¶	Begin a new paragraph	
no ¶	Run two paragraphs together	
(SP)	Spell out (e.g., 20 ft.)	
tr	Transpose	
lc	Lowercase a Capital letter	
cap	capitalize a lowercase letter	
o/	Correct an error	
⌃	Superior number	
⌄	Inferior number	

∧	Caret (placed within the text to indicate the point at which a marginal addition to be inserted)	
⊙	Period	
⌃	Comma	
:/	Colon	
;/	Semicolon	
∛/	Apostrophe or single quotation mark	
❝/❞	Quotation marks	
?/	Question mark	
!/	Exclamation point	
=	Hyphen	
⊥/M	Dash	
(/)	Parentheses	
[/]	Brackets	

PRENTICE-HALL, INC., Englewood Cliffs, N.J.

FIFTH EDITION

Prentice-Hall
Handbook for Writers

Glenn Leggett
Grinnell College

C. David Mead
Michigan State University

William Charvat
Late of Ohio State University

Design by Walter Behnke

Prentice-Hall International, Inc., *London*
Prentice-Hall of Australia, Pty. Ltd., *Sydney*
Prentice-Hall of Canada, Ltd., *Toronto*
Prentice-Hall of India Pvt. Ltd., *New Delhi*
Prentice-Hall of Japan, Inc., *Tokyo*

Current printing (last number):
10 9 8 7 6 5 4 3 2

13-695718-8

Preface

*T*he *Prentice-Hall Handbook* is both a reference work for the individual writer and a text for class use. As a summary of grammatical usage and elementary rhetoric, it provides the essentials of clear writing. Its format provides the student with a convenient reference tool for both the preparation and the review of his written work. It provides the instructor assistance in reading papers, allowing him to direct attention readily to specific essentials. Ample illustrations and exercises provide ready help in study, review, or class discussion.

Throughout the book the emphasis is on the practical problems the student needs to consider when he is writing. The introductions to the main divisions are designed to explain many of the basic assumptions and principles underlying the standards of writing— to make clear why most of the rules of writing are necessary.

The Introduction and Sections 1–5 lay the groundwork of language and grammar. The Introduction sketches the growth of the language to its present character and discusses the standards of good English. "Grammar" (Sections 1–5) outlines basic materials— the structure of sentences, parts of speech, case, tense and principal parts, and so forth. "Basic Sentence Faults" (Sections 6–14) reviews the recurrent problems in sentence construction which most seriously interfere with clarity and effectiveness—fragments and comma splices, misplaced and dangling constructions, shifts, and faulty reference and agreement.

"Manuscript Mechanics" (Sections 15–18) and "Punctuation" (Sections 19–30) describe the conventions of manuscript form and of punctuation, and the principles upon which those conventions rest. "Manuscript Mechanics" outlines the conventions of manuscript form, of writing numbers, of using abbreviations, and of word division (syllabication). "Punctuation" clarifies basic principles by dividing the problems into those of end punctuation (Section 19), internal punctuation (Sections 20–25), and word punctuation (Sections 27–30). Throughout, the emphasis is upon the understanding and solution of persistent problems.

Sections 31–44 turn from the more elementary problems of grammar, punctuation, and mechanics to the basic rhetorical questions of writing, the questions of skill and effectiveness in building and using well the writer's resources as opposed to the questions of correctness and clarity. "Larger Elements" (Sections 31–32) discusses the planning and organization of the complete paper and the structure of paragraphs. "Effective Sentences" (Sections 33–36) describes the principles of rhetorically sound sentences, from the elementary one of subordination to the more subtle one of emphasis. "Logic" (Section 37) discusses briefly how illogical thinking interferes with clear and honest communication. Information on dictionaries and on ways of improving vocabulary appears in the first two sections (38–39) under "Words." The last sections under "Words" (40–44) discuss the three principles of word choice (exactness, directness, appropriateness), include a glossary of troublesome words, and provide both exhortation and practical help for poor spellers.

The remaining sections of the *Handbook* deal with special matters. "The Library" (Section 45) describes the organization of a library and its facilities for research. "The Research Paper" (Section 46) gives instruction on research technique and provides a facsimile paper, with comment and analysis. Section 47 discusses the principles of summarizing, or *précis*-writing. Section 48, the last, is an index to grammatical terms.

The *Handbook* is designed particularly to be a useful and easy reference guide in the preparation, correction, and revision of papers. It classifies the standards and conventions of writing and provides reference to them in three ways: (1) through a full index, (2) through a detailed table of contents, and (3) through the charts on the endpapers of the book. Each major rule is given a number and a symbol, and each subrule is designated by the number of the major rule plus a letter (5a, 16b, 22c, etc.). Thus in writing a paper the student may readily check any specific convention about which he is doubtful. The instructor, in reading papers, may conveniently call attention to a specific convention or to general principles by using either numbers or symbols, so that the student may refer quickly to the proper section of the *Handbook*.

For an illustration of this procedure, consider the two copies of the specimen paper on the next pages. Specimen A shows the paper after it had been marked with *Handbook* numbers by an instructor. Specimen B shows the paper after it had been revised by the writer.

Specimen Paper A

THE IDEAL EDUCATION   ⟨31b⟩

More than ever before, a good education is required if one is
going to seek the fortunes of opportunity. The past few years college ⟨13a⟩
enrollments have been increasing steadily because people are realizing
the importance of higher education. The best jobs are held by people
who have an advanced education, therefore the value of education can- ⟨7a⟩
not be stressed too much.

⟨12b⟩   In choosing a college to enter, the differences of colleges must
be considered. For instance, a student considering Normal State must
⟨44a⟩ realise that this university has many thousands of students. When a
student comes to State, he feels as though he is coming to live in a
⟨26e⟩ new town. Right away he finds that he is on his "own." He feels that
high school was more like kindergarten. The college with a small enrollment is more compact, which helps the new student considerably at ⟨9c⟩
⟨37b⟩ first. He always receives more personnel attention from the faculty ⟨44d⟩
than he would at a college as large as Normal St. ⟨17b⟩

⟨10b⟩   Now that we have seen the big differences between large and small
universities, you probably see that there are advantageous aspects to ⟨41a⟩
both or they would not be in existence. At Normal State the student
⟨44d⟩ sacrifices personnel attention for the better equipment he has to work
with. At a small college the situation is reversed. Irregardless, the ⟨41c⟩
fact remains that the student coming from high school is facing a new
situation and needs guidance in many cases. ⟨41a⟩

viii

A Small College or a Large University?

THE IDEAL EDUCATION ~~31b~~

More than ever before, a good education is required if one is going to seek the fortunes of opportunity. *In* The past few years college 13a enrollments have been increasing steadily because people are realizing the importance of higher education. *Because* The best jobs are held by people who have an advanced education, ~~therefore~~ the value of education cannot be stressed too much. 7a

12b In choosing a college to enter, *one must consider* the differences. ~~of colleges must be considered.~~ For instance, a student considering Normal State must 44a *realize* ~~realize~~ that this university has many thousands of students. When a student comes to State, he feels as though he is coming to live in a 26e new town. Right away he finds that he is on his "own." He feels that high school was more like kindergarten. The college with a small enrollment is more compact, *a circumstance* which helps the new student considerably at 9c 37b first. He ~~always~~ *usually* receives more ~~personnel~~ *personal* attention from the faculty 44d than he would at a college as large as Normal ~~St~~ *State.* 17b

10b Now that we have seen the big differences between large and small universities, ~~you~~ *we* probably see that there are ~~advantageous aspects~~ *advantages* to 41a both or they would not be in existence. At Normal State the student 44d sacrifices ~~personnel~~ *personal* attention for the better equipment he has to work with. At a small college the situation is reversed. ~~Irregardless~~ *Regardless*, the 41c fact remains that the student coming from high school is facing a new situation and need*s* guidance. *may* ~~in many cases~~ 41a

Acknowledgments

For suggesting ways to improve the fourth edition of the *Handbook for Writers,* we are grateful to many persons, but especially to Helen Barnes, Pasadena City College; H. Alan Dirlam, State University of New York Agricultural and Technical College at Alfred; Jack Franzetti, St. John's University, Jamaica, N. Y.; Frederick Harrison, Portland State College; Grace T. Kitchens, Georgia State College; James Mason, Indiana State University; Lucretia Parlin, Modesto Junior College; Donald C. Rigg, Broward Junior College; Joseph B. Roberts, Jr., Troy State University; and R. B. Thomas, Lamar State College of Technology. In addition, particular credit is due Richard S. Beal, Boston University.

Special thanks are due to Miss Francesca Tillona, Boston University, for help in revising the exercises, and to both Miss Tillona and Mrs. Mary Leonard for assistance in revising the material on the research paper. We are also grateful to Mrs. Norma Olmer for help in typing portions of the manuscript.

In addition, we thank the staff of Prentice-Hall, Inc., especially Cecil Yarbrough for his many suggestions as well as for his constant patience and guidance.

Throughout the *Handbook* we have quoted from copyrighted material, and we are grateful to the copyright holders who gave their permission for its use. Quotations are from the following works:

Frederick Lewis Allen, *Only Yesterday* (Harper & Brothers, 1931). By permission of Harper and Row, Publishers.

Jacques Barzun, *Teacher in America.* By permission of Atlantic-Little, Brown and Company.

Monroe C. Beardsley, *Practical Logic.* Copyright 1950 by Prentice-Hall, Inc.

Isaiah Berlin, *Mr. Churchill in 1940.* By permission of the author and John Murray (Publishers) Ltd.

Pierre Berton, *The Klondike Fever* (Alfred A. Knopf, Inc., 1958).

Newman and Genevieve Birk, *Understanding and Using English.* By permission of The Odyssey Press, Inc.

Crane Brinton, *Ideas and Men.* Copyright 1950 by Prentice-Hall, Inc.

Erich Fromm, *Man for Himself.* By permission of Holt, Rinehart and Winston, Inc.

Alice Glasgow, *Sheridan of Drury Lane.* By permission of J. B. Lippincott Company.

Eric F. Goldman, *The Crucial Decade and After: America, 1945–60.* By permission of Alfred A. Knopf, Inc.

A. Whitney Griswold, *Liberal Education and the Democratic Ideal.* By permission of Yale University Press.

Edith Hamilton, *The Greek Way.* Copyright 1930, 1943 by W. W. Norton and Company, Inc.; renewed 1958 by Edith Hamilton. By permission of the publisher.

Harlan Hatcher, *Lake Erie.* Copyright 1945. By permission of Bobbs-Merrill Company, Inc.

Ernest Hemingway, "Big Two-Hearted River," from *In Our Time;* and *A Farewell to Arms.* By permission of Charles Scribner's Sons.

W. H. Ittelson and F. P. Kilpatrick, "Experiments in Perception," *Scientific American,* August 1951.

D. C. Jarvis, *Folk Medicine.* Copyright © 1958 by D. C. Jarvis. By permission of Holt, Rinehart and Winston, Inc.

Wendell Johnson, "You Can't Write Writing." Reprinted from *Language, Meaning, and Maturity,* ed. S. I. Hayakawa, by permission of Mr. Hayakawa.

Okakura Kakuzo, *The Book of Tea.* By permission of Charles E. Tuttle Company.

Donald Keene, *Japanese Literature.* By permission of Grove Press, Inc.

Murray Kempton, "The March on Washington," *New Republic,* September 14, 1963.

Elaine Kendall, "An Open Letter to the Corner Grocer," *Harper's* Magazine, December 1960. By permission of the author, Harper & Brothers, and The Sterling Lord Agency.

George F. Kennan, "Training for Statesmanship," *The Atlantic,* May, 1953.

Joseph Wood Krutch, *The Desert Year,* copyright 1952, used by permission of William Sloane Associates, Inc.; *Human Nature and the Human Condition,* © copyright 1959 by Joseph Wood Krutch, used by permission of Random House, Inc.; "Should We Bring Literature to Children, or Children to Literature?" *New York Herald Tribune Book Review,* July 22, 1951, © copyright 1951 by New York Herald Tribune, Inc., used by permission of the author and the publisher.

Susanne K. Langer, "The Lord of Creation," *Fortune,* January 1944. Copyright 1944 by Time, Inc.

D. H. Lawrence, *Sons and Lovers.* By permission of Mrs. Frieda Lawrence, William Heinemann Ltd., and The Viking Press, Inc.

W. J. Lederer, *All the Ships at Sea.* Copyright 1950. By permission of William Sloane Associates, Inc.

Henry S. Leonard, *Principles of Right Reason.* By permission of Holt, Rinehart and Winston, Inc.

Deems Taylor, *Of Men and Music.* By permission of Simon and Schuster, Inc.

James Thurber, "There's an Owl in My Room" and "Something to Say," from *The Middle-Aged Man on the Flying Trapeze.* By permission of the author and *The New Yorker.*

H..W. Troyer, ed., *Five Travel Scripts.* By permission of Columbia University Press.

Mark Twain, *Life on the Mississippi.* By permission of Harper & Brothers.

Hendrik Willem Van Loon, *Van Loon's Geography.* By permission of Simon and Schuster, Inc.

Paul Velde, "Psychedelics: You Can't Bring the Universe Home," *The Village Voice,* October 6, 1966.

Gerald Weales, "The Bogart Vogue," *Commonweal,* March 11, 1966.

E. B. White, *One Man's Meat.* By permission of Harper & Brothers.

Leslie A. White, *The Science of Culture.* By permission of Farrar, Straus and Giroux, Inc.

A. N. Whitehead, *The Aims of Education,* copyright 1929; *Science and the Modern World,* copyright 1925. By permission of The Macmillan Company.

Benjamin Lee Whorf, "Language, Mind, and Reality," *Theosophist,* April 1942. By permission of the Theosophical Publishing House.

Thomas Wolfe, *Look Homeward, Angel.* By permission of Charles Scribner's Sons.

Contents

Blot out, correct, insert, refine,
Enlarge, diminish, interline;
Be mindful, when invention fails,
To scratch your head, and bite your nails.

—JONATHAN SWIFT

Introduction

All life therefore comes back to the question of our speech, the
medium through which we communicate with each other; for all
life comes back to the question of our relations with one another.
— HENRY JAMES, *The Question of Our Speech*

The origin and growth of English.

All languages change constantly, and English is no exception. The language we speak and write today is the creation of all generations that have gone before us, and we in turn help create the English of future generations. The most obvious kind of change occurs in vocabulary. A glance at a drugstore counter is enough to remind us that a decade ago *Compose, Contac,* and *Excedrin* were uncoined names for unborn products of our pill-happy age. But language changes in more complex and subtle ways also. We have our own opinion of the status of the man who says "She won't never do nothing." But Shakespeare's *nor this is not my nose neither* was good Elizabethan English; and when Chaucer wanted to be emphatic about the perfection of his knight, it was perfectly natural for him to say that *He nevere yet no vileynye ne sayde.* Even the sounds of language change. For Shakespeare, *deserts* rhymed with *parts, reason* sounded much like our *raisin,* the vowels of *face* and *glass* were much the same, and the *l* in such words as *would* and *should* was pronounced; and for Dryden and Pope, *join* rhymed with *line,* and *seas* with *surveys.*

Few of us realize that English is basically a Germanic language, descended from the language of the Germanic tribes (the Angles, Saxons, and Jutes) who invaded the British Isles in the fifth and sixth centuries A.D. Some of the surviving specimens of this language —now called Old English—hardly seem like English at all. The following sentence is taken from King Alfred's preface to his translation of a work entitled *Pastoral Care.* He is writing in the latter part of the ninth century and is talking about the fact that very little of the earlier learning in England, before his own troubled times, had been translated into English.

Ða ic þa ðis eall gemunde   ða wundrade ic swiðe swiðe
When I then this all remembered, then wondered I exceedingly

þara godena wiotona þe   giu   wæron   giond   Angelcynn ond
of the good wise men who formerly were throughout England, and

þa bec ealla be fullan geliorned hæfdon, þaet hie hiora þa
the books all completely learned had, that they of them then

nænne dæl noldon   on hiora agen geðiode wendan.
no   part did not wish into their own language to turn.

2

In the more than 1,000 years since that sentence was written, English has clearly altered immensely. Its vocabulary, particularly, has been continuously enriched and modified by external influences. Even before the time of King Alfred, the coming of Christianity had left its Latin mark in such words as *angel, candle, priest, school,* and many others. The Danes, who repeatedly attacked their Germanic cousins from the eighth century until the eleventh, left their imprint on the language. The evidence survives in such place names as those ending in -*by* and -*thorp,* in such common nouns and adjectives as *skull, skin, sky, anger, root, ill,* and *happy,* and even in such basic words as the pronouns *they, them,* and *their,* all of which supplanted earlier words of Germanic origin.

But the first really great growth and change in English vocabulary came after 1066 when William, then Duke of Normandy, made good his claim to the English throne at the Battle of Hastings. For several centuries thereafter the rulers of England were kings whose native language was French. Though English continued to be spoken by the common people, French became the language of the law, of the court, and of the upper classes. For a century at least it was the only language that was written, except Latin, which continued to be the language of learning and of the church. Even after French ceased to be the native language of anyone in England, it remained the language of fashion, the second language of the cultivated and educated classes. Thus French words continued to pour into the English vocabulary long after French rule was a thing of the past.

The borrowed vocabulary touched almost every corner of life: fashion, dress, and social life (*gown, veil, satin, dance, conversation*); court, government, and legal procedures (*tax, parliament, liberty, mayor, justice, jury, fraud*); the church (*prayer, clergy, religion, faith*); war (*battle, soldier, lieutenant, besiege*); the arts (*painting, beauty, cathedral, poet, tragedy, preface, paper, geometry, surgeon*). In addition to such classifiable groups of words, an endless variety of common words of all kinds came into use from the French: *very, age, gentle, final, flower, sure, surprise.* The lists could be extended by the thousands, and the borrowing process continued for four centuries until by 1500 many English speakers surely must have known more French than English words. That the proportion of French words in today's English remains high is clear from the large number of typical words listed above which we would find indispensable.

Yet in spite of this almost overwhelming influx of French words, English remained essentially English, and by the latter half of the fourteenth century the law courts and Parliament returned to the use of English for the conduct of their business. More important, writers such as Chaucer, Langland, and Malory chose to write in English, and under the influence of John Wyclif the Bible was translated into English for the first time since the Old English period. By 1400, the time of Chaucer's death, not only was English established as the language of the land, but also the English spoken in London—by now the largest commercial center and seaport of the country, as well as the meeting place of Parliament and the center of government—was rapidly becoming the standard.

In another century, by 1500, English was firmly established, recognizably modern in a great many respects, and entering upon the period of Modern English. But the great wave of classical influence that swept English culture and thought during the sixteenth and seventeenth century Renaissance exerted another strong influence upon the language. Perhaps attuned to the habit of borrowing by their long contact with French, Englishmen borrowed with almost greater readiness from the Latin and Greek which they came to respect so highly and study so avidly. Thousands upon thousands of classical words flooded the vocabulary, until Sir Thomas Browne complained in the early seventeenth century that "if elegancy still proceedeth . . . we shall, within a few years, be fain to learn Latin to understand English." There is no way of estimating the total number of words borrowed, though the estimate of one scholar that English took over fully a quarter of the entire Latin vocabulary seems a reasonable one. A random selection of a few words that seem vital today might contain *industry, maturity, admiration, education, insane, emancipate, exist, extract, confidence, anticipate, illustrate, multiply, benefit, paragraph, contradict,* and *dedicate.*

The kinds of change in English at which we have been glancing have the excitement of history. They are largely the story of how invasion and conquest, shifting political fortunes, and changing patterns of civilization and culture have molded our language. But they do not touch upon the deeper internal changes that alter the very shape of language over long periods of time and that, like the external changes, go on continuously, sometimes rapidly, sometimes slowly, depending upon external events. These changes are more complicated to explain, but knowing a little about them can help a good deal in understanding some important things about our language.

We can learn a good deal by looking briefly at some selections taken from earlier periods of English. Let us first go back nearly a thousand years and look at a familiar selection as it would have appeared to our Germanic forefathers about 1000 A.D. The Lord's

Prayer is convenient because, since we already know it, it requires no translation.

Fæder ure þu þe eart on heofonum, si þin nama gehalgod. Tobecume þin rice. Gewurþe ðin willa on eorðan swa on heofonum. Urne gedæghwamlican hlaf syle us to dæg. And forgyf us urne gyltas swa swa we forgyfað urum gyltendum. And ne gelæd þu us on costunge, ac alys us of yfele.

Some of the differences between this and Modern English are simply differences in spelling. The letters þ and ð represent the sounds we spell *th*. The digraph æ represents a sound about like the *a* in *hat*. Generally, Old English spelling was much more phonetic than ours; that is, there were few if any silent letters. Differences in sound are difficult to describe briefly, but we can note as examples that the first vowel sound of *ure*, which is the modern *our*, was pronounced like the vowel of *too*, and that the sound spelled *y*, a sound we no longer have, is something like a short *i* pronounced with the lips rounded.

Neither differences in spelling nor those in sound are nearly as important for us as differences in the forms of words and in word order. *Ure, urne,* and *urum,* for example, are all different case forms of our word *our*. Similarly, such endings as *-um, -an,* and *-as,* which appear on *heofonum (heaven), gyltendum (guilt-doers), eorðan (earth),* and *gyltas (guilts),* are case endings of nouns. The *-að* that appears at the end of *forgyfað (forgive)* is a conjugational ending indicating the third person plural form of the verb.

In vocabulary this particular passage does not seem as far removed from Modern English as other earlier and less familiar passages might. With a little effort, we can see our *heaven* in *heofonum,* our *hallowed* in *gehalgod.* Our *become* is contained within *tobecume. Alys,* which meant *loosen* or *release,* is related to our words *lose* and *loose.* Perhaps the only words in the passage that have left no trace on today's vocabulary are *costunge,* for which we have substituted the Latin borrowing *temptation,* and *rice,* which we now translate *kingdom,* though many of us know its German cognate *Reich* in other contexts. Two other words, *hlaf* and *syle,* we still have, though their meanings are changed: *hlaf* is our word *loaf,* which we use only for bread shaped in a special way, and *syle* is our *sell,* the connotation of which today makes it highly inappropriate to a prayer.

Closely associated with the greater number of inflectional endings in Old English is the freer word order, which strikes us as

5

being different from ours. *Father our, be thy name hallowed, our daily bread give us,* and *not lead thou us in temptation* are the major examples in the selection above. A single sentence from the preface to King Alfred's *Anglo-Saxon Chronicle,* written in the latter part of the ninth century, will illustrate more strikingly the differences between Old English and Modern English word order:

Ða gemette hie Æþelwulf aldorman on Englafelda, ond him þær
Then met them Aethelwulf alderman in Englefield, and them there

wiþ gefeaht ond sige nam.
against fought and victory won.

The number of inflectional endings and what seems to us a higgledy-piggledy word order go hand in hand. Every language must have ways of showing what relationships the speaker or writer intends among the words he puts together. One of the major differences between Old English and Modern English is simply that our ancestors depended heavily on inflections to show relationships among words, where we depend mainly on word order. When we discuss grammar later we shall see that it is important to understand this difference if we are to manage our own language well.

Let us now look quickly at our gospel selection as it appears about four hundred years later, in the translation of John Wyclif:

Oure fadir that art in heuenes, halwid be thi name; Thu kyngdom cumme to; be thi wille don as in heuen and in erthe; ȝif to vs this day oure breed ouer other substance; And forȝeue to vs oure dettis, as we forȝeue to oure dettours; And leede vs nat in to temtacioun, but delyuere vs for yuel.

Of course we still notice differences between this and the version we know. The letter ȝ is strange to us. This sometimes represents the sound we usually spell with a *y* in such words as *young,* and sometimes another sound like that in Modern German *Nacht.* The letter *v* sometimes occurs where we would use *u,* and *u* where we would use *v; i* and *y* seem almost interchangeable.

Some words continue to have endings that are completely gone in Modern English: *-e* in *oure,* and *-es* in *heuenes,* for example; but these are few compared to the number in our Old English version. Word order, though not always entirely familiar, seems unusual only in one or two places. The greatest difference is perhaps in the words we call prepositions—*as in heuen, forȝeue to us, delyuere us for yuel.* In spite of these differences between Wyclif's language and ours, clearly the language has changed enormously in the four hundred years that separate John Wyclif from the Old English translator whose handiwork we examined above.

The following selections, arranged chronologically, will give us some idea of English as it continued to grow and change from the time of Wyclif to the late sixteenth century:

> But now, if so be that dignytees and poweris be yyven to gode men, the whiche thyng is full selde, what aggreable thygnes is there in tho dignytees or power but oonly the goodnesse of folk that usen them?
> —CHAUCER, from the translation of BOETHIUS, c. 1380

> And so as sir Mordred was at Dovir with hys oste, so came kyng Arthur wyth a greate navy of shyppis and galyes and carykes, and there was sir Mordred redy awayting uppon hys londynge, to lette hys owne fadir to londe uppon the londe that he was kynge over. Than there was launching of greate botis and smale, and full of noble men or armys; and there was muche slaughtir of jantyll knyghtes, and many a full bolde barown was layde full lowe, on both partyes.
> —SIR THOMAS MALORY, from *Morte d'Arthur,* c. 1470

> I late consideringe (moste excellent prince and myne onely redoughted soveraigne lorde) my duetie that I owe to my naturall contray with my faythe also of aliegeaunce and othe . . . I am (as God juge me) violently stered to devulgate or sette fourth some part of my studie, trustynge therby tacquite me of my dueties to God, your hyghnesse, and this my contray.
> —SIR THOMAS ELYOT, from *The Governour,* 1531

> A Proude Man contemneth the companye of hys olde friends, and disdayneth the sight of hys former famyliers, and turneth his face from his wonted acquayntaunce. —HENRY KERTON, *The Mirror of Man's Life,* 1576

By the end of the sixteenth century, English was truly a national language, as the English translation of the Bible in 1611 very well indicates. Among other influences, the introduction of printing into England toward the end of the fifteenth century rapidly increased the number of people who could read and write, thus contributing greatly to the standardization of the language; and the growth of a national spirit in the sixteenth century gave dignity and vigor to the language. But though change since that time has been less dramatic and radical, the language has nonetheless continued to grow in important ways.

Early in the seventeenth century, England began that vital expansion which took its language into all corners of the globe. The language was established firmly in America in that century. Later it became a vital second language in India, and the language of Canada, New Zealand, and Australia. Still later it became an important second language in such countries as Japan and in many of the newer colonies of Africa, which have continued to rely upon it for their common language after their independence. As a result of this expansion, English has become probably the major world language today.

During its expanding contact with other languages, English has continued its free-wheeling habit of borrowing; our vocabulary to-day, therefore, is enlarged by words from many sources besides the French, Latin, and Greek that greatly enriched it earlier. The language has played no favorites in its modern borrowings, draw-ing on Hungarian (*coach, goulash, paprika*); Arabic (*alcohol, assassin, harem*); Hebrew (*kosher, matzo*); East Indian (*bandanna, bungalow, jungle, pajamas, yoga*); Chinese and Japanese (*tea, pongee, chop suey, geisha, kimono, tycoon*); and many others.

The borrowing process continues endlessly into our own day. But in the past hundred years two other developments have had major consequences for English. The first is the rapid development of mass education and the resulting rise in literacy. The second is the rise of science and technology. Both of these developments have had complex effects upon our language and will doubtless continue to exert great influence in the future. Though the effect of the first is difficult to measure, it is dramatically clear that a language which can reach the great majority of its users in print, and an even greater number with the immediacy of radio and television, will develop differently than a language in which writing is addressed to a small and special minority, and in which speech occurs largely in face-to-face daily exchange. The effect of the technological revo-lution and the rapid specialization in many fields of knowledge is clearer. It has given us a burgeoning vocabulary of technical terms ranging from the names of the drugs our doctors prescribe for our daily ills to the almost incredible increase in specialized words in every area from do-it-yourself kits to space-engineering. An interesting and important by-product of the current rapid in-crease in scientific and technical terms, perhaps much more signifi-cant in the long run than we imagine, is that many of them appear in widely various languages with only minor changes in spelling and pronunciation.

Changes in grammar since the sixteenth century, though very minor compared with the great loss of inflections and the accom-panying fixing of word order that came earlier, have continued in Modern English. Since the sixteenth century, word order has become even more fixed. Questions in the form of *Consents he?* and negations in the form of *I say not, I run not* have disappeared, to be replaced by the use of the auxiliary verb *do* as in *Does he consent, I do not say, I do not run.* Verb forms with *be* in the pattern of *He was speaking, We are going, It is being built* have multiplied greatly. In our own immediate period we can observe such changes as the increase in the number of verbs made up of verbs combined with adverbs or prepositions on the pattern of *He looked up the word, He looked over Bill's new house, The fireplace was smoking up the room;* and the increase, at least in some kinds of writing, of nouns as modifiers of other nouns on the pattern of *college student, radio station, mathematics course, ice-cream stand.* Though but a few of the developments of Modern English, these make it clear that change in our language is unending.

The following passages, though less strikingly dissimilar than those we saw earlier, will help make clear that language was hardly static between 1600 and 1900. Many of the differences among these selections are those of idiom or style rather than of grammar, strictly speaking. The distinctions involved are important, but less important for us than the basic fact that the differences are representative of some of the kinds of language change that are continuous.

I had often before this said, that if the Indians should come, I should chuse rather to be killed by them than taken alive but when it came to the tryal my mind changed; their glittering weapons so daunted my spirit, that I chose rather to go along with those (as I may say) ravenous Bears, then that moment to end my dayes; and that I may better declare what happened to me during that grievous Captivity, I shall particularly speak of the severall Removes we had up and down the Wilderness.

—MARY ROWLANDSON, *The Narrative of the Captivity,* c. 1682

About the twelfth year of my age, my Father being abroad, my Mother reproved me for some misconduct, to which I made an Undutifull reply & the next first-day, as I was with my Father returning from Meeting, He told me he understood I had behaved amis to my Mother, and Advised me to be more careful in future.

—JOHN WOOLMAN, *The Journal,* 1756

My elder brothers were all put apprentices to different trades. I was put to the grammar-school at eight years of age, my father intending to devote me, as the tithe of his sons, to the service of the Church. My early readiness in learning to read . . . and the opinion of all his friends, that I should certainly make a good scholar, encouraged him in this purpose of his.   —BENJAMIN FRANKLIN, *The Autobiography,* 1771

To go into solitude, a man needs to retire as much from his chamber as from society. I am not solitary whilst I read and write, though nobody is with me. But if a man would be alone, let him look at the stars. The rays that come from those heavenly worlds will separate between him and what he touches.   —RALPH WALDO EMERSON, *Nature*, 1836

I had stopped in Boston at the Tremont House, which was still one of the first hostelries of the country, and I must have inquired my way to Cambridge there; but I was sceptical of the direction the Cambridge horsecar took when I found it, and I hinted to the driver my anxieties as to why he should be starting east when I had been told that Cambridge was west of Boston.

—WILLIAM DEAN HOWELLS, *Literary Friends and Acquaintances*, 1894

During the eighteenth century, some things occurred which influenced the history of English in a way somewhat different from those we have been looking at. During this period, English grammarians set about trying to standardize and refine English. They did not have much effect on the actual history of our language, but they had a great effect upon our attitudes toward language and our use of it. They prepared dictionaries in an attempt to fix the spellings and meanings of words, and some of them tried to force English into the mold of Latin. Not understanding very well the inevitability of change in language, and believing that all such change was undesirable, they strove hard to stop it. Since they greatly admired Latin, and since Latin was highly inflected, they felt that loss of inflections in English was especially bad. Thus they developed a host of rules to preserve distinctions between *who* and *whom* and other pronoun forms, between the principal parts of verbs such as *begin, began,* and *begun,* and other irregular forms that had come down from earlier, inflected periods of the language but contributed little if anything to clarity any longer. Some of these rules died of neglect. But others won acceptance and were considered vital to "correct" English. Educated speakers and writers, even when they did not in fact observe such rules, subscribed wholeheartedly to the belief that they were important.

Even today a great many users of English feel that the language obeys (or at least ought to obey) a kind of abstract logic instead of doing what it obviously does and must do: follow the actual usage of people who speak and write it. The distaste that purists still feel for split infinitives, for prepositions at the end of sentences, for *Who did you see, It's me,* and so on, grows out of the "eighteenth century" attitude toward English. This attitude has passed into the subconsciousness of many English and American people and makes it difficult to discuss the "standards" of Modern English realistically.

The standards of Modern English.

What do we mean by the STANDARDS of Modern English? Remove from your typewriter the letter you have just written to your best friend. Now write another letter to a man you have never seen who can give you a job you are eager to get. Compare the two letters. In the first, you spoke of the *great job* you are *after*. In the second, the job becomes a *position*. In the first, you were sure you had *the stuff to make a go of it*. In the second, you *assure* the man that you have had *excellent training* which will *enable you to succeed*. In the first you hoped *to get together* with your friend over *Xmas for a blast or two*. In the second, you *suggest* that the *Christmas holidays might provide an opportunity for an interview*.

You might assume that in the second letter you were writing "good" English and that in the first you were writing "poor" English. But it is not so simple as that. Some authorities might even argue that the English in your first letter was better because it was more "natural." The trouble with this argument is that "natural" is a relative term, and really describes the kind of English you were using in both letters. In one letter you were communicating "naturally" with a friend; in the other you were, consciously or not, adjusting your English to a different audience and situation, and being just as "natural." Each is "good" English because it is <u>appropriate</u> to the audience and situation for which it was written.

Good English, in short, varies not only from period to period, as we have seen in our glance at the history of the language, but also from area to area, from social group to social group, and from one kind of speaking and writing to another. The most important kinds of variation are those between STANDARD and NONSTANDARD English and between FORMAL and INFORMAL English. These differences are sometimes referred to as differences between CULTURAL LEVELS and FUNCTIONAL VARIETIES of English.

The distinction between standard and nonstandard English rests on the cultural status (or ambitions) of the people using the language.* STANDARD ENGLISH describes the speaking and writing of cultivated people. It is the variety of spoken and written language which enjoys cultural prestige, and which is the medium of education, journalism, and literature. Competence in its use is

---

*The words *acceptable* and *unacceptable* are often equated with *standard* and *nonstandard*, respectively. The equation is frequently accurate, but before assuming that *nonstandard* English is always unacceptable, we ought to ask "unacceptable to whom?"

necessary for advancement in many occupations. NONSTANDARD ENGLISH describes the writing and speaking habits of the uncultivated. Nonstandard speakers usually have had little formal education and are normally employed in jobs that require little or no writing. Here are some illustrations of standard and nonstandard English:

STANDARD

Today, as never before, the sky is menacing. Things seen indifferently last century by the wandering lamplighter now trouble a generation that has grown up to the wail of air-raid sirens and the ominous expectation that the roof may fall at any moment. Even in daytime, reflected light on a floating dandelion seed, or a spider riding a wisp of gossamer in the sun's eye, can bring excited questions from the novice unused to estimating the distance or nature of aerial objects.

—LOREN EISELEY, "Little Men and Flying Saucers," 1956

Society never advances. It recedes as fast on one side as it gains on the other. It undergoes continual changes; it is barbarous, it is civilized, it is christianized, it is rich, it is scientific; but this change is not amelioration. For everything that is given something is taken. Society acquires new arts and loses old instincts. What a contrast between the well-clad, reading, writing, thinking American, with a watch, a pencil and a bill of exchange in his pocket, and the naked New Zealander, whose property is a club, a spear, a mat, and an undivided twentieth of a shed to sleep under! But compare the health of the two men and you shall see that the white man has lost his aboriginal strength. If the traveller tell us truly, strike the savage with a broad-axe and in a day or two the flesh shall unite and heal as if you struck the blow into soft pitch, and the same blow shall send the white to his grave.

—R. W. EMERSON, "Self-Reliance," 1841

NONSTANDARD

So I said to him, I said, "You was dead wrong thinking you'd get away with that dough. We had you spotted from the beginning, smart boy. And we was sure when we seen you put that roll in your pocket." So I starts to move in on him, easy-like, and all at oncet he grabs in his pocket and comes out with a gun. "Don't nobody move," he yells, and starts for the door. But he trips over his own big feet and goes down, hard. Right then I lets him have it with five quick shots. He was the deadest doublecrosser you ever seen.

By FUNCTIONAL VARIETIES, on the other hand, we refer to different uses or functions of language within standard English. The chief functional varieties are INFORMAL and FORMAL. In broadest terms, INFORMAL describes the English of conversation, of private correspondence, of ordinary everyday writing and speaking. FORMAL describes the language of books and articles on serious subjects, of reports in industry, business, and science, most legal writing, and literary prose. It is more characteristic of written than of spoken English, but it is found in formal lectures, speeches, and serious discussions. Until a generation or two ago most schoolteachers and textbooks in English recommended formal usage. Formal English was equated with standard English. Informal English, though obviously then as now the real workaday language of educated people, was suspected of being not quite proper. This state of affairs was unrealistic, and it led some people to assume that only pretentious-sounding English was "good English." Nowadays we recognize that both informal and formal usage are standard English and that neither is necessarily "more correct" than the other. Everything depends on its suitability to audience and situation: appropriateness is the real measure of "good English."

Of course the line between formal and informal is not sharply drawn, and there are wide ranges of degree in each kind of writing. In general, as we approach improvised speech we become more informal. At the extreme of informality is the casual speech of educated people and the kind of writing that attempts to catch the flavor of such speech. At the extreme of formality is careful scientific, scholarly, and legal writing in which the need for exactness is most important. In the examples below, note the more elaborate sentence structure of the more formal selections, their Latinate vocabulary, and their obviously serious purpose. As the examples move toward the informal, note the increasingly relaxed sentences, the everyday vocabulary, and the conversational tone. But if you catch yourself thinking that one is better than the other, remember that the purpose, subject matter, audience, temperament, and hence style of each author are quite different.

FORMAL

An antibiotic is a chemical substance, produced by microorganisms, which has the capacity to inhibit the growth of and even destroy bacteria and other microorganisms. The action of an antibiotic against microorganisms is selective in nature, some organisms being affected and others not at all or only to a limited degree; each antibiotic is thus characterized by a specific antimicrobial spectrum. The selective action of an antibiotic is also manifested against microbial vs. host cells. Antibiotics vary greatly in their physical and chemical properties and in their toxicity to animals. Because of these characteristics, some antibiotics have remarkable chemotherapeutic potentialities and can be used for the control of various microbial infections in man and in animals. —Quoted in SELMAN A. WAKSMAN, *The Actinomycetes and Their Antibiotics*

Dean Donne in the pulpit of old Paul's, holding his audience spellbound still as he reversed his glass of sands after an hour of exposition and application of texts by the light of the church fathers, of mortification for edification, of exhortation that brought tears to the eyes of himself and his hearers, and of analogies born of the study, but sounding of wings— there was a man who should have had wisdom, surely. For if experience can bring it, this was the man. —R. P. T. COFFIN and A. M. WITHERSPOON, "John Donne," in *Seventeenth Century Prose*

INFORMAL

All scientists are not alike. Look at any laboratory or university science department. Professor Able is the kind of man who seizes an idea as a dog seizes a stick, all at once. As he talks you can see him stop short, with the chalk in his fingers, and then almost jump with excitement as the insight grips him. His colleague, Baker, on the other hand, is a man who comes to understand an idea as a worm might understand the same stick, digesting it a little at a time, drawing his conclusions cautiously, and tunneling slowly through it from end to end and back again.

—JOHN RADAR PLATT, "Style in Science"

Of all the common farm operations none is more ticklish than tending a brooder stove. All brooder stoves are whimsical, and some of them are holy terrors. Mine burns coal, and has only a fair record. With its check draft that opens and closes, this stove occupies my dreams from midnight, when I go to bed, until five o'clock, when I get up, pull a shirt and a pair of pants on over my pajamas, and stagger out into the dawn to read the thermometer under the hover and see that my 254 little innocents are properly disposed in a neat circle round their big iron mama.

—E. B. WHITE, *One Man's Meat*

The colossal success of the supermarkets is based upon the fact that nobody, but nobody, can sell you something as well as you can by yourself. As a result, supermarkets now stock clothing, appliances, plastic swimming pools, and small trees. The theory is that if you succumb to an avocado today, tomorrow you may fall for an electronic range or a young poplar. —ELAINE KENDALL, "An Open Letter to the Corner Grocer"

The term COLLOQUIAL is sometimes used in discussing levels and varieties of English. It has sometimes been misunderstood as referring to nonstandard usage, with a suggestion of disreputability. But *colloquial* simply means *spoken*, being related to *eloquent* and *loquacious*. In this sense, it may refer to any spoken English, whether "culturally" standard or nonstandard, whether "functionally" formal or informal. Most students of language, however, use the word to refer to the everyday speech of educated people, and to the kind of writing that has the easy unpretentious vocabulary, the loose constructions, the contractions, and the other characteristics of that speech. Charles Fries, one of the editors of the *American College Dictionary*, defines as colloquial those words and constructions

... whose range of use is primarily that of the polite conversation of cultivated people, of their familiar letters and informal speeches, as distinct from those words and constructions which are common also in formal writing. The usage of our better magazines and of public addresses generally has, during the past generation, moved away from the formal and literary toward the colloquial.

In this sense *colloquial* may be applied to the more informal kinds of style illustrated by the selections from E. B. White and Elaine Kendall above.

The existence of "levels" and "varieties" of English means, then, that there is no absolute standard of correctness. But it does not mean that we can do without standards at all, or that what is good enough for familiar conversation is appropriate for all kinds of communication. It is true that if people were to write as naturally as they talk, they might rid their writing of a great deal of affectation. But it is also true that conversational English depends for much of its force upon the physical presence of the speaker. Personality, gesture, and intonation all contribute to the success of spoken communication.* Written English, on the other hand, whether formal or informal, requires a structure that makes for clarity without the physical presence of the writer. It must communicate through the clarity of its diction and the orderliness of its sentence and paragraph structure and the relative fullness of its detail. In short, the writer must meet certain standards if he is to get his meaning across.

A handbook somewhat arbitrarily classifies standards of "good English" into rules or conventions that cannot always be defended on logical grounds. Rather, they reflect the practices—some old, some new—of English and American writers. Most of these conventions are quite flexible. The rules for punctuation, for instance, permit many variations, and so do the standards for diction and sentence structure and paragraphing. The truth is that the rules of writing represent "typical" or "normal" practices. Skillful writers interpret them very loosely and occasionally ignore those that seem too restrictive for their purposes. For most writers, how-

---

* Let anyone who disagrees test this assertion by arranging for a tape recording of an ordinary argument or discussion—without informing the speakers. The transcript will probably seem absurd and only partly intelligible.

ever, the rules are a discipline and a security. Observing them will not make a writer great, but it will help make his writing clear and orderly. And clarity and order are the marks of all good writing.

Books for reference and further study.

Baugh, Albert C. *A History of the English Language.* 2nd ed. New York: Appleton-Century-Crofts, 1957.

Bryant, Margaret C., ed. *Current American Usage.* New York: Funk and Wagnalls Company, Inc., 1962.

Evans, Bergen and Cornelia. *A Dictionary of Contemporary American Usage.* New York: Random House, 1957.

Fowler, Henry W. *A Dictionary of Modern English Usage.* New York: Oxford University Press, 1926.

Fries, Charles C. *American English Grammar.* New York: Appleton-Century-Crofts, 1940.

Greenough, J. B., and George L. Kittredge. *Words and Their Ways in English Speech.* New York: The Macmillan Company, 1923.

Jespersen, Otto. *Growth and Structure of the English Language.* 9th ed. Garden City, N. Y.: Doubleday & Company, Inc., 1955.

Laird, Charlton. *The Miracle of Language.* New York: World Publishing Co., 1953.

Marckwardt, Albert H. *American English.* New York: Oxford University Press, 1958.

Mathews, Mitford M. *Words: How to Know Them.* New York: Henry Holt and Company, Inc., 1956.

Mencken, H. L. *The American Language: The Fourth Edition and the Two Supplements,* abridged and ed. by Raven I. McDavid, Jr. New York: Alfred A. Knopf, Inc., 1963.

Myers, L. M. *The Roots of Modern English.* Boston: Little, Brown and Company, 1966.

The MLA Style Sheet. Rev. ed. New York: Modern Language Association of America, 1951.

Nicholson, Margaret. *A Dictionary of American-English Usage.* New York: Oxford University Press, 1957.

Partridge, Eric. *A Dictionary of Slang and Unconventional English.* 5th ed. New York: The Macmillan Company, 1961.

Potter, Simeon. *Our Language.* Baltimore: Penguin Books, Inc., 1950.

Pyles, Thomas. *Words and Ways of American English.* New York: Random House, 1952.

Robertson, Stuart, *The Development of Modern English.* 2nd ed., rev. by Frederic G. Cassidy. New York: Prentice-Hall, Inc., 1954.

Summey, George. *American Punctuation.* New York: The Ronald Press, 1949.

The University of Chicago Press. *A Manual of Style.* 12th ed. Chicago: The University of Chicago Press, 1969.

Whitehall, Harold. *Structural Essentials of English.* New York: Harcourt, Brace & Company, Inc., 1956.

Basic

Grammar

= GR

Good grammar is not merely grammar which is free from unconventionalities, or even from the immoralities. It is the triumph of the communication process, the use of words which create in the reader's mind the thing as the writer conceived it; it is a creative act. . . .   —JANET AIKEN, *Commonsense Grammar*

Grammar is a systematic description of the way a language works. A grammarian describes the kinds of individual words that occur in a language, the forms they take, and the ways speakers and writers put them together in meaningful combinations. If his description is a good one, his generalizations will help guide us in using our language more efficiently. We can think of his generalizations as "rules" as long as we are careful to remember that they are statements about the way speakers and writers use the language and not statements about how they ought to use it. It is a grammatical "rule" in English that most nouns form plurals by adding *-s* to the singular. Since we all know this, we are pretty sure that if a person can have *one hackbut,* he could have *two hackbuts,* even though we don't have any idea what a *hackbut* might be. There is nothing either good or bad about this way of forming noun plurals; other languages form them in different ways. But this is the way English does it, and it is a fact—or a "rule"—that if you decide suddenly to try saying *two hackbutera* or *two hackbuti,* people will not understand you even if they do know what a *hackbut* is.

There are several good reasons for studying the grammar of one's language. First, if one begins to see grammar as an overall description of the way one's language works rather than as a set of trivial and only vaguely related details, it is interesting. Language is, after all, the most remarkable and intricate invention of man, and if one can get over being frightened by it and start examining it objectively, it can prove to be at least as interesting as Roman history, abnormal psychology, and rockets, none of which could have existed without it.

Second, an understanding of the basic grammar of our language can give us some useful guidelines for improving our own writing. If we know, for example, that modifying words and word groups in English are tied to the words they modify mostly by position, we are likely to be more careful about writing such confusing sentences as *The short man in the black shoes with the sandy hair knocked on the door* or *While enjoying our hamburgers and coffee, the halfback broke away for his third touchdown.*

Third, a knowledge of basic grammar and grammatical terms is almost indispensable for talking about our writing with those who are trying to help us improve it. An instructor's comment which suggests that we *need to combine simple sentences more frequently, and use phrases and clauses to subordinate less important ideas* won't help us much if we don't know what *simple sentences, phrases, clauses,* and *subordinate* mean. We wouldn't expect to play baseball without knowing a *strike* from a *ball,* poker without knowing a *flush* from a *straight,* or the piano without knowing a *scale* from a *chord* or *pianissimo* from *forte.* No more can we expect to talk about language without knowing a dangling modifier from a finite verb.

The following pages outline some of the details about English grammar which have proven useful to less experienced writers. One basic concept about language may be helpful in keeping these details in perspective. Any language is composed of individual words and of GRAMMATICAL DEVICES for putting them together into larger meaningful combinations. A series of words such as *age, buggy, the, and, horse* is pretty much just a series of isolated words in English. Each word makes sense, but they aren't related to one another in any particular way. But *the horse-and-buggy age* makes a quite different kind of sense; the words have been put together into a meaningful combination. English has several devices for putting words into meaningful combinations, and it is useful to keep these in mind. The three most important are word order, function words, and inflections.

In English, grammatical meaning is determined to a large extent by WORD ORDER. *Blue sky* and *sky blue* mean different things: in the first, *blue* modifies *sky;* in the second, *sky* modifies *blue.* We can see the principle in action in the following:

The thief called the lawyer a liar.
The lawyer called the thief a liar.
The liar called the lawyer a thief.

Our new neighbors bought an old house.
Our old neighbors bought a new house.

FUNCTION WORDS, sometimes called GRAMMATICAL WORDS, are words such as *the, and, but, in, to, at, because,* and *while,* the main use of which is to express relationships among other words. Compare the following:

I am lonely *at* dark.   The cook prepared *a* rich feast.
I am lonely *in the* dark.   The cook prepared *the* rich *a* feast.

INFLECTIONS, less important in Modern English than they were in earlier stages of the language, are changes in the form of words which indicate differences in grammatical relationship. Inflections account for the differences in the following:

The boys walk slowly.   Stop bother*ing* me.
The boy walk*s* slowly.   Stop*s* bother me.

These three grammatical devices—word order, function words, and inflections—are the principal ones we must learn to control if we are to write clearly and effectively.

A distinction is sometimes made between grammar and usage. GRAMMAR, strictly speaking, is concerned with generally applicable principles about a language. USAGE, in contrast, is concerned with alternative choices, particularly with differences between standard and nonstandard English, and between formal and informal English. The differences between *tile floor* and *floor tile, home run* and *run home, tiger tails* and *tiger's tail,* and *he walks* and *he walked* are grammatical differences. On the other hand, the differences between *I saw* and *I seen, he doesn't* and *he don't, he ought to do it* and *he had ought to do it,* and *let me do it* and *leave me do it* are differences between standard and nonstandard English. They identify those persons who use them as educated or uneducated. But they do not mean different things. The differences between them are usage differences rather than grammatical differences. Since this book is concerned with providing guidelines for writing standard English, it is concerned with both grammar and usage. And since many questions of grammar and usage overlap, the two are not set apart sharply.

We can make useful generalizations about some usage differences. It is true, for instance, that, in standard English, verbs almost always agree in number with their subjects, and that the objective case is almost always used for pronouns that are the objects of verbs and prepositions. But a good many matters of usage are not readily reducible to neat "rules." For one thing, writing is slower to change and more orderly than speech. For another, the language an educated person uses in writing differs in a good many rather slight but important ways from the language he uses in casual and hasty conversation. Finally, the habits of language are simply not as regular and logical as we might like them to be.

Speakers of standard English in most sections of the country regularly use *It's me/him/them/us,* for example, but in writing they tend strongly to prefer *It's I/he/they/we.* Standard English allows double negatives of the form *not infrequently* and *not uncommon,* but rejects completely *can't scarcely* and *can't hardly. Anywheres* is sometimes used by educated speakers in some parts of the country, but only *anywhere* appears in written English.

However minor such annoying quirks of our language as these and dozens of others may seem, they are real and important. A college student concerned with acquiring the ability to write as other educated people do must be willing to learn and to observe these differences and to turn to some reference such as this book when in doubt about what forms or words standard English uses. He must also be willing to acquire (if he has not already done so) enough knowledge of the basic grammar of English to be able to judge where difficulties may arise in his writing; enough understanding of English sentences to see how he may work effectively toward greater flexibility in his writing; and enough grammatical terminology to discuss his writing efficiently.

Properly understood and applied, such a knowledge of basic grammar, and of its relation to problems of usage, can be a very useful tool rather than a burdensome collection of trivial and confusing detail.

1 Sentence Sense* = SS

1a Recognizing sentences.

A sentence is grammatically independent and complete. It may contain words that we cannot fully understand unless we check the preceding or succeeding sentence, but it is grammatically self-sufficient even when lifted out of context and made to stand alone.

> Old Dinger's ghost was said to live in the surrounding hills.
> It had been seen several times from the tavern window.

Both sentences are grammatically complete. True, the full meaning of the second sentence depends on our identifying the subject *it* with its antecedent *Old Dinger's ghost* in the first sentence. But the

---

* The grammatical terms used in these sections are defined in the Index to Grammatical Terms, pp. 450–461.

second sentence is structurally independent because the pronoun *it* is an acceptable substitute for *Dinger's ghost*.

The main ingredients of the typical English sentence are a subject and a predicate. Usually the SUBJECT names something or someone; the PREDICATE tells something about the subject. In the simplest sentence form the subject is a noun or a pronoun, and the predicate is a verb, which may be either a single word, or a group of words such as *was going, has been eating, will have finished*.

SUBJECT	VERB
The boys	scurried.
Bugs	bite.
Myrtle	has disappeared.
She	is dancing.

Though sentences as simple as this are relatively rare in mature writing, they show the pattern for all English sentences, no matter how complex. When we think, we think about something; and we think something about that something. When we write, we follow this same pattern.

A great many English sentences have one or two objects or a complement after the verb. An OBJECT is a noun or a pronoun or a group of words serving as one. It indicates something that receives the action of the verb or something that is affected by what the subject does.

SUBJECT	VERB	OBJECT	OBJECT
Dogs	eat		bones.
His wife	bought	him	a dishwasher.
Henry	called	John	a traitor.

Note that all the verbs in these sentences are action words. Such verbs are called TRANSITIVE verbs, meaning that they can pass their action along to their objects.

In another common kind of English sentence, the verb does not indicate action, but merely links the subject with descriptive words that follow the verb. Such verbs are called LINKING verbs, and the words that follow them are COMPLEMENTS, indicating that they complete, or describe, the subject.

SUBJECT	VERB	COMPLEMENT
Napoleon	was	a Frenchman.
She	may become	president.
This book	seems	obscene.
The cloth	felt	soft.

22

As these sentences indicate, the describing word, or complement, in this pattern may be either a noun (*Frenchman, president*) or an adjective (*obscene, soft*).

These three sentence patterns—a subject and a verb; a subject, an action verb, and one or two objects; and a subject, a linking verb, and a complement—are the most important patterns of the English sentence. Three other patterns, though less frequent in writing, are important because they change the usual order and relation of subject and predicate. ~ *not used often —try to advoid*

The first of these is the PASSIVE pattern, in which the object in an active sentence is made the subject.

SUBJECT	PASSIVE VERB
The demonstrators	will be held.
The meat	may have been adulterated.
Fred	was defeated.

Notice that the verb in all such sentences consists of some form of the AUXILIARY or helping verb *be* and the PAST PARTICIPLE.

The second pattern allows us to postpone the subject of a sentence until after the verb by beginning with the EXPLETIVE *there* or *it:*

EXPLETIVE	VERB	COMPLEMENT	SUBJECT
It	is	doubtful	that they will arrive.
There	is		no reply.
There	are		seven students.
There	will be		an opportunity.

The third pattern omits the subject. This is the pattern used for commands (the IMPERATIVE MOOD):

VERB	OBJECT OR COMPLEMENT
Open	the can.
Be	obedient.
Know	thyself.
Keep	calm.

The overwhelming majority of written English sentences follow one of the patterns we have described above. Occasionally, the order of subject and verb is inverted, as in *Happy am I,* or *Up the hill raced John,* but such inversions are relatively infrequent. Questions, which are much less frequent in writing than in speaking, have patterns of their own which are modifications of the basic patterns. The most common kinds of question patterns are those in which the subject and verb are inverted, as in *Will he run?* and those in which a function word precedes the basic pattern, as in *Does he run?* The great variety of English sentences is created not by variety in the basic sentence patterns but by the addition of modifying words and word groups, and by the use of various kinds of word groups in the position of subject and object.

Learning to recognize the subjects and predicates of sentences and to distinguish the verbs and objects or complements within the predicate is the first step in analyzing sentences.

EXERCISE 1a.   Indicate the subjects and verbs in the following sentences by underlining the subject once and the verb twice. Be prepared to indicate which of the basic patterns each sentence follows.

1. The classroom door squeaks.
2. Are you old enough to vote?
3. Not everyone thinks Pop Art is here to stay.
4. The marchers hoisted their signs and fell into line.
5. The dangers of cigarette-smoking have been adequately proven.
6. A dictionary, to be useful, must be used.
7. The streets of most seaside resorts are strangely desolate in winter.
8. Of all the mistakes students make on examinations, misreading directions is the most notable.
9. Even if everyone eligible to vote were registered at the polls, offered a ride to the polls, and fined for not voting, we would still not have a 100 percent turnout at election time.
10. Some students maintain that smoking marijuana helps to counteract the tensions generated by our modern society.
11. Driving along by myself, I suddenly wondered what would happen if a tire went flat.
12. Because they find it increasingly difficult to cope with the bustle of the Western world, many young people are finding refuge in the religions and philosophies of the East.
13. Working too many hours a week while attending college may affect the grades of some students.
14. To write the greatest American novel of all time is probably every English major's secret wish.
15. Allowing students to participate in the college decision-making process may help to bridge the generation gap on the American campus.

1 b   **Recognizing parts of speech.**

One important part of the basic grammar of any language is its word classes, or PARTS OF SPEECH. These are basic categories into which words can be divided, according to their distinctive character. Grammarians can classify words as particular parts of speech in three ways: (1) by their grammatical function, such as subject or modifier; (2) by their grammatical form, such as the distinctive -*s* of most nouns in the plural, or the -*ed* of most verbs in the past tense; (3) by their type of meaning, such as the name of a thing, or the statement of an action.

The class we assign a particular word to may differ according to which kind of classification we use. In such a construction as *the army cannon,* for example, *army* is an adjective if we ask what function it performs (that of modifying *cannon*), but a noun if we ask what form it can take (a plural, *armies*). In *She seemed tired, seemed* is a verb clearly enough if we have defined verbs as words that can form a past tense with -*ed* or the equivalent; but one might question whether *seemed* states an action.

However we divide up the words in English, some will occur as more than one part of speech. A great number of words in English can function in more than one way, and a good many can have more than one set of forms. Note, as an example, the following uses of the word *place:*

NOUN	The *place* to be is New York.
	The *places* to be are New York and San Francisco.
VERB	*Place* the book on the desk.
	He *placed* the book on the desk.
MODIFIER	She bought *place* mats for the table.

How we decide to define our parts of speech depends partly on what we want to do with the classification. In English, it turns out that for our purposes it is most useful to classify words according to their most common function (keeping in mind that some words will belong to more than one part of speech), and to note their other characteristics as convenient ways of identifying them when we have any doubt. The basic functions in English are naming (performed principally by nouns and pronouns); predicating— that is, stating or asserting (performed by verbs); modifying (performed principally by adjectives and adverbs); and connecting (performed by conjunctions and prepositions). Nouns and verbs are the basic elements, being necessary to the typical sentence patterns we have described. Modifying and connecting words permit the expansion and refinement of these basic patterns. One other part of speech, the interjection (*Oh, Ouch*), is used to express emotion and is grammatically independent of other elements.

1. *Nouns.* Words that function as the basic part of sentence subjects are most commonly nouns (*Carl, Detroit, studio, committee, courage, wealth*). Nouns also characteristically function as objects of verbs and prepositions (*Send John to the store*). The overwhelming majority of nouns name or classify things, people, places, activities, concepts, and the like. They normally change form to make a plural (*boy, boys; man, men*), although some are irregular (*sheep, sheep; deer, deer*), and others (like *courage,* which names a quality, and *Detroit,* which names a particular place) belong to special subclasses that do not usually have plurals. The great majority of nouns show a possessive in writing by adding an *-s* preceded by an apostrophe in the singular, or in some cases merely by adding an apostrophe (*cow's horns, the committee's decision, Archimedes' law*).

2. *Pronouns.* The most common pronouns substitute for nouns. We can usually discover the full meaning of a pronoun only by referring to the noun that serves as its antecedent. In the sentence *Clara Barton is the woman who founded the American Red Cross,* the pronoun *who* refers to its antecedent, *woman.* In the sentence *Whichever he chooses will be acceptable,* we can tell what *whichever* means only if we know from a larger context what is referred to. In such sentences as *He who hesitates is lost,* the meaning is implied by the context itself; that is, *he* refers to any person who hesitates to take action. Words called indefinite pronouns (*anybody, everybody, somebody*) act like nouns and require no antecedent.

The personal pronouns *I, we, he, she,* and *they,* and the pronoun *who,* which is used either to relate one group of words to another or to ask a question, have distinctive case forms for the nominative, possessive, and objective cases; *you* and *it* have distinctive forms for the possessive only.

3. *Verbs and verbals.* Verbs serve as the heart of sentence predicates; they are the indispensable minimum of the second part of the typical English subject–predicate word group. The overwhelming majority of verbs make some sort of statement or assertion about their subjects. Typical verbs are *eat, give, call, describe, demand, criticize, exist, seem, appear, become.* In meaning, verbs normally indicate some sort of action, the occurrence of something, or the presence of some condition.

Verbs can usually be recognized by their ability to change from the plain form, or infinitive, to a form with *-s* in the third person singular of the present tense (*I run, he runs; we criticize, he criticizes*); by their ability to form a past tense by adding *-ed* or making an equivalent change (*he walks, he walked; I criticize, I criticized*); and by the characteristic positions in which they occur, as immediately after words like *please* and *let's*, and after simple noun subjects: *Please go, Let's eat, John hit Henry.* Verbs can combine with AUXIL-IARIES, which precede the main verb form, to make a variety of verb phrases such as *is eating, should have been eating, should have been eaten,* and *will be eating,* which convey special shades of meaning. Verbs have special forms, called VERBALS, which have some of the characteristics and abilities of verbs but *cannot function as predicates by themselves.* Verbals are classified as INFINITIVES, usually marked by a preceding *to* (*to eat, to run, to describe*); PARTICIPLES, which end in *-ing* (*eating, running, describing*) in the present form, and either end in *-ed* (*described*) or *-en* (*eaten*), or make an internal change (*begun, flown*) in the past form; and GERUNDS, which have the same *-ing* form as the present participles. The distinctive name *gerund* is given to *-ing* forms only when they function as nouns. Their typical forms and uses may be seen in the following:

INFINITIVE (*to* form of a verb, used as noun, adjective, or adverb)
To see is to *believe.*   (Both used as nouns.)
It was time *to leave.*   (Used as adjective.)
I was ready *to go.*   (Used as adverb.)
PARTICIPLE (verb form used as adjective)
Screaming, I jumped out of bed. (Present participle.)
Delighted, we accepted his invitation. (Past participle.)
GERUND (*ing* form of a verb, used as noun)
Swimming is healthful exercise.
His wife enjoyed *nagging.*

Although verbals can never function by themselves as predicates, they can, like verbs, take objects and complements, and like verbs they are characteristically modified by adverbs. Note the following:

To hear him is *to believe him.*
It was time *to leave the house.*
Screaming loudly, I jumped out of bed.
Completely delighted, we accepted his invitation.
Swimming in the Atlantic is healthful exercise.
His wife enjoyed *nagging him.*

4. *Adjectives and adverbs.* Adjectives and adverbs are the principal modifiers in English, adjectives modifying nouns or their equivalents and adverbs modifying other words or whole sentences. Typical adjectives are the underlined words in the following: *brown dog, Victorian dignity, yellow hair, beautiful girl, one football, reasonable price.* Adjectives have distinctive forms in the COMPARATIVE and

SUPERLATIVE: *happy, happier, happiest; beautiful, more beautiful, most beautiful; good, better, best.* Typical adverbs are the underlined words in the following: *stayed outside, walked slowly, horribly angry, fortunately the accident was not fatal.*

The term PREDICATE ADJECTIVE is used to describe the adjective which follows a LINKING VERB and serves as a modifier of the subject in sentences such as *Hepzibah is happy,* or *The grapes seemed sour.* The most common verbs with which predicate adjectives occur are *be, seem, become, appear,* and the verbs pertaining to the five senses, *look, smell, taste, sound,* and *feel.*

For a discussion of the special forms by which adjectives and adverbs show comparison, and of certain distinctions between the two, see Section 4.

5. *Prepositions and conjunctions.* Prepositions and conjunctions are the connecting words of English. A PREPOSITION relates a noun, pronoun, or phrase to some other part of the sentence.

> He was young *in* spirit. (*Spirit* is related to the adjective *young.*)
>
> See the shower *of* sparks. (*Sparks* is related to the noun *shower.*)
>
> I apologized *to* her. (*Her* is related to the verb *apologized.*)
>
> We ate sukiyaki *with* our wooden chopsticks. (*Our wooden chopsticks* is related to the verb *ate.*)

Over the centuries, English nouns have gradually lost their case endings; noun functions are now shown by the use of prepositions and objects. The object of the preposition is in the objective case (*between you and him; to John and me*). Even the last-remaining use of the inflected noun, the possessive, is often replaced by a preposition and its object (*day's end, end of the day*). Some of the more common English prepositions are *at, between, by, for, from, in, of, on, through, to, with.*

A CONJUNCTION is a word used to join words, phrases, or clauses. Conjunctions show the relation between the sentence elements that they connect.

Coordinating conjunctions (*and, but, or, nor, for*) join words, phrases, or clauses of equal grammatical rank. (See 1d, "Recognizing Clauses."*)

WORD JOINED	We ate ham *and* eggs.
PHRASES JOINED	Look in the closet *or* under the bed.
CLAUSES JOINED	We wanted to go, *but* we were too busy.

---

* For a discussion of the punctuation of clauses separated by a coordinating conjunction, see Section 20.

Subordinating conjunctions (*because, if, since, when, where,* etc.) join subordinate clauses with main clauses. (See 1d, "Recognizing Clauses."*)

We left the party early *because* we were tired.
If the roads are icy, we shall have to drive carefully.

6. *Interjections.* An INTERJECTION is an exclamatory word that expresses emotion. It has no grammatical relation to other words in the sentence. Mild interjections are usually followed by a comma. *Oh, is that you? Well, well, how are you?* Stronger interjections are usually followed by an exclamation point. *Ouch! You are hurting me. Oh! I hate you!*

EXERCISE 1b. Indicate the part of speech of each word in the following sentences.

1. From the crowd at the rally came a loud cheer.
2. Stop! I've heard that joke before.
3. Playing records is a good way to spend a rainy afternoon.
4. "Jeepers," said the starlet, "I'm really just a simple farm girl at heart."
5. Since there are so many prerequisites for a major in biochemistry, Bill decided that a major in physical education would do just as well.
6. Einstein said that a man has at the most only one or two ideas in his lifetime.
7. The pollution of air and water continues unabated, although scientists warn that it poses a threat to the survival of man.
8. There have been several assaults on poverty through the years, but it has not yet been conquered.
9. It is sometimes difficult to draw the line between "literature" and "pornography"; even legal definitions reflect that difficulty.
10. It is impossible to experiment with psychedelic drugs cautiously, because true caution would preclude their use entirely.

1c Recognizing phrases.

A phrase is a group of related words without a subject or predicate and used as a single part of speech. Typical phrases are a preposition and its object (*I fell on the sidewalk*), or a verbal and its object (*I wanted to see the parade*).

Prepositional phrases are classified, according to function, as adjective, adverb, and noun phrases. An adjective phrase modifies a noun or pronoun. (*He is a man of action.*) An adverb phrase modi-

---

* For a discussion of the punctuation of subordinate clauses, see Section 21.

29

fies a verb, adjective, or adverb. (*The train arrived <u>on time</u>. We were ready <u>at the station</u>. She came early <u>in the morning</u>.*) A noun phrase is used as a noun. (<u>*Before breakfast*</u> *is <u>the best time for calisthenics</u>.*)

Verbal phrases are classified as participial, gerund, or infinitive phrases. A participial phrase functions as an adjective, modifying a noun or pronoun. (*The man <u>sitting on the porch</u> is my father. The dog <u>found in the street</u> was homeless.*) Such phrases are formed with the present participle of a verb (*seeing, calling*) or the past participle (*seen, called*). A gerund phrase is used as a noun. (<u>*Collecting stamps*</u> *is my hobby.*) Since both gerunds and present participles end in *-ing*, they can be distinguished only by their separate functions as nouns or adjectives. An infinitive phrase is used as an adjective, adverb, or noun. (*It is time <u>to go to bed</u>. We were impatient <u>to start the game</u>. I wanted <u>to buy a house</u>.*)

EXERCISE 1c. In the following sentences identify the prepositional phrases by underlining them once and the verbal phrases by underlining them twice.

1. He was happy to hear the lecture end.
2. The man with the smile is the candidate.
3. Organizing a budget, personal or national, requires careful planning.
4. Playing bridge is a pleasant pastime.
5. Gaining approval from her group was more important to Jane than showing loyalty to a principle.
6. Suddenly the tornado hit the town, ripping roofs away from houses, wrenching trees from the ground.
7. Even little girls dream of becoming astronauts.
8. She became interested in social work through her summer job in a camp for underprivileged children.
9. For many years the gap between rich and poor in South America has been gradually widening.
10. Rising in a graceful arc, the spaceship swung into orbit around the earth.

1 d   Recognizing clauses.

A clause is a group of words containing a subject and a predicate. The relation of a clause to the rest of the sentence is shown by the position of the clause or by a conjunction. There are two kinds of clauses: (1) subordinate or dependent clauses, and (2) main or independent clauses.

1. *Subordinate clauses.* Subordinate clauses are frequently introduced by a subordinating conjunction (*as, since, because,* etc.) or by a relative pronoun (*who, which, that*). A subordinate clause functions as an adjective, adverb, or noun, and expresses an idea that is less important than the idea expressed in the main clause. The exact relationship between the two ideas is indicated by the subordinating conjunction or relative pronoun that joins the subordinate and the main clause.

a. An adjective clause modifies a noun or pronoun.

This is the jet *that broke the speed record.* (The subordinate clause modifies the noun *jet.*)

Anybody *who is tired* may leave. (The subordinate clause modifies the pronoun *anybody.*)

Canada is the nation *we made the treaty with.* (The subordinate clause modifies the noun *nation,* with the relative pronoun *that* understood.)

b. An adverb clause modifies a verb, adjective, or adverb.

The child cried *when the dentist appeared.* (The subordinate clause modifies the verb *cried.*)

I am sorry *he is sick.* (The subordinate clause modifies the adjective *sorry,* with the subordinating conjunction *that* understood.)

He thinks more quickly *than you do.* (The subordinate clause modifies the adverb *quickly.*)

c. A noun clause has the function of a noun. It may serve as subject, predicate nominative, object of a verb, or object of a preposition.

What John wants is a better job. (The subordinate clause is the subject of the verb *is.*)

This is *where we came in.* (The subordinate clause is a predicate nominative.)

Please tell them *I will be late.* (The subordinate clause is the object of the verb *tell.*)

He has no interest in *what he is reading.* (The subordinate clause is the object of the preposition *in.*)

EXERCISE 1d(1). Underline the subordinate clauses in the following sentences and identify each as an adjective, adverb, or noun clause.

1. The new politicians are those who substitute organization for charisma.
2. He was a scientist who kept searching for solutions.
3. What one thinks at twenty seems naïve at thirty.
4. If success depended solely on hard work, most poor people would be millionaires.

5. The police were annoyed by the jeers of the crowd.
6. The students felt that the administration had been evasive.
7. What upsets young people most is the older generation's tendency to sermonize.
8. We tried out our new speedboat when the sea was calm.
9. She had the quality of innocence that the director had been looking for.
10. Many parents are under the impression that education is to be gotten only in school.

2. *Main clauses.* A main clause also has both subject and verb but is not introduced by a subordinating word. A main clause makes an independent statement. It is not used as a noun or as a modifier.

The number of main or subordinate clauses in a sentence determines its classification: *simple, compound, complex,* or *compound–complex.*

A SIMPLE SENTENCE has a single main clause.

The wind blew.

A COMPOUND SENTENCE has two or more main clauses.

The wind blew and the leaves fell.

A COMPLEX SENTENCE has one main clause and one or more subordinate clauses.

When the wind blew, the leaves fell.

A COMPOUND–COMPLEX SENTENCE contains two or more main clauses and one or more subordinate clauses.

When the sky darkened, the wind blew and the leaves fell.

EXERCISE 1d(2). Indicate whether each of the following sentences is simple, compound, complex, or compound-complex.
1. Before elections, it is every politician's opinion that taxes must be cut.
2. Thinking is an activity that requires practice.
3. An addict needs more and more heroin, and needs it all the time.
4. Even though I enjoy pastoral beauty, bugs scare me and flowers make me sneeze.

5. What would you do if you found yourself in a miniskirt in a snowstorm?

6. The professor told the class he was retiring that year, and there was a burst of applause.

7. Anyone who likes rock music wants to hear it all day long.

8. Teachers frown on the idea of cramming the night before an exam, but it's better than flunking.

9. He tries to be a sophisticated man of the world, but he does not succeed.

10. Although Elvis Presley's heyday is over, he is still popular in some sections of the country.

EXERCISE 1d(3). In the following sentences point out the main and subordinate clauses. Indicate the function of each subordinate clause as an adjective, an adverb, or a noun.

1. The day she developed laryngitis was the happiest of her husband's life.

2. As the class ended, the teacher heaved a deep sigh of relief.

3. Many of the hard-core unemployed lack the skills that are needed for jobs in modern industry.

4. One of the major objections to capital punishment is not that it is ineffective as a deterrent to crime, but that it is so inconsistently administered.

5. The argument for the legalization of marijuana rests on the contention that the drug is not addictive.

6. It is difficult to estimate the impact of televised violence upon young children.

7. Students are demanding a larger role in university decisions because, they claim, they are the university.

8. An educated person is one who knows not only the extent of his knowledge but also its limits.

9. One result of the space program has been the rise of phrases and expressions that were unknown only a decade ago.

10. The ideal summer job is one that involves very little work and a great deal of money.

2 Case = CA

Case is a grammatical property showing the function of nouns and pronouns within a sentence. In the sentence *He gave me a week's vacation,* the nominative case form *he* indicates that the pronoun is being used as subject; the objective case form *me* shows that the pronoun is an object; the possessive case form *week's* indicates that the noun is a possessive.

In some languages, such as German, both adjectives and nouns have special endings to indicate the nominative, possessive, dative, and objective cases. Old English too was highly inflected. Case endings were extremely important in showing the function of a word and its meaning in a sentence.

Modern English, however, retains only a few remnants of this complicated system. Nouns have only two case forms, the possessive (*student's*), and a common form (*student*) that serves all other functions. The personal pronouns *I, we, he, she,* and *they,* and the relative or interrogative pronoun *who,* are inflected in three cases—nominative, possessive, and objective; the personal pronouns *you* and *it* have distinctive forms in the possessive.

PERSONAL PRONOUNS

	Nominative	*Possessive*	*Objective*
		SINGULAR	
FIRST PERSON	I	my, mine	me
SECOND PERSON	you	your, yours	you
THIRD PERSON	he, she, it	his, her, hers, its	him, her, it
		PLURAL	
FIRST PERSON	we	our, ours	us
SECOND PERSON	you	your, yours	you
THIRD PERSON	they	their, theirs	them

RELATIVE OR INTERROGATIVE PRONOUN

SINGULAR	who	whose	whom
PLURAL	who	whose	whom

In contrast, adjectives, which were once declined in five cases, now have no case endings at all. Consequently, English has had to rely increasingly on word order to show the relation of a particular word to other parts of the sentence. For example, the object of a verb or preposition normally follows the verb or preposition and thus is easily identified. In the following sentences, the nouns are identical; it is the position of each noun that determines its function.

Jack threw Bill the ball.   Bill threw Jack the ball.

2a **Nominative case.**

1. _Use the nominative case for the subject of a verb._ No English speaker is likely to say "Us are happy" or "Him is tired" instead of "We are happy" and "He is tired." But there are several types of sentence in which the subject is not easily recognized and can be confused with the object.

Ellipsis **a.** _In formal English use the nominative case of the pronoun after the conjunctions_ as _and_ than _if the pronoun is the subject of an understood verb._

In informal English there is a growing tendency to use _as_ and _than_ as prepositions.

FORMAL	He is taller than _I_ (am). (_I_ is the subject of the verb _am_, which must be supplied by the reader.)
INFORMAL	He is taller than _me_.
FORMAL	She is as rich as _they_ (are).
INFORMAL	She is as rich as _them_.

b. _Remember that the pronoun_ who _used as subject of a verb will not be changed by parenthetical elements intervening between it and its verb._

He is a man _who_ I think deserves praise. (_Who_ is the subject of _deserves._)

We invited only the people _who_ he said were his friends. (_Who_ is the subject of _were._)

c. _Use the nominative case for any pronoun that is the subject of a clause, even though the whole clause may function as an object of a verb or preposition._

I shall welcome _whoever_ wants to attend. (_Whoever_ is the subject of _wants._ The object of _welcome_ is the entire clause _whoever wants to attend._)

A reward is offered to _whoever_ catches the escaped lion. (The entire clause is the object of the preposition _to._)

2. _In formal English use the nominative case of the personal pronoun after forms of the verb_ be, _such as_ is, are, were, have been.

The use of the objective case of the personal pronoun after forms of _be_, however, has gained widespread acceptance in informal usage. "It's me" is freely used by good speakers. The prejudice against _us, him,_ and _them_ after _be_ is yielding to a strong tendency to use the objective form of the pronoun after a verb, regardless of what the verb may be. The objective forms occur most frequently with contractions.

FORMAL	It was *I*. I thought it was *he*. It was not *we*.
INFORMAL	It's *me*. I thought it was *him*. It wasn't *us*.

3. *In formal English use the nominative case for a pronoun following the infinitive* to be *when the infinitive has no expressed subject.*

Informal English commonly uses the objective case of the pronoun in this construction.

FORMAL	I would not want to be *he*. (The infinitive *to be* has no expressed subject.)
INFORMAL	I would not want to be *him*.

2b Possessive case.

1. *Generally, use the* s-*possessive* (boy's, Paul's) *with nouns denoting animate objects, but an* of-*phrase for the possessive of nouns denoting inanimate objects.*

ANIMATE	a man's hat; the ladies' coats; Jack's wife
INANIMATE	the floor of the house; the power of the machine; the point of the joke

The *s*-possessive is commonly used in expressions that indicate time (*moment's notice, year's labor*) and in many familiar phrases (*heaven's sake, heart's content*). Which possessive form to use may also depend on sound or rhythm: The *s*-possessive is more terse than the longer, more sonorous *of*-phrase (*morning's beauty, beauty of the morning*).

2. *In formal English use the possessive case for a noun or pronoun preceding a gerund.*

In informal English, however, the objective case rather than the possessive case is often found before a gerund.

FORMAL	What was the excuse for *his* being late?
INFORMAL	What was the excuse for *him* being late?
FORMAL	He complained of *Roy's* keeping the money.
INFORMAL	He complained of *Roy* keeping the money.

Even in formal English the objective case is frequently used with plural nouns.

The police prohibited *children* playing in the street.

The choice of case sometimes depends on the meaning the writer intends to convey.

Fancy *his* playing the violin. (The act of playing the violin is emphasized.)
Fancy *him* playing the violin. (The emphasis is on *him*. *Playing* is here used as a participle modifying *him*.)

And note the difference in the meaning of the following sentences:

I hate that *woman* riding a bicycle.
I hate that *woman's* riding a bicycle.

We must confess, however, that the illustrations above are a little artificial. A person wishing to state his dislike for a *woman's riding a bicycle* would say *I hate the way that woman rides a bicycle.*

3. *Use* which *to refer to impersonal antecedents. However, substitute* whose *in cases where the phrase* of which *would be awkward.*

We saw a house *whose* roof was falling in. (*Compare:* We saw a house the roof of which was falling in.)

This is the car *whose* steering wheel broke off when the driver was going seventy miles an hour. (*Compare:* This is the car the steering wheel of which broke off when the driver was going seventy miles an hour.)

2c Objective case.

1. *Use the objective case for the object of a verb, verbal, or preposition.*

OBJECT OF A VERB

I saw *him*. *Whom* did you see?

OBJECT OF A VERBAL

Visiting *them* was enjoyable. (*Them* is the object of the gerund *visiting*.)
Whom does he want to marry? (*Whom* is the object of the infinitive *to marry*.)

OBJECT OF A PREPOSITION

Two of *us* policemen were wounded. With *whom* were you dancing?

Formal English usage requires *whom* in the objective case. Informal English uses *who* in similar situations.

FORMAL	*Whom* are you discussing? (*Whom* is the object of *are discussing*.)
INFORMAL	*Who* are you discussing?
FORMAL	*Whom* are you looking for? (*Whom* is the object of the preposition *for*.)
INFORMAL	*Who* are you looking for?

The following sentences illustrate the use of the pronoun in the objective case after the conjunction *and*.

He found Tom and *me* at home. (Not "Tom and *I*." *Me* is an object of the verb *found*.)

He must choose between you and *me*. (Not "between you and *I*." *Me* is an object of the preposition *between*.)

She had dinner with *him* and *me*. (*Him* and *me* are objects of the preposition *with*.)

2. *After the conjunctions* than *and* as, *use a pronoun in the objective case if it is the object of an understood verb.*

She needs him more than [she needs] *me*.
I called him as well as [I called] *her*.

3. *When the infinitive* to be *has an expressed subject, both that subject and the object of the infinitive are in the objective case.*

He took *him* to be *me*. (*Him* is the subject of the infinitive; *me* is its object.)

EXERCISE 2. In the following sentences correct the errors in case in accordance with formal usage. Be prepared to give reasons.

1. Burgess was the candidate who all educated people voted for.
2. I will consider whomever applies for the position, regardless of creed or color.
3. It was her who was elected to the student council.
4. Let's you and I get engaged, sweetheart.
5. When we heard the doorbell, we knew it was him.
6. The teacher reported Dick as well as I for cheating.
7. I appreciate soul music without him telling me what to listen for.
8. We discovered Mark and she in the swimming pool.
9. Sometimes I think everybody knows more than me.
10. The police told about him testifying against his friends.

3 Tense and Mood = T

TENSE

Tense is a grammatical property indicating the time of the action expressed by a verb.

English verbs are usually thought of as having three PRINCIPAL PARTS, or forms: a PLAIN FORM, or INFINITIVE (*talk*), a PAST TENSE FORM (*talked*), and a PAST PARTICIPLE (*talked*). In most English verbs the past tense and the past participle are identical, both being created by adding *-ed* to the plain form: *smoked, hammered, played, worked.* Such verbs are called "regular" verbs. Other English verbs indicate their past tense and past participle forms by more individualistic changes, frequently a vowel change within the word: *grow, grew, grown; swim, swam, swum.* Such verbs are called "irregular." A few verbs have only one form for all three principal parts (*burst, cost, split*). By themselves these verbs cannot indicate differences in time but depend entirely on auxiliary verbs (*I was splitting the wood*) or modifying words or phrases (*I split the wood yesterday*).

With few exceptions the distinction between present and past in English is shown by a difference in the form of the verb. All other time relationships indicated by verbs are manifested by combining these forms with auxiliaries. Future time is shown by using the auxiliaries *shall* and *will* with the plain, or infinitive, form. The perfect tenses, which usually indicate that an action is completed prior to a given point in time, are formed by combining the various forms of *have* (and, for the future perfect, the auxiliaries *shall* and *will*) with the past participle. Still another kind of time construction is made by using the forms of the auxiliary *be* with the present participle, or *-ing* form. The basic system can be seen in the outline of the verbs *drag* and *drive* on page 40.

The most common uses of the various tenses of the active verb forms are illustrated in the following:

PRESENT TENSE (expressing a present or habitual action)

He *is talking* to the gun club now. He *talks* to the gun club at least once every year.

PAST TENSE (expressing an action that was completed in the past)

He *talked* to the gun club yesterday.

FUTURE TENSE (expressing an action yet to come)

He *will talk* to the gun club tomorrow.

PRESENT PERFECT TENSE (expressing a past action extending to the present and not necessarily completed)

He *has talked* to the gun club every day.

PAST PERFECT TENSE (expressing a past action completed before some other past action)

This morning I saw the speaker who *had talked* to the gun club last month.

FUTURE PERFECT TENSE (expressing an action that will be completed before some future time)

He *will have talked* to the gun club before next Thursday.

PARADIGM OF REGULAR AND IRREGULAR VERBS

ACTIVE VOICE

	Simple Form	*Progressive Form*
PRESENT	I drag/drive	I am dragging/driving
PAST	I dragged/drove	I was dragging/driving
FUTURE	I shall/will drag/drive	I shall/will be dragging/driving
PRESENT PERFECT	I have dragged/driven	I have been dragging/driving
PAST PERFECT	I had dragged/driven	I had been dragging/driving
FUTURE PERFECT	I shall/will have dragged/driven	I shall/will have been dragging/driving

PASSIVE VOICE

PRESENT	I am dragged/driven	I am being dragged/driven
PAST	I was dragged/driven	I was being dragged/driven
FUTURE	I shall/will be dragged/driven	I shall/will be being dragged/driven
PRESENT PERFECT	I have been dragged/driven	I have been being dragged/driven
PAST PERFECT	I had been dragged/driven	I had been being dragged/driven
FUTURE PERFECT	I shall/will have been dragged/driven	I shall/will have been being dragged/driven

The passive forms indicate that the subject is the object or receiver rather than the doer of the action. Note that they can be formed only with verbs that can take objects in the active voice; We can say *The elephant dragged him,* or *He was dragged by the elephant; The poison drove him mad,* or *He was driven mad by the poison;* but only *He talked,* not *He was talked.*

The progressive forms of the verb indicate that the action referred to by the main verb is continuing at the time indicated by the auxiliaries.

3a **Make sure that the tense of the verb in a subordinate clause is logically related to the tense of the verb in the main clause.**

FAULTY	As the day *ends,* a few stars *appeared* in the sky.
REVISED	As the day *ends,* a few stars *appear* in the sky.
REVISED	As the day *ended,* a few stars *appeared* in the sky.
FAULTY	If he *tried,* he *could have avoided* the accident.
REVISED	If he *had tried,* he *could have avoided* the accident.

3b **Use a present infinitive after a verb in a perfect tense. A perfect infinitive may sometimes be used after a verb not in a perfect tense.**

FAULTY	I would have liked *to have gone.*
REVISED	I would have liked *to go.* (At the time indicated by the verb, I desired *to go,* not *to have gone.*)
REVISED	I would like *to have gone.*
FAULTY	I hoped *to have visited you.*
REVISED	I had hoped *to visit* you.

3c **Use the present tense in statements that are generally true or that have no reference to time.**

Brevity *is* the soul of wit.
Corn *grows* rapidly in warm, humid weather.

3d **Distinguish carefully between the principal parts of irregular verbs.**

If you are in doubt about the principal parts of a particular verb, go to your dictionary. There you will find the present infinitive (*begin*), the past tense (*began*), and the past participle (*begun*) of irregular verbs. For regular verbs, which form the past tense and past participle simply by adding -d or -ed (*live, lived, lived*), you will find only the present infinitive.

The principal parts of some irregular verbs are listed below. Add to the list any other verbs that you may have used incorrectly.

PRESENT INFINITIVE	PAST TENSE	PAST PARTICIPLE
begin	began	begun
blow	blew	blown
break	broke	broken
bring	brought	brought
burst	burst	burst
choose	chose	chosen
come	came	come
dive	dived, dove	dived
do	did	done
draw	drew	drawn
drink	drank	drunk
drive	drove	driven
eat	ate	eaten
fall	fell	fallen
fly	flew	flown
forget	forgot	forgot, forgotten
freeze	froze	frozen
get	got	got, gotten
give	gave	given
go	went	gone
grow	grew	grown
hang (*suspend*)	hung	hung
hang (*execute*)	hanged	hung
know	knew	known
lead	led	led
ride	rode	ridden
ring	rang, rung	rung
rise	rose	risen
run	ran	run
see	saw	seen
sing	sang, sung	sung
sink	sank, sunk	sunk
speak	spoke	spoken
steal	stole	stolen
swim	swam	swum
swing	swung	swung
take	took	taken
tear	tore	torn
throw	threw	thrown
wear	wore	worn
write	wrote	written

Two pairs of irregular verbs—*lie, lay,* and *sit, set*—are particularly troublesome. The principal parts of *lie* (meaning *to recline*) are *lie, lay, lain.* The principal parts of *lay* (meaning *to place*) are *lay, laid, laid.* The distinction between the two verbs continues to be quite carefully observed in standard English.

LIE

Present	*Lie* down for a while and you will feel better.
Past	The cat *lay* in the shade and watched the dog carefully.
Present participle	His keys were *lying* on the table where he dropped them.
Past participle	After he *had lain* down for a while, he felt better.

LAY

Present	*Lay* the book on the table and come here.
Past	He *laid* the book on the table and walked out the door.
Present participle	*Laying* the book on the table, he walked out the door.
Past participle	*Having laid* the book on the table, he walked out the door.

The principal parts of *sit* (meaning *to occupy a seat*) are *sit, sat, sat;* the principal parts of *set* (meaning *to put in place*) are *set, set, set.*

SIT

Present	*Sit* down and keep quiet.
Past	The little girl *sat* in the corner for half an hour.
Present participle	*Sitting* down quickly, he failed to see the tack in the chair.
Past participle	*Having sat* in the corner for an hour, the child was subdued and reasonable.

SET

Present	*Set* the basket on the table and get out.
Past	Yesterday he *set* the grocery cartons on the kitchen table; today he left them on the porch.
Present participle	*Setting* his spectacles on the table, he challenged John to wrestle.
Past participle	*Having set* the basket of turnips on the porch, Terry went to play the piano.

EXERCISE 3a-d. Correct the verb forms in the following sentences. Consult your dictionary when necessary.

1. The protesters laid in front of the Pentagon for days.
2. The Kennedy family use to live in Boston.

3. The first man to set foot on the moon become quite famous.
4. He was depressed and hung himself.
5. Plans for the space launch were began in the spring.
6. How are students suppose to learn when teachers can't teach?
7. After the government declared amnesty, hundreds of political prisoners come rushing out of jail.
8. The spy denied that he had stole the microfilm.
9. My new bikini shrunk when it was washed.
10. Even Republicans were moved when Lyndon Johnson bid the nation farewell.

MOOD

MOOD is that property of a verb which indicates how a writer or speaker regards a statement, that is, as fact, supposition, command, and so on. English has three moods, the INDICATIVE, expressing a statement (*He is happy*); the IMPERATIVE, expressing a command or request (*Be happy*); and the SUBJUNCTIVE, expressing doubt, condition, wish, or probability (*I wish he were happy*). Although some languages have a variety of verb forms to express distinctions in mood, Modern English does not. One set of special verb forms does occur in the subjunctive, however, and although these forms are disappearing from informal writing and speaking they are still often used in more formal usage.

Distinctive forms for the subjunctive mood occur in formal English in the present tense, first and third person singular and plural, of the verb *be* (*If I be, If they be*); in the past tense, first and third person singular, of *be* (*If I were, If he were*); and in the third person singular of all verbs (*I demand that he give a report*).

3e Use the subjunctive mood in formal idioms.

Come what may, I have to leave college.
We can always walk, *if need be.*

Such idioms have survived from earlier times, when the subjunctive was more common in English.

3f In formal English use the subjunctive in stating conditions contrary to fact, and in expressing doubt, regrets, or wishes.

FORMAL   If I *were* tired, I would go home.
INFORMAL   If I *was tired,* I would go home.

FORMAL	The elm tree looks as if it *were* dying.
INFORMAL	The elm tree looks as if it *was* dying.
FORMAL	If this man *be* guilty, society will condemn him.
INFORMAL	If this man *is* guilty, society will condemn him.
FORMAL	I wish that I *were* taller.
INFORMAL	I wish that I *was* taller.

3g **Use the subjunctive in** *that* **clauses which express formal demands, resolutions, or motions.**

I demand that he *resign* his position.
Resolved, that Mr. Smith *investigate* our financial condition.
I move that the meeting *be* adjourned.

EXERCISE 3e-g. In the following sentences make whatever changes are demanded by formal usage. Indicate those sentences that would be acceptable in informal English.

1. The revolution might have succeeded, if the people was ready to fight.
2. World peace will be assured when the leaders of all nations set down and talk to one another.
3. Any woman would love her husband even more if he was a millionaire.
4. The Arabs and the Israelis haven't spoke to one another for years.
5. After the cars collided, the injured were laying all over the highway.
6. The *Titanic,* which was considered unsinkable, sunk in a matter of hours.
7. He couldn't swim very well, but he dove beautifully.
8. She raised from her seat in a rage.
9. I won't invite them again because they drunk a whole case of beer at my last party.
10. Roosevelt lead the nation through some very difficult times.

4 Adjectives and Adverbs = AD

Both adjectives and adverbs are modifying words. The characteristic use of adjectives is to modify nouns, and their normal position is adjacent to the nouns they modify. The characteristic use of adverbs is to modify verbs, adjectives, or other adverbs. When they modify adjectives or other adverbs, they are adjacent to the words they modify. When they modify verbs, they are frequently but not always adjacent to the verbs. Most uses of adjectives and adverbs are common to both standard and nonstandard English and to all levels. But formal English makes more frequent use of distinctive adverb forms than ordinary conversation. Since certain distinctions in the use of adjectives and adverbs are especially clear markers of differences between standard and nonstandard, and between formal and informal English, they must be observed closely.

Most adverbs are distinguished from their corresponding adjectives by the ending *-ly: strong–strongly, happy–happily, doubtful–doubtfully, hasty–hastily, mad–madly.* But the *-ly* ending is not a dependable indication of the adverb since some adjectives also end in *-ly* (*gentlemanly, friendly*);* some adverbs have two forms (*quick, quickly; slow, slowly*); and still others have the same form as adjectives (*fast, much, late, well*).

Where there is a choice between a form with *-ly* and a form without it, formal English prefers the *-ly* form: *runs quickly* rather than *runs quick, eats slowly* rather than *eats slow,* even though the shorter forms are widely used in informal English, particularly in such commands as *Drive slow.* Note particularly that *good* and *bad* used as adverbs are nonstandard. The sentence *He talks good but writes bad* is nonstandard. Standard English requires *He talks well but writes badly.*

4a Do not use an adjective to modify a verb.

> INCORRECT He writes *careless.*
>
> CORRECT He writes *carelessly.* (The adverb *carelessly* is needed to modify the verb *writes.*)
>
> INCORRECT She talks *modest.*
>
> CORRECT She talks *modestly.* (The adverb is needed to modify the verb).

4b Do not use an adjective to modify another adjective or an adverb.

> INCORRECT He was *terrible* wounded.
>
> CORRECT He was *terribly* wounded. (The adverb *terribly* is needed to modify the adjective *wounded.*)
>
> INCORRECT She works *considerable* harder than he does.
>
> CORRECT She works *considerably* harder than he does. (The adverb *considerably* is needed to modify the other adverb *harder.*)

* The ways in which adjectives are formed from nouns are discussed in Section 39, "Vocabulary."

The use of adjectives in place of adverbs is more common in conversation than in writing. Indeed, the use of the adjective *real* as an emphatic *very* to modify adjectives and adverbs is often heard in educated speech.

FORMAL   You will hear from me *very* soon.
COLLOQUIAL* You will hear from me *real* soon.

4c Use an adjective to modify the subject after a linking verb.

The common linking verbs are *be, become, appear, seem,* and the verbs pertaining to the senses: *look, smell, taste, sound, feel.* Modifiers after such verbs often refer back to the subject and should be in the adjectival form. In each of the following sentences, for example, the predicate adjective modifies the subject. The verb simply links the two.

Jane looks *pretty* tonight. (*Pretty* modifies *Jane.*)
The butter smells *sour.* (*Sour* modifies *butter.*)

One of the most frequent errors in this construction is *I feel badly* in place of the correct subject–linking verb–predicate adjective form *I feel bad.* Though *badly* is common even in educated speech, *bad* is strongly preferred by many speakers.

FORMAL   He feels bad (*ill*).
COLLOQUIAL He feels *badly.*

FORMAL   He felt *bad* about it.
COLLOQUIAL He felt *badly* about it.

4d Use an adverb after the verb if the modifier describes the manner of the action of the verb.

He looked *suspiciously* at me. (The adverb *suspiciously* modifies the verb *looked.* Contrast *He looked suspicious to me.*)
The thief felt *carefully* under the pillow. (The adverb *carefully* modifies the verb *felt.*)

In these examples the verbs *look* and *feel* express action, and must be modified by adverbs. But in constructions like *He looks tired* or *He feels well,* the verbs serve not as words of action but as links between the subject and the predicate adjective. The choice of ad-

* We use the term *colloquial* to signify the qualities of familiar spoken English.

47

jective or adverb thus depends on the function and meaning of the verb—in other words, on whether or not the verb is being <u>used as a linking verb</u>. Ask yourself whether you want a modifier for the <u>subject</u> or for the <u>verb</u>.

4e Distinguish between the comparative and superlative forms of adjectives and adverbs.

Adjectives and adverbs show degrees of quality or quantity by means of their positive, comparative, and superlative forms. The positive form (*slow, quickly*) expresses no comparison at all. The comparative, formed by adding *-er* or by prefixing *more* to the positive form (*slower, more quickly*), expresses a greater degree or makes a comparison. The superlative, formed by adding *-est* or by putting *most* before the positive form (*slowest, most quickly*), indicates the greatest degree of a quality or quantity among three or more persons or things. Some common adjectives and adverbs retain old irregular forms (*good, better, best; badly, worse, worst*).

Whether to use *more* or *most* before the adjective or adverb or to add the *-er, -est* endings depends mostly on the number of syllables in the word. Most adjectives and a few adverbs of one syllable form the comparative and superlative with *-er* and *-est*. Adjectives of two syllables often have variant forms (*fancier, more fancy; laziest, most lazy*). Adjectives and adverbs of three or more syllables always take *more* and *most* (*more beautiful, most regretfully*). Where there is a choice, select the form that sounds better or that is better suited to the rhythm of your sentence.

Some adjectives and adverbs, such as *unique, empty, dead, perfect, entirely,* are absolute in their meaning and thus cannot logically be compared. Logically there are no degrees of *uniqueness, deadness,* or *perfection.* In informal usage, however, such words are often compared.

FORMAL	His diving form is *more nearly perfect* than mine.
INFORMAL	His diving form is *more perfect* than mine.
FORMAL	The new stadium is *more nearly circular* than the old one.
INFORMAL	The new stadium is *more circular* than the old one.

4f In formal usage, use the comparative to refer only to one of two objects; use the superlative to refer only to one of three or more objects.

COMPARATIVE	His horse is the *faster* of the two.
SUPERLATIVE	His horse is the *fastest* in the county.

| COMPARATIVE | Ruth is the *more* attractive but the *less* good-natured of the twins. |
| SUPERLATIVE | Ruth is the *most* attractive but the *least* good-natured of his three daughters. |

EXERCISE 4. In the following sentences correct any errors in the use of adjectives and adverbs in accordance with formal usage.

1. I felt very badly about having missed him.
2. The President appears on television most every week.
3. Student leaders should take their obligations more serious.
4. He saw the truck coming and luckily he was driving slow.
5. At first even the critics didn't understand *Lolita* because it's a very unique book.
6. The South Pole is the coldest of the two Poles.
7. Our society is based on the belief that all men are created equally.
8. It is Shakespeare, I believe, who said that a rose by any other name would smell as sweetly.
9. The lecture was poor because the teacher didn't feel very good.
10. John is the taller of all three brothers.

5 Diagraming Grammatical Relationships

Diagrams can be used in grammar for the same general purpose that they are used in the sciences: to help us visualize the way the parts of something work or go together. The chemist represents the structure of molecules by diagrams. The grammarian may construct diagrams to represent his conception of how the parts of a sentence go together. The kind of diagram which either the chemist or the grammarian draws will depend, of course, on his ideas of how, in fact, the parts of what he is representing <u>do</u> go together. We must remember that neither of them uses diagrams as ends in themselves. A diagram can only add a graphic dimension to our understanding of how something works or is constructed, be it a molecule or a sentence. But by so doing, it sometimes enables us to grasp more readily an abstraction that would otherwise remain vague.*

The conception of a sentence presented in this book is that it consists of a subject and a predicate, the latter consisting of a verb alone, or of a verb plus one or two objects or a complement. (See "Basic Grammar," pp. 21–24.) Such sentences as *Boys play, Boys ride bicycles, Boys give parents trouble, Boys consider teachers unnecessary*, and *Boys are trouble* are basic sentence types. These basic sentences can be expanded by three means. First, the parts may be modified by adding words that qualify or restrict one or more of the basic parts. Second, word groups—clauses, or verbal or prepositional phrases—may be substituted for one or more of the basic parts, or for a single-word modifier. Third, any one of the basic parts or modifiers can be compounded; that is, another similar part may be added to it.

A well-developed system which translates this conception of the sentence into diagrams has long been in use. Essentially, it consists of four devices. First, the basic sentence parts—subject, verb, and objects or complements—are represented on a horizontal base line. Second, modifiers of the basic parts are placed below the line and attached to one of the basic parts. Third, word groups that function as subjects, objects, or complements are placed above the base line. Fourth, compound parts of any kind are placed in parallel arrangements. The mechanics of the system can be seen in the following.

The basic sentence.

The subject–predicate division is indicated by a vertical line cutting the base line to suggest the major division within the sentence. Direct objects are indicated by a vertical line extending upward from the base line.

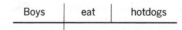

---

*The great usefulness of some sort of diagram as a way of making grammatical conceptions clear can be seen from an examination of their use by linguists. The "Chinese box" diagrams of W. Nelson Francis (see p. 55) and the various diagrams of Eugene A. Nida and others are examples. One of the readiest ways to "see" some of the basic differences between different grammatical descriptions is to compare their various diagrammatic representations. That diagrams have sometimes been misused as ends in themselves, or that unrealistic claims have been made for what they can accomplish, ought not to deter us from their judicious use to clarify systems of grammatical analysis.

Complements after linking verbs and objective complements (see Section 48) after direct objects are indicated by a line slanted back toward the words they complete.

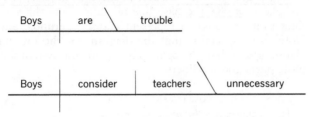

Modifiers.

Modifiers are always placed below the base line, attached by slant lines to the words they limit or describe.

The white rooster crowed proudly.

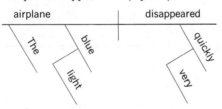

Continuing this principle, words that modify modifiers are attached to the words they modify.

The light blue airplane disappeared very quickly.

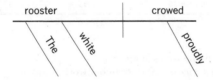

Since an indirect object is thought of as equivalent to a modifying phrase beginning with *to* or *for,* it is also placed below the line, as follows:

We gave him money.

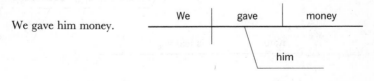

Word groups that function as basic sentence parts and as modifiers.

Word groups that function as subjects, objects, or complements are placed above the base line on stilts. Note the special kinds of lines that are used to represent clauses, gerunds, and infinitives. Note also, especially, that the diagram for the internal parts of a clause or a verbal phrase merely repeats the system for diagraming basic parts and modifiers.

NOUN CLAUSE AS COMPLEMENT

His weakness was *that he had no ambition.*

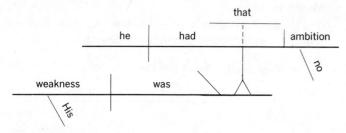

GERUND PHRASE AS SUBJECT

Breaking a forest trail is strenuous work.

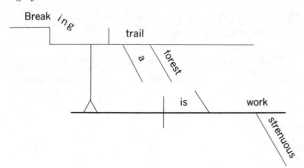

INFINITIVE PHRASE AS OBJECT

Kate is learning *to drive an automobile.*

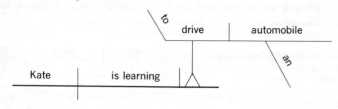

Word groups that function as modifiers are placed, in accordance with the principle for modifiers, below the base line. The connecting slant line carries the connecting word.

PREPOSITIONAL PHRASE USED AS AN ADJECTIVE
He is the owner *of the store.*

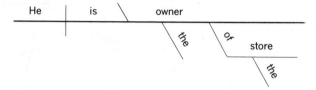

PREPOSITIONAL PHRASE USED AS AN ADVERB
The cow jumped *over the moon.*

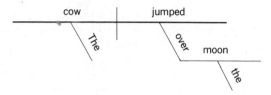

PARTICIPIAL PHRASE
Having made his fortune, he retired.

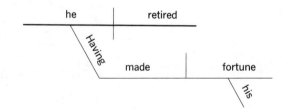

ADJECTIVE CLAUSE
The girl *who won the contest* is a college freshman.

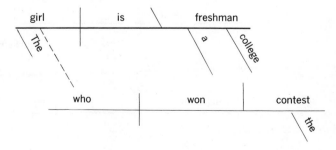

ADVERB CLAUSE
We will meet him *when the train arrives.*

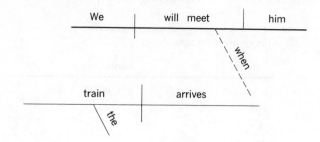

Compound constructions.

Compound constructions are always represented in parallel arrangements. If a connecting word is present, it is indicated on the line that joins the compound parts.

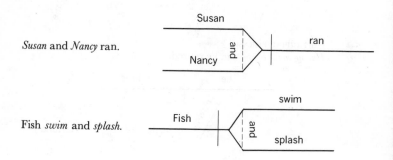

Susan and *Nancy* ran.

Fish *swim* and *splash.*

Hawkeye *was pursued* by Indians, but they *did* not *catch* him.

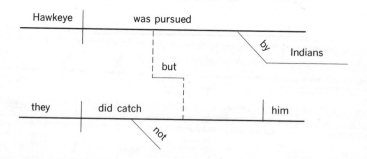

54

This system of diagraming offers devices for representing other elements also, such as absolutes, expletives, words of direct address, and the like. In its complete form it provides a means of representing almost all English sentences in graphic form.*

Other types of diagrams.

We can, of course, think of the grammatical structure of an English sentence differently from the representation in the diagrams we have been looking at. Many grammarians do think of it differently today, and have devised other kinds of diagrams to help make their ideas clear.

The idea of the sentence we have been diagraming is essentially that of a basic subject and predicate to which other less important parts are somehow attached. Suppose we think instead of the subject and predicate each as divisible into two parts, just as the sentence is divisible into a subject and a predicate. And then suppose we think of these parts in turn as again divisible, and so on until we reach individual words. The principle may be represented in this way:†

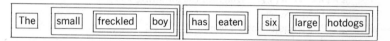

If we were to carry such a system of diagraming through so that it would permit us to make blueprints of all sentences, we should have to devise conventional ways for indicating all the different kinds of grammatical relations, just as the traditional system of diagraming has. We might, for instance, decide to show modification by an arrow connecting two boxes, and the subject–predicate relation by a *P* between boxes:

Obviously we should have to develop ways of indicating various kinds of objects and complements, compound constructions, and the like. And the finished system would have to let us always represent

---

our sentences in accordance with the basic idea that any sentence is successively divisible into two parts until we reach single words, just as traditional diagraming is consistent with its basic ideas about sentence construction.

Naturally, if we didn't like either of the kinds of diagrams above, we could try inventing others. If we wished, we could borrow a different kind of trick from the mathematicians and the logicians; instead of working with diagrams, we could work out formulas for our grammar. To do this, we would have to agree on symbols to represent each kind of word, word group, and grammatical relation. But once we had worked out our symbols, we could then reduce our statements about grammar to a set of formulas. Some recent grammarians have done something like this, trying to develop convenient shorthand ways of talking about some of the more complicated problems of language.

Such devices as these are not grammar, of course; they are merely convenient ways of understanding our language better.

EXERCISE 5(1).   Diagram the following sentences.

1. Men work.
2. Men and women work.
3. Birds eat worms.
4. Life is short.
5. Russia invaded Czechoslovakia.
6. Marijuana offered them escape.
7. The wounded cowboy slipped off the horse slowly.
8. The rising floodwaters overflowed the riverbanks.
9. The rebels carefully surveyed the terrain.
10. The outdated regulations irritated the students severely.

EXERCISE 5(2).   Which word groups in the following sentences would go <u>above</u> the base line on stilts? Which would be attached by slant lines <u>under</u> the base line?

1. The frightened boy wanted to run and hide.
2. The teacher is always willing to help.
3. The suspect refused to talk.
4. Castro was the leader of a rebel army.
5. Balancing the national budget is a difficult task.
6. The excited reporters besieged him with questions.
7. His ambition was to marry well and retire soon.
8. His passion was hunting for antiques.

9. China seems eager for war.
10. To ignore others' misery is to aggravate it.

EXERCISE 5(3). Which of the clauses in the following sentences would be placed <u>above</u> the base line? Which <u>below</u> it? For those below, indicate the words to which they would be attached.

1. A minority group's main problem is that it has little power.
2. They are refugees who escaped from oppression.
3. When the police arrived, the students had taken over the school building.
4. This is the mixed economy toward which both communism and capitalism are moving.
5. The student militants insisted that their demands were nonnegotiable.
6. The continent of Africa is now divided into nations, but tribal divisions are more faithfully observed.
7. Nixon's campaign promise was that he would end the war in Vietnam.
8. The candidate who won the last election also promised to end the war in Vietnam.
9. What were you doing when you heard that Robert Kennedy had been assassinated?
10. Martin Luther King's basic principle was that violence is not a viable alternative.

"BASIC GRAMMAR" REVIEW EXERCISE (Sections 1 through 5). Correct the grammatical errors in the following sentences according to formal usage.

1. Our hopes for a Cold War "thaw" sunk when Soviet troops invaded Czechoslovakia.
2. The morale of the Arab nations fell real low after the 1967 Six-Day War with Israel.
3. After that war ended, the belligerents all begin making plans for the next one.
4. Whom do you think suffered most when the New York City schoolteachers went on strike?
5. All the people of the world will be grateful to whomever discovered a way to halt the arms race.
6. NASA was sure delighted when the space shot proceeded on schedule.
7. When the moon became an object of scientific exploration, its hard to think of it in the romantic terms we use to.
8. Federal law forbade states imposing a poll tax.
9. It's quite possible that LBJ sometimes wishes he was back in the White House.

10. Most students are annoyed by those kind of teachers who fail to make their courses relevant.
11. Cleveland was the first major American city that has a black mayor.
12. Many policemen feel badly over newspaper accounts of police brutality.
13. It would be interesting to have watched a debate between William Buckley and Stokely Carmichael.
14. After De Gaulle left office, he asked his countrymen to abjure parties on the extreme left and right.
15. The U.S. could only protest about the East Germans building the Berlin Wall.

Basic Sentence Faults = *SEN FLT*

There is a high order of correlation between beauty and clarity of expression. A slovenly designed and constructed sentence is an unsafe container of knowledge.

—JOHN J. O'NEIL

*T*he purpose of writing is to communicate facts, feelings, attitudes, and ideas clearly and effectively. Having something to say, thinking about it clearly, developing general ideas with ample fresh, specific, and accurate details—these are all indispensable to effective writing. But so also are many details of basic sentence structure and punctuation. Unless our sentences observe the limits of English grammar and conform to the conventions of written English, we are not likely to have any readers to ask whether our ideas are interesting and our writing vivid. A reader confronted, for instance, with *In Yellowstone Park driving down the road some bears were seen having climbed down from the trees* doesn't worry much about effectiveness. He worries about the basic grammatical difficulties which make the statement such an incoherent mishmash. And the writer, if he wishes to be read, must worry about them, too.

6 Sentence Fragment = FRAG

The usual written sentence contains both a subject and a verb. But writers sometimes decide, for reasons of emphasis or economy, to omit either one or the other. Conversational language abounds in questions, answers, and exclamations that do not follow the usual sentence pattern. "Really?" "Yes." "How absurd!" Familiar expressions such as "The sooner, the better," or transitional phrases such as "So much for this point. Now for my second argument" are used even in formal English. Although these sentences are fragments, they are perfectly acceptable in a suitable context.

Writers occasionally omit the verbs in descriptive passages, particularly in recording a series of sense impressions. Here is an example:

> Howland & Gould's Grocery. In the display window, black, overripe bananas and lettuce on which a cat was sleeping. Shelves lined with red crepe paper which was now faded and torn and concentrically spotted.
> —SINCLAIR LEWIS, *Main Street*

Similarly, writers sometimes omit the verbs in passages that reflect a person's thoughts.

> He looked at the old photograph and was suddenly unhappy. The old gang all split up now. Smitty in L.A., Frank in Berlin, Joe on a two-year stretch in Alaska. Weather observer. Good joke that one. Heard Joe say once he'd never live north of Miami. Serves him right. Never second-guess destiny.

In good expository writing, however, sentences that do not conform to the normal subject–verb pattern are very infrequent. A phrase or subordinate clause usually is meaningless unless it is closely related to an independent clause. If you punctuate such phrases and clauses as complete sentences, you sacrifice meaning and effectiveness. Note this example:

> He leaped through the window with a crash. Because there was no other way of escaping the fire.

Here the meaning of the *because*-clause depends directly on the main clause. Punctuating the subordinate clause as though it were a complete sentence results in a PERIOD FAULT and sometimes reflects the writer's inability to determine what a complete sentence is. There are several ways of correcting the error.

> He leaped through the window with a crash, because there was no other way of escaping the fire.
> He leaped through the window with a crash; there was no other way of escaping the fire.
> He leaped through the window with a crash. There was no other way of escaping the fire.

EXERCISE 6. In the following sentences eliminate ineffective fragments (1) by combining them with the main clause or (2) by making them into complete sentences.

1. The Soviet delegate walked out of the meeting. Which was his way of avoiding the issue.
2. Nixon's first national budget was the largest in history. Though he had promised to cut it.
3. Violence is becoming a tool of political dissent. Chiefly because non-violence can so easily be ignored by the country as a whole.
4. Many doctors refuse to prescribe birth control pills. Some women have had serious side effects after using the pills.
5. The Beatles decided to stop giving concerts. Just as they were at the peak of their fame.

6. Soul music was gaining popularity. But many people still didn't know what it was.
7. The climax of many new films is the nude scene. Even when it adds nothing at all to the particular story.
8. The two candidates have identical platforms. The only difference is their party.
9. The cortege at President Kennedy's funeral was a long one. Rich and poor, young and old, all marching side by side.
10. Many young people are considering social work as a career. Not for the money, but for the sense of satisfaction it provides.

7   Comma Splice = CS or CF
and Run-together or Fused Sentence = FS

7a   Comma splice = CS or CF.

Do not connect two main clauses with only a comma. The use of a comma between two main clauses without a coordinating conjunction results in the COMMA FAULT or COMMA SPLICE. If two main clauses are joined by a coordinating conjunction *(and, but, for, or, nor, yet)*, a comma may precede the conjunction. If no conjunction is used, the two clauses must be separated by a semicolon or a period.

Comma splices may be corrected in one of the following ways:

1. Connect the main clauses with a coordinating conjunction.
2. Replace the comma with a semicolon.
3. Make a separate sentence of each main clause.
4. Change one of the main clauses to a subordinate clause.

COMMA SPLICE	The witness was unwilling to testify, he was afraid of the accused man.
REVISED (1)	The witness was unwilling to testify, *for* he was afraid of the accused man.
REVISED (2)	The witness was unwilling to testify; he was afraid of the accused man.
REVISED (3)	The witness was unwilling to testify. He was afraid of the accused man.
REVISED (4)	Because he was afraid of the accused man, the witness was unwilling to testify.

Revision 4 would ordinarily be the most effective, for it not only corrects the comma splice but also indicates a specific relationship between the clauses. A good revision of a comma-splice error often entails reworking the sentence rather than merely inserting a punctuation mark. The kind of revision you choose will depend on the larger context in which the sentences occur.

A comma splice can sometimes be justified if it joins two clauses that are in balance or contrast:

> As I have said elsewhere, a journalist's work is not important, it is only indispensable. —BERNARD DE VOTO

But note that in this sentence a dash would serve the same purpose as a comma. The inexperienced writer will be wiser to follow the more common convention.

NOTE: Do not allow a conjunctive adverb (words like *accordingly, also, consequently, furthermore, however, instead, likewise, moreover, nevertheless, otherwise, then, therefore, thus*) or a transitional phrase (such as *for example, in fact, on the other hand, that is*) to lead you into a comma splice. When such words and phrases connect main clauses, they are always preceded by a semicolon.

> Everything seemed quiet; then the explosion came.
> John must be sick; otherwise he would be here.
> He disliked college; however, he studied every day.
> He wanted a job; in fact, he needed a job very badly.

7b Run-together or fused sentence = FS.

Do not omit punctuation between main clauses. Such omission results in run-together or fused sentences—that is, two grammatically complete thoughts with no separating punctuation. Correct these errors in the same way as the comma splice.

FUSED	Balboa gazed upon the broad Pacific his heart was filled with awe.
REVISED	Balboa gazed upon the broad Pacific, and his heart was filled with awe.
REVISED	Balboa gazed upon the broad Pacific; his heart was filled with awe.
REVISED	Balboa gazed upon the broad Pacific. His heart was filled with awe.
REVISED	When Balboa gazed upon the broad Pacific, his heart was filled with awe.

EXERCISE 7. Eliminate comma splices and run-together sentences from the following items.

1. The U.S.S.R. and Red China are technically allies however they have been having quite a few problems lately.
2. General Eisenhower wrote a book about his World War II experience, he called it *Crusade in Europe.*
3. Throughout the 1960's, when civil rights bills were being passed, Senator Fulbright was considered a liberal, in spite of this he always voted against them.
4. The North Koreans allowed the crew of the *Pueblo* to return home, they kept the ship.
5. Most of Hemingway's novels have similar themes, love and war are two of the most frequent.
6. The best way to publicize a movie is to say it's "For Adults Only" then teen-agers will flock to see it.
7. The pollution of water resources is proceeding rapidly, the next generation of Americans may be drinking rationed water.
8. The black students decided they wanted a dormitory reserved to their use, some white students called it "reverse segregation."
9. It's confusing to try to remember all the organizations called by their initials, CIA, CIO, and USIS are just a few.
10. Some students question whether literature is relevant to them, they should really be asking whether they are relevant to literature.

8   Faulty Agreement = AGR

Agreement is the grammatical relationship between a subject and a verb, or a pronoun and its antecedent, or a demonstrative adjective and the word it modifies. Since Modern English nouns and verbs have few inflections, or special endings, agreement usually presents few problems. However, there are some grammatical patterns, such as the agreement in number of a subject and verb, or a pronoun and its antecedent, that you must watch carefully.

8a   Make every verb agree in number with its subject.

Sometimes a lack of agreement between subject and verb is merely the result of carelessness in composition or revision. But more often, writers use a singular subject with a plural verb or a plural subject with a singular verb, not because they misunderstand the general rule, but because they are uncertain of the number of the subject. This problem in agreement is most likely to arise when other words intervene between the subject and verb.

1. *Do not be confused by words or phrases that intervene between the subject and verb. Find the subject and make the verb agree with it.*

> The first two *chapters* of the book *were* exciting. (The verb agrees with the subject, *chapters*, not with the nearest noun, *book*.)
> The *size* of the bears *startles* the spectators.

Singular subjects followed by such expressions as *with, together with, accompanied by,* and *as well as* take singular verbs. The phrases introduced by such expressions are not part of the subject, even though they do suggest a plural meaning.

> FAULTY   The *coach,* as well as the players, *were* happy over the victory.
> REVISED   The *coach,* as well as the players, *was* happy over the victory.
>
> FAULTY   The horse *thief,* with his two accomplices, *have been hanged.*
> REVISED   The horse *thief,* with his two accomplices, *has been hanged.*

2. *Remember that singular pronouns take singular verbs.*

All speakers observe this convention when pronouns such as *everyone* and *nobody* immediately precede a verb. No English speaker is likely to say *Everyone are present,* or *Nobody win all the time.* But formal and informal English differ in their handling of pronouns that refer to antecedents such as *anyone, everyone, nobody.* Informal English frequently has sentences such as *Everyone took off their coats,* and *Nobody ate their dinner.* Formal English, however, clearly prefers *Everyone took off his coat,* and *Nobody ate his dinner.* (See Section 8b [1].)

None, either, neither, any may be followed by either a singular or a plural verb, depending on whether you intend a singular or a plural meaning.

> SINGULAR   *None* but a fool *squanders* his time.
> PLURAL   *None* but fools *squander* their time.

3. *Use a plural verb with two or more subjects joined by* and.

A dog and a cat *are* seldom friends.

But use a singular verb when the two parts of a compound subject refer to the same person or thing.

My friend and benefactor *was* there to help me.

4. *Use a singular verb with two or more singular subjects joined by* or (*or* nor). *If the subjects differ in number or person, make the verb agree with the subject nearer to it.*

Either the dean or his assistant *was* to have handled the matter.
Neither the farmer nor the chickens *were* aware of the swooping hawk.
Either you or he *has* to be here.

5. *When the verb precedes the subject of the sentence, be particularly careful to find the subject and make the verb agree with it.*

There *are* only a chair and a table left to auction.
In the balcony there *are* many seats.

In informal English a singular verb is often used when it is followed by a compound subject.

FORMAL   As a result, there *are* confusion, trouble, and uncertainty.
INFORMAL   As a result, there *is* confusion, trouble, and uncertainty.

6. *Use a singular verb with* COLLECTIVE NOUNS *to indicate that the group is considered as one unit. Use a plural verb to indicate that the individual members of the group are acting separately.*

The committee *is* meeting today.
The committee *are* unable to agree on a plan of action.

7. *Make the verb agree with its subject, not with a predicate noun.*

The best part of the program *is* the vocal duets.
Men *are* a necessity in her life.

8. *With relative pronouns use a singular verb when the antecedent is singular, a plural verb when the antecedent is plural.*

He is the only one of the councilmen who *is opposed* to the plan. (The antecedent of *who* is *one*, not *councilmen*.)
He is one of the best baseball players that *have come* from Texas. (The antecedent of the relative pronoun *that* is *players*, not *one*.)

Expressions like *one of the best baseball players that* commonly take a singular verb in informal usage. Although the antecedent of *that* is the plural noun *players,* the writer or speaker is influenced in his choice of a verb by the fact that *one* is singular.

FORMAL	He is one of those people who *are* afraid to act.
INFORMAL	He is one of those people who *is* afraid to act.

EXERCISE 8a. In the following sentences correct any errors in agreement in accordance with formal usage. Place an *I* before the sentences that might be correct in informal English.

1. A United States Senator's first interest is his constituents.
2. There is several Nobel Prize winners at the University of Chicago.
3. Each of the Congressmen have a special purpose for making this inspection tour.
4. Either the President or the members of his cabinet was ill-advised about the distribution of farm subsidies.
5. Among my favorite books are *Nine Stories* by J. D. Salinger.
6. There is a good many reasons for the tensions between Arabs and Israelis.
7. The burden of sales taxes fall on the shoulders of the consumer.
8. In an ideal society, everybody would be carrying their own weight.
9. The crux of the urban problem are overcrowding and unemployment.
10. The farmer, and not the city dweller, feel downhearted when agricultural prices fall.
11. Ten dollars are more than a poor family can afford to pay for a pair of shoes.
12. The main complaint of most college students are the many required courses forced upon them.
13. The Vietnam conflict is only one of several wars that have evoked public dissent.
14. Norman Mailer is one of the best writers who have ever run for mayor of New York City.
15. A theme of many of Truman Capote's novels are what has come to to be called "Southern Gothic."

8b Use a singular pronoun in referring to a singular antecedent. Use a plural pronoun in referring to a plural antecedent.

SINGULAR	The small *boy* put *his* penny in the collection box.
PLURAL	The *cows* lost *their* way in the storm.

Ambiguity in the use of pronouns is an offense against clarity. The following general rules will help you select proper pronouns;

1. In formal writing use a singular pronoun to refer to antecedents such as *person, man, woman, one, any, anyone, anybody, someone, somebody, each, every, everyone, everybody, either, neither.*

Informal English frequently uses a plural pronoun to refer to antecedents such as *any, every,* and their compounds, and *each, someone, somebody, either, neither,* especially when a plural meaning is suggested.

FORMAL	*Everybody* held *his* breath.
INFORMAL	*Everybody* held *their* breath.
FORMAL	He asked *each* of us to bring *his* own lunch.
INFORMAL	He asked *each* of us to bring *our* own lunch.

2. *With a collective noun as an antecedent, use a singular pronoun if you are considering the group as a unit, a plural pronoun if you are considering the individual members of the group separately.*

The *militia* increased *its* watchfulness.
The *band* raised *their* instruments at the conductor's signal.

3. If two or more antecedents are joined by *and,* use a plural pronoun to refer to them. If two or more singular antecedents are joined by *or* or *nor,* use a singular pronoun to refer to them. If one of two antecedents joined by *or* or *nor* is singular and one plural, make the pronoun agree with the nearer.

Jack and Jim *have* finished *their* work.
Neither Jack nor Jim *has* finished *his* ~~work~~.
Neither the instructor nor the students *have* finished *their* work.

EXERCISE 8b.   In the following sentences make every pronoun agree with its antecedent in accordance with formal usage. Then place an *I* before any sentence that would be acceptable in familiar speech or informal writing.

1. Everybody has their own solution to the race problem.
2. None of the students in the psychology class could analyze their own dreams.
3. Anyone should have the right to vote after they reach the age of eighteen.
4. The citizens' group submitted their report to the mayor.
5. Neither of the world leaders was willing to compromise on their demands.
6. If either a black man or a white man were qualified, they would get the job.

68

7. No teen-ager appreciates their parents' sacrifices for them until later in life.
8. If a physician or a lawyer came to this town, they would make a good living.
9. Every American citizen should have the right to live wherever they can afford to live.
10. The Kennedy family carried on in spite of their tragedies.

→ **8c** **Make sure that a demonstrative adjective** *(this, that, these, those)* **agrees in number with the noun it modifies.**

These adjective forms seldom cause difficulty. One frequent error, however, occurs when the demonstrative adjective is used with *kind of* or *sort of* followed by plural nouns. Here you must remember that the demonstrative adjective modifies the singular noun *kind* or *sort* and <u>not</u> the following plural noun. Thus a singular demonstrative is used.

NONSTANDARD	*These kind* of strawberries taste sweet.
STANDARD	*This kind* of strawberry tastes sweet.
NONSTANDARD	*These sort* of watches are expensive.
STANDARD	*This sort* of watch is expensive.

EXERCISE 8c. In the following sentences correct every error of agreement in accordance with formal usage.

1. Adam Clayton Powell is one of those kind of politicians who is usually described as "flamboyant."
2. Congress should pass a law that everyone must vote or they will be fined.
3. The committee on admission of new members does not approve the nomination of Mr. Smith.
4. The President with his cabinet members are touring South America.
5. Ignorance is one of the major forces that encourage crime.
6. Two solutions to national traffic problems have been offered but neither have been tried.
7. Poverty is still one of the major problems that afflict our society.
8. The NAACP is only one of the groups that are trying to better conditions for black Americans.
9. The college president told the militant students he would not put up with these sort of tactics.
10. After thirty, one loses both the rebelliousness and the inventiveness of their earlier years.
11. A chorus of jeers and catcalls were the response to the Vice-President's appearance.
12. Although everyone wants the right to vote, they don't all exercise that right at election time.

13. If world peace is to be assured, either the Eastern bloc or the Western bloc must alter their position.
14. The Democratic party lost several of their congressional seats in the last election.
15. If someone wants to "do their thing," they should be allowed to.

9 Faulty Reference of Pronouns = REF

A pronoun depends for meaning upon a noun or another pronoun. Insure clarity in your writing by making pronoun antecedents clear and obvious. Place pronouns as close to their antecedents as possible and make pronoun references exact.

9a Avoid sentences in which there are two possible antecedents for a pronoun.

AMBIGUOUS   Jack told Carl that he was ungrateful. (Is *he* Jack or Carl?)
CLEAR   Jack said to Carl, "You are ungrateful."
CLEAR   Jack said to Carl, "I am ungrateful."
CLEAR   Jack confessed to Carl that he was ungrateful.

AMBIGUOUS   After Mrs. Henry scolded little Sylvia, she regretted her rudeness. (To whom do *she* and *her* refer?)
CLEAR   After Mrs. Henry scolded her, little Sylvia regretted her rudeness.
CLEAR   After scolding little Sylvia, Mrs. Henry regretted her own rudeness.

EXERCISE 9a. Revise the following sentences by eliminating the ambiguous reference of pronouns.

1. When President Kennedy met with Premier Khrushchev in 1960, he was very disappointed by his reaction.
2. He gave his brother a copy of *Ulysses,* which was one of his favorite books.
3. He dropped the record on the phonograph arm and broke it.
4. Her second husband told her first husband that he should never have married her.
5. The American people have had a number of inadequate presidents, but Congress has kept them from ruining the country.
6. If Hitler had behaved differently with Stalin, he might not have had to take the action he did.

7. Joan told her friend that she should take speech lessons.
8. George had a dog with fleas which he was always scratching.
9. John Steinbeck should have written a biography of Martin Luther King after he won the Nobel Prize.
10. When Leon visited his father he was very angry.

9b **Avoid references to an antecedent which is remote from the pronoun, or so placed as to confuse the reader.**

REMOTE   The birds sang in the forest where the undergrowth was thick, and a brook wound slowly in the valley. *They* were of many colors. (The pronoun *they* is too far removed from its antecedent, *birds*.)

CLEAR   . . . The *birds* were of many colors. (Confusion in meaning avoided by repetition of the noun.)

CLEAR   The *birds*, which were of many colors, sang in the forest. . . . (Elimination of the remote reference by changing the second sentence of the example into a subordinate clause.)

VAGUE   When the President's committee was established, he appointed student representatives. (Reference to an antecedent in the possessive case is confusing.)

CLEAR   When the President established his committee, he appointed student representatives.

VAGUE   He leaned over the bench for hours working on the blueprints. It was too low to be comfortable. (Confusing: The reference of *it* is not clear until the reader completes the sentence.)

CLEAR   He leaned over the bench for hours working on the blueprints. The bench was too low to be comfortable.

EXERCISE 9b. Revise all sentences in which pronouns are too remote from their antecedents.

1. The school belongs to the community. Students and their parents should work closely with faculty and administrators in developing programs of instruction and recreation. It could be the meeting place for all community activities.
2. The delegates arrived in twos and threes for the emergency session at the UN. Interested spectators were also streaming in. They stopped only to pose for the press photographers at the entrance.
3. The crowd watched as the computer projected the election returns all across the nation. It moaned. It groaned. It was an unexpected defeat.
4. He argued that marijuana is simply a means of achieving relaxation, and that artists, writers, and even office workers find it necessary.
5. He and his opponent made promises to the people of the nation to augment and revitalize the various poverty programs. But they were soon forgotten after the election.

9c **Avoid the vague use of** *this, that,* **or** *which* **to refer to the general idea of a preceding clause or sentence.**

Informal English frequently uses *this, that,* or *which* to refer to the general idea of a preceding clause or sentence. Even relatively formal written English accepts such general antecedents when the reference is unmistakably clear. In general, however, it is preferable that a pronoun refer to a particular word in the sentence.

FORMAL   His *joining* a fraternity, *which* was unexpected, pleased his family. (*Which* refers specifically to *joining*.)

INFORMAL   He joined a fraternity, *which* was unexpected and pleased his family. (The reference is clear, although *which* refers to the entire preceding clause, not to any specific word.)

Eliminate a vague pronoun reference by (1) recasting the sentence to eliminate the pronoun, or (2) supplying a specific antecedent for the pronoun.

VAGUE   The profits from the investment would be large, *which* I realized almost immediately.

CLEAR   I realized almost immediately that the profits from the investment would be large. (The pronoun is eliminated.)

CLEAR   The profits from the investment would be large, a *fact that* I realized almost immediately. (A specific antecedent is supplied for the pronoun *that*.)

EXERCISE 9 c.   Revise all sentences in which the reference of pronouns is vague.

1. In the hockey playoffs at the 1964 Olympics, the Soviets were beaten by the Czechs, which made them very angry.
2. Martin Luther King was dedicated to nonviolence, which influenced him to become a minister.
3. People should always vote on election day. This is an indication of their desire to have good government.
4. Marlon Brando mumbles his lines and scratches his nose, which he learned at the Actor's Studio.
5. The government pays farmers not to grow crops. This is not helping to solve the problem of hunger among poor people.
6. The migrant farm worker is not protected by minimum wage laws, and this should be corrected immediately.
7. The campus paper proposed that the administration provide birth control pills, which upset school officials very much.
8. The Arabs and Israelis are constantly poised on the edge of war. This adds much to international tension.

9. There is a part on the far side of the museum, which is open to the public.
10. She was self-conscious about her money. But this didn't bother her real friends.

9d **Do not use a pronoun to refer to a noun that is not expressed but is merely implied by the preceding construction.**

WEAK   Because we put the wire fence around the chicken yard, *they* cannot escape. (The sentence implies the antecedent *chickens,* but the word is not expressed.)

CLEAR   Because we put the wire fence around the chicken yard, the *chickens* cannot escape.

WEAK   Tom's brother is an engineer, and *this* is the profession Tom wants to study. (*This* cannot logically refer to *engineer.*)

CLEAR   Tom's brother is an engineer, and *engineering* is the profession Tom wants to study.

EXERCISE 9d. In the following sentences eliminate all references to unexpressed antecedents.

1. She is a meticulous housekeeper because she learned it when she was a child.
2. He took the shutters off the window frames and painted them.
3. Because Lucy had never worked a potter's wheel, she supposed it was easy.
4. Dad told Ross that he stayed up watching television too late.
5. There is a police station near the church, and we called them when we saw broken windows in the basement.
6. The orange trees were covered with cloths and fanned by the warmth of smudge pots. This was due to the frost that had settled over Florida.
7. After hearing a lecture on underwater sound experimentation, Mr. Eldon had great admiration for them.
8. Whenever Shirley meets Rose, she seems annoyed.
9. Take the baby out of the bathwater and throw it away.
10. We plucked off the feathers before we roasted them.

9e **Avoid the indefinite use of** *they, you,* **and** *it.*

The indefinite use of *they, you,* and *it* is very common in spoken English, but is generally avoided in all but the most informal written English.

FORMAL   In less industrialized areas, the problems of the city are not understood.

INFORMAL   In less industrialized areas, *they* do not understand the problems of the city.

Don't be indefinite!

FORMAL   In some states motorists are not permitted to drive faster than fifty miles an hour.

INFORMAL   In some states *you* are not permitted to drive faster than fifty miles an hour.

FORMAL   The newspaper says that Monday will be warmer.

INFORMAL   *It* says in the newspaper that Monday will be warmer.*

EXERCISE 9e.   Revise the following sentences to avoid the indefinite use of *they, you,* and *it.*

1.   In the armistice agreement it says that neither party will violate the new boundaries.
2.   In every society you have to expect that some people will not be able to provide for themselves.
3.   The government pays out money everywhere except where it is needed.
4.   In France they count heavily on tourism as a source of income.
5.   In Central America you hear of revolutions every few months.
6.   In the Victorian era, they never talked about sex in public.
7.   When I called the CIA, they said they didn't have any openings for summer jobs.
8.   In every generation, you find a "generation gap."
9.   In the first few verses of the Bible, it describes the creation of the world.
10.   In Wisconsin they produce a lot of cheese.

10   Shifts in Point of View = PV and Mixed Constructions = MIX

POINT OF VIEW is said to be consistent when we continue the use of one subject, one person and number in pronouns, and one tense, mood, or voice in verbs, as far are grammar allows. Needless shifts in any of these elements, by forcing the reader to shift gears, will impair the effectiveness of your sentences.

---

* The indefinite use of *it* is appropriate in such idioms as *It is cloudy, It is too late to go.*

10a Do not shift the subject of a sentence or the voice of the verb.

FAULTY Frogs could be heard croaking as we neared the swamp. (The subject shifts from *frogs* to *we.* The verb shifts from passive to active voice.)

REVISED We heard frogs croaking as we neared the swamp.

FAULTY Ellen stayed at a mountain resort, and much of her time was spent in painting. (The subject shifts from *Ellen* to *much.* The verb shifts from active to passive voice.)

REVISED Ellen stayed at a mountain resort and spent much of her time in painting.

(See Section 36 for the weakness of the passive voice in many constructions.)

EXERCISE 10a. Revise the following sentences by eliminating all needless shifts in subject or voice.

1. If the bag doesn't match the hat, you can dye it.
2. He marked the distance from the crosswalk to the curb, and then a heavy yellow line was painted across the area.
3. David was a fine archer, but his strength was not great enough to pull that heavy bow.
4. Mr. Jones put putty around all the window panes, and then the broken window sashes were repaired.
5. When we neared the campus, the carillon tower was seen.
6. After a path was dug through the snow by the children, they began coasting on their sleds.
7. The Yankees will play the Mets; they have a great team.
8. The most plentiful supply of gold in the world is found in South Africa while Mexico leads in silver mining.
9. If you use highly fired china in your dishwasher, it will last longer.
10. After a hot fire was built by the campers, they dried their wet clothing.

10b Do not shift person or number.

FAULTY When *you* have good health, *one* should feel fortunate. (A shift from second to third person.)

REVISED When *you* have good health, *you* should feel fortunate.

REVISED When *one* has good health, *he* (or *one*) should feel fortunate.

FAULTY If a *person* practices diligently, *they* can become an expert archer. (A shift from singular to plural number.)

REVISED If a *person* practices diligently, *he* can become an expert archer.

EXERCISE 10b.   Revise the following sentences by eliminating all needless shifts in person or number.

1. No matter what political party one belongs to, you should listen to all the candidates.
2. You should install a safety belt in your car because they help to save lives.
3. A public opinion poll is based on a cross section of the population, but they have occasionally been wrong.
4. When one is feeling tired, a candy bar will give you some quick energy.
5. Leonard Bernstein once said of the New York Philharmonic that they were second to none.
6. Everyone should have access to birth control information, if their religious convictions permit.
7. The average black American today feels it is less important to imitate white people than for them to develop a feeling of racial pride in themselves.
8. Most people enjoy a novel by Tolstoy because their characters are so interesting.
9. If one is dissatisfied with the way the government is being run, you should write to your congressman more often.
10. I tried cigarette-smoking but they made my throat sore.

10c   Do not shift tense or mood.

FAULTY   He *sat* down at his desk and *begins* to write. (The verb shifts from past tense to present tense.)

REVISED   He *sat* down at his desk and *began* to write.

FAULTY   *Hold* the rifle firmly against your shoulder, and then you *should take* careful aim. (The verb shifts from imperative mood to indicative mood.)

REVISED   *Hold* the rifle firmly against your shoulder and then *take* careful aim.

EXERCISE 10c.   Revise the following sentences by eliminating all needless shifts in tense or mood.

1. When I smoked cigarettes, they don't do me any good.
2. First you should learn about the issues, and then vote for a candidate.
3. *Great Expectations* was exciting to read, but Miss Haversham is totally unrealistic.
4. You may prefer to travel by plane, but if the weather is bad, you might have to go by bus.
5. Since I explained to the professor why I hadn't done the work, I expect him to pass me.
6. The Sunday drivers were out in full force, and suddenly there is an accident.

7. I shall be delighted to attend if my husband might accompany me.
8. The university is attempting to revise its curriculum and the students were asked to submit suggestions.
9. The library has an intricate system of ordering books, but I might find what you wanted.
10. The store manager decided to offer free samples, and suddenly the store is packed with customers.

10d Do not use mixed constructions.

A mixed construction is one in which a writer begins a sentence with one construction and then shifts to another.

> The fact that John was a good student he received many offers for well-paying jobs.
>
> As a college town many students have their own rooms here.
>
> I think the use of DDT was by far the most dangerous in this county.

This error may occur when you are writing longer and more complex sentences than you commonly write. Careful proofreading of your papers is the best remedy, for once you are aware of the error, you can easily correct it.

MIXED	Take, for example, in the strip-mines of southeastern Ohio, the blaster has one of the best-paying jobs.
REPAIRED	For example, in the strip-mines of southeastern Ohio, the blaster has one of the best-paying jobs.
MIXED	If we here in America cannot live peaceably and happily together, we cannot hope that nations that have different living conditions to live peaceably with us.
REPAIRED	If we here in America cannot live peaceably and happily together, we cannot expect that other nations that have different living conditions will live peaceably with us.
MIXED	Every few hundred feet a test sample of the layer of earth a bit of it is analyzed to determine the distance from oil.
REPAIRED	Every few hundred feet a test sample of the layer of earth is analyzed to determine the distance from oil.

A more specific kind of mixed construction springs from the use of an improper verb tense in indirect quotations.

MIXED	The manager told me he would have my car for me as soon as he can get the service garage.
REPAIRED	The manager told me he would have my car for me as soon as he could get the service garage.

EXERCISE 10d. Eliminate any mixed constructions in the following sentences.

1. As a center for the performing arts, most young actors and actresses yearn to go to New York.
2. I tried to explain the generation gap to my parents who, from their attitudes, one would think they hadn't read anything in years.
3. In every effort the student made to explain the problem to his instructor got him more confused.
4. By allowing black Americans to develop and enforce their unique culture will increase their sense of racial pride and identity.
5. Wage increases are regular but the way the cost of living is rising they don't make much difference.
6. By introducing sex education in the elementary school young people could approach marriage with understanding and maybe they would last longer.
7. LSD might be a useful drug, but the way it is used by young people it seems to do more harm than good.
8. Much help came from the instructor tried a second time to explain the idea to his students.
9. The law requires you to go to high school until of a certain age, besides being an accepted policy that all children go through at least high school.
10. By sitting down to talk together, many family problems could be avoided altogether.

11 Misplaced Parts = MIS PT

Modern English, as we have seen in our discussion of grammar, relies heavily upon word order to show relations among words. The Latin sentences *Puella amat agricolam* and *Agricolam amat puella* have the same literal meaning: *The girl loves the farmer.* Even though the positions of subject and object are reversed, the special endings (*-a* and *-am*) make the meaning of the sentence unmistakable. But if the English equivalents of the Latin words are reversed, so is the English meaning: *The girl loves the farmer; The farmer loves the girl.* Word order, in short, is crucial to meaning in our language.

Just as word order is the principal means by which we keep our subject–verb–object relations clear, so it is the principal grammatical means by which we keep many of our modifiers attached to the words they modify. We have to be especially watchful of phrases and clauses that modify nouns, since they normally attach to the nearest noun preceding them. Consequently, unless we are careful we can write sentences such as:

> He bought a horse from a stranger with a lame hind leg.
> We met a boy from the college in New York.

Context usually—though not always—allows the reader to work out the meaning intended in such sentences. But by the time he does so, he is, at best, distracted from the point.

11a **Be sure that adverbs such as** *almost, even, hardly, just, merely, only, nearly, scarcely* **refer clearly and logically to the words they modify.**

The misplacement of these modifiers—particularly *only*—does not always result in confusion. The misplaced *only,* in fact, is rather common in informal English. However, if you are to avoid ambiguity in meaning you must exercise care in placing modifiers.

FORMAL	We caught *only* three fish.
INFORMAL	We *only* caught three fish.
ILLOGICAL	She *nearly* blushed until she was purple.
CLEAR	She blushed until she was *nearly* purple.
MISPLACED	I *almost* read half the book.
CLEAR	I read *almost* half the book.

EXERCISE 11a. In the following sentences, place the adverbs nearer the words they modify.

1. He almost seemed amused.
2. The *U. S. Constitution* just docked here last week.
3. Since she had never appeared on a stage before, she nearly was faint from fright.
4. The Cub Scouts only have meetings once a week.
5. She merely refused our offer of help because she wanted to be independent.
6. The earthquake victims needed nurses to bandage their wounds badly.
7. Reports will only be mailed after all the final examinations are finished.
8. For ten years we almost knew nothing about the prisoner's condition.
9. They scarcely planted any crops on the farm last spring.
10. The convict nearly terrorized the captive guards for four hours.

11b   Be sure that modifying phrases refer clearly to the words they modify.

ILLOGICAL	Who is the woman who gave you the candy *in the pink dress?*
CLEAR	Who is the woman *in the pink dress* who gave you the candy?
ILLOGICAL	This poison attracts mice *with the smell of cheese.*
CLEAR	This poison *with the smell of cheese* attracts mice.

EXERCISE 11b. In the following sentences, place the modifying phrases nearer the words they modify.

1. The President announced that he would confer with his cabinet at his press conference last week.
2. The audience watched the go-go dancers with admiring eyes.
3. He dropped out of school after three years' attendance on Friday.
4. The furnace exploded after the patrons left the theater with a loud crash.
5. The government is watching the cost of living spiral upwards without doing anything.
6. The demonstrators took over the park with their banners flying.
7. The astronauts looked forward to landing on the moon for several years.
8. In old-style Westerns, the hero kisses the horse with a smile.
9. The boy was rescued after he was nearly drowned by a lifeguard.
10. The library informed me I had to return the book on the enclosed card.

11c   Be sure that modifying clauses refer clearly to the words they modify.

ILLOGICAL	She borrowed an egg from a neighbor *that was rotten.*
CLEAR	From a neighbor she borrowed an egg *that was rotten.*
ILLOGICAL	There was a canary in the cage *that never sang.*
CLEAR	In the cage there was a canary *that never sang.*
ILLOGICAL	A dog is good company *that is well trained.*
CLEAR	A dog *that is well trained* is good company.

EXERCISE 11c. In the following sentences, place the modifying clauses nearer the words they modify.

1. He bought a sports car from a dealer that had been completely re-hauled and repainted.
2. We watched the quiz program on the TV that our college team won.
3. She uses hair coloring on her hair which she buys wholesale.

4. I took a bus at Times Square that was going uptown.
5. He bought a Great Dane from a neighbor that was already house-broken.
6. He secured a job with the government after he graduated from college which lasted twenty years.
7. She was knitting socks for her children that were warm.
8. She bought an alarm clock for her husband that was guaranteed for life.
9. The new house was next to the park with three bedrooms.
10. He tried to get to know girls with a new approach.

11d **Avoid "squinting" modifiers.**

A "squinting" modifier is one that may modify either a preceding word or a following word. It squints at the words on its right and left, and leaves the reader confused.

SQUINTING	His physician told him *frequently* to exercise.
CLEAR	His physician *frequently* told him to exercise.
CLEAR	His physician told him to exercise *frequently*.
SQUINTING	The committee which was studying the matter *yesterday* turned in its report.
CLEAR	The committee which was studying the matter turned in its report *yesterday*.
CLEAR	The committee *which spent yesterday* studying the matter turned in its report.
SQUINTING	She promised *on her way home* to visit him.
CLEAR	*On her way home*, she promised to visit him.
CLEAR	She promised to visit him *on her way home*.

EXERCISE 11d. Recast the following sentences to eliminate squinting modifiers.

1. The motorcycle he was riding happily skidded off the road.
2. Even the student who works hard occasionally flunks.
3. The person who succeeds in nine cases out of ten is intelligent.
4. The instructor told his students when the class was over they could ask their questions.
5. The President said today taxes would be cut.
6. The passengers were told when it was noon the plane would take off.
7. Religious faith without doubt is a comfort to many people.
8. I promised Jack I would meet him at the corner with the book.
9. The men who were beating on the wall wildly began shooting.
10. I promised when the movie was over I would tell her all about it.

11e Do not split infinitives awkwardly.

An infinitive is split when an adverbial modifier separates the *to* from the verb. There is nothing ungrammatical about splitting an infinitive, and sometimes a split is necessary to avoid awkardness. But most split infinitives are unnecessary.

AWKWARD   She tried *to* not carelessly *hurt* the kitten.

CLEAR   She tried not *to hurt* the kitten carelessly.

AWKWARD   You should try *to,* if you can, *take* a walk every day.

CLEAR   If you can, you should try *to take* a walk every day.

On the other hand, in the following examples the sentence with the split infinitive is the less awkward.

CLEAR   Needing an advantage in the race, he expected *to* more than *gain* it by diligent practice. (Awkwardness results if *more than* is moved to any other position in the sentence.)

AWKWARD   Needing an advantage in the race, he more than expected *to gain* it by diligent practice.

EXERCISE 11e. Revise the following sentences by eliminating awkward split infinitives.

1. The President promised to, if the budget permits, consider instituting a wage-supplement law.
2. The owner of the discotheque asked the boys to immediately produce proof of their age.
3. The availability of birth control information helps to effectively reduce the number of unwanted children.
4. The student body voted to for once and for all abolish fraternities from campus.
5. Black Americans are determined to never again settle for subordinate status.
6. The president of the university tried to tactfully and quietly intervene between students and police.
7. The problem in Vietnam is to successfully resolve the differences between North and South.
8. The major nations of the world regularly decide to one day in the near future reduce their armaments complex.
9. It's helpful to immediately send in your tax return after the first of the year.
10. You have to willingly accept the idea that you are your brother's keeper, or the condition of man will never improve.

11f In general, avoid separations of subject and verb, verb and object, or parts of verb phrases unless such separations add greatly to the effectiveness of the sentence.

EFFECTIVE SEPARATION	The captain, *seeing the ominous storm clouds gathering overhead,* ordered the crew to take in the sail.
EFFECTIVE SEPARATION	And so Pilate, *willing to content the people,* released Barabbas unto them, and delivered Jesus, *when he had scourged him,* to be crucified.
	—*St. Mark* 15: 15
EFFECTIVE SEPARATION	Only when a man is safely ensconced under six feet of earth, *with several tons of enlauding granite upon his chest,* is he in a position to give advice with any certainty, and then he is silent.
	—EDWARD NEWTON
AWKWARD SEPARATION	She *found,* after an hour's search, the *money* hidden under the rug.
CLEAR	After an hour's search, she *found* the *money* hidden under the rug.
AWKWARD SEPARATION	At the convention I saw Mr. Ward, whom I *had* many years ago *met* in Chicago.
CLEAR	At the convention I saw Mr. Ward, whom I *had met* many years ago in Chicago.

EXERCISE 11f. Revise the following sentences by eliminating the unnecessary separation of related sentence elements.

1. The President announced, after answering several questions, the plan to recognize Red China.
2. You should, if you ever see a drunken driver, immediately contact the police.
3. He handed her the box from the top of the stairs.
4. Migrant workers, because they are not protected by minimum-wage laws, are underpaid.
5. The seniors bade farewell to the campus where through four long years they had spent so many happy hours.
6. The Soviets tried, although they did not succeed, to establish a missile base in Cuba.
7. In a primitive hospital in the jungles of Africa, Albert Schweitzer for many years lived and worked.
8. The administration, discovering that the students had taken over the building, decided to call in the police.
9. The uninvited guest slipped in the door during the party that was nearest the garden.
10. She made, after years of smoking heavily, an effort to stop.

12 Dangling Constructions = DGL

A dangling construction is a phrase or clause that either modifies nothing in the sentence or that seems to modify a word to which it is not logically related. A dangling construction is most often the result of carelessness in writing or thinking. Eliminate a dangling construction by (1) making the modifier apply clearly to the word it modifies or (2) expanding the dangling phrase into a subordinate clause.

12a   Avoid dangling participles.

A participle, though it does not make an assertion, nonetheless does imply an actor. Failure to identify this actor creates misleading —and sometimes humorous—effects.

Plastic sheeting is used to keep a baby on the rear seat of a car from rolling off and also to protect the seat itself. The sheeting is fashioned to fit the seat and extend upward at the front to fasten to window frames. *Being transparent,* the sleeping baby is always visible.

Having been shot in the stern, the captain ordered the ship towed back to the port.

DANGLING	*Driving* through the mountains, several bears were seen. (The participle *driving* modifies nothing, although it seems to modify *bears,* to which it is not logically related.)
REVISED	*Driving* through the mountains, *we* saw several bears. (*Driving* clearly modifies *we,* the subject of the main clause.)
REVISED	When *we drove* through the mountains, *we saw* several bears. (The modifying phrase is expanded into a subordinate clause.)
DANGLING	*Riding* my bicycle, a dog chased me. (*Riding* modifies nothing; it cannot logically modify *dog.*)
REVISED	*Riding* my bicycle, *I* was chased by a dog. (*Riding* clearly modifies *I,* the subject of the main clause.)
REVISED	While *I was riding* my bicycle, a dog chased me. (The modifying phrase is expanded into a subordinate clause.)

EXERCISE 12a. Revise the following sentences to eliminate the dangling participial phrases.

1. Los Angeles is impressive, viewing it through a veil of smog.
2. Knowing little about Asian customs, the first Presidential tour was not entirely successful.
3. Sitting at an outdoor cafe, Paris reveals its eternal variety.
4. The scenery was monotonous, passing flat plains without a tree in sight for miles.
5. Lying on the sidewalk, the police arrested the derelict.
6. Being made of glass, I handled the tabletop carefully.
7. Driving along at top speed, the road took an unexpected turn to the left.
8. Spanning the Narrows, I realized the Verrazano Bridge was one of the longest in the world.
9. Fearless and uncaged, visitors to game preserves must be careful not to excite the animals.
10. The airport delays were endless, waiting for the fog to lift.

12b Avoid dangling gerunds.

A gerund is an -*ing* verb form used as a noun. Like the participle, the gerund implies an actor, and once again you must identify that actor clearly in order to avoid confused or ludicrous meanings.

DANGLING After *putting* a worm on my hook, the fish began to bite.

REVISED After *putting* a worm on my hook, *I* found that the fish began to bite. (*Putting* clearly refers to *I,* the subject of the main clause.)

DANGLING Before *exploring* the desert, our water supply was replenished. (*Exploring* cannot logically refer to *supply*, the subject of the main clause.)

REVISED Before *exploring* the desert, *we* replenished our water supply. (*Exploring* refers to *we,* the subject of the main clause.)

EXERCISE 12b. Revise the following sentences to eliminate the dangling gerund phrases.

1. On receiving the draft notice, tears filled his mother's eyes.
2. By reading constantly, the doctor was forced to prescribe glasses.
3. After releasing the suspect, new evidence was submitted to the police.
4. In packing the bedroll, a blanket was forgotten by the camper.
5. Upon opening the closet door, the boxes on the shelf tumbled down.
6. In choosing a teaching career, opportunities for work were bright.
7. Before transferring to the new school, his mother took him in to meet his future classmates.

8. By riding in an airplane, the landscape acquires a new beauty.
9. By checking the answer sheet, my errors became clear to me.
10. In preparing the launch, the space ship was examined several times.

12c Avoid dangling infinitives.

DANGLING   *To write* effectively, practice is necessary. (*To write* cannot logically refer to *practice,* the subject of the main clause.)

REVISED   *To write* effectively, *one* must practice. (*To write* logically refers to *one,* the subject of the main clause.)

REVISED   If *one wishes to write* effectively, *he* (or *one*) must practice.

DANGLING   *To examine* the brakes, the wheel must be removed. (*To examine* cannot logically refer to *wheel.*)

REVISED   *To examine* the brakes, *one* must remove the wheel. (*To examine* refers to *one.*)

REVISED   If *you wish to examine* the brakes, *you* must remove the wheel.

EXERCISE 12c. Revise the following sentences to eliminate the dangling infinitive phrases.

1. To plan a college program, career goals must be kept in mind.
2. To become a concert pianist, many years of study are required.
3. To be a good citizen, some knowledge of government procedure is necessary.
4. To eliminate malnutrition, foodstamps were issued to the poor.
5. To be appreciated properly, the volume on the record player should be high.
6. To find out why the wheel shakes, the car must be driven over 50 miles an hour.
7. To be completely immune to polio, several innoculations may be necessary.
8. To be a financial success, a minimum of 100 performances of a play is necessary.
9. To impress a prospective employer, a neat appearance is essential.
10. To be extra safe, the lock on the new apartment door was changed.

12d Avoid dangling elliptical clauses.

An elliptical clause is one in which the subject or verb is implied rather than stated. The clause dangles if its implied subject is not the same as the subject of the main clause. Eliminate a dangling elliptical clause by (1) making the dangling clause agree with the subject of the main clause, or (2) supplying the omitted subject or verb.

DANGLING   *When a baby,* my grandfather gave me a silver cup.

REVISED   *When a baby, I* was given a silver cup by my grandfather.
           (The subject of the main clause agrees with the implied
           subject of the elliptical clause.)

REVISED   *When I was a baby,* my grandfather gave me a silver cup.
           (The omitted subject and verb are supplied in the elliptical
           clause.)

DANGLING   *While rowing on the lake,* the boat overturned.

REVISED   *While rowing on the lake,* we overturned the boat. (The sub-
           ject of the main clause agrees with the implied subject of the
           elliptical clause.)

REVISED   *While we were rowing on the lake,* the boat overturned (*or we
           overturned the boat*). (The elliptical clause is expanded into a
           subordinate clause.)

EXERCISE 12d. Revise the following sentences to eliminate the
dangling elliptical clauses.

1. If sighted, the astronauts would report that the man in the moon
   really did exist.
2. When well stewed, you drain off the juice.
3. While planning the takeover of the administration building, the
   police barged in.
4. If highly polished, you may slip on the floor.
5. The car proved hard to drive when drinking heavily.
6. When making use of birth control information, the child can arrive
   exactly when planned.
7. My bicycle tire went flat while hurrying to the dentist.
8. If well oiled, I find my motorcycle easier to handle.
9. Although a minor, the judge suspended the sentence.
10. If lost, we shall pay a reward for the ring.

13 Omissions = OM
and Incomplete
and Illogical Comparisons = COMP

A sentence will fail to communicate clearly if the writer omits
words necessary to his meaning. Some such omissions result merely
from carelessness.

> The opportunities for men television repair are varied.
> Many millions people were unemployed last depression.
> Learning by imitation is one of the most common in early life.

In the first two of these sentences, one suspects that the writer has simply failed to write the necessary words: *in* after *men* in the first, and *of* before *people* and *during the* before *last* in the second. The only cure for this sort of ill is more careful proofreading. The third sentence, although somewhat more complex, is probably of the same sort. The sentence clearly requires something like *methods of learning* after *common*. Very probably the writer thought out the sentence with such a phrase and, again, was merely careless in getting his idea down on paper.

Another kind of omission results from failing to follow through fully the logic of what one is saying. Note the following:

> If you miss chapel, either because of sickness or will power, you must account for your absence.
> Having spent most of my first year in college in mathematics and chemistry has made me a bit wary of English.

In the first of these the writer seems to be referring to the possibility of missing chapel *because of will power;* presumably the thing that would be parallel to sickness is not *will power* but rather *lack of will power.* The problem is not one of grammar or usage but of logic. The second sentence presents a more complicated problem, but still one of logic. The reader has a right to expect that wariness of English courses would come from experience with English courses, not with mathematics or chemistry courses. We have the same kind of puzzled reaction to the sentence as we would have to the statement *Having eaten biscuits, I am afraid of jam.* We feel we might be able to make something out of it, but we can't be at all sure what. In such constructions it is perhaps less the sentence itself than the writer's ideas that are confused and incomplete.

A final kind of omission results from carrying over into writing certain kinds of constructions which, though common in much spoken English, are less precise than most forms of written English require. Such constructions as *We became friends spring semester,* or *The trouble was the paper had not been turned in,* are common in speech and extremely informal writing; but more exact writing strongly prefers that constructions be filled out to avoid any possible ambiguity for the reader. The careful writer would prefer *We became friends during the spring semester,* and *The trouble was that the paper had not been turned in.*

13a **Carefully proofread your manuscripts to catch careless omissions.**

CARELESS   The ball sailed over back fence and out of sight.

CORRECTED   The ball sailed over *the* back fence and out of sight.

CARELESS   The officers of the fraternity were brought before the dean and asked explain the incident.

CORRECTED   The officers of the fraternity were brought before the dean and asked *to* explain the incident.

EXERCISE 13a. Supply the words omitted in the sentences below. Put an *I* before any sentence that you think would be acceptable in informal speech.

1. The trouble was the Viet Cong was not prepared to negotiate.
2. This type novel is difficult to understand.
3. Space travel the last few years has proved expensive but rewarding.
4. He made it seem he wanted to be caught.
5. The past few years more and more young men have been questioning the legality of military service.
6. The estimate from the contractor gave the committee an idea how extensive repairs would be.
7. This quality merchandise would not be sold in a reputable store.
8. I have been trying to decide which make car I would buy if I had the money.
9. He made a supreme effort senior year and graduated with his class.
10. Which brand toothpaste reduces cavities?

13b **Do not omit or leave incomplete any constructions or words that are necessary to the clarity of a sentence.**

CONFUSING   In college as compared with high school, teachers are more equal with students instead of a statue on a high pedestal.

REVISED   College teachers often treat their students as equals; high school teachers often set themselves above their students.

INCOMPLETE His ideas were sound and adopted without discussion.

REVISED   His ideas were sound and *were* adopted without discussion. (*Were* needs to be repeated since the two verbs are not parallel; the first *were* is used as a main verb; the second is used as an auxiliary with *adopted*.)

INCOMPLETE Henry was interested and skillful at photography.

REVISED   Henry was interested *in* and skillful at photography. (*Interested* idiomatically requires the preposition *in;* if it is not inserted, we tend to read *interested at.*

89

CONFUSING   The instructor noticed the students in the examination
             were anxious to start.

REVISED   The instructor noticed *that* the students in the examination
             were anxious to start. (The omission of *that* leads the reader
             momentarily to take *students* as the direct object of *noticed;*
             the inclusion of *that* indicates immediately that the whole
             clause is the direct object.)

EXERCISE 13b. Improve the following sentences.

1. Ability to make decisions and discipline mark the difference between a child and an adult.
2. He was both afraid and fascinated by the idea of skin-diving.
3. She majored in primary education because she was interested and capable with young children.
4. Being a traveling salesman is difficult, for by the time he gets home he is too tired to talk or play with his children.
5. I never will and never have ridden in an airplane.
6. He finally decided to and eventually wound up giving up smoking.
7. Ghetto children deserve to and should be getting a better education.
8. Joining the Peace Corps was something he never dreamed would happen to him.
9. Having spent large sums for defense has left the government with fewer resources to help the poor.
10. He wanted to and would have taken her home if his car had not broken down on the country lane.

13c Provide all necessary transitions within sentences.

The adept use of transitional words and phrases is one of the
distinguishing marks of a good writer. A careful control of transitions from sentence to sentence is indispensable to paragraph coherence (see Section 32d) and to the smooth and logical movement
of writing from one idea to the next. Many times, however, clarity
demands that the writer use connecting words within a sentence to
make explicit the relation he intends between its parts. Often, of
course, such relations are clear from the larger context in which
a sentence occurs, and may be better left implied. The writer, however, must be careful to determine when logic and context will
make the precise relation clear and when it is necessary to use
connecting words. Note the following:

CONFUSING   The captain had had many adventures; he once had been
             lost in the African jungle.

REVISED   The captain had had many adventures; once, for instance,
             he had been lost in the African jungle.

The original sentence invites a confusion between the *many* in the first part of the sentence, and what is apparently *one* in the second part. The revision, by including the connecting *for instance,* makes it immediately clear that the second part of the sentence is to be understood as one of several possible examples.

CONFUSING   I have lived in several large cities, New York and Chicago.

REVISED   I have lived in several large cities such as New York and Chicago.

REVISED   I have lived in several large cities, among them New York and Chicago.

REVISED   I have lived in New York and Chicago, and in other large cities.

The original sentence is confusing because it is not immediately clear that New York and Chicago are introduced as examples of the large cities the writer has lived in.

QUESTIONABLE   He lives in Florida; the setting of his poems is in Vermont.

REVISED   He lives in Florida, but the setting of his poems is in Vermont.

REVISED   He lives in Florida, yet the setting of his poems is in Vermont.

The original sentence may be clear and effective if the context has prepared the reader for the contrast between the two parts of the sentence. If it has not, the revisions, which make the contrast between the two main statements explicit, will be more effective.

EXERCISE 13c. Study the following sentences. Write one or more revisions of each. Be prepared to explain which ones require revision and which ones can stand as they are.

1. The temperature soared; the public beaches were closed because of water pollution.
2. I have climbed several high mountains, Mt. McKinley and Mont Blanc.
3. The job market is expanding; unskilled workers are unemployed.
4. Many students major in psychology; they want to understand themselves and others better.
5. Hemingway lived in Paris; the setting for his stories was Africa.
6. Faulkner wrote of the South; his was a universal message.
7. Hippies pledged themselves to nonconformity; they all looked alike and thought alike.
8. Premarital sex is gaining acceptance; some people still frown on it.

9. Candidates make many campaign promises; most of them are not fulfilled.
10. A young man who sincerely objects to war may refuse to serve in the army; the penalties are severe.

13d Avoid the illogical use of *than any of* or *any of.*

If you say in conversation *I like Wednesday better than any day of the week* when you mean *than any other day of the week,* you are not likely to be called illogical; the words disappear quickly into the atmosphere. But if you write *I like "Mending Wall" better than any of Robert Frost's poems* when you mean *better than any other,* you exhibit your careless logic more or less permanently on paper.

ILLOGICAL	He is the best singer of any in the chorus.
REVISED	He is the best singer in the chorus.

13e Do not compare items that are not logically comparable.

ILLOGICAL	The buildings here are as impressive as any other city.
REVISED	The buildings here are as impressive as those in any other city.

13f Complete all comparisons.

An incomplete comparison occurs if you make the final part of a comparison depend for its meaning upon a word or words in a preceding parenthetical element. (For example, in the first sentence below, the omission of the parenthetical phrase would result in *He is as strong than I am.*) In colloquial English, incomplete comparisons are quite common. But they are seldom appropriate in formal usage.

1. *Omission of a necessary* as *or* than.

INCOMPLETE	He is as strong, if not stronger, than I am.
REVISED	He is as strong as, if not stronger than, I am.
REVISED	He is as strong as I am, if not stronger.

2. *Incomplete use of the superlative.*

INCOMPLETE	She is a very kind, if not the kindest, woman I know.
REVISED	She is one of the kindest women I know, if not the kindest.

13g **Give both terms of the comparison.**

INCOMPLETE   I admire her more than Jane.
REVISED   I admire her more than I admire Jane.
REVISED   I admire her more than Jane does.

13h **State the basis of comparison.***

INCOMPLETE   Our new automobile uses less gasoline.
REVISED   Our new automobile uses less gasoline than our old one did.

EXERCISE 13d-h.   Make the comparisons logical and complete.

1. He is the best President of any.
2. Rock and roll is more pleasant.
3. His face is like a movie actor.
4. I like her more than her sister.
5. I like James Baldwin better than any writer.
6. She is as pretty, if not prettier, than her mother.
7. Humphrey was as well known, if not more so, than any Vice-President in history.
8. The business element was more heavily represented in Nixon's cabinet.
9. Water colors are much easier.
10. Midwesterners are as friendly as any section in the U.S.

14 Awkwardness = AWK
and Obscurity = OBSC

Some sentences are so clumsy or meaningless that they cannot be repaired by minor surgery. They contain so many errors in basic structure that statements like "lack of parallelism," "poor subordination," or "vague reference" only begin to diagnose their ills.

---

* Advertisers are especially guilty of violating this rule: "Smoke Dromedaries—they're better!" Here the violation is obviously intentional. In colloquial English, the basis of comparison is often omitted.

Such sentences are beyond hope. Discard them, rethink what it is you want to say, and then recast your whole statement. Assume that you have written this:

> The heart, an essential in any organism, to me has the same significance to the organism in comparison with hope and man.

Don't try to touch it up. Strike out the whole sentence and start over again.

Some obscure sentences are not necessarily awkward or ungrammatical, but are so absurd as to be meaningless.

> Even though our material possessions are destroyed, we know tomorrow will be different.

Again, don't try to touch it up. Discard it and start over.

14a   Recast awkwardly phrased sentences.

AWKWARD	Some farmers plow their land in the fall of the year, and this is better they think.
RECAST	Some farmers prefer to plow their land in the fall.
AWKWARD	An education will enable me to read good books which in turn will provide happiness on my part.
RECAST	An education will provide me with the opportunity to read the good books I feel are necessary to my happiness.
AWKWARD	Each student has different problems because each has a different reason for coming and place to live.
RECAST	The problem of each student is different from that of the others because his home life and his reasons for coming to college are different.

EXERCISE 14a.   Recast the following sentences.

1. This would be a much more pleasant world if everyone could do the things he wanted to instead of because he had to.
2. College requires that the student learn to think for himself and use self-discipline, as was not so in high school for instance.
3. An employee entering the company will find himself surrounded by a new way of computing and life.
4. My parents don't understand me—they keep telling me to settle down, get a job, get married, and many other instances which really irk me.
5. Thinking of others rather than of ourselves would make a big difference in all our lives if we could do this every day.

6. On Saturday mornings there are few students in the library, which is quite pleasant if you have a lot of work to do.
7. When I walked through the college gates, I entered something I knew nothing about and of which I had no knowledge.
8. He got his summons to military service on the morning of the exam, which was to begin on the first of July.
9. Astronauts have to adjust in space to a new way of moving and how to get their bearings.
10. He liked her because she was both pretty and clever: she had blonde hair, blue eyes, and a green thumb.

14b **Rethink and recast sentences whose meaning is obscure or illogical.**

It would not do a person any good to boast of a college education if he had accomplished nothing and had nothing at the time.

I have always thought that the present time was a rather unhappy time because there are always worries, but as the time went on I looked back at these times as the only happy times.

In the first sentence the statement *It would not do a person any good* is meaningless in its context. *Good* is too ambiguous a word to have real meaning here. The writer of the second sentence probably meant to say that experience grows more pleasant in retrospect. But his sentence structure does not permit him to move from the present to the future and then to the past, as he wants to. We would have to say of the sentence, as did the confused young boy trying to give directions to some travelers, "You can't get there from here."

There is a kind of illogical sentence which, in a proper context, may make sense—and in fact strike appreciative readers or listeners as sophisticated and witty. For example, the sentence *His bad temper is a lot like his father's, only more so* might impress acquaintances of the father and son as an extremely apt description. Similarly, a sentence like *He is more or less crooked, mostly more* could be either clever or inane, depending on the speaker and the circumstances. But such a sentence as *Our feeling was the closest feeling to love, maybe even closer* is likely to strike readers as absurd. Be sure your attempted wit hits its mark.

EXERCISE 14b. Recast the following sentences.

1. A small town is not much friendlier but it is smaller.
2. The first impressions I had of the party were very noticeable to me.
3. The first sound to strike the ears of space travelers will probably be the awesome silence of space.
4. A senior will always feel nostalgic at his graduation, be it high school or college.

5. If you live in the country, a drive-in is both cheaper and more accessible.

6. Her eyes were not set too far apart or too close together, and the two together, apart from her face, were beautiful.

7. The first difference a college freshman learns is how little he knows.

8. He worked a lot with delinquent boys, which wasn't easy work, but each day he found it more so.

9. When a college teacher has a group of boys and girls of college age, the instructor tends to let them on their own.

10. Most of the unknown facts about space are quite complicated; others are quite basic.

"BASIC SENTENCE FAULTS" REVIEW EXERCISE   (Sections 6–14).
Indicate what strikes you as the principal error in each of the following sentences (faulty agreement, faulty reference, misplaced parts, etc.) and then revise the sentence.

1. Harvard generally accepts more students from the northeast than others.

2. Having been pickled in formaldehyde for a week, the lab instructor distributed the frogs for dissection.

3. Because Manhattan is an island, you have to take a bridge from New Jersey.

4. Having been battered to a pulp, the referee told the boxers the bout was over.

5. When a teen-ager begins to lecture to his parents, it always makes them feel uncomfortable.

6. He had forgotten how tall the skyscrapers were after a year in Vietnam he had grown more used to thatched huts.

7. However much he wanted to get there on time, and with all possible modes of transportation at his disposal.

8. The letter was mailed an hour ago by the new clerk with the red miniskirt in the corner mailbox.

9. She likes her better than any of the other girls.

10. Millicent went to work in the theater after being graduated from college as a chorus girl.

Manuscript Mechanics = MS

It was very pleasant to me to get a letter from you the other day. Perhaps I should have found it pleasanter if I had been able to decipher it.

—THOMAS BAILEY ALDRICH

A good many of the practices of written English are merely conventions. Logic does not justify them; they represent instead standard ways of doing things. The "mechanics" of manuscript form, of writing numbers and abbreviations, of word division (syllabication) are such conventions. We observe them chiefly because generations of readers have come to expect writers to observe them. To be ignorant of these conventions, or to violate them, is by no means to commit a cardinal sin—it is only to make nuisances of ourselves to our readers, who expect that anyone seeking their attention with a piece of writing will have the graciousness at least to do the little things properly.

15 Manuscript Form = MS

15a Use suitable materials for your manuscripts.

1. *Paper.* Your instructor will probably require you to use standard theme paper (8½ by 11 inches) with lines about one-half inch apart. Unless specifically told to, do not use narrow-lined notebook paper for themes. If you typewrite your manuscript, use either regular typewriter paper or the unruled side of theme paper. Do not use onionskin paper.

2. *Typewriter.* Use a black ribbon and keep the keys clean.

3. *Pen and ink.* Write only on the ruled side of the paper. Use a good pen and black or blue-black ink. Do not write in pencil.

15b Make sure your manuscripts are legible.

1. *Typewritten manuscripts.* Use double-spacing. Leave one space between words and two spaces between sentences.

2. *Handwritten manuscripts.* Provide adequate spacing between words and between lines. Avoid unnecessary breaks between letters and syllables at the ends of lines. Form all letters distinctly, with clear and conspicuous capitals. Cross all *t*'s. Dot all *i*'s with real dots, not with decorative circles. Avoid artistic flourishes. If your handwriting tends to be excessively large and sprawling, or small and cramped, or precariously tipped to right or left, make a conscious effort to improve it.

15c **Keep your manuscripts physically uniform and orderly.**

1. *Margins.* Leave a uniform one-and-a-half-inch margin at the top and at the left side of each page and about one inch at the right side and bottom. Resist the temptation to crowd words in at the right or bottom of the page.

2. *Title.* Center the title about two inches from the top of the page, or on the first line. Leave a blank line between the title and the first paragraph. Capitalize the entire title, or if your instructor prefers, <u>capitalize the first word and all other words in the title</u> except the articles, *a, an, the,* and short prepositions or conjunctions. <u>Do not underline the title or put it in quotation marks unless it is an actual quotation.</u> Use no punctuation after titles except when a question mark or exclamation point is required. Do not repeat the title after the first page.

3. *Indenting.* Indent the first line of each paragraph about an inch, or five spaces on the typewriter. Indent lines of poetry one inch from the regular margin, or center them on the page. If you are typewriting, use single-spacing for poetry you are quoting.

4. *Paging.* Number all pages, after the first, in the upper right-hand corner. Use Arabic numerals (2, 3, 4, etc.).

5. *Endorsement.* The endorsement usually appears on the outside sheet of the folded composition and includes your name, the course, the date, plus any other information required by your instructor. Below is a specimen:

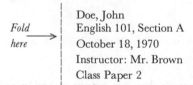

Fold here →

Doe, John
English 101, Section A
October 18, 1970
Instructor: Mr. Brown
Class Paper 2

15d **Carefully proofread your manuscripts before submitting them.**

Give every manuscript a close, almost finicky reading before turning it in. Allow a cooling-off period between composition and proofreading. If you know you are poor in spelling, punctuation, or some other area, give your paper a separate reading for each kind of error. If your proofreading reveals a great many errors, rewrite your composition. When rewriting is not necessary, make specific changes as follows:

1. If you want to delete words, draw a horizontal line through them. Do not use a series of parentheses to cancel words.

2. If you want to begin a new paragraph within an existing paragraph, put the sign ¶ or *Par.* before the sentence that is to begin the new paragraph. When you want to remove a paragraph division, write *No* ¶ or *No Par.* in the margin.

3. If you want to make a brief insertion, write the new material above the line and indicate the point of insertion by placing a caret (ʌ) below the line.

15e After your instructor has returned a manuscript, make the necessary corrections and submit it again.

Correcting your own errors is invaluable practice. Your instructor designates errors by means of numbers or symbols that refer to specific parts of this handbook. Study these parts carefully before making revisions. Note that your instructor may not indicate all errors. Be alert to eliminate all faults before returning your corrected paper. Pay especial attention to comments on plan and development, which are far more important than details of mechanics and grammar.

For an example of a composition with an instructor's markings, before and after correction, see Specimen Papers A and B in the Preface.

16 Numbers = NOS

16a Spell out numbers or amounts that can be expressed in one or two words; use numerals for other numbers or amounts.

> He spent two hundred dollars for a camera.
> Miriam is twenty-two years old.
> The boy saved $4.53.
> On their vacation they drove 2,468 miles.

16b Ordinarily, use numerals for dates.

The letters *st, nd, rd,* and *th* should not be used after the days of the month if the year is given. If the year is not given, they may be used. Write out the year only in formal social correspondence.

May 4, 1914; July 2, 1847
March 1, March first, March 1st

16c **Use numerals for street numbers, decimals and percentages, page numbers, and hours followed by** A.M. **or** P.M.

13 Milford Avenue; 57 121st Street.
The bolt is .46 inches in diameter.
The price was reduced 15 percent.
The quotation was in Chapter 4, page 119.
A train arrived from Chicago at 11:20 A.M.

16d **Except in legal or commercial writing, do not repeat in parentheses a number that has been spelled out.**

COMMERCIAL   The interest on the note was fifty (50) dollars.
STANDARD   The boys caught three fish.
              Henry ran six miles.

16e **Spell out numbers that occur at the beginning of a sentence.**

AWKWARD   217 bales of hay were lost in the fire.
REVISED   Two hundred seventeen bales of hay were lost in the fire.

If necessary, recast a sentence to eliminate numerals at the beginning.

AWKWARD   2,655 entries were received in the puzzle contest.
REVISED   In the puzzle contest 2,655 entries were received.

EXERCISE 16. In the following sentences make any necessary corrections in the use of numbers.

1. John Kennedy was inaugurated on January 20th, 1961, at the age of 44.
2. The students' strike lasted ten (10) days.
3. The satellite model measured five and nineteen-hundredths inches in circumference.
4. Steven spent 2 years in the Peace Corps.
5. The seminar met at two-thirty P.M.
6. Some students spend as much as $.95 for bus fare daily.
7. 85,000 people viewed the President's press conference.
8. Labor Day is the 1st Monday in September.
9. Retail prices were found to be nearly fifteen percent higher in the ghetto than in other areas of the city.
10. Nearly 400 people joined the protest march.

17 Abbreviations = AB

Save for a few standard exceptions, abbreviations should be avoided in ordinary writing. The following sections describe standard exceptions, as well as some forms that should not be used.

17a **The following abbreviations are appropriate in both formal and informal writing.**

1. *Titles before proper nouns.*   Use such abbreviations as *Mr., Mrs., Dr.* only when the surname is given: *Dr. Hart* or *Dr. F. D. Hart.*

INAPPROPRIATE   He has gone to consult the Dr.

REVISED   He has gone to consult Dr. Hart (*or* the doctor).

Use *St.* (Saint) with a Christian name: *St. James, St. Theresa.*

Use abbreviations such as *Hon., Rev., Prof., Sen.* only when both the surname and given name or initials are given: *The Hon. O. P. Jones,* but not *Hon. Jones.* In more formal usage spell out these titles and use *The* before *Honorable* and *Reverend.*

INFORMAL   Rev. W. C. Case delivered the sermon.

FORMAL   The Reverend W. C. Case delivered the sermon.

2. *Titles after proper names.*   Use the following abbreviations only when a name is given: *Jr., Sr., Esq., M.D., D.D., LL.D., Ph.D.* You may, however, use academic titles by themselves.

John Nash, Jr. received an M.A.

He is now studying for his Ph.D.

3. *Abbreviations used with dates or numerals.*   Use the following abbreviations only when specific dates and numerals are given: B.C., A.D., A.M., P.M., *No.*, $.

INAPPROPRIATE	What was the No. of the play the coach discussed yesterday P.M.?
REVISED	What was the number of the play the coach discussed yesterday afternoon?
APPROPRIATE	He was No. 2 on the list posted at 6:30 P.M.

4. *Latin abbreviations.* Latin abbreviations such as *i.e.* (that is), *e.g.* (for example), *etc.* (and so forth) are common in most writing. In formal writing the English equivalent is increasingly used. Do not fall into the habit of using *etc.* as a catch-all term or to save yourself the time and trouble of completing your sentences. *Etc.* is meaningless unless the extension of ideas it implies is immediately and unmistakably clear.

CLEAR	The citrus fruits—oranges, lemons, etc.—are rich in Vitamin C. (The reader has no difficulty in mentally listing the other citrus fruits.)
INEFFECTIVE	We swam, fished, etc. (The reader has no clues to the implied ideas.)
REVISED	We swam, fished, rode horses, and danced.

Use such abbreviations as *Bros.,* and *Inc.,* and the ampersand (*&*) for *and* only in names of firms (*Barnes & Noble, Inc.,* for example) where they are used in the official titles.

17b In formal writing spell out personal names and the names of countries, states, months, and days of the week.

| INAPPROPRIATE | Geo., a student from Eng., joined the class last Wed. |
| REVISED | George, a student from England, joined the class last Wednesday. |

17c In formal writing spell out the words *street, avenue, company,* and references to a subject, volume, chapter, or page except in special contexts such as addresses and footnotes.

INAPPROPRIATE	The Perry Coal Co. has an office at Third Ave. and Mott St.
REVISED	The Perry Coal Company has an office at Third Avenue and Mott Street.
INAPPROPRIATE	The p.e. class is reading ch. 3 of the textbook.
REVISED	The physical education class is reading the third chapter (*or* Chapter 3) of the textbook.

EXERCISE 17. In the following sentences correct all faulty abbreviations.

1. At two o'clock post meridian, the rocket was launched.
2. The Pres. and Amb. Smith discussed U.S. policy in the So. Pacific.
3. He enrolled in the U. of Me. because he liked the New Eng. climate.
4. Mister Turner spent his Aug. vacation working with a civil rights group in Ala.
5. Mister Downs noted the license No. of the motorcycle.
6. After yrs. of study in chem. he decided to become a Dr.
7. Many mt. passes are closed in the winter in Switz.
8. The Eng. prof. asked the students to draw on their personal experiences in writing comps.
9. The urban renewal project will cover the area from Main St. to Mich. Ave.
10. Next fall the university will offer courses in Black Lit. and Black Hist.
11. The dr. told his patient to take 3 tsp. of medicine every 2 hrs.
12. The shortest day of the year is in Dec.
13. Rev. Paul Crocker's sermons draw upon his training in phil.
14. The rds. are impassable because of a flood this A.M.
15. The capt. spent all his $$ on his Oct. furlough.

18 Syllabication = SYL

When you find that you can write only part of a word at the end of a line and must complete the word on the next line, divide the word between syllables. Use a hyphen to indicate the break. When you are in doubt about the syllabication of a word, consult a good dictionary.

The following list shows the proper syllabication of a few two- and three-syllable words.

bankrupt	bank-rupt	*grammar*	gram-mar
barren	bar-ren	*hindrance*	hin-drance
collar	col-lar	*pageant*	pag-eant
defraud	de-fraud	*puncture*	punc-ture
either	ei-ther	*theism*	the-ism

caliber	cal-iber	OR	cali-ber
collective	col-lective	OR	collec-tive
definite	def-inite	OR	defi-nite
malignant	ma-lignant	OR	malig-nant

18a Never divide words of one syllable.

WRONG   thr-ee, cl-own, yearn-ed, plough-ed

REVISED   three, clown, yearned, ploughed

18b Never divide a word so that a single letter stands alone on a line.

WRONG   wear-y, e-rupt, a-way, o-val

REVISED   weary, erupt, away, oval

18c When dividing a compound word that already contains a hyphen, make the break where the hyphen occurs.

AWKWARD   pre-Shake-spearean, well-in-formed, Pan-Amer-ican

REVISED   pre-Shakespearean, well-informed, Pan-American

EXERCISE 18.   Which of the following words may be divided at the end of a line? Indicate permissible breaks with a hyphen.

drowned	enough	walked
swimmer	twelve	automobile
learned	through	exercise
abrupt	acute	open
envelope	ex-President	preeminent

"MANUSCRIPT" REVIEW EXERCISE   (Sections 15 through 18). Correct the errors in the following sentences.

1. Some stores put a service charge on bills that are not paid within thirty (30) days.
2. I try not to enroll in classes that begin before ten forty-five a.m.
3. The vice-pres. of the Student Council is occasionally asked to act as chmn. of the mtgs.
4. The new Center for African Studies will be located at Maple and Main Sts.
5. 3 boxtops must accompany every request for a "free" sample.
6. Paperback books, which once sold for a quarter, now cost as much as five dollars and ninety-five cents.

7. The local movie house will show a Bogart film on the 1st. Mon. of every mo.
8. Most tourists in N.Y. go to see the Empire St. Bldg. first.
9. Several states have considered extending suffrage to 18 yr. olds.
10. Students should have a voice in curriculum development, course selection, etc.
11. The Moore Mfg. Co. gave all old customers a five percent reduction on snow tires.
12. All heavyweight boxers must be over 175 lbs.
13. All perch measuring under 5 in. must be thrown back into Lk. Mendota.
14. Rev. Winters performed the marriage ceremony at the Lutheran Ch.
15. Mr. & Mrs. Hone entered their 3 yr. old filly in the race.

Punctuation

= P

Punctuation is far from being a mere mechanical device. It is mechanical as a matter of course, like word-spacing or the use of initial capitals; but punctuation is much more than that. It is an integral part of written composition.

—GEORGE SUMMEY, JR.

*W*hen we speak, we use pauses and gestures to emphasize our meaning, and we vary the tempo, stress, and pitch of our voices to mark the beginning and end of units of thought. In other words, we "punctuate" our speech. We punctuate writing for the same purposes, drawing on a whole set of conventional devices we have developed to give the reader clues to what we are trying to communicate.

The first of these devices is SPACING: that is, closing up or enlarging the space between letters or words. For example, we do not runwordstogetherthisway. Instead, we identify a word <u>as a word</u> by setting it off from its neighbors. Spacing is the most basic of all punctuating devices.

Spacing has other uses as well. Writers of advertising copy use space to focus the reader's eye on the name of a product, a trademark, or a slogan. Novelists and poets manipulate the spacing between words and sentences to produce certain rhetorical effects. John Dos Passos reproduces in words the rush of an assembly line when he writes:

> . . . The Taylorized speedup everywhere, reach under, adjust washer, screw down bolt, shove in cotterpin, reachunder adjust washer, screwdownbolt, reachunderadjustscrewdownreachunderadjust. . . .
>
> —*The Big Money*

In more ordinary writing, we use spacing for less dramatic effects:

1. To set off and distinguish words.
2. To set off paragraphs.
3. To list items in a series (just as we are doing here).

Though important, spacing is naturally not the only punctuation you need. What, for example, can you understand from this string of words:

> yes madam jones was heard to say to the owl like old dowager without a doubt the taming of the shrew by shakespeare would be a most appropriate new years present for your husband

To make this passage intelligible, we need to add two other kinds of punctuation: (1) CHANGES IN THE SIZE AND DESIGN OF LETTERS (capitals and italics); and (2) MARKS OR "POINTS" (periods, commas, quotation marks, apostrophes, and other special signs).

> "Yes, Madam," Jones was heard to say to the owl-like old dowager, "without a doubt, *The Taming of the Shrew* by Shakespeare would be a most appropriate New Year's present for your husband."

Now you know at once that we are reproducing the words of a speaker named Jones; that Jones is probably not a female himself but is addressing someone who is; that Jones is speaking not to an owl but to a lady who looks like one; that *without a doubt* is spoken by Jones and not by the person who is quoting Jones; that Shakespeare did not tame a shrew but wrote a play about one; that *new* is not an ordinary adjective but part of a proper noun; and finally that *years* is not a plural noun but a singular possessive.

This example reveals the four functions of punctuation:

1. *End punctuation.*   Capitals, periods, question marks, and exclamation points indicate sentence beginnings and endings.

2. *Internal punctuation.*   Commas, semicolons, colons, dashes, and parentheses within sentences show the relationship of each word or group of words to the rest of the sentence.

3. *Direct-quotation punctuation.*   Quotation marks and brackets indicate speakers and changes of speaker.

4. *Word punctuation.*   Capitals, italics, quotation marks, apostrophes, and hyphens indicate words that have a special character or use.

The "owl-like old dowager" passage illustrates a conventional, fixed use of each punctuation mark needed to convey accurate meaning. In many instances, however, you may choose with equal correctness among punctuating devices. The statement

> He closed his eyes and jumped. Then he felt the waters close over him.

might just as "correctly" be punctuated

> He closed his eyes and jumped; then he felt the waters close over him.

or even

> He closed his eyes and jumped—then he felt the waters close over him.

Each of these statements makes a slightly different impression on the reader. The first emphasizes the equal importance of the two actions. The second emphasizes their close and immediate relationship. The third emphasizes the element of suspense between the two actions. Yet each interpretation is really the result of our

109

personal tastes and our understanding of the writer's "intention." In questions of punctuation there is often no absolute standard, no authoritative convention, to which you can turn for a "correct" answer. But there are two general rules that serve as reliable guides:

First, remember that punctuation is an *aid to* and *not a substitute for* clear and orderly sentence structure. Before you can punctuate a sentence properly, you must have constructed it properly. No number of commas, semicolons, and dashes will redeem a poorly written sentence.

Second, observe conventional practice in punctuation. Though many of the rules are not hard and fast, still there is a community of agreement about punctuating sentences. Learning and applying the punctuation rules that follow will help you observe these conventions.

19 End Punctuation = END P

Periods, question marks, and exclamation points signal the end of a sentence. Use a period to terminate plain assertions or commands; use a question mark to terminate interrogative statements; use an exclamation point to terminate strongly emotional assertions or ejaculations. Ordinarily, the character of the sentence dictates the proper end punctuation. Occasionally, however, you must determine for yourself just what you <u>intend</u> the character of a sentence to be. Notice the different intentions behind these three sentences:

He struck out with the bases loaded.
He struck out with the bases loaded?
He struck out with the bases loaded!

THE PERIOD

19a Use a period to signal the end of an assertion or a command.

ASSERTION   He mowed the hay with easy strokes.
COMMAND   Mow the hay with easy strokes.

19b **Use a period after an abbreviation.**

> Dr.   Mr.   Mrs.   R.N.   C.P.A.   Sen.   B.A.

You may omit the period after certain abbreviations, particularly those of organizations or government agencies (NEA, AFL, UNESCO, AMA, TVA). If you are in doubt about whether or not to use periods in an abbreviation, consult a good dictionary for the standard practice.

19c **Use a series of three spaced periods (. . .) to indicate an ellipsis within a sentence.**

An ellipsis is an intentional omission of words from quoted material. If you decide that it is unnecessary to reproduce all the words of the author you are quoting, use spaced periods to let your reader know that you have left something out.

For example, the first selection below is taken without any omissions from Donald Keene's *Japanese Literature* (New York, 1955), p. 2. The second selection shows how a writer quoting from the original passage might use the ellipsis. Notice that when the ellipsis comes at the end of a sentence, four periods are used. Three indicate the ellipsis, and the fourth is the usual sentence ending.

> The Korean Confucianists, on the other hand, tended towards extreme orthodoxy, and a chance remark attributed to Confucius, that the superior man did not talk while he ate, resulted in centuries of silent meals in Korea, though not in China, much less in Japan.

> The Korean Confucianists . . . tended towards extreme orthodoxy, and a chance remark attributed to Confucius, that the superior man did not talk while he ate, resulted in centuries of silent meals in Korea. . . .

THE QUESTION MARK

19d **Use a question mark after a direct question.**

Direct questions often begin with an interrogative pronoun or adverb (*who, when, what,* etc.), and have an inverted word order with the verb before the subject.

> Did you study *Ivanhoe* in high school?
> You want to make a good impression, don't you?
> Do you ever wonder what your future will be?

Who do you think will win the game?
What are you studying?

19e **Use a question mark inside parentheses (?) to indicate doubt or uncertainty about the correctness of a statement.**

The device shows that, even after research, you could not establish the accuracy of the fact. It does not serve as a substitute for checking facts.

John Pomfret, an English poet, was born in 1667 (?) and died in 1702.

Rather than using (?) you may simply say *about:*

John Pomfret, an English poet, was born about 1667 and died in 1702.

Do not use this mark as a form of sarcasm.

She was a very charming (?) girl.

19f **Do not use a question mark after an indirect question.**

An indirect question is a statement implying a question but not actually asking one. Though the idea expressed is interrogative, the actual phrasing is not. (See Section 19d for direct questions.)

They asked me whether I had studied *Ivanhoe* in high school.
He asked me whether I wished to make a good impression.
I wonder what my future will be.

A polite request phrased as a direct question is often followed by a period rather than a question mark.

Will you please return this book as soon as possible.
May we hear from you at your earliest convenience.

THE EXCLAMATION POINT

19g **Use the exclamation point after an interjection or after a statement that is genuinely emphatic or exclamatory.**

Fire! Help! Absolutely not!
What a vicious war!
The examination has been stolen!

19h Do not overuse the exclamation point.

Used sparingly, the exclamation point gives real emphasis to individual statements. Overused, it either deadens the emphasis or introduces an almost hysterical tone in your writing.

War is hell! Think of what it does to young men to have their futures interrupted and sometimes cut off completely! Think of what it does to their families! Think of what it does to the nation!

EXERCISE 19(1). Supply the appropriate punctuation marks in each of the following sentences. If you feel that a choice of marks is possible, state why you chose the one you did.

1. The reporter asked, "Mr President, could you clarify that remark please"
2. "Yes," he replied, "let me make that absolutely clear"
3. Mr C P Johnson, who formerly worked with the law firm of Herrick, Noble, and Snow, is now with the U S Army
4. He has a Ph D from U C L A, but he earned his M A from M I T
5. I would live in N Y C if I could afford to live on Fifth Ave and E 68th St
6. The N A A C P has led the fight for civil rights in the U S, but in recent years S N C C has been gaining more attention
7. Is Mrs or Miss the abbreviation for Mistress
8. "May I quote you on that, Mr President" asked the reporter
9. "Oh, why do you insist on quoting everything" he cried
10. The guard yelled "Halt"

EXERCISE 19(2). Assume that in quoting the following passage you wish to omit the following elements: the phrase "when I was a boy"; the clause "kill the savages, kill 'em"; and the sentence beginning "But it takes time to become free." Show how you would indicate to a reader that you were omitting these elements.

I remember that when I was a boy, I used to go to see Tarzan movies on Saturday. White Tarzan used to beat up the black natives. I would sit there yelling, "Kill the beasts, kill the savages, kill 'em!" I was saying: Kill *me*. It was as if a Jewish boy watched Nazis taking Jews off to concentration camps and cheered them on. Today, I want the chief to beat hell out of Tarzan and send him back to Europe. But it takes time to become free of the lies and their shaming effect on black minds.

—STOKELY CARMICHAEL, "What We Want"

20-25 Internal Punctuation = INT P

End punctuation indicates whether a writer wants you to read a whole sentence as a question, an assertion, or an expression of emotion. Internal punctuation indicates the relations and relative importance of elements within the sentence. Five punctuation marks are used for this purpose: commas, semicolons, colons, dashes, and parentheses. The most important uses of these marks are indispensable to clarity, and like the uses of end punctuation are repeated over and over again. But a skillful use of internal punctuation serves not only basic clarity; it can also help a writer communicate the precise shade of balance and emphasis he wishes the reader to get. Here is one example of the skillful use of internal punctuation.

> People who do not understand pigeons—and pigeons can be understood only when you understand that there is nothing to understand about them—should not go around describing pigeons or the effects of pigeons. Pigeons come closer to a zero of impingement than any other birds. Hens embarrass me the way my old Aunt Hattie used to when I was twelve and she still insisted that I wasn't big enough to bathe myself; owls disturb me; if I am with an eagle I always pretend that I am not with an eagle; and so on down to swallows at twilight who scare the hell out of me.
>
> —JAMES THURBER, *There's an Owl in My Room**

Notice how the use of dashes serves to emphasize the parenthetical thought beginning *and pigeons can be.* Commas would have weakened the humorous force of the aside, and parentheses would have made it seem too formal. The second sentence is emphatic because it is brief and simple in contrast to the longer sentences on either side of it. This contrast appears in subject matter, too, with just one bird discussed in the second sentence and four discussed in the third sentence.

What is the point of this illustration? Simply that internal punctuation is basically a rhetorical, not a mechanical, matter. In other words, it is impossible to talk about the punctuation of a sentence

* First published in *The New Yorker*.

without talking about the <u>meaning</u> of that sentence. On any level of writing, punctuation is an integral part of the meaning of a sentence. In studying the punctuation rules that follow, notice not only how each mark is used but also how it contributes to the total meaning of the sentence.

20 Main Clauses

20a Use a comma to separate main clauses joined with a coordinating conjunction (*and, but, or, nor, for, yet,* **and** *so*).*

> The patrol planes were delayed by a heavy rain, and they barely had enough fuel to get back to the carrier.
>
> The patrol planes were delayed by a heavy rain, but they succeeded in making safe landings on the carrier deck.
>
> The patrol planes could land near the enemy lines, or they could risk night landings on the carrier deck.
>
> The return of the patrol planes must have been delayed, for they made night landings on the carrier deck.

Exceptions:
1. In compound sentences, when one or both main clauses are very short, you may omit the comma.

> Ask no questions and you'll be told no lies.
> The scene changes but the inspiration of men of good will persists.
> —VANNEVAR BUSH

2. You may use a semicolon to separate main clauses joined by a coordinating conjunction, especially when you have already used commas within the clauses themselves.

> Babe Ruth, the greatest of home run hitters, was the most colorful figure in baseball; but many people think Ty Cobb was a better player.

* In formal English *yet* is sometimes used to mean *but.* Spoken English often uses *so* as a coordinating conjunction, but written English tends to be very sparing of its use as a coordinator.

The life of every man is a diary in which he means to write one story, and writes another; and his humblest hour is when he compares the volume as it is with what he vowed to make it. —SIR JAMES BARRIE

I first gave it a dose of castor-oil, and then I christened it; so now the poor child is ready for either world. —SIDNEY SMITH

3. You may use a semicolon in place of a comma to separate long coordinated clauses or to indicate a stronger pause between clauses.

We haven't all had the good fortune to be ladies; we haven't all been generals, or poets, or statesmen; but when the toast works down to the babies, we stand on common ground. —MARK TWAIN

The cook was a good cook as cooks go; and as cooks go she went. —H. H. MUNRO

20b Use a semicolon to separate main clauses not joined by a coordinating conjunction.

Children begin by loving their parents; as they grow older they judge them; sometimes they forgive them. —OSCAR WILDE

To educate a man is to educate an individual; to educate a woman is to educate a family.

Okinawa is sixty miles long and from two to ten miles wide; it is the largest of the Ryukyu Islands.

Exception: You may use a comma to separate very short main clauses not joined by coordinating conjunctions.

I stopped, I aimed, I fired.

20c Use a semicolon to separate main clauses joined with a conjunctive adverb.

Americans spend millions of dollars for road-building; however, our roads are rapidly deteriorating.

Note that when the conjunctive adverb comes within the second main clause instead of at the beginning, the clauses still must be separated by a semicolon, and the conjunctive adverb set off by commas.

Americans spend millions of dollars for road-building; our roads, however, are rapidly deteriorating.

CONJUNCTIVE ADVERBS are different from SUBORDINATING CON-
JUNCTIONS. A conjunctive adverb is primarily a transitional word
carrying the thought from one MAIN CLAUSE to the next. Subordinating conjunctions introduce SUBORDINATE CLAUSES. This list,
though incomplete, will aid you in distinguishing between the two:

CONJUNCTIVE ADVERBS	SUBORDINATING CONJUNCTIONS
however	when
nevertheless	although
moreover	though
therefore	since
consequently	if
hence	because
indeed	so that
likewise	as
furthermore	after
namely	in order that
still	while
then	unless

20d **Use a colon to separate two main clauses the second of which
amplifies or explains the first.** *

His reasons are as two grains of wheat hid in a bushel of chaff: you shall
search all day ere you find them, and when you do they are not worth
the search. —WILLIAM SHAKESPEARE

A gentleman of our day is one who has money enough to do what every
fool would do if he could afford it: that is, consume without producing.
—G. B. SHAW

Over the piano was printed a notice: Please do not shoot the pianist. He
is doing his best. —OSCAR WILDE

NOTE: The first word of a complete sentence following a colon may
be capitalized or not. If the sentence is in quotation marks, the first
word is always capitalized.

EXERCISE 20(1). Separate the main clauses in the following
sentences, applying the most appropriate rule in each case.

1. The morning edition made clear the newspaper's stand it would
   back the Republican candidate.

* Some writers prefer to use a dash instead of a colon, particularly when they wish
to give an emotional emphasis to the amplifying statement. (See also Section 24b.)

2. The Senator's record showed that he had consistently voted against every civil rights bill introduced during his term of office so the voters turned against him in the next election.

3. Space scientists are highly knowledgeable in engineering, physics, and mathematics however, they may not be capable of replacing a burnt-out light bulb at home.

4. During the period around 1960, interiors of buildings were more ornately decorated but some interiors, notably those in the IBM and Winnematic buildings, clung to the old simple, modern look.

5. Edward Albee commemorated the great blues singer Bessie Smith in his play *The Death of Bessie Smith* although the emphasis of the play is on racial prejudice and not the blues.

6. Mayor Daley of Chicago is a great believer in law and order therefore the 1968 Democratic Convention held in that city was one of the most orderly in history.

7. The difference between men and women is a simple one men earn the money and women spend it.

8. Every spring the fear of urban riots is renewed therefore city administrators take strong measures they announce plans to build a swimming pool in the ghetto.

9. Public apathy reached a new high in the recent campaign the results nevertheless were described as "a strong mandate."

10. Many scientists believe that marijuana is no more harmful or addictive than alcohol nevertheless alcohol is legal while marijuana is not.

EXERCISE 20(2). In each of the following sentences, make the change requested. Then correct the punctuation accordingly.

1. Change *but* to *still*
   Public opinion polls indicated that Mrs. Kennedy's popularity had declined after her marriage to Onassis, but it was not clear whether this was the sole reason.

2. Change *therefore* to *consequently*
   European housewives shop daily; therefore they do not have leftover food to throw away.

3. Omit *because*
   Because student demonstrations were becoming increasingly violent, school administrators adopted a "get tough" attitude.

4. Change *but* to *still*
   There were some congested areas on the highway, but for the most part traffic flowed smoothly.

5. Change *who* to *they*
   The witness was positive that these were the men who had rushed into the bank in broad daylight and held the employees at gunpoint.

6. Change *otherwise* to *or*
   Strong efforts must be made to bridge the gap between the races; otherwise this nation will be split into two separate societies.

7. Change *when* to *then*

   The reporters waited patiently for the President until noon, when they began to batter the press secretary with questions.
8. Change *and* to *also*

   Governor Wallace was very embarrassed by some of his running mate's statements and his popularity was declining rapidly.
9. Change *however* to *although*

   At that time, the Smiths thought nothing of the occasional signs of oil on the floor of the garage; however, they recalled later that their oil tank needed constant refilling.
10. Omit the first *and*

    The thundershower ended as quickly as it had begun and the spectators filed back into their seats and the baseball game was resumed.

21 Subordinate Phrases and Clauses

21a **Use a comma to separate introductory clauses and phrases from a main clause.**

When I saw the grizzly bear coming toward me, I raised the gun to my shoulder and took aim.

As soon as he finished his dessert, he left.

After his long exile to France during the Commonwealth, Charles II returned to England in 1660.

In his indifference to criticism from those who could not hurt his political chances, he revealed his callousness and vicious self-interest.

If you wish to avoid foreign collision, you had better abandon the ocean.

—HENRY CLAY

The comma is frequently omitted after very short introductory clauses or phrases. Note, however, that even when the introductory clause or phrase is very short, a comma will be necessary if its omission can cause misreading.

CLEAR   When he arrived she was taking the cat out of the piano.

CLEAR   After his defeat he retired from public life.

CONFUSING   When he returned, home was not what it used to be.

CONFUSING   After dark fireflies came in large numbers.

21b **Use a comma to set off a beginning participial phrase modifying the subject or an absolute phrase before the subject.**

Having been a teacher for fifty years, he felt perfectly relaxed among young people.
Exhausted, the swimmer fell back into the pool.
To be quite honest about it, that dog has been known to climb trees.

NOTE: Do not confuse verbal modifiers with verbals used as subjects.

Having been a teacher for fifty years made him perfectly relaxed among young people.

21c **Use a comma to set off phrases and clauses following the main clause and explaining, amplifying, or offering a contrast to it. Do not set off such clauses if they are closely related to the main clause.**

Adverbial phrases and clauses, to which this rule applies (see Section 22 for adjectival modifiers), usually <u>restrict</u> the meaning of the main clauses to which they are joined. They are therefore essential to the meaning of the main clause and are not set off by a comma when they follow the main clause. When they merely introduce additional <u>nonrestrictive</u> information, however, a comma is used to indicate that they are not essential to the meaning. The writer must be guided by the logic of his sentence and the meaning he intends. Note the following.

You will not pass the examination unless you study carefully.
You did not pass the examination, although I am sure you studied carefully.

The first of these sets up *unless you study carefully* as an essential condition for passing the examination. In the second, the main clause makes an unqualified statement of fact; the *although* clause merely adds some sympathy not immediately related to the fact of the main clause.

Jane loves John because he tolerates her petty moodiness.
Jane knows that she loves John, because she can tolerate his petty moodiness.

The first of these states that John's toleration is an essential condition of Jane's love for him. In the second, the *because* clause merely introduces explanatory information about how Jane knows that she loves John.

Note that in some constructions a comma or the lack of one will determine whether the reader will understand a phrase or a clause as a modifier of a final noun in the main clause or as an adverbial modifier.

> He has visited all the small towns in Pennsylvania.
>
> He has visited *all* the small towns, in Pennsylvania, in Ohio, in almost every state of the union.

In the first of these, *in Pennsylvania* restricts the location of the small towns and is an adjectival modifier of *towns*. In the second, however, the *in* phrase is additional information amplifying the assertion of the main clause but not essential to it.

EXERCISE 21(1).   Supply commas where necessary.

1. We could see the whole city from our hotel window.
2. After he had studied acting for many years and worked in summer stock he finally landed a part in a Broadway play.
3. Having completed a course in gourmet cookery she began to give a series of large dinner parties.
4. After visiting several mental institutions I became interested in pursuing a career in mental health.
5. For all the talk of "redeeming social value" most of the new films and plays are really involved with prurience.
6. In spite of their best efforts to keep up with the problems of youth most modern parents are at a loss to understand their own children.
7. Because of the high incidence of fatal injuries motorcyclists in most states are required to wear helmets.
8. Can you imagine putting a leg in a splint without any first-aid training?
9. On graduation day when he walked up to receive his degree he suddenly realized how brief the college years had been.
10. Few white people know and even fewer try to learn how difficult the life of the average black American has been.

EXERCISE 21(2).   Indicate whether the following sentences are punctuated correctly. If they are not, state why.

1. When the exam sheet was placed in front of him he realized how much he had neglected to study.
2. With the shift to Daylight Time in spring, everyone loses an hour's sleep.
3. Many psychiatrists argue that television has a bad effect on children because it makes them think that violence is justifiable.

4.   During his final exile on the remote island of St. Helena Napoleon was poisoned many believe.
5.   His program rejected by the French people De Gaulle resigned the presidency.
6.   Annoyed by the coughing in the audience John Barrymore once stalked off the stage during a performance.
7.   After the assassination of President Kennedy gun-control legislation was proposed but it was defeated.
8.   After they had followed their guru to India the Beatles decided that there was no place like home.
9.   Having lost the race for governor of California in 1962 Nixon vowed he would never again seek public office.
10. College students flocked to the aid of Eugene McCarthy during the primary campaigns of 1968.

22 Nonrestrictives
and other Parenthetical Elements

A NONRESTRICTIVE element in a sentence is a word or group of words that is an addition to, rather than an integral part of, the basic word or group of words it modifies. RESTRICTIVE elements identify or designate in some particular way that which they modify. Nonrestrictive elements introduce amplifying information beyond what is necessary for the purpose of identification. An illustration will help make our meaning clear.

RESTRICTIVE   A man *who is honest* will succeed.
NONRESTRICTIVE   Jacob North, who is honest, will succeed.

In the first sentence the clause *who is honest* identifies the kind of man who will succeed; it restricts the subject of *will succeed* to men *who are honest* as opposed to *men who are not honest*. In other words, the clause is <u>restrictive</u>. It is thus <u>not</u> set off with commas. In the second sentence, however, the proper noun *Jacob North* identifies or designates the particular man who *will succeed;* the fact that Jacob North *is honest* is merely amplifying information about a person already sufficiently identified. The clause is <u>nonrestrictive</u>. It <u>is</u> set off with commas.

We have italicized all the nonrestrictives in the following example. We have not italicized the restrictives. Notice that although the nonrestrictives contribute to the humor, they could be eliminated without destroying the basic meaning of the main clauses.

One day not long ago, *idling through the pages of a sophisticated 35-cent monthly while waiting for the barber to give me my sophisticated 65-cent monthly haircut,* I was suddenly oppressed by the characteristic shortness of breath, *mingled with giddiness and general trepidation,* that results whenever one gets too near an advertisement for Tabu. This exotic scent, *in case you have been fortunate enough to forget it,* is widely publicized as "the 'Forbidden' Perfume," which means, *when all the meringue is sluiced away,* that it is forbidden to anyone who doesn't have $18.50 for an ounce of it.

—S. J. PERELMAN, *Keep It Crisp*

22a **Set off nonrestrictive elements with commas, dashes, or parentheses; do not set off restrictive elements.**

Ordinarily you will use commas to set off nonrestrictives, though you may sometimes decide to use dashes or parentheses if you want to indicate a greater break in the sentence.

NONRESTRICTIVE   Zachariah Wheeler, *the town marshal,* was once a professional wrestler.

NONRESTRICTIVE   The town marshal, *Zachariah Wheeler,* was once a professional wrestler.

In each of these sentences the words to which the italicized phrases refer are sufficient by themselves to identify the person being talked about; the italicized phrases simply give additional or extra information about him. These phrases are nonrestrictive.

Now notice the differences among these sentences:

RESTRICTIVE   The ex-professional wrestler Zachariah Wheeler is the town marshal.

NONRESTRICTIVE   An ex-professional wrestler, Zachariah Wheeler, is the town marshal.

NONRESTRICTIVE   This (or that) ex-professional wrestler, Zachariah Wheeler, is the town marshal.

The first sentence indicates by the use of the definite article *the* that one particular person is meant. We need to know that person's name to identify him and complete the meaning of the sentence. Thus, *Zachariah Wheeler* here is <u>restrictive</u>—it is essential to the meaning of the sentence.

In the second sentence, the indefinite article *an* indicates that the writer's purpose is to make a general statement about an ex-professional wrestler's being town marshal; the marshal's name is merely incidental. Here, then, *Zachariah Wheeler* is <u>nonrestrictive</u>—it is not essential to the meaning of the sentence.

In the third sentence, the demonstrative adjective *this* (or *that*) indicates that the person is identified by being pointed out; again his name is incidental. Here again, then, *Zachariah Wheeler* is <u>nonrestrictive</u>—it is not essential to the meaning of the sentence.

Here is a rule of thumb to use in identifying restrictives and non-restrictives: If the words in question may be omitted without seriously impairing the sense of the sentence, they are nonrestrictive and must be set off by punctuation marks. If they may not be omitted without impairing the sense of the sentence, they are restrictive and must not be set off by punctuation marks.

In some cases, depending on the writer's intention, a sentence might be punctuated either way:

NONRESTRICTIVE Oklahomans, *who have oilwells in their backyards,* can afford the hotel's high prices. (Applies to all Oklahomans.)

RESTRICTIVE Oklahomans *who have oilwells in their backyards* can afford the hotel's high prices. (Applies only to those who have oilwells.)

NOTE: Always use <u>two</u> commas to set off a nonrestrictive unless it begins or ends the sentence:

NOT The old mare, half-blind and lame was hardly able to stand in the traces.

BUT The old mare, half-blind and lame, was hardly able to stand in the traces.

OR Half-blind and lame, the old mare was hardly able to stand in the traces.

22b **Set off nonrestrictive appositives with commas or dashes. Do not set off restrictive appositives.**

An appositive is a noun (or group of words used as a noun) that renames another noun in the sentence. Appositives immediately follow the noun they rename. Often they are nonrestrictive because they merely give additional information not essential to the meaning of the sentence. The italicized appositives in the following sentences are nonrestrictive and are therefore set off by commas.

The professor, *an elderly and gentle man,* led the student from the class by the ear.

Daisy Mae, *our old Irish setter,* has never missed or won a fight.

"Hello, Mitty. We're having the devil's own time with McMillan, *the millionaire banker and close personal friend of Roosevelt.*"

—JAMES THURBER, *The Secret Life of Walter Mitty*

Some appositives are restrictive because they give needed information. They are not set off by commas.

The poet *Bryant* was a leader in New York literary circles.

Among the holiday visitors were Doris, Wilma, and my Aunt *Martha.*

BUT NOTICE   Among the holiday visitors were Ted Stevens, Gertrude Williams, and my aunt, Martha Johnson. (The speaker has only one aunt. Had he more than one he might have said "and Martha Johnson, my aunt.")

To prevent confusion, use dashes rather than commas to set off compound appositives. In the following sentence, it is difficult to determine whether *Bill, Dave, and Blacky* are three additional men— or perhaps dogs or tame bears—or whether these are, in fact, the names of the men who were in the office.

Three men, Bill, Dave, and Blacky, were sitting in the office with their feet on the desk.

But when the commas are replaced by dashes, the meaning becomes clear:

Three men—Bill, Dave, and Blacky—were sitting in the office with their feet on the desk.

22c **Use commas to set off words or expressions that slightly interrupt the structure of the sentence.**

1. *Words in direct address.*

Yes, *Louise,* you should file your fingernails.

2. *Mild interjections.*

Oh, I never get *A*'s—always *C*'s and more *C*'s!

3. *Parenthetical explanations, transitions, and afterthoughts.*

Horses, *unlike tractors,* must be fed in winter.
You may, *if you wish,* leave your teeth in the bathroom.
Christians, *on the other hand,* are opposed to violence.
"The grave's a fine and private place,
But none, *I think,* do there embrace."
— ANDREW MARVELL, "To His Coy Mistress"

22d **Use dashes or parentheses to set off parenthetical expressions that abruptly interrupt the structure of the sentence.**

The choice here is largely one of personal taste. Most writers use dashes to set off statements that they wish to emphasize, and parentheses to set off less emphatic statements.

EMPHATIC PARENTHETICAL STATEMENT	The power of the *Tribune*—one million people read it daily—is enormous.
UNEMPHATIC PARENTHETICAL STATEMENT	The power of the *Tribune* (one million people read it daily) is enormous.

NOTE: Always use two commas to set off a parenthetical element unless it begins or ends a sentence.

NOT   She insisted, however that he bring her home before midnight.
BUT   She insisted, however, that he bring her home before midnight.
OR   She insisted that he bring her home before midnight, however.

EXERCISE 22(1). Punctuate the following sentences. If a choice of marks is possible, be prepared to explain why you chose the one you did.

1. John L. Lewis an aggressive union leader was a self-educated man.
2. The result of her attempt to win him back was as you can guess humiliating.
3. Greta Garbo whose films are constantly being shown on television is almost as popular now as she was thirty years ago.
4. Ronald Reagan after a successful career in the movies began an equally successful career in politics.
5. Queen Elizabeth II ignoring the threats of Welsh nationalists invested her son as Prince of Wales.
6. The President was explaining or rather trying to explain why taxes had to be increased.
7. Commuters who know what they are talking about complain bitterly over the current state of public transportation facilities.

8. Although he is still a very young man Julian Bond is being watched with interest by older politicians.

9. Choosing their words carefully the student leaders explained to the administration officials the nature of their grievances.

10. Few Americans know very much about our nearest and best neighbor Canada.

EXERCISE 22(2). Indicate which of the following sentences are correctly punctuated. Correct those that are incorrectly punctuated.

1. Uranium, which is one of our most valuable elements is capable of fission therefore it is necessary in hydrogen bombs.

2. An atomic reactor may be used for destructive purposes but it may also be used to benefit mankind.

3. Heart transplants once confined to science fiction are now becoming standard medical practice.

4. U.S. policy is, as you know to prevent the proliferation of atomic weapons.

5. The Christmas shopping season which all merchants look forward to begins earlier and earlier each year.

6. Traveling in Asia, if one is willing to experiment with new foods can be a very exciting experience.

7. Most dress designers expected and some were trying to encourage women to become bored with miniskirts.

8. Black studies programs, although they are being instituted primarily for black students will prove interesting to white students as well.

9. The seizure of the *Pueblo* by the North Koreans unexpected and unprecedented, set off waves of international alarm.

10. Few people know that Lincoln did not really write the Gettysburg Address on a train.

23 Items in a Series

23a Use commas to separate three or more words, phrases, or clauses that form a coordinate series.

He talked fluently, wittily, penetratingly.

He is honest, he is courageous, and he is experienced.

There is not a more mean, stupid, dastardly, pitiful, selfish, spiteful, envious, ungrateful animal than the Public. It is the greatest of cowards, for it is afraid of itself. —WILLIAM HAZLITT

Informal practice permits the omission of the comma before the *and*, unless it is required for clarity.

I'll have roast beef, potatoes and salad.

A comma before the last item in a series, however, is sometimes necessary to prevent an illogical grouping.

Our resort is equipped with comfortable cabins, a large lake with boating facilities, and a nine-hole golf course.

I am interested in a modern, furnished apartment with two bedrooms, kitchenette, living room, bathroom with shower, and garage.

If we omit the comma after *facilities* in the first sentence, the sentence seems to suggest that the resort has a lake with a golf course in it. If we omit it after the *shower* in the second sentence, the writer seems to be saying that he wishes an apartment with a garage in the bathroom.

23b **Use commas to separate coordinate adjectives in a series; do not use commas to separate adjectives that are not coordinate.**

Adjectives in a series are coordinate if each adjective modifies the noun separately. They are not coordinate if each adjective in the series modifies the total concept that follows it.

COORDINATE   You are a *greedy, thoughtless, insensitive* prig.
NOT COORDINATE   The boys are planning an *exciting holiday canoe* trip.

In the first sentence each adjective is more or less independent of the other two; the three adjectives might be rearranged without seriously affecting the sense of the sentence: *thoughtless, insensitive, greedy prig; insensitive, greedy, thoughtless prig.* Moreover, the conjunction *and* could be inserted in place of the commas and the basic meaning would remain—*greedy* and *thoughtless* and *insensitive* prig. But in the second sentence the adjectives are interdependent. Their order may not be changed, nor may *and* be substituted, without making hash of the original meaning—*canoe holiday exciting* trip; *holiday exciting canoe* trip; *exciting* and *holiday* and *canoe* trip. The adjectives in the second sentence constitute, in effect, a <u>restrictive</u> phrase, as distinct from the <u>nonrestrictive</u> quality of the adjectives in the first sentence, and therefore are not separated from one another by commas.

It must be said, however, that actual usage in punctuating co-

ordinate adjectives varies a great deal. Though few writers would
punctuate the sentences above other than we have, many of them
would be unable to choose between the punctuation of the sentences below.

He presented the ambassador with a *dirty, yellowed, gnarled* hand to shake.
He presented the ambassador with a *dirty yellowed gnarled* hand to shake.

Some writers feel that the meaning of the two sentences is slightly
different: that the latter sentence suggests a more unified image
than the former. That is, they feel that in the latter case the three
adjectives partake of one another's qualities—*dirty-yellowed-gnarled*
rather than *dirty and yellowed and gnarled.*

23c **Use commas to set off items in dates, addresses, and geographical names.**

DATES   I was born on July 17, 1941, the day the municipal hospital
            burned down.

BUT   I was born in July 1941.

The military services and some other organizations now observe
the practice of putting the day of the month before the name of
the month, as 17 July 1931, 6 August 1950. If you follow this practice, remember <u>not</u> to put a comma after the day of the month.

ADDRESSES   He gave 39 West 46th Street, Olean, New York, as his
                 forwarding address.

GEOGRAPHICAL   He pretended to make the grand tour in three months,
NAMES   but he spent a whole month at Bremen, Germany, and
                 the rest of the time in Tunbridge Wells, Kent, a small
                 village in England.

23d **Use semicolons to separate the items of a series if the items themselves contain commas** (see "Main Clauses," Section 20a[2]).

The following people were present: John Smith, the doctor; Paul Brown,
the dentist; and Elmer Wilson, the psychiatrist.
The bureaucracy consists of functionaries; the aristocracy, of idols; the
democracy, of idolaters.   —G. B. SHAW

EXERCISE 23.   Supply the appropriate punctuation marks in the
sentences below.

    1.   Among the countries I visited last summer were Rumania Bulgaria
         and Poland all behind the Iron Curtain.

2. The telephone operator reported that there was no 33 Pine Drive in Austin that there is no Michael Stone listed at any other address and that there is no telephone exchange beginning with 254 in that area.

3. To pursue a career in the theater one must have talent a great deal of energy and a supreme confidence in himself.

4. If TV commercials are to be believed the American dream consists of a new car a color television set and a mate who uses an effective mouthwash.

5. Fletcher Christian's men after taking over the *Bounty* seemingly disappeared from the face of the earth nearly twenty years were to pass before their hiding place was found.

6. Taking off his wrinkled old white cap lowering his tattered black umbrella and scraping his tennis shoes on the doormat he rang the bell.

7. The sculpture was dominated by two large poles overhanging several round objects that appeared to represent a crowd of people but we were not certain if our guess was correct.

8. Medical insurance plans are not keeping pace with rising medical costs the people hardest hit are the poor and the aged.

9. After he left office, former President Johnson said he was going back to Texas to rediscover the joy of hunting fishing playing with his grandchildren and just relaxing.

10. The Prudential Center in Boston is the tallest building on the mainland of North America but only if one remembers that Manhattan Island is not strictly speaking part of the mainland.

24 Final Appositives and Summaries

24a Use a dash to set off a short final appositive or summary.*

He had only one pleasure—eating.

These are the two culprits—Joe Green and Miller Berg.

Each person is born to one possession which overvalues all his others—his last breath.   —MARK TWAIN

So I leave it with all of you: Which came out of the opened door—the lady or the tiger?   —FRANK STOCKTON

*The comma is sometimes used:

The human species, according to the best theory I can form of it, is composed of two distinct races, the men who borrow, and the men who lend.   —CHARLES LAMB

The dash, however, makes the writer's intention more immediately clear.

24b **Use a colon to set off a long or formal appositive or summary, or a series or statement introduced by the words** *the following* **or** *as follows.*

Out of these things, and many more, is woven the warp and woof of my childhood memory: the dappled sunlight on the great lawns of Chowderhead, our summer estate at Newport, the bitter-sweet fragrance of stranded eels at low tide, the alcoholic breath of a clubman wafted on the breeze from Bailey's Beach.　　　—s. j. perelman, *Keep It Crisp*

Men hang out signs indicative of their respective trades; shoemakers hang out a gigantic shoe; jewelers, a monster watch; and the dentist hangs out a gold tooth; but up in the mountains of New Hampshire, God Almighty has hung out a sign to show that there He makes men.

　　　—daniel webster

I had three chairs in my house: one for solitude, two for friendship, three for society.　　　—henry david thoreau

Humanity has but three great enemies: fever, famine and war; of these by far the greatest, by far the most terrible, is fever.　—sir william osler

The great secret, Eliza, is not having bad manners or good manners or any other particular sort of manners, but having the same manner for all human souls: in short, behaving as if you were in Heaven, where there are no third-class carriages, and one soul is as good as another.

　　　—g. b. shaw

If you are interested in reading further on the subject, I would recommend the following books: Mencken, *The American Language;* Baugh, *A History of the English Language;* and Bryant, *Modern English and Its Heritage.*

To check out a book from our library, proceed as follows: (1) check the catalog number carefully, (2) enter the catalog number in the upper left hand corner of the call slip, (3) fill out the remainder of the call slip information, and (4) hand in the call slip at the main desk.

EXERCISE 24. Supply the appropriate punctuation marks in the sentences below. If a choice of marks is possible, explain why you chose the one you did.

1. Of all the things I relish eating, this is first steak.
2. She came back from New York a new woman her hair was bleached her face lifted and her nose shortened.
3. The mechanical errors many students have the most difficulty mastering are run-on sentences punctuation with semicolons and colons and reference of pronouns.
4. Of all the countries I visited last summer the one I liked best was Greece that's the one country I think I could live in.
5. If you live in a city you must observe speed limits therefore it seems pointless to buy a sports car.

6. National boundaries in Africa do not coincide with tribal boundaries therefore it is inevitable that these new nations must endure some internal frictions during the first few years of independence.

7. The Maoist doctrine of constant revolution finds little acceptance in Europe even the Soviet Union is made uneasy by it.

8. The staunchest support for Red China does not come from any of the major Communist nations in Europe but from the smallest and least significant Albania.

9. It was a sad day for Brooklyn when the Dodgers moved to Los Angeles but now Brooklynites' attention is focused on a new favorite the Mets.

10. Aging movie stars talk of "waiting for the right script" the truth is probably that they haven't been offered a role in years.

25   Superfluous Internal Punctuation

Do not use a comma unless you have a definite reason for doing so. Occasionally you will need to use a comma for no other reason than to prevent misreading.

Long before, she had left everything to her brother.
Pilots who like to see sunbathers, fly low over apartment houses.
Inside the house, cats are sometimes a nuisance.

The omission of a comma after *before* in the first sentence would be momentarily confusing; we get off to a false start by reading *Long-before-she-had-left* without interruption. If there were no comma in the second sentence, we might think we were reading about flying sunbathers. A similar difficulty arises in the third sentence if *house* is not separated from *cats*. Often it is best to rewrite such sentences to avoid confusion.

Too many punctuation marks, however, clutter sentences and confuse readers. The "comma-rash" is especially prevalent among untrained writers. The reader of the following sentence, for example, is constantly jarred by the unnecessary punctuation:

The people of this company, have, always, been aware, of the need, for products of better quality, and lower price.

Not one of the commas is necessary.

25a **Do not separate a single or final adjective from its noun.**

> NOT He was a discourteous, greedy, deceitful, boy.
> BUT He was a discourteous, greedy, deceitful boy.

25b **Do not separate a subject from its verb unless there are intervening words that require punctuation.**

> NOT The worth of real estate, is determined by the demand for it.
> BUT The worth of real estate is determined by the demand for it.
> OR The worth of real estate, tangible property, is determined by the demand for it. (The commas set off an appositive.)

25c **Do not separate a verb from its complement unless there are intervening words that require punctuation.**

> NOT After the meeting, Bob was, of the opinion that fraternities should be ruled off the campus.
> BUT After the meeting, Bob was of the opinion that fraternities should be ruled off the campus.
> NOT The boys always made Peanut, the butt of their pranks.
> BUT The boys always made Peanut the butt of their pranks.
> OR The boys always made Peanut, an undersized and immature smart aleck, the butt of their pranks.

25d **Do not separate two words or phrases joined by a coordinating conjunction.**

> NOT He is very honest, and patient.
> BUT He is very honest and patient.
> NOT I decided to work during the summer, and relax in the fall.
> BUT I decided to work during the summer and relax in the fall.

25e **Do not separate an introductory word, brief phrase, or short clause from the main body of the sentence unless clarity requires it.**

> NOT On Wednesday, the ice in the river began to break up.
> BUT On Wednesday the ice in the river began to break up.

Occasionally, however, a comma must be inserted to prevent misreading (see introduction to Section 25).

NOT   Notwithstanding *Drums at Dusk* is a worthy successor to *Black Thunder*.

BUT   Notwithstanding, *Drums at Dusk* is a worthy successor to *Black Thunder*.

25f **Do not separate a restrictive modifier from the main body of the sentence** (see "Nonrestrictives," Section 22a).

NOT   The girl, who slapped my face, also kicked my shins.

BUT   The girl who slapped my face also kicked my shins.

NOT   The band, in the park, played the same tired old marches we had heard, for fifteen years.

BUT   The band in the park played the same tired old marches we had heard for fifteen years.

25g **Do not separate indirect quotations, or single words or short phrases in quotation marks, from the rest of the sentence.**

CORRECT   After drinking ten bottles of pop Henry said he could drink ten more.

CORRECT   Claude said he was "weary of it all" and that he had "absorbed" his "fill of monotony."

EXERCISE 25.   Eliminate any superfluous commas in the sentences below.

1. Group therapy is useful for mental patients, because it allows them to verbalize their problems, and to interact with others.
2. Percussion instruments carry the repetitive theme of the symphony, and many critics, who are conservative about new sounds, are bound to object.
3. Nudity on the public stage, once undreamed of, but now commonly accepted, may eventually run out its course, and be received only with apathy.
4. The Job Corps, a federal program to aid the uneducated and unskilled, was forced, because of a reduced budget, to make proportionate reductions in its services.
5. The troops on the island of Malaita, and on Guadalcanal, were shocked to hear the natives talk about "the long pig," the white man, which the cannibals relished.
6. Many responsible citizens believe that the laws prohibiting abortion should be changed, and made more flexible.
7. The senator replied slowly, because he had not expected the question, and he really didn't know what to say.

8. The United States is slowly taking over the world, not with guns, but with Coca-Cola and television reruns.

9. The apparent increase in cancer and heart disease, arises from the fact that these are the diseases of old age, and more people are living longer.

10. The disenchantment with urban renewal, stems from the fact that, frequently, it is merely a matter of building new slums, to replace the old.

"INTERNAL PUNCTUATION" REVIEW EXERCISES (Sections 20 through 25).

EXERCISE A. Correct the internal punctuation of the following sentences where necessary.

1. No I have no idea where she went but I do know she packed her ski clothes.

2. Students were allowed to bring their textbooks to the final exam if they so desired.

3. Mr. Goldberg, who was once U.S. Ambassador to the UN was also once an Associate Justice of the Supreme Court.

4. Before he was elected President John F. Kennedy had been the junior senator from Massachusetts.

5. There's only one problem involved in "doing your own thing: that's that everyone else may want to do his own thing as well.

6. A noted wit observed recently in all seriousness that England was gradually sinking giggling into the sea.

7. Some extreme conservatives fear that outrageous programs such as Social Security Medicare and Aid to Dependent Children are like unemployment insurance gradually turning this country into a socialist state.

8. It's relatively easy to borrow money it's much harder to pay it back.

9. Jealousy, a debilitating emotion, can wreck a relationship for without genuine trust there can be no real love.

10. There is some evidence to show that Christopher Columbus was not the first European to visit America recent discoveries reveal that there may have been Viking settlements on the northeastern tip of the continent.

EXERCISE B. Analyze the internal punctuation in the following passages just as we analyzed the selection from Thurber on page 114.

1. In the long history of the world, only a few generations have been granted the role of defending freedom in its hour of maximum danger. I do not shrink from this responsibility; I welcome it. I do not believe that any of us would exchange place with any other people in any other generation. The energy, the faith, the devotion which we bring to this endeavor will light our country and all who serve it, and the glow from that fire can truly light the world.   —JOHN F. KENNEDY

2. The various codes which were presented to you at Crossgates—religious, moral, social and intellectual—contradicted one another if you worked out their implications. The essential conflict was between the tradition of nineteenth-century asceticism and the actually existing luxury and snobbery of the pre-1914 age. On the one side were low-church Bible Christianity, sex puritanism, insistence on hard work, respect for academic distinction, disapproval of self-indulgence; on the other, contempt for "braininess" and worship of games, contempt for foreigners and the working class, an almost neurotic dread of poverty, and, above all, the assumption not only that money and privilege are the things that matter, but that it is better to inherit them than to have to work for them. Broadly, you were bidden to be at once a Christian and a social success, which is impossible. At the time I did not perceive that the various ideals which were set before us cancelled out. I merely saw that they were all, or nearly all, unattainable, so far as I was concerned, since they all depended not only on what you did but on what you *were*. —GEORGE ORWELL

3. The houses were left vacant on the land, and the land was vacant because of this. Only the tractor sheds of corrugated iron, silver and gleaming, were alive; and they were alive with metal and gasoline and oil, the disks of the plows shining. The tractors had lights shining, for there is no day and night for a tractor and the disks turn the earth in the darkness and they glitter in the daylight. And when a horse stops work and goes into the barn there is a life and a vitality left, there is a breathing and a warmth, and the feet shift on the straw, and the jaws champ on the hay, and the ears and the eyes are alive. There is a warmth of life in the barn, and the heat and smell of life. But when the motor of a tractor stops, it is as dead as the ore it came from. The heat goes out of it like the living heat that leaves a corpse. Then the corrugated iron doors are closed and the tractor man drives home to town, perhaps twenty miles away, and he need not come back for weeks or months, for the tractor is dead. —JOHN STEINBECK

26 Punctuation of Quoted Material = Q

Direct speech and material quoted verbatim from other sources must always be set off distinctly from a writer's own words. Such distinctions are usually indicated by quotation marks, although longer quotations may be indicated merely by different spacing and indentation. The following sections describe conventional usage in punctuating quoted material.

26a **Use double quotation marks to enclose a direct quotation whether from a written or spoken source.**

DIRECT   He said, "Don't dive from that rock."

DIRECT   Our handbook says, "Direct speech and material quoted ver-batim from other sources must always be set off distinctly from a writer's own words."

Remember *not* to punctuate indirect quotations.

He said not to dive from that rock.

Our handbook says that direct speech and material quoted verbatim from other sources must always be set off distinctly from a writer's own words."

plagiarism

26b **Use single quotation marks to enclose a quotation within a quota-tion.**

She turned and said, "Remember Grandfather's advice, 'When other people run, you walk.' "

Notice that the end punctuation of the sentence within single quotation marks serves also as the end punctuation for the entire sentence unit of which it is a part.

26c **If a quotation is relatively long—more than four lines—it is usually indented from both right and left margins, and not enclosed in quotation marks.** *

In one respect a cavalry charge is very like ordinary life. So long as you are all right, firmly in your saddle, your horse in hand, and well armed, lots of enemies will give you a wide berth. But as soon as you have lost a stirrup, have a rein cut, have dropped your weapon, are wounded, or your horse is wounded, then is the moment when from all quarters enemies rush upon you. Such was the fate of not a few of my comrades in the troops immediately on my left. Brought to an actual standstill in the enemy's mass, clutched at from every side, stabbed at and hacked at by spear and sword, they were dragged from their horses and cut to pieces by the infuriated foe. But this I did not at the time see or understand.

—WINSTON CHURCHILL

* If quotation marks, rather than the usual indentation, are used for a passage of two or more paragraphs, they are placed at the beginning of each paragraph and at the end of the last; they are not placed at the end of intermediate paragraphs.

26d **Use quotation marks to set off titles of poems and songs, and of articles, short stories, and other parts of a longer work.**

(For the use of italics to set off titles, see "Italics," Section 27a.)

"Preparing the Manuscript" is a chapter in *Report Writing*, a text for engineers.

"The Easy Chair" is a section of informal literary review appearing in *Harper's*.

"Wintergreen for President" is a song from the musical play *Of Thee I Sing*.

26e **Words used in a special sense may be set off by quotation marks.**

When a new book comes into the library, it is first of all "accessioned." Is this what you call "functional" architecture?

"Anarchy" means "without a leader," hence "without government."

(*Or:* Anarchy means *without a leader*, hence *without government*. See Section 27c).

NOTE: Do not use quotation marks around common nicknames. Do not use them apologetically to enclose slang, colloquialisms, or trite expressions. If a word is appropriate to your writing, it should stand without apology. If it is not suitable, you should replace it.

26f **Use brackets to set off editorial remarks in quoted material.**

You will sometimes want to insert an explanatory comment in a statement you are quoting. By enclosing such comments in brackets, you let the reader know at once that you are speaking rather than the original author.

John Dryden, a famous English poet, said, "Those who accuse him [Shakespeare] to have wanted knowledge, give him the greater commendation; he was naturally learned."

The favorite phrase of their [English] law is "a custom whereof the memory of man runneth not back to the contrary."

—RALPH WALDO EMERSON

In bibliographical notations, use brackets to enclose the name of a writer reputed to be the author of the work in question. For an illustration of this practice, see page 142.

26g Use the word *sic* ("thus it is") in brackets to indicate that a mistake or peculiarity in the spelling or the grammar of a foregoing word appears in the original work.

> The high school paper reported, "The students spoke most respectively [*sic*] of Mrs. Higginbottom."

26h Always place a comma or a period inside the quotation marks.

> Commas are generally used to separate direct quotations from unquoted material.

> "There is no use in working," he complained, "when it only makes me more sleepy than usual."

Note that this rule <u>always</u> applies regardless of the reason for using quotation marks.

> According to Shakespeare, the poet writes in a "fine frenzy."
> While he insisted that he was a "beatnik," I certainly got tired of hearing him say that everything was "cool."

26i Always place a colon or a semicolon outside the quotation marks.

> According to Shakespeare, the poet writes in a "fine frenzy"; by "fine frenzy" he meant a combination of energy, enthusiasm, imagination, and a certain madness.

26j Place a dash, question mark, or exclamation point inside the quotation marks when it applies only to the quotation; place it outside the quotation marks when it applies to the whole statement.

> He said, "Will I see you tomorrow?"
> Didn't he say, "I'll see you tomorrow"?
> "You may have the car tonight"—then he caught himself abruptly and said, "No, you can't have it; I need it myself."

When a mark applies to both quotation and sentence, use it only once.

> Has he ever asked, "May I come in?"

26k In punctuating explanatory words preceding a quotation, be guided by the length and formality of the quotation.

NO PUNCTUATION	He yelled "Stop!" and grabbed the wheel.
PUNCTUATION WITH A COMMA	The old man said very quietly, "Under no circumstances will I tell you where my money is hidden."
PUNCTUATION WITH A COLON	The speaker rose to his feet and began: "The party in power has betrayed us. It has not only failed to keep its election promises but has sold out to the moneyed powers."

26l Use a comma to separate an opening quotation from the rest of the sentence unless the quotation ends with a question mark or an exclamation point.

"The man is dead," he said with finality.

"Is the man dead?" he asked.

"Oh, no!" he screamed hysterically. "My brother can't be dead!"

26m When a quotation is interrupted by explanatory words (*he said*, or their equivalent), use a comma after the first part of the quotation. In choosing the punctuation mark to place after the explanatory words, apply the rules for punctuating clauses and phrases.

"I am not unaware," he said, "of the dangers of iceboat racing."

"I have always worked hard," he declared. "I was peddling newspapers when I was eight years old."

"John has great capacities," the foreman said; "he has energy, brains, and personality."

EXERCISE 26. Supply the appropriate punctuation in each of the following sentences.

1. The letter said tartly, The fault is not with our product but with your skin; it appears to be super-sensitive.
2. Perhaps you might like to do a study of the sexual imagery in Shakespeare the professor suggested.
3. How long have you noticed this condition the doctor asked.
4. As the history professor said in class yesterday There is no real evidence that Marie Antoinette ever said Let them eat cake!
5. He said, When the policeman asked me Where's the fire? I felt like giving him an equally sarcastic answer.

6. The song Aquarius is from the controversial musical *Hair*.
7. Arthur Schlesinger, Jr., says John Stuart Mill wrote a century ago, The greatness of England is now all collective; individually small, we appear capable of anything great only by our habit of combining.
8. The salesgirl said, Madam I would exchange this sweater, but, she added, it has already been worn.
9. One day, just as I was going out to Rahul's house, I heard her shouting outside the door of the study. The director is a busy man! she was shouting. She had her back against the door and held her arms stretched out; M. stood in front of her and his head was lowered. Day after day you come and eat his life up! she said.

   —R. PRAWER JHABVALA, "My First Marriage"
10. I climbed up in the bar yelling, Walsh, I'm shot. I'm shot. I could feel the blood running down my leg. Walsh, the fellow who operated the fish-and-chips joint, pushed me off the bar and onto the floor. I couldn't move now, but I was still completely conscious. Walsh was saying, Git outta here, kid. I ain't got no time to play. A woman was screaming, mumbling something about the Lord, and saying, Somebody done shot that poor child.

    —CLAUDE BROWN, *Manchild in the Promised Land*

27-30 Word Punctuation = WORD P

Italics, capitals, apostrophes, and hyphens identify words that have a special use or a particular grammatical function in a sentence.

> Our two-week reading program, assigned in Wednesday's class, is Shakespeare's *King Lear*.

Here the italics set off the words *King Lear* as a single title. The capitals identify *Wednesday, Shakespeare, King* and *Lear* as proper names. The apostrophes indicate that *Shakespeare* and *Wednesday* are singular possessives and not plurals. The hyphen between *two* and *week* makes the two words function as a single adjective.

27 Italics

Strictly speaking, italics are type faces that slope toward the right. In typed or handwritten manuscript, however, indicate italics by underlining.

On the printed page: *italics*
In typewritten copy: **italics**

In handwritten copy: *italics*

Three centuries ago printers italicized words pretty much as they pleased. They set off important words and phrases in italics and sometimes used italics in place of quotation marks.

> The *Gravity* and *Piety* of their looks, are of great Service to these *American* Christians: It makes strangers that come amongst them, give Credit to their Words. And it is a Proverb with those that know them, *Whosoever believes a* New-England Saint, *shall be sure to be Cheated: And he that knows how to deal with their trades, may Deal with the Devil and fear no Craft.*
> —[NED WARD], *A Trip to New England* (1699)

Now, however, the use of italics is carefully distinguished from that of capitals and quotation marks.

27a Italicize the titles of books, newspapers, magazines, and all publications issued separately.

"Issued separately" means published as a single work and not as an article or story in a magazine, nor as a chapter or section of a book. (For the proper punctuation of such titles, see 26d.)

The New York Times	*Commentary*
The Lord of the Flies	*Death of a Salesman*

Webster's Seventh New Collegiate Dictionary

Be careful not to add the word *The* to titles unless it belongs there, and not to omit it if it does belong.

NOT   *The Reader's Digest*   NOT   the *Red Badge of Courage*
BUT   the *Reader's Digest*   BUT   *The Red Badge of Courage*

27b   Italicize the names of ships, aircraft, works of art, and movies.

the *Titanic*   H.M.S. *Queen Elizabeth 2*   the *Spirit of St. Louis*
the *Sistine Madonna*   *Bonnie and Clyde*

27c   Italicize letters, words, and numbers used as words.

Your *r*'s look very much like your *n*'s.
I can't tell your *7*'s from your *1*'s.
The early settlers borrowed Indian words like *moccasin, powwow,* and *wigwam.*

27d   Italicize foreign words and phrases that have not yet been accepted into the English language.

The Communists staged a *coup d'état* in Hungary.
Many of the works of the *fin de siècle* that seemed so sensational when they were written appear to us now as innocent.

You may sometimes feel that a foreign word or phrase expresses your meaning more aptly or concisely than an English one. If you are sure that your readers will understand the expression, use it. But to overuse such words is pedantry. Many foreign words have been accepted into the English language and need no longer be italicized. The following words, for example, are no longer aliens and do not require italics:

bourgeois   milieu   denouement   liqueur

To determine whether a foreign word should be italicized, consult a good dictionary. (See discussion on spelling under "The Uses of a Dictionary," pp. 292–293.)

27e   Use italics to give a word special stress.

The idea that knowledge follows interest is a scandalous half-truth; it is a better-than-half-truth that *interest follows knowledge.*
I heard him say once that in a democracy (a *democracy,* mind you) a division of opinion cannot be permitted to exist.

27f   **Avoid the overuse of italics.**

Distinguish carefully between a real need for italicizing and the use of italics as a mechanical device to achieve emphasis. The best way to achieve emphasis is to write effective, well-constructed sentences. The overuse of italics will only make your writing seem immature and amateurish, as in the following:

> Any good education must be *liberal.*
>
> America is a *true* democracy, in every sense of the word.
>
> This book has what I call *real* depth of meaning.

EXERCISE 27.   Italicize words and phrases where necessary in the following sentences.

1. James Earl Jones, the eminent black actor, received a Tony award for his Broadway performance in The Great White Hope.
2. H.M.S. Queen Elizabeth, for years the flagship of the Cunard Line, was finally retired from service.
3. Are you supposed to pronounce the p in coup d'état?
4. Some Americans use the word simpatico as though it meant sympathetic, but its meaning is really closer to that of the English word charming.
5. Is T.S. Eliot's The Wasteland included in The Oxford Book of English Verse?
6. His travels had brought him greater understanding of himself and just a touch of savoir-faire.
7. Webster's Third New International Dictionary lists more than half a dozen pronunciations of lingerie.
8. I am constantly forgetting what eclectic means.
9. New Englanders tend to add an r to words that end in a and to omit the r in words that do end in r.
10. Thus, in Boston, Cuba becomes Cuber, while river becomes riva.

28   Capitals

Modern writers capitalize less frequently than did older writers, and informal writing permits less capitalization than formal writing. Two hundred years ago, a famous author wrote:

Being ruined by the Inconstancy and Unkindness of a Lover, I hope a true and plain Relation of my Misfortune may be of Use and Warning to Credulous Maids, never to put much Trust in deceitful Men.

> —JONATHAN SWIFT, "The Story of the Injured Lady"

A modern writer would eliminate all capitals but the initial *B* and the pronoun *I*.*

28a **Capitalize the first word of a sentence and the first word of a line of poetry.**

Education is concerned not with knowledge but the meaning of knowledge.

True ease in writing comes from art, not chance.
As those move easiest who have learned to dance.

> —ALEXANDER POPE, *Essay on Criticism*

Some modern poets ignore the convention of capitalizing each line of poetry, perhaps because they feel that an initial capital letter gives a word unwanted emphasis.

a man who had fallen among thieves
lay by the roadside on his back
dressed in fifteenthrate ideas
wearing a round jeer for a hat

> —e. e. cummings, "a man who had fallen among thieves"

28b **Capitalize the pronoun *I* and the interjection *O*.**

Do not capitalize the interjection *oh* unless it is the first word of a sentence.

---

* The practice of capitalizing nouns persisted long after Swift. The nineteenth century poet Byron wrote:

> Near this spot are deposited the remains of one who possessed Beauty without Vanity, Strength without Insolence, Courage without Ferocity, and all the Virtues of Man without his Vices. This Praise, which would be meaningless Flattery if inscribed over human ashes, is but a just tribute to the Memory of Boatswain, a Dog.

Some modern humorous or satiric writers sometimes capitalize nouns as a way of personifying abstractions and pointing up irony:

> "Well," she said hesitatingly, "the idea is to reduce all employees to a Curve."
> —STEPHEN LEACOCK, *Frenzied Fiction*

28c Capitalize proper nouns, their derivatives and abbreviations, and common nouns used as proper nouns.

1. *Specific persons, races, nationalities.*

William	Bob	George A. Smith	Negro
Asiatic	American	Mongolian	Cuban
Canadian	English	Latin	Zulu

2. *Specific places.*

Dallas	Jamestown	California	Lake Erie
Newfoundland	Iran	Jerusalem	Ohio River

3. *Specific organizations, historical events, and documents.*

Daughters of the American Revolution   the French Revolution
the Locarno Pact   NAACP
Declaration of Independence

4. *Days of the week, months, holidays.*

Thursday	April	Christmas	Sunday	Thanksgiving

5. *Religious terms with sacred significance.*

the Virgin	God	Heavenly Father	the Saviour

6. *Titles of books, plays, magazines, newspapers, journals, articles, poems.* Capitalize the first word and all others except articles, and conjunctions and prepositions of fewer than five letters. (See also Sections 26d and 27a.)

Gone with the Wind	*The Country Wife*	*Pippa Passes*
Paradise Lost	*Atlantic Monthly*	*War and Peace*
Journal of Higher Education	*Much Ado About Nothing*	

7. *Titles, when they precede a proper noun.* Such titles are an essential part of the name and are regularly capitalized.

Professor Wilson	Secretary Hawkins
Dr. James Spence	Mr. Gottschalk
President Nixon	Judge Paul Perry

When titles <u>follow</u> a name, do not capitalize them unless they indicate high distinction:

> Robert F. Jones, president of the National Bank
> J. R. Derby, professor of English
> BUT   Abraham Lincoln, President of the United States
> John Marshall, Chief Justice, United States Supreme Court

"High distinction" is, however, becoming more and more broadly interpreted. Some people write*

> Robert F. Jones, President of the National Bank
> J. R. Derby, Professor of English

8. *Common nouns used as an essential part of a proper noun.* These are generic names such as *street, river, avenue, lake, county, ocean, college.*

> Vine Street   Fifth Avenue   Pacific Ocean   Lake Huron
> General Motors Corporation   Penn Central Railroad
> Hamilton College   Mississippi River

When the generic term is used in the plural, it is not usually capitalized.

> Vine and Mulberry streets   Hamilton and Lake counties
> the Atlantic and Pacific oceans

28d   **Avoid unnecessary capitalization.**

A good general rule is not to capitalize unless a specific convention warrants it.

1. *Capitalize* north, east, south, west *only when they come at the beginning of a sentence or refer to specific geographical locations.*

> Birds fly south in the winter.
> BUT   She lives in the western part of the Old South.

---

* This practice is at variance with the trend toward less capitalization, but is perhaps explained by (1) a writer's desire to seem polite, and (2) copying the style of capitalization used in formal letters, as

Robert F. Jones
President of the National Bank
West Third Avenue
Kokoma Hills, Georgia

2. *The names of seasons need not be capitalized.*

fall   autumn   winter   midwinter   spring   summer

3. *Capitalize nouns indicating family relationships only when they are used as names or titles or in combination with proper names. Do not capitalize* mother *and* father *when they are preceded by possessive adjectives.*

I wrote to my father.	My uncle has ten children.
BUT I wrote Father.	BUT My Uncle Ben has ten children.

4. *Ordinarily, do not capitalize common nouns and adjectives used in place of proper nouns and adjectives.*

I went to high school in Cleveland.
BUT   I went to John Adams High School in Cleveland.
I left for Washington by railroad.
BUT   I left for Washington by the Penn Central Railroad.
I am a university graduate.
BUT   I am a Columbia University graduate.
I took a psychology course in my senior year.
BUT   I took Psychology 653 in my senior year.

EXERCISE 28. Capitalize words as necessary in the following sentences. Remove unnecessary capitals.

1. Last Summer he worked with the job corps, which was part of a larger Federal Program.
2. The reverend Martin Luther King, jr. first came to public attention as a leader of the Civil Rights sit-ins in the south.
3. The late Robert Kennedy had been attorney general of the United States before being elected senator from the state of New York.
4. It has been predicted that power in the un will eventually shift from the security council to the general assembly.
5. The Boston symphony orchestra is not to be confused with the Boston pops orchestra.
6. All Math Majors who were preparing to teach Elementary School students were required by the math department to take courses in the New Math.
7. The organization of American states is designed to encourage co-operation and understanding among the nations of the western hemisphere.
8. Michael O'hara, president of the student congress, addressed the meeting.
9. Many of the aberdeen angus cattle come from the state of nebraska.
10. It was the fall of the Roman empire which ushered in the middle ages.

29 Apostrophe

29a **Use an apostrophe to show the possessive case of nouns and indefinite pronouns.**

1. *If a word (either singular or plural) does not end in* s, *add an apostrophe and* s *to form the possessive.*

the woman's book	the women's books
the child's book	the children's books
the man's book	the men's books
someone's book	people's books

2. *If the singular of a word ends in* s, *add an apostrophe and* s *unless the second* s *makes pronunciation difficult; in such cases, add only the apostrophe.*

	Lois's book	James's book
BUT	Moses' leadership	Sophocles' dramas

(The addition of a second *s* would change the pronunciation of *Moses* to *Moseses* and *Sophocles* to *Sophocleses*.)

3. *If the plural of a word ends in* s, *add only the apostrophe.*

the girls' books
the boys' books
the Smiths' books (referring to at least two persons named Smith)

4. *In compounds, make only the last word possessive.*

father-in-law's book (*singular possessive*)
mothers-in-law's books (*plural possessive*)
someone else's book

5. *In nouns of joint possession, make only the last noun possessive; in nouns of individual possession, make both nouns possessive.*

John and Paul's book (*joint possession*)
John's and Paul's books (*individual possession*)

Here is a list of standard spelling forms:

SINGULAR	PLURAL
child	children
man	men
lady	ladies
father-in-law	fathers-in-law
passer-by	passers-by

POSSESSIVE SINGULAR	POSSESSIVE PLURAL
child's	children's
man's	men's
lady's	ladies'
father-in-law's	fathers-in-law's
passer-by's	passers-by's

29b Use an apostrophe to indicate the omission of a letter or number.

doesn't   can't   won't   o'clock   the blizzard of '89

In reproducing speech, writers frequently use an apostrophe to show that a word is given a loose or colloquial pronunciation.

"An' one o' the boys is goin' t' be sick," he said.

A too-frequent use of the apostrophe for such purposes, however, clutters up the page and annoys the reader.

29c Use an apostrophe and *s* to form the plurals of letters, numbers, and words used as words. (In such cases, the letters, numbers, and words are also italicized, but the *s* is not.)

Cross your *t*'s and dot your *i*'s.
Count to 10,000 by *2*'s.
Tighten your sentence structure by eliminating unnecessary *and*'s.

29d Do not use the apostrophe with the possessive form of personal pronouns.

The personal pronouns *his, hers, its, ours, yours, theirs,* and the pronoun *whose* are possessives as they stand and do not require the apostrophe.

his father; a book of *hers;* a friend of *theirs.*

Be particularly careful not to confuse the possessive pronoun *its* with the contraction *it's* (it is).

We couldn't find *its* nest.
We know *it's* a robin.

EXERCISE 29. Insert apostrophes as necessary in the following sentences.

1. One of my most prized possessions is the Supremes first record album.
2. Its hard to believe that in a country as rich as ours, some people still go to bed hungry every night.
3. The chairmans secretary has assured all members of the department that theyll have their class schedules in two weeks time.
4. Most modern cities havent the resources with which to keep up with their expanding populations.
5. He had asked for a months leave of absence, but he was allowed to take only the three days sick leave that were due him.
6. Hers was the better way, mine was the quicker.
7. Whats the point of experimenting with mind-expanding drugs when they can do terrible damage to ones mind?
8. A rock groups career, as show business goes, is relatively short.
9. The greatest years of *The New Yorker* were those under Harold Ross editorship.
10. Its hard to keep up with the Joneses when you dont have Mr. Jones income.

30 Hyphen

The hyphen has two distinct uses: (1) to form compound words, and (2) to indicate that a word is continued from one line to the next. The proper use of the hyphen for (2), commonly called "syllabication," is arbitrarily fixed. (See "Syllabication," Section 18.) But the proper use of the hyphen to form compound words is continually changing as the language grows and new word combinations are accepted.

30a **Use a hyphen to form compound words that are not yet accepted as single words.**

The spelling of compound words that express a single idea passes through successive stages. Originally spelled as two separate words, then as a hyphenated word, a compound word finally emerges as a single word.

> base ball *became* base-ball *became* baseball
> post man *became* post-man *became* postman

There is no way of determining the proper spelling of a compound at any given moment. Even the best and most up-to-date dictionaries tend to be too conservative in the matter; they hyphenate many compounds that in actual practice are written as single words. However, the dictionaries are the most authoritative references we have.

30b **Use a hyphen to join two or more words serving as a single adjective before a noun.**

Do not hyphenate such an adjective if it follows the verb as a predicate adjective.

> a well-known speaker
> BUT   The speaker was well known.
> a grayish-green coat
> BUT   The coat was grayish green.

Omit the hyphen when the first word is an adverb ending in *-ly*.

> a slow-curving ball   a quick-moving runner
> BUT   a slowly curving ball   BUT   a quickly moving runner

30c **Use a hyphen to avoid an ambiguous or awkward union of letters.**

> NOT   belllike   NOT   recreate
> BUT   bell-like   BUT   re-create (create anew)

In commonly used words, the hyphen is omitted.

> coeducational   coordinate   readdress

30d **Use a hyphen to form compound numbers from twenty-one through ninety-nine, and to separate the numerator from the denominator in written fractions.**

> twenty-nine   fifty-five   two-thirds   four-fifths

30e Use a hyphen with the prefixes *self-, all-, ex-,* **and the suffix** *-elect.*

    self-important   all-Conference   ex-mayor   governor-elect

Do not capitalize the prefix *ex-* or the suffix *-elect,* even when used in titles that are essential parts of a name.

    ex-Mayor Kelley   Governor-elect Jones   ex-President Truman

EXERCISE 30. Insert hyphens as needed.

1. In choosing a car, you should remember that a well tuned motor is more important than white wall tires.
2. He boasts that he is self made and self educated but he forgets to add that he is also self centered.
3. The life long dream of most Americans is fulfilled when they move into a four bedroom house with a two car garage.
4. He changed a twenty dollar bill into twenty dollar bills and distributed them among the children.
5. In a well planned maneuver, the students reentered the administration building and retook their position in the corridors.

EXERCISE 27-30(1). Supply the necessary italics, capitals, apostrophes, and hyphens in the sentences below.

1. ex governor spiro Agnew of maryland became vice president of the United States.
2. Playboy magazine is designed to appeal to the would be man about town type.
3. More of the mothers receiving welfare would seek employment if they were assured that their children would be well cared for in their absence.
4. Its a well know fact that most old age pensions are inadequate for the present day needs of senior citizens.
5. its hard to believe that that old timer was once all american fullback of 1910.

EXERCISE 27-30(2). Correct the punctuation in the following sentences.

1. Steinbecks novel, the grapes of Wrath, *written* in the 1930s, helped him to win the nobel prize for literature.
2. Barbra Streisands first big break in show business was in the Broadway play I can get it for you Wholesale.
3. That young mans heart is not yours, nor mine, nor hers.
4. The four American delegates carefully prepared proposal was rejected by the Soviet unions spokesman.

5. Long before Israel was declared a nation, it's people had *yearned* for a home of their own.

6. Although eighteen year olds are subject to the draft, my brothers friend wasnt called until he was twenty one years old.

7. The Fall Semester began mid september this year so that freshman could complete their preentrance orientation Program.

8. All surviving members of the Pueblo's crew were besieged by fact seeking newsmen.

9. The Huntley-Brinkley-Show is one of nbc's major attractions.

10. The four cylinder sixty horsepower car was'nt able to pull Jones custom built limousine out of the ditch.

"PUNCTUATION" REVIEW EXERCISES   (Sections 19 through 30).

EXERCISE A. Supply all necessary punctuation in each of the following sentences.

1. The most famous sentence from President Kennedys inaugural speech is the one that begins ask not what your country can do for you. . .

2. Her term paper consisted of nothing more than a series of quotations from the works of Shakespeare Marlowe and Milton strung together with some ill thought out and half baked comments of her own.

3. De Gaulles chief virtues or faults as the case may be were a supreme self confidence an inability to compromise and a strong resistance to any kind of criticism of his or his appointees ideas.

4. Something must be wrong with the school system it has a tremendous number of drop outs and truants.

5. I have just received an un-expected letter from the director of the bureau of internal revenue.

6. Although I am not a member of the democratic party I am very democratic in my relationships with people.

7. Ruth wanted a Pontiac Francis a Ford Donna a Chrysler and Alice a raleigh bicycle.

8. The late Will Rogers favorite saying was Ive never met a man I did'nt like.

9. At least two states allow eighteen year olds to vote Kentucky I think is one or is it Georgia?

10. Judy Garland is best remembered for her role in the 1930s film The Wizard of Oz.

11. During the 1968 presidential campaign, Spiro Agnews remark, when you've seen one slum you've seen them all, considerably distressed his running mate.

12. The students were asked to read two books, Candy and Portnoy's Complaint, but they failed to find in either any so called redeeming social significance.

13. Does anyone remember who said Absolute power corrupts absolutely?

14. I make it a point to read the New York Times every day and Life Magazine every week only rarely however do I get around to Time or Newsweek.

15. You can't do that, she cried hysterically, you can't you can't.

EXERCISE B. Supply all the necessary punctuation in the passages below.

1. it is astonishing in retrospect how constantly and boldly this irish catholic president this young man so publicly committed to things like patriotism and public affairs lampooned politicians politics notions men systems myths himself even his church when the wall street journal criticized nixon kennedy said it was like l'obsservatore romano criticizing the pope and speaker john mccormack denies that kennedy called him archbishop he called me cardinal mccormack recalls when the vatican implied some criticism of kennedys campaign effort to prove himself free of papal influence kennedy said ruefully to a pair of reporters now i understand why henry the eighth set up his own church   —TOM WICKER, "Kennedy Without Tears"

2. trip describes the psychedelic experience very well it is gratuitous an extra day in the week one saying goes and the sense of this experience being unearned is perhaps the common feature of all the attitudes that have grown up around it it shapes the disbelief of those who have not experienced it and paradoxically it confirms the belief that something quite so rich in life experience must somehow always be a gift and unmerited the view of ordinary life is nearly always altered after a trip but this does not mean the style of post psychedelic life is set or naturally follows egos are still distinct twins in their variety and the egoless genuine lsd head cant really be said to have returned from his trip you cant bring the universe home with you perhaps all you can do is choose your home
   —PAUL VELDE, "Psychedelics: You Can't Bring the Universe Home"

3. the other pitfall blocking the path of the new left is the cultures skill at amiably absorbing all manner of rebels and turning them into celebrities to be a radical in america today is like trying to punch your way out of a cage made of marshmallow every thrust at the jugular draws not blood but sweet success every hack at the roots draws not retaliation but fame and affluence the cultures insatiable thirst for novelty and titillation insured leroi jones television interviews norman mailer million dollar royalties and paul goodman fat paychecks as a government consultant yesterdays underground becomes todays vaudeville and tomorrows cliche if the draft super patriots and the justice department dont wreck the new left masscult may kill it with kindness and then deposit its carcass in the cemetery of celebrities alongside of jane holzer liberace and jack kerouac
   —JACK NEWFIELD, *A Prophetic Minority*

EXERCISE C. In the following sentences determine which marks of punctuation are used correctly, which marks are used incorrectly, and what additional punctuation is needed. Be prepared to give reasons for your decisions.

1. I've seen the play Hello Dolly twice, but I still find it's plot fascinating.
2. We like to think that the spoils system went out with Andrew Jackson, but actually it's still in effect: in federal, state, and municipal government.
3. Is'nt it time we all ignored our own personal problems and cooperated with one another in making this world a better place to live in.
4. She watches television all day long; and in the evening too.
5. Should one judge a candidate from the speeches he makes? from the printed matter he distributes? or from the ideas he generates?
6. Blacks and whites must learn to live and work together; otherwise, this country is doomed.
7. The Presidents daughters activities are always reported in the press, so are his wifes.
8. I think I recognize that actor, wasn't he on the television show My Three Sons?
9. I wanted to make that perfectly clear, the President said, Have I made it so?
10. As one pundit once observed of Senator Dirksen, He certainly couldn't be accused of using any greasy kid stuff!

Larger

Elements

If you wish to be a writer, write.
　　　　　—EPICTETUS

Anyone who wishes to become a good writer should endeavor, before
he allows himself to be tempted by the more showy qualities, to be
direct, simple, brief, vigorous, and lucid.
　　　　　　　　　　　　　　—H. W. FOWLER

31   **The Whole Composition** = PLAN

Two difficulties face every writer: Can he say what he really means, and can he make that meaning clear to his readers? There are no pat solutions to this double problem, no easy rules, no short cuts. Every writer has to decide first what he wants to write, and second how he wants to write it. And then, having written it, he has to stand off and look at the results of his labor from the point of view of a reader. Does his writing have readability and clarity? A sense of direction and purpose? If not, he has failed as a writer.

Although there is no safe generalization about "how to write," there are some useful guiding principles:

1. Decide what you are going to write about. (See Section 31a on selecting a subject, and Section 31b on limiting the subject.)

2. Make a rough but full list of ideas, assertions, facts, and illustrations that may have some bearing on your subject. (See Section 31c on making a preliminary outline.)

3. Frame a statement of what you want to say about your subject. (See Section 31d on framing a thesis statement.)

4. Sort out the items in your rough outline, putting together all the ideas that belong together and eliminating all those that seem irrelevant. (See Section 31e on making a complete outline.)

5. Try to find a concrete instance, illustration, anecdote, or example for a good opening statement. If you can think of nothing appropriate to your purposes, proceed to the next step immediately. (See Section 31f on beginning the paper.)

6. Begin to write. Don't let problems of wording and phrasing slow you down, or you will lose momentum and direction. (See Section 31g on writing a first draft.)

7. Once you have finished the first draft, go back over it and polish your words, sentences, and paragraphs. Check the ending to make sure that it gives the impression of finality and completeness. (See Section 31h on ending the paper and 31i on writing a second draft.)

8. If possible, put your paper aside for a few days before making final revisions. You will gain perspective in this way and will spot errors in logic and presentation more readily. (See Section 31j on making final revisions.)

In brief, the writing process consists of two basic steps: (1) planning what you are going to say, and (2) writing and rewriting it. Remember that the first step is fully as important as the second. Good writing requires careful planning.

31a **Select a subject that interests you.**

In a college writing course, some assignments prescribe your subject, and some even the specific method of handling it. Others will give you either complete freedom or a range of choice. If you are given a choice, select a subject that captures your interest and about which you have or want to have ample knowledge. Begin by reviewing your own experience and abilities. Can you clean a gun, make a model airplane, build a set of shelves, repair an automobile, put together a hi-fi set, make a dress? What interesting people have you known? What teachers have you liked and why? What sports do you enjoy playing or watching? What books have you read recently? Which ones have you liked? What do you want to know more about? Such subjects, close to everyday experience, make interesting writing if you dig for the details that really describe them. Indeed, no writing will be interesting unless you do dig for the details that make it concrete, and you are much more likely to dredge up the material for a paper describing your own house than for one describing a South Sea sunrise.

Remember that good writing about abstract subjects is not made up of great billowing generalizations unsupported by details, examples, illustrations, and explanations. You can't say much that is meaningful about prejudice, for instance, without tying your paper down to examples; and examples bring you back to your own experience. This approach is likely to lead you to some such topic as "prejudice against traffic laws in my home town," "my prejudice against dentists," or "my roommate's prejudices."

The list below may be helpful, not only for the specific subjects it gives, but also for those it brings to mind.

GENERAL	SPECIFIC
1. Fashions in Clothes	Casual Dress on _____ Campus.
2. Science Fiction	Themes in Ray Bradbury's Novels
3. Conformity in College	Why Should We All Follow the Leader?
4. Moms and Momma's Boys	Homesickness in College
5. The College Newspaper	Student Editorials
6. Women Think for Themselves	Why Should Girls Have Curfew?
7. Will Americans Pay for Education?	Teachers' Salaries in My Home Town
8. Home-built Furniture	A Simple Coffee Table Design

GENERAL	SPECIFIC
9. Fun in Photography	Using a Polaroid Camera
10. Are We Progressing Backwards?	Six New Ways of Being Sick
11. Should Anti-Abortion Laws Be Liberalized?	The Aftereffects of the Thalidomide Scandal
12. The U.S. Space Effort	Did We Have to Go to the Moon?
13. Racial Prejudice in the U.S.	Black Militancy and the White Backlash
14. Civil Disobedience	Whatever Happened to Passive Resistance?
15. Changing Sexual Mores in the U.S.	The Pill and Its Effects on Teen-Age Morality
16. Drug Addiction	If Dad Drinks Gin, Why Can't I Smoke Pot?
17. Campus Democracy	Why Students Should Have a Hand in Designing the Curriculum
18. Urban Congestion	Riding the Subway During Rush Hour
19. Black Power	The Role of the NAACP
20. Military Service	Why I Decided to Stay in College

EXERCISE 31a(1). Make a list of five titles suggested by your tastes in motion pictures—for example, "Why Are 'Westerns' so Popular?" or "The Appeal of the Art Film."

EXERCISE 31a(2). List five titles suggested by the advantages or disadvantages of living in a large city—for example, "Horses: You Can Have Them; I'll Take a Buick," or "Lawn Mowers Are Not for Me."

EXERCISE 31a(3). List five titles suggested by your hobbies or your interest in sports—for example, "The World's Most Expensive Stamp," "The Time I Did <u>Not</u> Strike Out with the Bases Loaded."

31b **Limit the subject you have chosen so that you can handle it in the time and space at your disposal.**

Don't try to do too much in a paper of three hundred to five hundred words, or you will end up in a series of vague and half-supported generalizations that never come into focus. It is attempts to solve world problems such as "NATO and Soviet Policy," "United States Involvement in the Far East," "The Future of Mass Media," or "Public Education, Past and Present" that lead to difficulties. Experienced writers are constantly aware of the limitations dictated by the time and space at their disposal. They will reject a subject like "The Problems of Television" for something like "My Nights with *Laugh-In*," or "The Army-Navy Game in Your Living Room," and a subject like "Swimming" for "How to Swim the Backstroke," or "Developing Speed in Swimming."

Five hundred or even a thousand words do not provide much space. Consider that a page of such a magazine as *Harper's* or *The Atlantic* carries seven hundred words or more. A typical newspaper column runs to a thousand words. Clearly these lengths are not sufficient for such topics as "The Idea of Freedom," "The Problem of Equality," "World Peace," and "Drugs in Modern Medicine." If you are tempted to tackle these or similar topics, discipline yourself to trim them down to the size you can hope to handle in the few hundred words you will usually be assigned.

Suppose, for example, that your family has always had pets—at various times a dog or two, three cats, a parakeet, some tropical fish, and once a few white mice. You decide that since you have had considerable experience with a variety of pets, you have a good potential topic. Your first temptation will be to write a paper entitled something like "Pets I Have Known." Resist it. A paper of this sort will almost surely become a list of your various pets, with a random comment or two on each. It will lack any focus, any center of interest. You must narrow it down. Consider such questions as which pet gave you the most satisfaction, what all pets had in common, which pet you liked least, what you gained by having a variety of pets, what difficulties you had in keeping tropical fish. Limit your subject to something you can talk about fully and interestingly in the space you have. Doing so, you may find that your best topics will lead you to titles such as "The Care and Feeding of Parakeets," "One Small Girl and a Tank of Tropical Fish," "White Mice Are for the Birds," "Every Boy Needs a Variety of Pets," or "No Pets Allowed." The important thing is to get a specific topic and keep it in focus, and not to choose a general subject in which you say less and less about more and more.

Be sure that the title of your paper reflects accurately the limitations you have set on your subject. Don't call a paper on the care of tropical fish "Tropical Fish," a report on the stories of H. P. Lovecraft "Fantasy Fiction," or a personal paper on working out your quarrels with your roommate "Roommates."

Keep in mind the character of the audience for which you are writing, for your audience always limits the way you treat a subject. Always try to focus on a specific audience, even if it is as large a group as "general readers." Then try to decide whether that audience will respond best to a simple or complex, a popular or technical, or a general or specific presentation. If you are honestly trying to communicate, you must adapt the nature of your subject matter, your point of view, the extent of detail and explanation that you introduce, and even your terminology, to the audience you are addressing. This does not mean that you should be pretentious or condescending; you must be yourself, but "being yourself" means first of all that you know what you are trying to say.

EXERCISE 31b(1). List five topics that would be appropriate for themes of several thousand words. Select a single aspect of each of these topics that would make an appropriate title for a theme of 200–300 words.

EXERCISE 31b(2). Refer to the topics suggested on pages 159–160. Choose five items from the general list and devise a more specific topic for each.

EXERCISE 31b(3). Write specific titles for five of the general topics listed below.

1. Mass Protest	6. Going on a Hike
2. Current Music	7. The U.S. Supreme Court
3. Teachers	8. At the Racetrack
4. A Scenic Wonder	9. TV Violence
5. Censorship	10. Political Conventions

EXERCISE 31b(4). Write a one-paragraph "open letter" on some subject that you think should be of general interest (e.g., taxes, traffic signs, a municipal memorial, fresh air in the classroom). Address it to a very small audience, such as a school board, the city council, your parents, or your fellow students in this course.

31c Gather materials and make preliminary notes.

Once you have decided on a reasonably limited topic, your next business is to get together the rough materials for your paper. A good many inexperienced writers make the mistake of thinking that once they have decided upon a topic such as "The Qualities of a Good Teacher" they should be able to sit down and dash off four or five hundred words. No one can do this. Any writer needs a kind of incubation period for even the simplest subject. For some writers, the work of incubation goes on half subconsciously. They think about about their topic over a cup of coffee, while they are walking between classes, while they are brushing their hair or shaving. For others it goes on with much chewing of pencils over a blank piece of paper. However it goes on, it must go on, for few people have on the top of their minds the kind of specific detail out of which a solid piece of writing, even about personal experiences, is made.

The material you need for a solid paper can come from a variety of sources, depending on the topic. For papers based on your own experience, you will need to dig around in your memory. A paper on the qualities of teachers whom you considered good will require you to ask such questions as: What teachers did you like? Why? What did they do that others did not? Were they more friendly? To everyone? To you in particular? In what ways? Did they know their subject matter better than other teachers? How did you know? What specific things did they do that made you like them? For papers based on observation you will need to do some closer looking and thinking than you are accustomed to. One part of the value of a composition course, indeed, is that it encourages you to look more closely, to see more than you ordinarily do. Each of us thinks he knows his own backyard, or the look of his best friend, or the shape of his favorite hideout until he tries to describe it on paper. When he does so, he finds that he has to work to see the specific details.

Most inexperienced writers discover that the best way to get their observations and ideas in order is to put them on paper. Making notes on paper is a way of finding out what you have to say on a subject. They help you select and evaluate your material and put it in order. Suppose you decide to write a paper on "The Scene," the discotheque where you usually go on Saturday nights. As a start, you might jot down the following:

1. Good selections of records
2. More exciting than fraternity dances
3. Very crowded dance floor
4. Good coffee
5. Psychedelic decor
6. Cheaper than a night club
7. Food badly prepared and selection limited
8. Waitresses pleasant, especially Liz
9. Good place to meet people
10. Makes a change from movies or TV
11. See some people you don't meet on campus
12. Close to the center of town and the campus
13. No alcoholic drinks
14. Owner keeps place clean
15. Too small
16. Customers always shouting above music

Or suppose you decide to write a paper on "Buying a Second-Hand Car." Your preliminary notes might consist of the following:

1. Used-car dealers in town
2. Down payment from Dad

3. Sources of used cars
4. Advantages of car loan over personal loan
5. Condition of car
6. Choosing the car
7. Price
8. Trade-in allowance for old car
9. Newspaper used-car ads
10. Comparison shopping
11. Criteria for choice

Clearly neither of these lists is more than a list of notations, without logical order or arrangement. But making a list is a valuable first step. It gets your beginning ideas down on paper and shows you what you have to work with.

EXERCISE 31c(1).   Make preliminary notes for two of the theme titles you prepared for Exercises 31a(1)–31a(3).

EXERCISE 31c(2).   Which of the suggested topics listed on pages 159–160 could you use for a 200- to 300-word theme without any further study or research? Make preliminary notes for three of them, to see whether you know as much about them as you think you do.

EXERCISE 31c(3).   Make preliminary notes of one subject you can write about from personal experience (for example, "Problems of an Oldest Child") and one you know about only from hearsay or guesswork (for example, "The Life of a Ranch Hand").

31d **Frame a thesis statement that will help you avoid irrelevancies in planning your composition.***

A THESIS STATEMENT sums up the central idea and purpose of a paper in one or two sentences. It serves as a guide to help you reorder and arrange the material in your preliminary notes. The very act of constructing a thesis statement forces you to clarify your thinking, to sift out pointless and irrelevant material, and to keep focused on the main point of your paper. The preliminary notes on "The Scene" suggest some such thesis statement as *In spite of its noise and confusion, "The Scene" is the best place to go on a Saturday night* or *In spite of some disadvantages, I prefer to spend Saturday nights at "The Scene" because it is an exciting and friendly place to be.* The preliminary notes for "Choosing a Second-Hand Car" suggest a thesis state-

---

* Practice in writing précis, or brief summaries of other people's works, is excellent training for framing clear thesis statements for your own writing. See Section 47.

ment such as this: *Although I needed a car for commuting to school, neither I nor my parents could have afforded a new one.* Notice that in each case the thesis statement catches most of the ideas in the preliminary notes and puts them in meaningful order. It defines central ideas and purposes so that the writer knows where he is going. Once these are clearly stated, the writer can begin to revise his preliminary notes.

EXERCISE 31d(1). Some of the following thesis statements define a clear central idea and purpose; others are too vague, general, or confused to provide good guides for papers. Comment upon each. Suggest revisions for those which you think are unsuccessful.

1. What a student gets out of college depends on the college.
2. Government today plays too large a role in business.
3. Freshmen ought to be allowed to select their own courses in college because they have not been able to in high school and they are now ready to.
4. Student government works only as well as the students make it work.
5. The indiscriminate use of insecticides must be stopped.
6. Objective examinations are limited because they give undue weight to memory and not enough weight to ability to relate facts to one another.
7. Mathematics ought to be a required course for everyone.
8. Collecting coins is an educational and profitable hobby.
9. The qualities of a good teacher are many.
10. Practicing the piano requires tedious repetition, coordination, good instruction, and sometimes patience on the part of your family.

EXERCISE 31d(2). Make a thesis statement for each of the two themes you outlined in Exercise 31c(1).

EXERCISE 31d(3). Write a thesis statement for an essay or a chapter assigned to you as outside reading.

EXERCISE 31d(4). Write thesis statements for paragraphs 1, 2, 7, 11, and 13 on pages 227–231.

31e **Prepare a complete outline in which you arrange details in logical order and perfect your overall plan.**

Make it a habit to construct a complete outline for every piece of writing you do. An outline provides you with a working plan for organizing your paper. It insures that your development of the subject will be logical and orderly, and enables you to distinguish clearly between important ideas and less important ones.

Outlines may vary from simple, informal notes for your own

guidance, to carefully worked out topic or sentence outlines for longer and more complex papers. The kind of outline you choose will depend upon your writing assignment. For a brief class paper on your high school preparation in English, for example, you might have time only for such scratch notes as the following:

1. More literature than composition
2. Emphasis on grammar in 10th grade
3. Wrote most papers on literature
4. Research papers in 11th and 12th grades
5. Enjoyed literature more than papers
6. Lack of contemporary literature
7. Not much comment on papers except 11th grade.

Even such a limited set of notes as this provides a guide for your paper. It suggests immediately two major divisions into composition and literature, and clarifies the fact that the main emphasis in high school was on literature. A glance at the notes suggests a scheme in which topics 1, 3, 5, and 6 go in one paragraph, and 2, 4, and 7 in another. The whole suggests some such thesis statement as *My high school preparation in English included work in both composition and literature, but the latter was the more thorough as well as the more enjoyable.* With this kind of start and your notes before you as you write, even a brief paper is likely to go more smoothly and logically. Such preliminary outlines are, of course, especially valuable in writing examinations.

The greater the number of notes you have to begin with, the greater the probability that a more formal outline will be useful.

In constructing your outline, follow some consistent principle of organization—chronological, general to specific (deductive), specific to general (inductive), spatial, and so on. Bring together all related ideas in one place and do not repeat them in other parts of the outline.

In the preliminary outline for "Buying a Second-Hand Car" (31c), notice that two of the items stand out as general headings: "Sources of used cars" and "Choosing the car." Notice too that a third general heading, "Financing" must be added; otherwise there would be no place to put such items as "Down payment from Dad" and "Advantages of car loan over personal loan." If we arrange all the details under these three major headings, we come up with the following outline:

BUYING A SECOND-HAND CAR

   I. Sources of used cars
      A. Used-car dealers in town
      B. Newspaper used-car ads

  II. Choosing the car
      A. Comparison shopping
      B. Criteria for choice
         1. Condition of car
         2. Price
         3. Trade-in allowance for old car

 III. Financing
      A. Down payment from Dad
      B. Advantages of car loan over personal loan

Such an outline will help you keep your plan in mind as you write your paper (adherence to purpose). It will indicate the order in which you want to discuss each idea (logical development) and the relative importance of each (proportion of material).

If you are to do an efficient job of organizing your material, you must know something of the formal mechanics of outlining, and the various types of outlining that your instructor may require.

1. *Use a consistent method for numbering and indenting major headings and subheadings.* For most outlines, it is unnecessary to divide sub-headings more than two degrees. Here is a conventional system of outline notation:

   I. . . . .
     A. . . . .
        1. . . . .
           a. . . . .
           b. . . . .
        2. . . . .
     B. . . . .
  II. . . . .

2. *Be sure that your outline is logically clear and consistent.* Do not use single headings or single subheadings in your outline. Any category of heading or subheading must have at least two parts. If you have a I, you must also have a II. If you introduce an A under a Roman numeral, you must also have a B under that Roman numeral. If you put a 1 under an A, you must also put a 2. And so on for any division. The reason for this procedure is sheer logic. Each breakdown of the outline is a division of a foregoing bigger point, and you cannot logically divide something into just one part. A single subheading reflects poor organization and should be incorporated into the heading of which it is logically a part.

We might illustrate the principle mathematically as follows:

TWO DOLLARS

   I. One dollar
     A. Fifty cents
     B. Fifty cents
       1. Twenty-five cents
       2. Twenty-five cents
  II. One dollar

The same principle requires that each group of subheadings be logically equal to the next larger heading under which they fall. If we wish, for instance, to divide the general heading "dogs," we can do so with the subheadings "house dogs" and "working dogs," or "large dogs" and "small dogs," or "poodles," "collies," "spaniels," and the like. But each one of these groups represents a different principle of classification, and if we mix them we will have an illogical outline.

3. *Use either the topic, the sentence, or the paragraph form throughout your outline.* In a topic outline the separate headings are expressed by a noun, or a word or phrase used as a noun, and its modifiers. In a sentence outline, which has the same structure as the topic outline, the separate headings are expressed in complete sentences. The sentence outline is more informative than the topic outline, because it states ideas more fully; but the topic outline is easier to read. The paragraph outline gives a summary sentence for each paragraph in the theme. It does not divide and subdivide headings into subordinate parts.

Before you start to outline, decide which of the three types of outline you are going to use and then follow it consistently. If, for example, you choose to make a sentence outline, remember that every statement in the outline must be expressed as a complete sentence. Remember, too, to make all parts of the outline parallel in structure (see "Parallelism," Section 35), as in the following models.

THE TELEGRAPHER: KEEPER OF THE KEYS

(*Topic Outline*)

  I. Importance of telegraphic communication
    A. International telegraphic networks
    B. Emergency means of communication

II. Telegrapher's instrument
    A. Manually operated key, or "bug"
        1. Appearance of the key
        2. Operation of the key
    B. Modern teleprinter
        1. Appearance of the teleprinter
        2. Operation of the teleprinter
III. Comparative skills of telegraphers
    A. Complex skills of the "bug" operator
    B. Simple skills of the teleprinter operator

THE TELEGRAPHER: KEEPER OF THE KEYS

(Sentence Outline)

I. Telegraphy is one of our most important means of communication.
    A. The nations of the world are bound together by telegraphic networks.
    B. The telegraph is of great value for sending emergency messages.
II. Telegraphic instruments are of two general types.
    A. The manually operated key, or "bug," is used in small or remote communication centers.
        1. The "bug" resembles a miniature stapler connected to a panel of sockets.
        2. The "bug" produces long and short electrical impulses, or dots and dashes.
    B. The modern teleprinter is used in large communication centers.
        1. The teleprinter is a complicated machine with a manually operated keyboard.
        2. The teleprinter records, or prints, messages.
III. Operators of the "bug" and the teleprinter have different skills.
    A. The "bug" operator sends, receives, and translates the International Morse Code.
    B. The teleprinter operator uses a keyboard like that of a typewriter.

THE TELEGRAPHER: KEEPER OF THE KEYS

(Paragraph Outline)

1. Telegraphers are the keepers of a worldwide network of communications.
2. The small key, or "bug," sends electrical impulses through a panel of sockets and out into the atmosphere.
3. The modern teleprinter, operated by a keyboard, records messages in large communication centers.
4. The "bug" operator must employ great skill in sending and receiving messages in the International Morse Code.
5. The teleprinter operator must have only the simple skill of using a typewriter keyboard.

4. *Cast all items in the outline in parallel grammatical constructions.*
Consistency of grammatical form emphasizes the logic of the outline and gives it clarity and smoothness. Inconsistency of form, on the other hand, makes a perfectly rational ordering of items seem illogical.

THE GAME OF TENNIS	THE GAME OF TENNIS
Nonparallel	*Parallel*
I. The playing court	I. Playing court
A. The surface materials for it	A. Surface materials
1. Made of clay	1. Clay
2. Grass	2. Grass
3. The asphalt type	3. Asphalt
B. Measuring the court	B. Measurements
1. For singles	1. Singles
2. Doubles	2. Doubles
C. Net	C. Net
D. Backstops necessary	D. Backstops
II. Equipment needed	II. Equipment
A. Racket	A. Racket
B. The tennis balls	B. Ball
C. The wearing apparel of players	C. Wearing apparel
III. Rules for playing tennis	III. Playing rules
A. The game of singles	A. Singles
B. Doubles	B. Doubles
IV. Principal strokes of tennis	IV. Principal strokes
A. Serving the ball	A. Serving stroke
B. The forehand	B. Forehand stroke
1. Drive	1. Drive
2. Lobbing the ball	2. Lob
C. The backhand stroke	C. Backhand stroke
1. The drive	1. Drive
2. Lob	2. Lob

5. *Avoid vague outline headings such as* introduction, body, *and* conclusion. Not only does the outline serve as a guide in your writing; submitted with your paper, it may also serve as a table of contents for your reader. To use such words as *introduction, body,* and *conclusion* as outline headings is meaningless, for they give no clue to what material is to come. If your paper is to have an introduction, indicate in the outline what will be in it. If your paper is to have a formal conclusion, indicate in the outline what conclusion you will draw.

EXERCISE 31e(1). Examine the following outlines. Suggest appropriate revisions for each, and revise one so that it will be fully consistent with the principles of outlining.

FINDING A SUMMER JOB

I. Examining the field
   A. Kinds of jobs available
      1. Camp jobs
      2. Part-time typing
      3. Caring for children
      4. Construction work
   B. Studying the newspapers
   C. The interview
      1. Arrangements by letter or telephone
      2. Things to avoid
         a. Jobs you are not interested in
         b. Jobs too far from home
         c. Talking yourself down
         d. Being overconfident

THE VALUE OF PUBLIC OPINION POLLS

I. Introduction
   A. Operation of public opinion polls
      1. Selection of an important issue
      2. Constructing a set of questions
         a. Scientific nature of this construction
      3. A cross section of the population is selected
   B. Replies are tabulated and results summarized
II. Importance of poll's results
      1. Attitudes of public revealed to lawmakers
      2. Power of present groups revealed
      3. Polls are a democratic process
         a. Polls reveal extent of people's knowledge

THE ADVANTAGES OF GOING TO COLLEGE

I. Liberal Education
   A. Science
   B. Literature
II. Preparation for Career
   A. General
   B. Specific
III. Extracurricular Activities
   A. Bull sessions
      1. Informal discussion valuable
      2. Subjects not discussed in class

    B. Sports
    C. Social activities
        1. Clubs
        2. Speakers and concerts
        3. Dances

THE ADVANTAGES AND DISADVANTAGES OF A CITY UNIVERSITY

I. Convenience of location
 A. Transportation
 B. Hotels
 C. People
 D. Stores
 E. Theaters
II. Advantages
 A. Center of travel
 B. Students learn to be more independent.
 C. More types of people
 D. Those who have never been in city get new view
 E. Opportunities for work
III. Disadvantages
 A. Tendency to become too interested in other things
 B. Too much for some to cope with
 C. Too close to other schools

EXERCISE 31e(2). Construct a complete outline for one of the titles suggested in Section 31a. Use each of the three forms just described: (1) topic, (2) sentence, (3) paragraph.

EXERCISE 31e(3). Write a topic outline for one of the theme titles you prepared for Exercises 31a(1) to 31a(3).

31f **Begin your paper effectively.**

The beginning of your paper should serve as a springboard into your subject and, if possible, attract the reader's interest. Of the two, getting started is more important than devising a catchy opening. If you have trouble writing a satisfactory opening sentence or paragraph, don't waste time over it in the early drafts of your paper. Important as your opening sentences will be in the final draft of your paper, don't worry about them in your first draft. After you have written your first draft, you will often discover that your purpose has become clearer and that it is then much easier to write good opening sentences. Indeed, you may frequently discover that the first few sentences you wrote are relatively useless warming-up and that with slight revision the fourth or fifth sentence is in fact a good beginning.

How long your beginning should be depends on the length and complexity of your paper. An extended discussion of the relative merits of engineering and teaching as possible careers may require a well-organized paragraph of introduction in which you state your thesis and indicate the general plan of your paper. But the briefer papers which you will be writing for the most part in a composition course usually require only a sentence or two to get started effectively. A long introductory paragraph for a five-hundred-word paper on the disadvantages of living in a dormitory is very likely to be wordy, repetitious, and ineffective. In general, confine your opening for brief papers to a sentence or two. A paper entitled "I Hate Cats" would well begin with *Cats are a menace to mankind. They should be exterminated.* Or a paper on how to build a ship model may well begin with *The best method of building a ship model is.* . . . In each instance you will have launched the subject forcefully and established yourself with the reader, and can then move right along with your development.

Here are some guides to help you in writing good beginnings.

1. *Make the beginning self-explanatory.* Make the first sentence self-sufficient without the title. Give the reader a clear idea of what you are talking about from the very outset. Do not, for example, begin a paper entitled "Atomic War" with *Everyone is against it.* The following paragraph is intelligible only if the title is read as part of the paper.

HOW TO BUILD A SHIP MODEL

The first thing to do is to lay all the parts on the table in front of you. Next, read the directions carefully, and identify each of the parts. Then arrange the parts in the following manner. . . .

2. *Avoid a rambling, decorative beginning that simply delays the introduction.*

FATHER KNOWS BEST

You probably wonder from my title what I am going to write about. Well, it's a long story. It started way back in 1952 when I was born. My mother announced to my father that I was a boy! "We're going to send him to State University!" my father exclaimed. So here I am at State, a member of the freshman class.

It was my father's idea from the first that I should come to State. He had been a student here in 1945 when he met my mother. . . .

Here the writer meant well, aiming at what newspapermen call a "human interest" beginning. But he succeeded only in rambling about and wasting the reader's time; he would have done better had he begun his paper with the second paragraph.

3. *Avoid beginnings which have nothing to do with the actual thesis of the paper.*

> Describing a building accurately is a very difficult task. Though it is a good assignment because it makes you look closely and observe details you would not otherwise notice, it takes considerable time and does not leave the student enough time to write the actual paper. I discovered this when I tried to observe and describe the university chapel.

This kind of beginning might be called the "complaint about the assigned subject" beginning. The author has used sixty words worrying about his topic and has not yet managed to get to his real opening.

> After trying unsuccessfully to write a paper describing my roommate, and then attempting to gather some new ideas on books I had read during the summer, I gave up and decided to write on my experience in reading *The Grapes of Wrath* by John Steinbeck. I hope this fits the assignment.

This is the characteristic "apology" opening. The modest author of such an opening paragraph, if he felt the need to apologize, should have done so in a note clipped to the paper he finally wrote.

4. *If you have trouble writing a good beginning, try one of the following techniques.*

a. *Repeat the title.*

FATHER KNOWS BEST

> I was not much taken with the idea that I should enter State University this year. After visiting the campus for a few days, however, I became convinced that Father knows best when it comes to matters of his alma mater. . . .

or

> I decided that my father knows best after he had persuaded me that State University was the place to go. . . .

b. *Paraphrase the title.*

COLLEGE FOOTBALL: A GAME OR A BUSINESS?

> How much longer must we pay lip service to the notion that big-time college football is a sport played for fun by amateurs? It is time. . . .

c. *Begin with a statement of fact.*

When I went to school I learned that the town I grew up in was once covered with water.

Hair was one of the most popular Broadway musicals of the past decade.

Ninety-two per cent of the students at State College live at home and commute daily.

d. *Begin with a short sentence that will startle the reader.*

Gone with the Wind is a readable, exciting book. But it is a bad book.

I do not believe in composition courses.

My grandmother believed in ghosts.

e. *Begin with an anecdote directly related to the subject of the paper.*

FATHER KNOWS BEST

When Mark Twain left home at an early age, he had no great respect for his father's intelligence. When he returned a few years later, however, he was astonished at how much his father had learned in the meantime. Similarly, it was only after I had been away from home for a few years that I became aware that Father knows best. . . .

EXERCISE 31f(1). Choose three titles from the list of suggested topics in Section 31a. Then write a beginning for each, using a different technique each time.

EXERCISE 31f(2). Comment upon the following beginnings.

1. One of the characters in *The Moon and Sixpence* remarked that he had faithfully lived up to the old precept about doing every day two things you heartily dislike; for, said he, every day he had got up and he had gone to bed. —CHRISTOPHER MORLEY, "On Going to Bed"
2. There is something to be said for a bad education.
—PHYLLIS MCGINLEY, "The Consolations of Illiteracy"
3. Come what may, I change my razor blade each Saturday morning, and as I did so on a hot one not long ago, I found myself worrying about the Civil War.
—ROBERT HENDERSON, "The Enamelled Wishbone"
4. There is nothing more alone in the universe than man.
—LOREN EISELEY, "The Long Loneliness"
5. The School System has much to say these days of the virtue of reading widely, and not enough about the virtues of reading less but in depth.
—JOHN CIARDI, "Robert Frost: The Way to the Poem"

31g Always write a preliminary rough draft of your paper.

Having completed your outline and having phrased an opening statement, you are ready to proceed with the actual writing of your paper. Be sure to allow time to write your papers at least twice. The first—or rough—draft gives you an opportunity just to *write*. In this draft you need not concern yourself with spelling, punctuation, mechanics, or grammar. Rather, you can devote your attention to getting your ideas, as directed by the outline, down on paper.

Remember that your paper is more than an outline. No matter how unified, clear, and coherent a paper is, it will be thin and weak unless it is adequately developed. Good writing is not made by orderly outlines alone. It is packed with specific detail, example, and illustration. The real failure of a great many student papers lies not in their lack of essential unity or coherence, but in their thinness. They say little or nothing because their writers have contented themselves with generalizations and have not been willing to dig for the sort of facts and examples that will make the subjects alive for a reader. The papers make good sense as far as they go; but they do not go far enough or deep enough to make good reading. Since the ways of developing papers are the same as the ways of developing paragraphs, which are their principal units of thought, this problem is considered in more detail in Section 32, "Effective Paragraphs."

31h End your paper effectively.

Just as a forceful opening gets your paper off to a good vigorous start, so a strong conclusion lends a finished note to your paper. An effective ending may bring your paper to a logical conclusion or tie it all together. A paper titled "How to Build a Ship Model" might end with this statement:

> If you have followed all the directions given here, you should now have an assembled ship model ready to be put in a place of honor in the family living room.

Here are some ideas to help you end your papers effectively.

1. *Conclude with a restatement of your thesis statement.* In the paper "Father Knows Best" this sort of ending might be effective:

> Now that I have been here and have seen the school for myself, I am convinced that Father *does* know best. I have decided to enroll for the next term at State.

2. *Summarize the major ideas you have brought out in the paper.* A summary serves the double purpose of bringing your paper to a good conclusion and of reminding your readers once more of the major points you have made. The paper called "Buying a Second-Hand Car" could effectively employ this sort of ending:

> Thus, it is clear that buying a second-hand car is a complex process. But anyone who investigates the sources of used cars carefully, chooses his car intelligently, and finances it soundly will have a car that lasts him for years.

3. *Draw a logical conclusion, inductively or deductively, from the facts you have presented.* This sort of conclusion is especially effective if you have set out to defend a point of view. If you have, for example, been exploring a controversial topic such as "Should the Franchise Be Extended to Eighteen-Year-Olds?" your conclusion might be a call for action to reinforce whichever side you had defended.

4. *Avoid weak endings.*

a. *Don't end your paper with an apology.* Such endings as *This is only my opinion, and I'm probably not really very well qualified to speak* or *I'm sorry that this isn't a better paper, but I didn't have enough time* spoil the effect of whatever you have written. If you feel that you have failed, your reader will probably think so too.

b. *Don't end your paper by branching off into another aspect of the topic or by introducing new material.* The end of your paper should conclude what you have already said. It is disconcerting to a reader to find new ideas introduced that are not explored further. Avoid such endings as: *There is a lot more I could say about this if I had more time* or *Another aspect of buying a second-hand car is convincing your parents you should have a car in the first place, but it would take another paper to tell about it.* This type of ending leaves the reader with the feeling that you have led him to no definite conclusion.

31i Prepare a finished second draft.

After a cooling-off period of several hours, you are ready to check, revise, and rewrite. Test the overall organization of your first draft by asking yourself the following questions:

1. Does the title fit the discussion?
2. Is the material divided into distinct sections?
3. Are these sections arranged in logical order? (Is there an orderly sequence of thought from one section to the next, and from the beginning to the end?)

4. Is all the material relevant to the central purpose of the paper?

5. Is the beginning direct and pertinent?

6. Does the ending of the paper give an impression of finality and completeness? (Or does it trail off in a cloud of minor details?)

Once you have answered these basic questions to your own satisfaction, check the individual paragraphs—that is, the units of discussion. Be sure that the topic of each paragraph is clear-cut and adequately developed (see Section 32). Test every generalization to insure that it is supported by sufficient evidence—facts, illustrations, examples. When you spot an opinion or assertion that lacks evidence, supply the evidence—or else discard the opinion entirely.

Now you can proceed with your rewriting. Recast clumsy sentences, repair faulty phraseology, make the diction more exact and precise. Supply needed transitions and check existing transitions for accuracy. Scrutinize every mark of punctuation and look up all questionable spellings. Then recopy or retype the whole paper in the required format (see "Manuscript form," Section 15).

31j Make final revisions.

Set your manuscript aside for a day or two before making final revisions. Then you can go back to it with some of the objectivity of a reader. Make minor revisions—punctuation, spelling, word substitution—directly (but neatly) on the manuscript. If you find that more fundamental revisions—paragraph and sentence structure—are needed, you may have to recopy one or more pages. Usually the reaction of an unofficial reader—a roommate, a friend, a parent, even a well-disposed stranger—is helpful. Ask whether or not your paper communicates clearly. The revisions your reader suggests may be minor: a word here, a punctuation mark there. If he spots more fundamental flaws, you may have to rewrite the whole paper. One final proofreading—if possible, aloud to yourself —is good insurance against handing in an imperfect paper. Good writers are patient, with an infinite capacity for revision.

EXERCISE 31j. On the following pages, you will find four specimen papers, the first of which has a critical commentary. After studying the papers carefully, write critical commentaries on the others.

Specimen Paper 1: Critical Commentary

"Government Censorship of TV Violence" is not a successful paper. Despite its correct spelling and punctuation and its competent sentence structure, the paper fails to accomplish what it sets out to do. The author's announcement of his subject in the title is all but forgotten in the process of the actual writing. The paper obviously was written without a preconceived plan—without even a tentative outline.

The first three sentences of the paper are concerned, not with television violence, but with movie heroes of the 1930's, nor is any attempt made by the writer to connect this in any way with the stated subject of his paper. The concluding sentence of the first paragraph, instead of providing a transition to the next, is an unsupported generalization that marks a further digression from the topic.

The second paragraph, without any transition from the one preceding it, launches finally into the subject with which, according to the title, the paper was to be concerned. But again the author's digressive tendencies prevail. Instead of discussing violence on TV, or government censorship, the paragraph veers into a consideration of psychiatric studies of the effects of TV violence on young children.

Paragraph 3 begins with an attempt to provide a transition between the effects of mass media on children and their effects on adults. The second sentence, however, leaps to another subject, violence in the society, and is furthermore an unsupported generalization. Only with the third sentence of this paragraph is the idea of government interest in TV introduced—and even then there is no indication that that interest is taking any form other than that of investigation and study.

The fourth paragraph, instead of tying up all the many loose ends of the paper, brings in a few more of its own. The author has forgotten that the paper was supposed to have been about government censorship. Instead, he is now attempting to fix the blame for the violence, a subject which could be done justice only in a paper of its own. Thus, although strong and provocative, the concluding paragraph does not fulfill its proper function here. When a paper ends, the reader wants to feel that a certain area has been covered thoroughly. In this paper, the end serves only to add to the haphazard selection of topics, and to the constant lack of connection among them.

Specimen Paper 1

GOVERNMENT CENSORSHIP OF TV VIOLENCE

In the 1930's, America acquired a new pantheon of heroes. Among them were James Cagney, Edward G. Robinson, and Humphrey Bogart. But the real heroes were the gangsters they portrayed, men beyond the reach of the law (except in the final scenes) and addicted to violence as a way of life. In a way, violence has always been a way of life in America.

There is an alarming amount of violence on TV. Most of us are too used to it to really notice it anymore, but it is there. Psychiatrists are increasingly concerned with the effect of TV violence on young children. Recent studies have shown that children tend, to a large extent, to adopt behavior patterns they have observed on the TV screen. It has been noted that children who are exposed to large doses of TV-watching exhibit more aggressive characteristics than children whose exposure to TV is more severely limited.

It is impossible to estimate how much effect the mass media have on adult behavior. But it is a well-known fact that crimes of violence are relatively far more frequent in the United States than in any other of the so-called civilized countries of the world. Several Senate subcommittees have already begun investigating the various causes of the continuing rise in violent crime in this country.

TV, with its constant access to the American home, is the greatest offender. The fault lies with the producers, with the networks, with the sponsors. But most of all it lies with the American public, which continues to watch it.

Specimen Paper 2

MY IDEA OF INTELLIGENT READING

Intelligent reading is a very important medium by which a person may educate himself and be well informed. Students, professional people, laborers, and people in all walks of life find intelligent reading to be a great asset. Intelligent reading is a way of getting an education, and if a person cannot afford a conventional education he can always educate himself by reading.

But what is intelligent reading? It means the kind of reading that forces a person to think. Intelligent reading is not just reading for fun. People who want to educate themselves by reading should select their materials carefully. They should select something that interests them, about which they wish to know more.

When a person has selected the right material, he should make himself comfortable. This means a comfortable chair and a good reading light. If the book is his own, he should read with a pencil in his hand, marking in the margin of the page or underscoring the important parts. He should make sure that he understands where the writer is taking him. When he begins to tire, he should stop reading, for that is a sign that his mind is tired and unable to absorb any more information.

The habit of reading a little each day is a good one. It provides a pattern and a direction, and a person who gets himself into such a habit will be surprised at the end of a year how much he has learned, how different he is intellectually from what he was before. He will know a great many more words and he will also know much more language in general. For he has exposed himself to a liberal education, and the effects of that exposure are more telling on him than he thought possible.

Specimen Paper 3

LET'S <u>NOT</u> LEGALIZE MARIJUANA

A lot of "enlightened" opinion these days is on the side
of the legalization of marijuana. Advocates of legalization
argue that marijuana is not addictive and that there is therefore no cause-and-effect relationship between the use of marijuana and the use of so-called hard drugs. The point is also
made that there is little difference between marijuana and
alcohol, which <u>is</u> legal. Finally, some argue, the use of marijuana should be left to the choice of the individual, because
it concerns only him and no one else.

These are ridiculous arguments, as this paper will show.
First of all, marijuana has been shown to be psychologically
addictive so that, although the body does not require it, the
mind may. Marijuana provides a temporary release from anxieties
and feelings of inferiority and a user of marijuana may try
to find, eventually, an even stronger release in hard drugs.

Also, marijuana is not like alcohol. A drinker eventually
reaches the point of passing out, but the marijuana smoker
never does. However marijuana is like alcohol in that both
affect the reflexes, making users dangerous drivers, and both
affect the personality, making users dangerous to society.

For this reason, marijuana should not be looked at as an
individual's private business. When a person becomes a danger
or a burden to society, what he does becomes the business of
society. So marijuana should not be legalized; instead an
even greater penalty should be placed upon those found using
it or selling it.

Specimen Paper 4

HUNTING ALONE

The day was beautiful and full of sunshine as I started, rifle in hand, on one of the many exciting days of my life. This was to be my first deer-hunting trip alone. Before I had always gone with my father, who was never very trusting.

Living in a little town on the Olympic Peninsula, where hunting is a way of life, didn't mean that I could go deer hunting by myself. My father figured that I might trip and fall on the rifle, thus suffering one of the many hazards of hunting. This time I had to prove that I could handle a rifle and compass properly. I took a course given by the Game Department, which taught me the proper use of and basic rules for handling of firearms. It was very educational.

When the deer season opened and I asked my father about going alone, he said, to my surprise, "OK," adding, without a trace of a smile, "Just be sure to bring back a deer so we'll have steaks this winter." So here I was, jogging along the highway. The birds sounded more cheerful than I did.

After turning off an old logging road, I took a bearing with my compass. I listened as I walked, trying to get any sound or sight that a deer had been this way. Suddenly, I spotted a hoofprint in the mud beside the road. But on closer examination, I found it to be at least two days old.

Then I noticed a berry bush that had been stripped of its berries. Could it have been a bear? No, there are no bears here, I thought. Then I saw the tracks—two, three, four sets of deer tracks beyond the bush. Then, through the bushes I saw them in a clearing, a watchful doe, her timid offspring, and a magnificent buck. I stood frozen to the ground. They caught my scent and were gone in the flicking of an eye.

Look to the paragraph and the discourse will look to itself. . . .
    —ALEXANDER BAIN

32   **Effective Paragraphs** = ¶

The purpose of paragraphing is to reveal the order and unity of the overall statement. A sentence is a group of words that makes a single statement; a paragraph is a group of sentences that are related to one another, and that, taken together, form a single coherent part of a larger unit.

Let us examine a good paragraph to see how each sentence serves as part of a larger unit. (The sentences are numbered for easy reference.)

(1) The outlook was bad. (2) The trail from Auche to Nhpum Ga was four-and-a-half miles long and followed the crest of a steep ridge; there was no way to move other than on the exposed trail, and though no Japanese were seen, the accuracy of the fire as the shelling searched up and down the column indicated that observers were controlling it. (3) The trail was all up hill or down; in places it was nearly as steep as the declivity on both sides of it. (4) Also it was slippery. (5) Whenever it rained—and it had been raining hard—the soil of those hills turned into mud of the exact consistency of butter. (6) While the shells whistled in and the jarring, nerve-shattering explosions cracked at front and rear and the wounded cried, men and mules slipped and fell and the morale of the marchers began to go. (7) Panic, the obsessive, uncontrollable urge to get the hell out that extinguishes every other consideration, threatened to wreak more havoc than the shelling itself.
    —CHARLES OGBURN, JR., *The Marauders*

First, all these sentences serve a single purpose. Sentence 1 establishes a generalization with a built-in personal attitude. Sentence 2 provides a physical setting that is both general (it is an obvious wartime scene) and specific (the concentration is on a particular trail important to both sides). Sentences 3 and 4 give further details about the trail, showing why it is dangerous as well as important. Sentence 5 adds a further, more vivid detail (the mud which has the *exact consistency of butter*); but it also shows how this factor in the physical setting makes the outlook of sentence 1 *bad*. Sentence 6 reinforces the same impression with further physical details: shells, explosions, cries of the wounded, the slipping feet and hooves. Sentence 7, with its emphasis on the psychological, sums up the entire paragraph by identifying the *bad outlook* of sentence 1 with a state of mind (*panic*) as well as with the physical setting. Thus, the generalization is made concrete by details both physical and psychological. Because all the sentences contribute directly to a single purpose, we say the paragraph has unity.

Second, the individual sentences are not only related to each other in subject matter; they are also specifically tied together by logic and grammatical structure. By isolating one element, a trail in wartime, sentence 2 justifies the broad generalization in sentence 1. This is why sentence 2 must be longer and more detailed: The writer is committed to "proving" why this particular situation is *bad*. Sentence 3 refers again to the trail, indicating the importance of the physical setting, and the pronoun *it* in sentence 4 ties that whole sentence to the preceding one, which contains its antecedent, *trail*. Moreover, sentences 2, 3, 4, and 5 are all connected, not by chronology or a sense of time, but by a sense of place. They all help to visualize the scene, each sentence going one step beyond its predecessor in vivid details. Sentence 6 brings all the details into focus with a sense of activity. Notice the uniform verb tense and the choice of several action verbs—*whistled, cracked, cried, slipped*. Thus, before sentence 7 the writer has established not only a sense of place but also a sense of activity at that place. Sentence 7, with its subject *panic* and its verb *threatened*, adds still another dimension to the physical setting and the overall state of mind. In short, the paragraph has coherence.

Third, the sentences in this paragraph give ample information about the subject. The author does not have to write extensively about warfare to make vivid his feelings in this restricted area of warfare. He satisfies us with enough information—the exposed trail watched by enemy patrols and the various discomforts and dangers of jungle fighting—so that we can believe that the platoon or regimental or battalion numbers, or names of the fighting men, would have merely cluttered up the paragraph; and perhaps, even worse, they might have buried the one thing the author wanted to write about. The paragraph therefore is adequately developed.

The elements of a good paragraph, then, are (1) UNITY, (2) COHERENCE, and (3) ADEQUATE DEVELOPMENT. For convenience we discuss these elements separately, but all three are interdependent. As the illustration above shows, a coherent paragraph is also unified and adequately developed. In other words, to support a topic sentence clearly and purposively, you must develop a paragraph adequately and connect its sentences logically. Making a good paragraph calls for several closely related skills, none of which is sufficient in itself.

EXERCISE 32(1).   Analyze the following paragraphs just as the paragraph above was analyzed.

1. (1) What people do not seem to realize is that the editors of the various "digests" do not simply delete a word here and there. (2) They do not cut only extraneous material. (3) Instead, they "blue pencil" paragraphs and pages. (4) We depend upon the discretion of these editors, and what seems of importance to them becomes the text we read. (5) We have no idea what has been cut. (6) What we do read may be so removed from its original context that the remainder of the article is completely distorted. (7) The reader, however, has no way of knowing of this distortion and thus reads his digest version in good faith. (8) Consequently, when he tries to discuss his mutilated concept with someone who has taken the time to read the unabridged version, he may find himself unfamiliar with a point that was the basis of the entire thesis.   —Student paragraph

2. (1) Any sort of problem can start us thinking: a stuck door, a rainy day, or a kiss. (2) But the problems that require hard and sustained thinking nearly always come to our attention through *language*. (3) The most perplexing problems we face, as citizens or as members of a family or as people doing some kind of job, are problems that require us to handle words. (4) A paragraph in a newspaper, an announcement over the air, a quarrel, a letter, a chapter in a book: these may be the occasion of thinking, or may turn up to be reckoned with before the thinking has reached its goal. (5) There is still a good deal of mystery about the exact relation between words and thoughts, but we know that the connection is intimate, and we can't talk very fruitfully about the one without talking about the other.
    —MONROE C. BEARDSLEY, *Practical Logic*

3. (1) The late 1920's were an age of islands, real and metaphorical. (2) They were an age when Americans by thousands and tens of thousands were scheming to take the next boat for the South Seas or the West Indies, or better still for Paris, from which they could scatter to Majorca, Corsica, Capri or the isles of Greece. (3) Paris itself was a modern city that seemed islanded in the past, and there were island

countries, like Mexico, where Americans could feel that they had escaped from everything that oppressed them in a business civilization. (4) Or without leaving home they could build themselves private islands of art or philosophy; or else—and this was a frequent solution —they could create social islands in the shadow of the skyscrapers, groups of close friends among whom they could live as unconstrainedly as in a Polynesian valley, live without moral scruples or modern conveniences, live in the pure moment, live gaily on gin and love and two lamb chops broiled over a coal fire in the grate. (5) That was part of the Greenwich Village idea, and soon it was being copied in Boston, San Francisco, everywhere.   —MALCOLM COWLEY,
Exile's Return: A Literary Odyssey of the 1920's

4. (1) As man proceeds toward his announced goal of the conquest of nature, he has written a depressing record of destruction, directed not only against the earth he inhabits but against the life that shares it with him. (2) The history of the recent centuries has its black passages—the slaughter of the buffalo on the western plains, the massacre of the shorebirds by the market gunners, the near-extermination of the egrets for their plumage. (3) Now, to these and others like them, we are adding a new chapter, and a new kind of havoc—the direct killing of birds, mammals, fishes, and indeed practically every form of wildlife by chemical insecticides indiscriminately sprayed on the land.   —RACHEL CARSON, *Silent Spring*

5. (1) The Bogart the books celebrate, the figure who looms a little larger than any one of his films, is chiefly a product of a handful of Warner movies made between 1941 and 1946, from "High Sierra" to "The Big Sleep." (2) He was a long time getting there. (3) Bogart played a number of minor roles on Broadway during the 1920's. (4) It is usually said that he spent those years dressed in white flannels, carrying a tennis racket, but the Bogart role that sticks in my mind from a later reading of the play is the prim and earnest young man in Larry E. Johnson's "It's a Wise Child" (1929), who, always willing to sacrifice romance to his career, loses the girl to Minor Watson. (5) Bogart made several unsuccessful bids for a Hollywood career (nine movies for four companies from 1930 to 1932), but it was not until his success as Duke Mantee in "The Petrified Forest" (1936), a repetition of his Broadway role, that his movie career began in earnest. (6) He was no star even then. (7) Featured, he appeared in five films in 1936, seven in 1937, six in 1938, seven in 1939, a functioning cog in the Warner machine, a busy bush-league gangster on the turf ruled by Cagney and Robinson. (8) He had played a gangster as far back as 1932, in "Three on a Match," in which he drove poor Ann Dvorak to suicide, but it was his Duke Mantee that convinced the Warner typecasters that they had a good thing. (9) Given that many movies in that short a time, he played a variety of parts, but the tough-guy roles predominated and became his identification tag.
    —GERALD WEALES, "The Bogart Vogue: Character and Cult"

Unity in the Paragraph = ¶ UN

32a **Write unified paragraphs.**

A unified paragraph has a clear intent, and its topic is either summed up in one of its sentences or strongly implied by the subject matter. Most paragraphs have a TOPIC SENTENCE—that is, a sentence that expresses the central idea of the paragraph. The following paragraphs illustrate various ways of placing the topic sentence.

1. *The topic sentence may be the first sentence of the paragraph.* Following the deductive method, such paragraphs state their topics first and then add supporting details.

> The tea-plant, a native of Southern China, was known from very early times to Chinese botany and medicine. It is alluded to in the classics under the various names of Tou, Tseh, Chung, Kha, and Ming, and was highly prized for possessing the virtues of relieving fatigue, delighting the soul, strengthening the will, and repairing the eyesight. It was not only administered as an internal dose, but often applied externally in the form of paste to alleviate rheumatic pains. The Taoists claimed it as an important ingredient of the elixir of immortality. The Buddhists used it extensively to prevent drowsiness during their long hours of meditation.
>
> —OKAKURA KAKUZO, *The Book of Tea*

Note that the initial sentence may combine a transition from the preceding paragraph with the statement of the new paragraph, as in the following example.

> Although it lay in the shadow of the Arctic Circle, more than four thousand miles from civilization, and although it was the only settlement of any size in a wilderness area that occupied hundreds of thousands of square miles, Dawson was livelier, richer, and better equipped than many larger Canadian and American communities. It had a telephone service, running water, steam heat, and electricity. It had dozens of hotels, many of them better appointed than those on the Pacific Coast. It had motion-picture theaters operating at a time when the projected motion picture was just three years old. It had restaurants where string orchestras played *Cavalleria Rusticana* for men in tailcoats who ate pâté de fois gras and drank vintage wines. It had fashions from Paris. It had dramatic societies, church

choirs, glee clubs, and vaudeville companies. It had three hospitals, seventy physicians, and uncounted platoons of lawyers. Above all, it had people. —PIERRE BERTON, *The Klondike Fever*

2. *The topic sentence may be the last sentence of the paragraph.* Following the inductive method, such paragraphs give details first and lead up to the main point in the final sentence.

Pasteur had already obtained direct evidence that germs of life are present in the air by concentrating the fine particles suspended in the atmosphere and observing them under the microscope. He had aspirated air through a tube in which was inserted a plug of guncotton which acted as a filter and intercepted the aerial germs. When at the end of the experiment, the guncotton plug was dissolved by placing it in a tube containing a mixture of alcohol and ether, the insoluble dust separated from the solvent and settled in the bottom of the tube. Under the microscope, the sediment was found to contain many small round or oval bodies, indistinguishable from the spores of minute plants or the eggs of animalcules; the number of these bodies varied depending upon the nature of the atmosphere and in particular upon the height above the ground at which the aspirating apparatus had been placed. The dust recovered from the alcohol and ether solution always brought about a rapid growth of microorganisms when it was introduced into heated organic infusions, despite all precautions taken to admit only air sterilized by heat. It was thus clear that the fine invisible dust floating in the air contained germs which could initiate life in heated organic fluids.

—RENÉ J. DUBOS, *Louis Pasteur*

Not until 1894 did Japan feel strong enough for a real test of arms. In that year she precipitated a war with China over the control of Korea. The Japanese easily seized Korea, destroyed the Chinese naval forces, overran Southern Manchuria, and even captured the port of Wei-hai-wei in China proper. The war ended in 1895. In the peace treaty China agreed to pay a large indemnity to Japan, recognized the full independence of Korea, and ceded to Japan the rich island of Formosa, the strategically placed Pescadores Islands between Formosa and the coast of China, and the Liaotung Peninsula at the southern tip of Manchuria. Japan had demonstrated that she had indeed become a modern military power, and had made a successful start in building an empire.

—EDWIN O. REISCHAUER, *Japan Past and Present*

3. *The topic sentence may appear first and last.* In such paragraphs the last sentence repeats the idea of the first, frequently restating it with some amplification or a slight difference in emphasis in the light of the intervening details or discussion.

Another principle underlying communicative writing is that clarity is a prerequisite to validity. It is to be considered that statements that flow beautifully and are grammatically superb may be, also, utterly devoid of factual meaning, or meaningful but vague, or precise but invalid. For writing to be effective, in the sense in which I am using this term, it may or may not be grammatically correct, but it must be both clear and valid. It can be clear without having validity, but if it is unclear its validity cannot well be determined. It must, then, first of all, be clear; it must be that before the question of its validity can even be raised. We ask the writer, "What do you mean?" before we ask, "How do you know?" Until we reach agreement as to precisely what he is writing about, we cannot possibly reach agreement as to whether, or in what degree, his statements are true. —WENDELL JOHNSON, "You Can't Write Writing"

The second meaning of thinking limits it to things not sensed or directly perceived, to things *not* seen, heard, touched, smelt, or tasted. We ask the man telling a story if he saw a certain incident happen, and his reply may be, "No, I only thought of it." A note of invention, as distinct from faithful record of observation, is present. Most important in this class are successions of imaginative incidents and episodes that have a certain coherence, hang together on a continuous thread, and thus lie between kaleidoscopic flights of fancy and considerations deliberately employed to establish a conclusion. The imaginative stories poured forth by children possess all degrees of internal congruity; some are disjointed, some are articulated. When connected, they simulate reflective thought: indeed, they usually occur in minds of logical capacity. These imaginative enterprises often precede thinking of the close-knit type and prepare the way for it. In this sense, a thought or idea is a mental picture of something not actually present, and thinking is the succession of such pictures.

—JOHN DEWEY, *How We Think*

4. *The topic sentence may be implied.* Narrative and descriptive paragraphs sometimes do not state a topic sentence directly; instead, the topic may be implicit in the details given. The implied topic of the paragraph below, for example, is *a description of the Grand Ball at Bath, England, in the late eighteenth century.*

The hour is just on nine. At six, with the playing of a minuet, the dancing had started; now there is the usual pause for the gentlemen to hand tea to the ladies, and for the musicians to wet their tired throats. Tonight being something of an occasion there will be supper as well, and behind screens footmen are busily laying a long table with cold ham and pheasant, biscuits, sweetmeats, jellies and wine. And now the Master of Ceremonies in plum satin and paste buckles offers his arm to the ranking lady present, Her Grace the Duchess of Marlborough, and together they swing across the room. Behind them rustle the others, Her Grace's inferiors. Countesses and ladyships, wealthy tradesmen's wives and daughters, the mothers and mistresses of bone-setters and shipbuilders and swindling gamesters, all come to Bath to taste the salubrious "Spaw" waters at the Pump Room, to take the cure, to ogle their partners at balls at the Assembly Rooms— and best of all, to be stared at themselves in return.

—ALICE GLASGOW, *Sheridan of Drury Lane*

EXERCISE 32a(1).　What is the topic sentence, expressed or implied, in each of the following paragraphs?

1.　One aspect of participatory democracy is the idea of parallel structures. The F[reedom] D[emocratic] P[arty] is a parallel political party, prompted by the conclusion that registration of Negroes in the regular Democratic Party of Mississippi is presently impossible. Freedom Schools were parallel schools, although delegates to the Freedom School Convention decided they would return to the public schools and seek to transform them rather than continue into the winter a parallel school system. In the North, neighborhood unions organized by SDS represent parallel antipoverty agencies, challenging the legitimacy of the top-down middle-class "community organizations" sponsored by urban renewal and antipoverty administrators.

—STAUGHTON LYND, "The New Radical and 'Participatory Democracy' "

2.　It is the fact that a word only "means" what its logical definition makes it mean but can call to life all sorts of associative ideas and emotions which makes language such an excellent material for poetry and, at the same time, such an imperfect and even dangerous instrument for any sort of discussion of a scientific or political nature. In poetry, the word *moonlight* is a highly effective word because, apart from meaning "the light of the moon," it also calls up visions of stillness, mystery, beauty, and perhaps love. That these visions are not absolutely the same for each reader of a poem to the moon is no disadvantage to the poet. On the contrary, the more varied the associative values of the word, the greater the number of readers to whom it may appeal in one way or another. In logical discussion, on the other hand, the peripheral elements of meaning represent a constant danger. Even if we tried, we could not keep our language free from words whose emotional value is strong enough to blunt our own mental functions and those of our listeners. As long as words express ideas and conditions about which we are concerned, the word can arouse exactly all the emotion of the thing of which it is the symbol. If, as is often the case, the two parties in a discussion use the same words with different connotations it becomes difficult to reach an agreement. Many scientific discussions have been prolonged and many political conflicts embittered by this insufficiency of language.

—ROBERT M. ESTRICH and HANS SPERBER, *Three Keys to Language*

3. The bright and serious students in this group are the ones who demand the most from the university. They get good grades, although they often feel cynical about the system. Many of them are genuinely more concerned with putting knowledge of the past to work in the present than regurgitating it on a final. In a sense they are always putting administrators on the spot, because they believe that the educational process should provide a continuum between ideas and social and political action. For instance, when these students sit in for Negro rights in San Francisco or go off to register Negro voters in Mississippi, they are convinced that they are only carrying out a literal application of the democratic ideals they are supposed to memorize in the classroom. Such behavior unnerves the administration, which has to soothe the ruffled feelings of taxpayers and their representatives who grow anxious about the threats their sons and daughters are posing to the Established order.

    —MICHAEL VINCENT MILLER, "The Student State of Mind"

4. The poor who came to America—the majority of the settlers—had fewer illusions to shed than had the gentry. They took a rationally pessimistic view of the world and did not expect to get anything for nothing. Whether they were solvent enough to pay their way (the mere cost of transportation was relatively very high indeed in those days), or sold themselves as indentured servants to earn, by seven years' serfdom, the passage to America, or were transported, free, by a vigilant government for offenses ranging from taking the wrong side in a rebellion to plain and fancy felonies, the move to America was important and final. They did not expect to go back; if they were religious or political refugees they did not want to. And the new world into which they came had to be made habitable by them.

    —D. W. BROGAN, *The American Character*

5. If the march was important, it was because it represented an acceptance of the Negro revolt as part of the American myth, and so an acceptance of the revolutionaries into the American establishment. That acceptance, of course, carries the hope that the Negro revolt will stop where it is. Yet that acceptance is also the most powerful incentive and assurance that the revolt will continue. The children from Wilmington, North Carolina, climbed back on their buses with the shining memory of a moment when they marched with all America—a memory to sustain them when they return to march alone. So it was, too, for all the others who came from Birmingham, Montgomery, Danville, Gadsden and Jackson—places whose very names evoked not only the cause but also the way it is being won.

    —MURRAY KEMPTON, "The March on Washington"

EXERCISE 32a(2).   Following are three topic sentences, each accompanied by a set of statements. Some of the statements are relevant to the topic, some are not. Eliminate the irrelevant ones, and organize the rest into a paragraph.

1.   Given my choice I would sooner be in the Air Force than any other service branch.
      1.   I am more interested in flying than in any other military occupation.
      2.   Opportunities for advancement are greater in the Air Force.
      3.   Wages in certain brackets of the Air Force are higher than in other branches.
      4.   There are many opportunities to travel.
      5.   The Navy gives one travel opportunities too.
      6.   My cousin has been in the Navy for two years, and he has sailed around the whole world.
      7.   I think, though, that I still like the Air Force better.
2.   The wreck on Route 64 at Mt. Nixon was caused entirely by careless and reckless driving by the driver of the Buick.
      1.   When the wreck occurred the lights were green for the cars coming off the side road.
      2.   A heavy truck loaded with hay was pulling out to cross the highway.
      3.   The Buick came speeding down the main road, went through the stoplight, and crashed into the truck.
      4.   You could hear the screeching of the tires and then the crashing and grinding of metal a quarter of a mile away.
      5.   You could hear it in our house up the road.
      6.   Both drivers were killed, and I will never forget how awful the accident was.
3.   We owe some of our notions of radar to scientific observation of bats.
      1.   Most people hate bats.
      2.   Women especially are afraid of them, since they have been told that bats are likely to get into their hair.
      3.   Bats are commonly considered unattractive, ugly creatures.
      4.   They really look more like mice with wings than anything else.
      5.   Scientists noticed that bats rarely collided with anything in their erratic flight.
      6.   Keen eyesight could not be the reason for their flying the way they do, since bats are blind.
      7.   It was found that bats keep sending out noises inaudible to people and that they hear the echoes of those noises.
      8.   This principle whereby they fly safely was found to be similar to the main principle of radar.

32b   **Be sure that every sentence in a paragraph bears on the central subject.**

Not only must you have a clear intent in writing a paragraph, you must also hold to that intent throughout the paragraph. The writer of the following paragraph, for example, changes his intent three times in the first three sentences; and he tacks on the last sentence as a kind of afterthought:

> Henry James' extensive travel during his early years greatly influenced his later writings. Born in New York in 1843, Henry was destined to become one of the first novelists of the world. He received a remarkable education. His parents took him abroad for a year when he was only an infant. He was educated by tutors until he was twelve, and then taken abroad for three more years by his parents. His father wanted him to absorb French and German culture. His older brother, William, received the same education.

One way of revising this paragraph would be to restrict its subject matter to the one major topic of James' childhood.

> Henry James, the novelist, had an unusual childhood. In 1844, while still an infant, he was taken abroad by his parents for a year. Upon his return, he and his older brother, William, were given private tutoring until Henry was twelve. At that time both boys were taken abroad to spend three years absorbing French and German culture.

Be careful not to violate the principle of unity by introducing new topics or points of view at the end of a paragraph. Notice in the following example how the last sentence, in which the writer deserts his earlier objectivity and takes sides in the argument, breaks the unity.

> In the years following World War II there has been much discussion on the question of lowering the minimum voting age to eighteen. Among those people who believe that the age limit should be lowered, the favorite statement is, "If a boy is old enough to die for his country, he's old enough to vote in it." Those people who want the age limit to remain at twenty-one think eighteen-year-olds will be unduly influenced by local ward-heelers who will urge them to vote a "straight ticket." But the young voter who has not had a chance to become a "dyed-in-the-wool" party member will tend to weigh the merits of the individual candidate rather than those of the party itself.

Revised, the paragraph might read:

In the years following World War II there has been much discussion on the question of lowering the minimum voting age to eighteen. Among those people who believe that the age limit should be lowered, the favorite statement is, "If a boy is old enough to die for his country, he's old enough to vote in it." Those people who want the age limit to remain at twenty-one think eighteen-year-olds will be unduly influenced by the promises of dishonest politicians.

EXERCISE 32b(1). Each of the following paragraphs violates the principle of unity. Discuss exactly where each paragraph goes wrong.

1. (1) Racial discrimination has existed in the United States for many years. (2) It began when the first white settler decided that the Indians were an inferior breed. (3) It was given impetus by the arrival of the first Negro slaves. (4) A civil war was fought largely because the spokesman of the North, Abraham Lincoln, believed that all men are created equal. (5) Slavery was abolished and the Negro set free by act of Congress.

2. (1) The life of Thomas A. Edison illustrates the truth of the old saying "Genius is ten percent inspiration and ninety percent perspiration." (2) Edison was born in Milan, Ohio, and was expelled from school because his teachers thought he was a moron. (3) So Edison was educated at home by his mother, who helped him build a laboratory in the basement. (4) Edison spent long hours here, sometimes working as long as sixteen hours a day.

3. (1) Hardy's *The Return of the Native* is one of the finest novels I have ever read. (2) I was amazed to see how Hardy makes his major and minor episodes culminate in a great climax, and how inextricably he weaves the fortunes of his chief characters with those of his lesser characters. (3) Moreover, his handling of the landscape—gloomy Egdon Heath—is masterful. (4) He makes it a genuine, motivating force in the story. (5) My favorite character, however, was Diggory Venn.

4. (1) Many people who use the word *fascism* in discussing current world problems confuse it with *communism*. (2) Both fascism and communism are totalitarian, but fascism is the economic antithesis of communism. (3) Fascism uses military force to sustain capitalism: communism uses force to suppress capitalism. (4) Obviously, no two systems of government could be more different. (5) But there has never been a clear explanation of the two systems. (6) The popular information media—newspapers, radio, and television—refer indiscriminately at times to communism and fascism in the same terms.

5. (1) The advantages of modern transportation are many. (2) An enormous amount of time is saved by the great speeds at which vehicles of today travel. (3) Cross-country trips are much more comfortable than they were, and they can be made in days rather than months. (4) For land travel today the automobile, motorcycle, and bus have taken the place of the horse and wagon, stage coach, and mule. (5) The railroad has been developed and extended since the use of the diesel. (6) Sailing ships are now chiefly a hobby and few consider them seriously as a means of transportation.

6. (1) If you intend to plant a strawberry bed, there are several things that you should consider. (2) Strawberries do best in a sandy loam or sandy clay that has been enriched with humus. (3) Blueberries and blackberries are better in acid soils. (4) Strawberries should be set out in an area that receives adequate drainage. (5) Too much moisture in the soil will kill them or interfere with their growth. (6) Other kinds of plants do better in marshy soils. (7) On account of frost dangers it is better to plant strawberries on a hillside or on a relatively high level area. (8) The effects of frost are rather peculiar; in general, plants in low-lying areas are more likely to be harmed by frost than those on hills. (9) The growth of young strawberries is actually increased if one pinches off the runners from the plants.

Coherence in the Paragraph = ¶ COH

A paragraph may be unified without being coherent. Unity depends upon selecting details and ideas relevant to the paragraph topic. Coherence depends upon organizing these details and ideas so that the reader can easily see *how* they are relevant. Even though all the sentences of a paragraph bear upon a single point, unless they are knit together and flow into one another so that their relation to that single point is clear, they will not be coherent. A coherent paragraph leads the reader easily from sentence to sentence. An incoherent paragraph confronts him with puzzling jumps in thought, events out of sequence, facts illogically arranged, or points in a discussion omitted. Coherence requires that sentences be logically arranged and clearly connected.

32c **To insure coherence in a paragraph, arrange the sentences in a logical order.**

Arrange all sentences within a paragraph according to some pattern that will make for an orderly, natural flow of ideas. One technique is to list events chronologically. Another is to establish a clear cause-and-effect relationship among the ideas. The following examples show how essential some sort of order is to coherence.

INCOHERENT

The Declaration of Independence was the instrument by which the thirteen colonies declared their independence of Great Britain. It was signed originally by only the president and secretary of the Continental Congress. When the declaration was originally voted on, June 28, 1776, the delegates from Pennsylvania and South Carolina refused to approve it until it carried an amendment. The declaration was written by Thomas Jefferson, who was one of a special committee of five assigned by Congress to draw up a form of declaration. The declaration was finally approved on July 4. The signatures of the delegates were added as their states confirmed the action of Congress.

COHERENT (*Chronological order introduced*)

The Declaration of Independence was the instrument by which the thirteen colonies declared their independence of Great Britain. It was written by Thomas Jefferson, one of a special committee of five assigned by the Continental Congress to draw up a form of declaration. When the declaration was originally brought before Congress on June 28, 1776, the delegates from Pennsylvania and South Carolina refused to approve it until it carried an amendment. That amendment was then written into the declaration, which was finally approved on July 4. Originally, only the president and secretary of the Continental Congress affixed their signatures; the delegates added their signatures as their individual states confirmed the action of Congress.

INCOHERENT

Juvenile delinquency is a major problem in this country. This problem became more serious after World War II. The war itself is one of the causes. Parents of youngsters born during these years either avoided their responsibility or were unable to maintain it. Everywhere we read about the vicious crimes committed by young people. During the war the newspapers and the movies depicted violence, cruelty, and bloodletting as heroic rather than vicious. The war inspired brutality by distorting and twisting humane values. It is no wonder that the younger generation has made a problem of itself. During the war many of them had fathers who were in the service; their mothers were working in war plants. Consequently, they were unhappy and undisciplined. Many of them are now organized in gangs and proud of their devotion to a life of crime.

COHERENT (*Clear cause-and-effect relationship introduced*)

Juvenile delinquency is a major problem in this country. Everywhere we read and hear about the vicious crimes committed by younger people. Many of them are organized in gangs and are proud of their devotion to a life of crime. Certainly this unfortunate situation grows partly out of the years of World War II. For one thing, the war itself inspired brutality in the young generation by distorting and twisting humane values. The newspapers and the movies depicted violence, cruelty, and bloodletting as heroic rather than vicious. For another, parents of youngsters born during the war either avoided their responsibilities or were unable to exercise them. Many fathers were in the service; mothers were often busy working in war plants. The result was an unhappy, undisciplined group of young people. It was no wonder they soon made a problem of themselves.

EXERCISE 32c(1).   Write a coherent paragraph that incorporates, in your own words, all the following information about Thomas Hardy.

1. He was an English novelist, short story writer, and poet.
2. He died in 1928, at the age of eighty-eight.
3. He is considered one of the most important of the writers who revolted against Victorian tradition at the end of the nineteenth century.
4. He is known for the pessimism of his ideas.
5. His most important prose works are novels of character and environment.
6. *The Return of the Native, Tess of the D'Urbervilles,* and *Jude the Obscure* are among his most important novels.
7. His best novels are studies of life in the bleak English countryside.
8. In his best novels individuals are defeated in their struggle against their physical and social environment.
9. Individuals in his best novels also struggle against the caprices of chance.

EXERCISE 32c(2).   Write a coherent paragraph that incorporates all the following information about Robert La Follette. Begin your paragraph with the topic sentence *Robert La Follette truly deserved the epithet "Fighting Bob."*

1. When he was twenty-five he ran for District Attorney of Madison County, Wisconsin, as a Republican but against the organized Republicans. He was elected.
2. After a term as District Attorney he ran for Congress and was elected.
3. While a student at the University of Wisconsin he became known as a debater, once winning an interstate contest.

4. In 1942 he ran for President and, although defeated, received 4½ million votes.

5. After serving three terms as Governor of Wisconsin, he was elected to the United States Senate, where he became known as a spokesman for small businessmen and farmers.

6. After graduation from college, he worked in a law office.

7. After serving one term as a Representative, he was elected Governor of Wisconsin, a position he used to help initiate laws of direct primary, referendum, and recall.

8. During the years just preceding the United States entry into World War I, La Follette set himself against the proposed neutrality legislation of Woodrow Wilson, arguing vehemently that such legislation would help get the United States into war.

EXERCISE 32c(3). Because of poor sentence arrangement the following paragraphs lack coherence. Rearrange each group of sentences to form a coherent paragraph.

1. (1) Once upon a time, before 1920, the whole American League hoped that by some freak of fortune the weak New York Yankees might be able to win a pennant. (2) The mighty Red Sox and Athletics, often tail-enders after 1920, were riding high. (3) Things move in cycles in sports, and a weak team five years ago may be a champion now. (4) So let's not lose interest in the home team; they may be up there again soon. (5) Even the Browns, the last team to play in a World's Series, were very strong in 1922 and finally won the pennant in 1942. (6) The standings are never the same two years straight, and second-division teams of last year often are strong contenders this year. (7) During the last eighteen years Detroit teams have ended up in all eight positions.

2. (1) There were various reasons for the popularity of canasta. (2) It could be played by different numbers of players. (3) Bridge, of course, required no more and no less than four. (4) Many people naturally continued to like bridge. (5) Some players found canasta more dramatic than bridge. (6) They liked the appeal of the different combinations of cards. (7) Canasta became popular about 1950. (8) Many card players liked the freedom of personal choice and independence from a partner's decisions.

3. (1) After World War II our leaders had various problems in framing our foreign policy. (2) Few experts could be sure of the policy of the U.S.S.R. (3) The strength and the determination of our proven allies were questionable. (4) Seemingly no one anticipated developments in Indo-China and Korea. (5) The attitudes of the defeated Germans, Italians, and Japanese were uncertain. (6) Whether the wartime cooperation with the Russians could be continued, no one knew. (7) The attitude of India and Pakistan on future developments was hard to determine.

32d **To insure coherence in a paragraph, make clear the relationships among sentences.**

Coherence requires not only that the sentences within a paragraph be related to each other, but also that their relationship be made clear. You can achieve clear relationships among sentences by: (1) being consistent in point of view, (2) using parallel grammatical structure, (3) repeating words or ideas, and (4) using transitional words or phrases.

1. *Maintain a consistent point of view.*   Avoid unnecessary shifts in person, tense, or number within a paragraph.

UNNECESSARY SHIFT IN PERSON

A pleasant and quiet place to live is essential for a serious-minded college student. If possible, you should rent a room from a landlady with a reputation for keeping order and discipline among her renters. Moreover, a student ought to pick a roommate with the same temperament as his own. Then you can agree to and keep a schedule of study hours.

UNNECESSARY SHIFT IN TENSE

Last summer I finally saw the movie *Around the World in 80 Days,* based on the novel by Jules Verne. I particularly enjoyed the main character, who is played by David Niven. He gives an excellent performance and really seemed intent on winning the wager he has made with his friends. His personal servant was played by the Mexican actor Cantinflas, who is very able in his part, too.

UNNECESSARY SHIFT IN NUMBER

Of great currency at the moment is the notion that education should prepare students for "life." A college graduate no longer goes out into the world as a cultivated gentleman. Instead students feel obliged to prepare themselves for places in the business world. Consequently, we are establishing courses on how to get and keep a mate, how to budget an income, and how to win friends and influence people—that is, how to sell yourself and your product. The study of things not obviously practical to a businessman is coming to be looked upon as unnecessary.

2. *Use parallel grammatical structure.*   Using parallel grammatical structure in successive sentences is one of the most important ways of connecting them. Just as parallel grammatical form in coordinate parts of a single sentence emphasizes the coordinate relation of the ideas, so parallel structure from sentence to sentence within a paragraph emphasizes the relation of these sentences to the single idea of the paragraph. Note the following examples:

We Americans have a strange—and to me disturbing—attitude toward the subject of power. We don't like the word. We don't like the concept. We are suspicious of people who talk about it. We like to feel that the adjustment of conflicting interests is something that can be taken care of by juridical norms and institutional devices, voluntarily accepted and not involving violence to the feelings or interests of anyone. We like to feel that this is the way our own life is arranged. We like to feel that if this principle were to be understood and observed by others as it is by us, it would put an end to many of the misunderstandings and conflicts that have marked our time. —GEORGE F. KENNAN, "Training for Statesmanship"

Conversation in this country has fallen upon evil days. The great creative art whereby man translates feeling into reason and shares with his fellow man those innermost thoughts and ideals of which civilization is made is beset by forces which threaten its demise. It is forsaken by a technology that is so busy tending its time-saving devices that it has no time for anything else. It is drowned out in singing commercials by the world's most productive economy that has so little to say for itself it has to hum it. It is hushed and shushed in dimly lighted parlors by television audiences who used to read, argue, and even play bridge, an old-fashioned card game requiring speech. It is shouted down by devil's advocates, thrown into disorder by points of order. It is subdued by soft-voiced censors who, in the name of public relations, counsel discretion and the avoidance of controversy, like so many family physicians breaking the news gently and advising their patients to cut down on their calories. It starves for want of reading and reflection. It languishes in a society that spends so much time passively listening and being talked to that it has all but lost the will and the skill to speak for itself. —A. WHITNEY GRISWOLD, *Liberal Education and the Democratic Ideal*

3. *Repeat key words and phrases.* The great majority of well-constructed paragraphs depend heavily upon the repetition of key words and phrases, many times with slight modification, to emphasize major ideas and carry the thought from sentence to sentence. Pronouns referring back to clearly established antecedents in the previous sentence function in the same way. In the following paragraphs the words and phrases that are repeated to provide clear links from sentence to sentence and produce a closely integrated whole are underlined.

In discussing the pre-Civil War South, it should be remembered that the large plantation owners constituted only a small part of the total Southern population. By far the greater part of that population was made up of small farmers, and of course the Negro slaves themselves. Some small farmers had acquired substantial acreage, owned three or four slaves, and were relatively prosperous. But most of the small farmers were terribly poor. They rented their land and worked it themselves, sometimes side by side with the slaves of the great landowners. In everything but social position they were worse off than the Negro slaves. But it must also be remembered that they were as jealous of that superior social position as the wealthy landowner himself.   —Student paragraph

Nobody has succeeded in explaining the connection between the private sources and the public functions of art. But art does have its public functions, though we often lose sight of them. In primitive agricultural societies, and even in Western Europe until the Renaissance, the functions were more clearly defined. It was the duty of the artist to celebrate the community in its present oneness, in its divine past, and in its glorious future. Thus he invented dances and rituals for the group, he retold the stories of its gods and heroes, he fashioned their images, and he persuaded the "people"—his own tribe that is, the only genuine persons—that they were reenacting the lives of the gods, who would some day return and reinstitute the golden age. Thus the artist played a recognized part in the daily life of the people.

—MALCOLM COWLEY, "Artists, Conscience, and Censors"

Nonconformity is not only a desirable thing, it is an actual thing. One need only remark that all art is based upon nonconformity—a point that I shall undertake to establish—and that every great historic change has been based upon nonconformity, has been bought either with the blood or with the reputation of nonconformists. Without nonconformity we would have had no Bill of Rights nor Magna Carta, no public education system, no nation upon this continent, no continent, no science at all, no philosophy, and considerably fewer religions. All that is pretty obvious.

But it seems to be less obvious that to create anything at all in any field, and especially anything of outstanding worth, requires nonconformity, or a want of satisfaction with things as they are. The creative person—the nonconformist—may be in profound disagreement with the present way of things, or he may simply wish to add his views, to render a personal account of matters.   —BEN SHAHN, *The Shape of Content*

Because they [the colonists] had first of all to survive, they took life with deadly seriousness. And in their seriousness they were able to record memorably life and living as they knew it. When their writing has distinguished style, as it often does, it is style which serves a higher purpose than itself; it is style which expresses the very seriousness of the colonial enterprise. Indeed, when one studies stylistically the best of colonial writing, one is studying the quality of colonial seriousness. The very forms of expression—sermons, histories, diaries, poems, and the like—themselves characterize the men who write, the society to which they write, and the occasion for writing. The difference between the writing of a Mather and of a Byrd, between that of a Sewall and of a Woolman, is in the style and form as well as the content. One can see not only what each believes in, but the quality of the belief. Theirs is the style and form which develop when an idea or an attitude is seriously put into action.

—ROY HARVEY PEARCE, *Colonial American Writing*

4. *Use transitional markers.* A transitional marker is a word or a phrase placed at or near the beginning of a sentence to indicate its relation to the preceding sentence. The coordinating conjunctions *and, but, or, nor, so,* and *yet* are often used this way, particularly in informal writing, for they provide easy bridges from one sentence to another. But English provides a wide variety of transitional markers, as suggested in the lists below. Good modern writing uses the more formal markers sparingly, and we should be wary of cluttering our writing with unnecessary *however*'s, *moreover*'s, and *consequently*'s. But we should be equally careful to know them and to use them when they make for clarity.

Here is a list of many of the common transitional words and phrases:

TO INDICATE ADDITION

again, also, and, and then, besides, equally important, finally, first, further, furthermore, in addition, last, likewise, moreover, next, second, third, too

TO INDICATE CAUSE AND EFFECT

accordingly, as a result, consequently, hence, in short, otherwise, then, therefore, thus, truly

TO INDICATE COMPARISON

in a like manner, likewise, similarly

TO INDICATE CONCESSION

after all, although this may be true, at the same time, even though, I admit, naturally, of course

TO INDICATE CONTRAST

after all, although true, and yet, at the same time, but, for all that, however, in contrast, in spite of, nevertheless, notwithstanding, on the contrary, on the other hand, still, yet

TO INDICATE SPECIAL FEATURES OR EXAMPLES

for example, for instance, incidentally, indeed, in fact, in other words, in particular, specifically, that is, to illustrate

TO INDICATE SUMMARY

in brief, in conclusion, in short, on the whole, to conclude, to summarize, to sum up

TO INDICATE TIME RELATIONS

after a short time, afterwards, as long as, as soon as, at last, at length, at that time, at the same time, before, earlier, of late, immediately, in the meantime, lately, later, meanwhile, presently, shortly, since, soon, temporarily, thereafter, thereupon, until, when, while

Transitional words and phrases are underlined in the following:

As I have remarked, the pilots' association was now the compactest monopoly in the world, perhaps, and seemed simply indestructible. And yet the days of its glory were numbered. First, the new railroad, stretching up through Mississippi, Tennessee, and Kentucky, to Northern railway-centers, began to divert the passenger travel from the steamboats; next the war came and almost entirely annihilated the steamboating industry during several years, leaving most of the pilots idle and the cost of living advancing all the time; then the treasurer of the St. Louis association put his hand into the till and walked off with every dollar of the ample fund; and finally, the railroads intruding everywhere, there was little for steamers to do, when the war was over, but carry freights; so straightway some genius from the Atlantic coast introduced the plan of towing a dozen steamer cargoes down to New Orleans at the tail of a vulgar little tugboat; and behold, in the twingling of an eye, as it were, the association and the noble science of piloting were things of the dead and pathetic past! —MARK TWAIN, *Life on the Mississippi*

Sometimes a question may be made still more clear or precise by an indication of the circumstances in which it occurs. Let us take an example. I ask, "How wide is this bookcase?" This certainly appears to be a straightforward question that could be answered simply enough by specifying the number of inches across its front. But when one undertakes to find the answer, several perplexing considerations may arise. What dimension is wanted: the length of the shelf? the outside dimension? at the widest point? or at some other typical point? Again, how accurate a measure is wanted?—for no measurement is entirely accurate; all we can expect is greater or less accuracy. All these questions could be more or less cleared up by indicating the circumstances under which the problem arose. It might be, for example, that I contemplate placing the bookcase against a certain wall and desire to know whether or not it is too wide to fit into the position under consideration. At once I realize that the widest outside dimension is the one required, and that a relatively high degree of accuracy is necessary only if the width of the wall and that of the bookcase are found to be nearly the same.

—HENRY S. LEONARD, *Principles of Right Reason*

Charles, however, had one advantage, which, if he had used it well, would have more than compensated for the want of stores and money, and which, notwithstanding his mismanagement, gave him, during some months, a superiority in the war. His troops at first fought much better than those of the Parliament. Both armies, it is true, were almost entirely composed of men who had never seen a field of battle. Nevertheless, the difference was great. The parliamentary ranks were filled with hirelings whom want and idleness had induced to enlist. Hampden's regiment was regarded as one of the best; and even Hampden's regiment was described by Cromwell as a mere rabble of tapsters and serving-men out of place.

The royal army, <u>on the other hand</u>, consisted in great part of gentlemen, high-spirited, ardent, accustomed to consider dishonor as more terrible than death, accustomed to fencing, to the use of firearms, to bold riding, and to manly and perilous sport, which has been well called the image of war. <u>Such gentlemen</u>, mounted on their favorite horses, and commanding little bands composed of their younger brothers, grooms, gamekeepers, and huntsmen, were, from the very first day on which they took the field, qualified to play their part with credit in a skirmish. The steadiness, the prompt obedience, the mechanical precision of movement, which are characteristic of the regular soldier, these gallant volunteers never attained. <u>But</u> they were at first opposed to enemies as undisciplined as themselves, and far less active, athletic, and daring. <u>For a time</u>, <u>therefore</u>, the Cavaliers were successful in almost every encounter.

—THOMAS MACAULAY, *The History of England*

EXERCISE 32d(1). Make a coherent paragraph of the following statements. First, put them in logical order. Second, give them a consistent point of view and link them smoothly with transitional words or phrases. Revise the wording of the statements if necessary, but use all the information given.

1. This attitude shows a naïve faith in the competency of secretaries.
2. Practicing engineers and scientists say they spend half their time writing letters and reports.
3. Many of us foolishly object to taking courses in writing.
4. College students going into business think their secretaries will do their writing for them.
5. A student going into the technical or scientific fields may think that writing is something he seldom has to do.
6. Young businessmen seldom have private secretaries.
7. Our notion that only poets, novelists, and newspaper workers have to know how to write is unrealistic.
8. Other things being equal, a man in any field who can express himself effectively is sure to succeed more rapidly than a man whose command of language is poor.

EXERCISE 32d(2). Using the topic sentence *The United Nations is a potential source of world peace,* arrange the following statements into a coherent paragraph with a logical order, a consistent point of view, and smooth transitions.

1. Seventy-four countries issued special stamps in 1959 in support of the UN proclamation of a World Refugee Year to emphasize the world refugee problem.
2. The UN investigated border tensions and accusations between Arabs and Israelis in 1947.
3. After China, France, Great Britain, Russia, and the United States and a majority of the other signing nations had ratified the Charter on October 24, 1945, the United Nations came into existence.

4. On two separate occasions, the UN has made a truce; one was in the Indonesia–Netherlands dispute, and the other was in the Korean War.

5. The UN troops have been active in the Congo, attempting to restore order since the Congo gained its independence from Belgium in 1960.

6. The United Nations High Commissioner for Refugees protects and helps refugees throughout the world by promoting international agreements on their legal status and by working with different governments for their admittance.

7. Financially, the UN is constantly having difficulty because some nations do not contribute sufficient funds to support it.

EXERCISE 32d(3).   Arrange the following statements into a coherent paragraph.

1. It takes a considerable amount of equipment to operate a ham radio.

2. There are 260,000 licensed amateur stations in the United States.

3. My cousin, Glenn Wade, had DRT as his signal code which he used to broadcast as Dirty Rotten Tomatoes.

4. Radio amateurs or hams send messages on their home radio stations to people all over the world.

5. The Federal Communications Commission has often praised these hams for their voluntary aid in times of emergencies such as floods or storms.

6. There are four types of licenses a ham may obtain from the FCC: (1) novice, (2) technician, (3) general class, and (4) extra class.

EXERCISE 32d(4).   The following paragraphs and paragraph parts are marred and made incoherent by shifts in person, tense, and number. Rewrite the paragraphs to insure consistency and coherence throughout.

1. Literature is a medium through which a person can convey his ideas towards or protests against different norms of society. Those works that deal with a moral issue are of particular importance in literature; they are written with a particular purpose in mind. A literary work with a moral issue will live on to be reinterpreted by different generations, such as Shakespeare's plays. These works involve the reader for he forms his own moral judgment towards the issue. Arthur Miller's *Death of a Salesman,* is a play which deals with moral issues.

2. It is difficult to feel compassion for people who do not deserve it. My neighbor, John Carroll, is a poor little rich boy who just can't find happiness and love. He had never been deprived of anything. The one thing he really wanted, a girl who had gone to high school with him, he couldn't get. His mother tells the story in such a way that you feel pity for this man because of this one thing that he couldn't attain. The people who least deserve compassion get more than their share of it.

3. Every time a nation is involved in a war it must face problems about its ex-soldiers after that war. The veteran is entitled to some special considerations from society, but treating them with complete fairness is a baffling problem. Livy reports that grants to the former soldier caused some troubles in the early history of Rome. There were many disagreements between them and the early Roman senators.

4. Preparing a surface for new paint is as important a step in the whole process as the application of paint itself. First, be sure that the surface is quite clean. You should wash any grease or grime from the wood-work. The painter may use turpentine or a detergent for this. One must be careful to clean off whatever cleanser they have used. Then sand off any rough or chipped paint.

5. One of the books I read in high school English was Dickens' *Tale of Two Cities.* In it the author tells of some of the horrors of the French Revolution. He spent several pages telling about how the French aris-tocrats suffered. The climax part of the book tells how a ne'er-do-well who had failed in life sacrifices himself for another. He took his place in a prison and went stoically to the guillotine for him.

Paragraph Development = ¶ DEV

32e **Construct every paragraph around a topic sentence.**

Once you have set forth the point of a paragraph in the topic sentence, you must then give reasons to support it or examples or details to clarify it. Failure to develop every paragraph around a clear-cut topic sentence will give you only a series of short, choppy paragraph fragments.

1. *Lack of reasons to support topic sentences.*

The president should be elected for an eight-year term. In a four-year term the president cannot establish a smooth-running administration. He has to spend much of his time being a politician rather than being an executive.

Representatives should also be elected for longer terms. Under the present situation, they no more than get elected when they have to begin preparations for the next election.

2. *Lack of examples and details to clarify topic sentences.*

English is made up of many words taken from early Church Latin. These words probably came into the language shortly after the Christianization of the British Isles in the seventh century. One such word is *altar;* another is *temple.*

It was the Norman Conquest, beginning in 1066, that had the greatest effect, however, on English. According to one authority about ten thousand French words came into the English language, about three-fourths of which still remain in the language.

EXERCISE 32e. Choose two of the following topic sentences and develop each into a meaningful paragraph by supporting it with reasons or examples.

1. A first impression is not always a reliable basis for judgment.
2. A book that is one man's meat may be another man's poison.
3. The first day of college is a nerve-shattering experience.
4. Making homemade furniture is less difficult than it appears.
5. Words are the most powerful drugs used by mankind.
6. There are three great advantages to air travel—speed, comfort, and thrills.
7. Harmony seldom makes the headlines.
8. Keeping a detailed budget is more trouble than it's worth.
9. A good hitter is far more valuable to a baseball team than a good fielder.
10. Fashions in clothes (books, drama, hairdress, slang, etc.) change from one year (decade, century) to the next.

32f Avoid excessively long and excessively short paragraphs.

The length of a paragraph is determined by the nature of the subject, the type of topic sentence, the intention of the writer, and the character of the audience. Ultimately, the length of a paragraph is a matter that you must determine for yourself. In general, however, avoid paragraphs that contain less than four or more than eight sentences. Too short a paragraph may mean that you are not developing your topic sentence adequately. Too long a paragraph may mean that you are permitting excessive detail to obscure your central aim.

Excessively long paragraphs may be revised either by a rigorous pruning of details or by division into two or more paragraphs. Insufficiently developed paragraphs usually show lack of attention to detail and an imperfect command of the full idea of the paragraph. The paragraphs below, for example, are all insufficiently developed. The arguments are undirected, and the generalizations are inadequately supported by reasons, examples, and details. Simply stitching these fragments together would not produce a coherent, unified statement; instead, the entire statement would have to be thought through again and then rewritten.

> I am in favor of lowering the minimum voting age to eighteen. I think the average eighteen-year-old has more good judgment to put to use at the polls than the average middle-aged person.
>
> Among the members of the two major parties there is too much straight-ticket voting. I think the candidate himself and not his party should be voted on. The young voter would weigh the virtues of the candidate and not his party.
>
> It is unlikely that the young voter would be influenced by corrupt politicians. The majority of eighteen-year-olds are high school graduates and would surely have learned enough about current affairs to use good judgment.
>
> If the question of lowering the voting age were put to a nationwide vote, I am sure it would pass.
>
> In conclusion I say give young Americans a chance. I am sure they will make good.

EXERCISE 32f(1). Group the following sentences into two or three paragraphs. You need not rewrite the sentences, even though they may need revision.

> Frederick Winslow Taylor was born in 1856. His mother was a cultured Easterner. She took the family abroad for three years. Fred's father was a lawyer. While at Exeter Fred was a star baseball player and head of his class. Fred began work as a machinist. He liked the men he worked with. He was short, heavily built, and sharp-tongued. When he became a foreman he forgot about his working pals. He thought up new ways of doing things. The idea of producing things efficiently went to his head. He divided up jobs. When he was thirty-four, he married. In six years he became chief engineer. Then he went to work for Bethlehem steel. This job did not last long. He began to play golf and entertain. He lectured on production techniques at various colleges. The reason he lost his job was that he was more interested in production than in profit. He died in 1915 of pneumonia. He was one of the first efficiency experts.

EXERCISE 32f(2). Rewrite the following material as one or two paragraphs, combining relevant ideas and eliminating irrelevant ones.

> The word *modern* has many meanings. It may mean something new-fashioned or something characteristic of present or recent times, as modern painting, modern automobiles, or modern poetry.
>
> To be modern means something pleasant, hard to understand, or something my grandmother never seemed to be.

A modern painting is a very unrealistic painting of something very realistic. It is unrealistic in the sense that the painter is trying to give you his interpretation of his impression of the object rather than a picture of the object itself. This is sometimes very exciting, but often hard to understand.

To many people, particularly middle-aged and ancient adults, *modern* is a word of condemnation. These people usually speak longingly of "the good old days" and anything modern is a "contraption," a device to make young people either sinful or lazy.

But to young people in general *modern* is a word of high praise. They use it to refer to things and ideas that are up to date, clever, speedy.

But I have little doubt that within twenty or thirty years these young-people-grown-old will be using the word just as their parents and grandparents use it now—as a word of condemnation.

32g Choose a method of paragraph development suitable to the subject matter and to your own intent.

The best development for a paragraph depends upon the nature of its topic and the way it is related to other paragraphs in the whole composition. A writer does not arbitrarily decide to develop his first paragraph by one method, his second by another, and so on. He must look to his subject matter and determine what method will express his thought most clearly and adequately at any particular point. Every paragraph will have its own problems of structure, and every writer must find his own solutions. But most well-wrought paragraphs depend on one of the following organizational principles or on some slight variation of it: (1) CHRONOLOGICAL, (2) SPATIAL, or (3) LOGICAL.

1. *Use chronological order to describe events or processes in the sequence of time in which they took place or should take place.*   The opening paragraph of Jonathan Swift's *Gulliver's Travels* is a classic illustration of the chronological method of narrating events, and Benjamin Franklin's famous instructions for making a kite are a classic illustration of the chronological method of describing how something is done.

> My father had a small estate in Nottinghamshire; I was the third of five sons. He sent me to Emanuel College in Cambridge at fourteen years old, where I resided three years, and applied myself close to my studies: but the charge of maintaining me (although I had a very scanty allowance) being too great for a narrow fortune, I was bound apprentice to Mr. James Bates, an eminent surgeon in London, with whom I continued four years; and my father now and then sending me small sums of money, I laid them out in learning navigation, and other parts of the mathematics, useful to those who intend to travel, as I always believed it would be some time or other my fortune to do. When I left Mr. Bates, I went down to my

father; where, by the assistance of him and my uncle John, and some other relatives, I got forty pounds, and a promise of thirty pounds a year to maintain me at Leyden: there I studied physics two years and seven months, knowing it would be useful in long voyages.

—JONATHAN SWIFT, *Gulliver's Travels* (1726)

Make a small cross of two light strips of cedar, the arms so long as to reach to the four corners of a large thin silk handkerchief when extended; tie the corners of the handkerchief to the extremities of the cross, so you have the body of a kite; which being properly accommodated with a tail, loop, and string, will rise in the air, like those made of paper; but this being of silk, is fitter to bear the wet and wind of a thunder-gust without tearing. To the top of the upright stick of the cross is to be fixed a very sharp-pointed wire, rising a foot or more above the wood. To the end of the twine, next the hand, is to be tied a silk ribbon, and where the silk and twine join, a key may be fastened. The kite is to be raised when a thunder-gust appears to be coming on, and the person who holds the string must stand within a door or window or under some cover, so that the silk ribbon may not be wet; and care must be taken that the twine does not touch the frame of the door or window. As soon as any of the thunder-clouds come over the kite, the pointed wire will draw the electric fire from them, and the kite, with all the twine, will be electrified, and the loose filaments of the twine will stand out every way, and be attracted by an approaching finger. And when the rain has wet the kite and twine, so that it can conduct the electric fire freely, you will find it stream out plentifully from the key on the approach of your knuckle. At this key the phial may be charged; and from electric fire thus obtained, spirits may be kindled, and all the other electric experiments be performed, which are usually done by the help of a rubbed glass globe or tube, and thereby the sameness of the electric matter with that of lightning completely demonstrated.

—BENJAMIN FRANKLIN, Letter to Peter Collinson (1752)

2. *Use spatial order to describe physical relationships among persons, places, or things.* Spatial order is well suited to stating such relationships as east to west, north to south, small to big, up to down, center to circumference, here to there, and so on. The author of the selection below, which gives an elementary but clear guide to a map of the British Isles, follows an east-to-west organization.

On the east, England is bounded by the North Sea, which is really nothing but an old depression which has gradually run full of water. Again a single glimpse at the map will tell you more than a thousand words. There on the right (the east) is France. Then we get something that looks like a trench across a road, the British Channel and the North Sea. Then the great central plain of England with London in the deepest hollow. Then the high mountains of Wales. Another depression, the Irish Sea, the great central Irish plain, the hills of Ireland, a few lonely rocks further toward the west, rearing their tops above the shallow sea. Finally the rock of St. Kilda (uninhabited since a year ago as it was too hard to reach) and then suddenly down we go, down, down, down, for there the real ocean begins and the last of the vast European and Asiatic continent, both submerged and semi-submerged, here comes to an end.

—HENDRIK WILLEM VAN LOON, Van Loon's Geography

3. *Use logical order to present details, examples, or reasons in support of the topic sentence.* There are several methods of logical organization. They are not confined to the paragraph as a form; they are rather the general patterns of organization and development by which exposition and argument proceed. If you will study them carefully, you will have at your disposal a set of patterns among which you can almost always find one suited to your purpose in a particular paragraph. The principal methods of logical development and organization are the following: (a) details, examples, and illustrations; (b) comparison and contrast; (c) repetition and restatement; (d) definition; (e) explanation of causes and effects; and (f) elimination of alternatives. Each of these is illustrated below.

a. *Details, examples, and illustrations.* One of the most common and convincing ways to develop a general statement is to provide concrete and specific details or illustrations that will convey to the reader a clear impression of what the general statement really means to the writer. In fact, a good many of the other methods of logical development depend more or less on the use of detail and example, for the latter are virtually indispensable to clear and lively writing.

A writer may support his topic sentence either by amassing a variety of specific details, by providing a few examples each stated in a sentence or two, or by describing at greater length a single extended illustration of his topic. The first of the paragraphs below is developed by specific detail; the second and third, by examples; and the fourth by an extended illustration.

Americans are still born free but their freedom neither lasts as long nor goes as far as it used to. Once the infant is smacked on the bottom and lets out his first taxable howl, he is immediately tagged, footprinted, blood-tested, classified, certificated, and generally taken in census. By the time that squawler has drawn the breath of adulthood he must have some clerk's permission to go to school or stay away, ride a bike, drive a car, collect his salary, carry a gun, fish, get married, go into the army or stay out, leave or re-enter the country, fly a plane, operate a power boat or a ham radio, buy a piece of land, build a house or knock one down, add a room to the house he has bought, burn his trash, park his car, keep a dog, run his business, go bankrupt, practice a profession, pick the wildflowers, bury the garbage, beg in the streets, sell whiskey in his store, peddle magazines from house to house, walk across a turnpike from one of his fields to another now that the state has divided him—the list is endless. Even in death his corpse must be certificated and licensed before the earth may swallow him legally. Freedom is no longer free but licensed.

—JOHN CIARDI, "Confessions of a Crackpot"

I have come to marvel at the instinct of animals to make use of natural laws for healing themselves. They know unerringly which herbs will cure what ills. Wild creatures first seek solitude and absolute relaxation, then they rely on the complete remedies of Nature—the medicine in plants and pure air. A bear grubbing for fern roots; a wild turkey compelling her babies in a rainy spell to eat leaves of the spice bush; an animal, bitten by a poisonous snake, confidently chewing snakeroot—all these are typical examples. An animal with fever quickly hunts up an airy, shady place near water, there remaining quiet, eating nothing but drinking often until its health is recovered. On the other hand, an animal bedeviled by rheumatism finds a spot of hot sunlight and lies in it until the misery bakes out.

—D. C. JARVIS, *Folk Medicine*

McCarthyism was permeating every state and every occupation, sometimes ridiculous, sometimes frightening, sometimes bordering on the incredible. Five distinguished ex-diplomats warned that the assaults on the State Department were having "sinister results. . . . A premium has been put upon reporting and upon recommendations which are ambiguously stated or so cautiously set forth as to be deceiving . . . the ultimate result is a threat to national security." The major drama publisher, Samuel French, announced a playwriting contest in which one of the conditions was that the sponsor "reserves the right at any time to declare ineligible any author who is, or becomes publicly involved, in a scholastic, literary, political, or moral controversy." The crackdown on scientists and teachers had reached the point where Albert Einstein was advising his correspondents to resort to the "way of non-cooperation in the sense of Gandhi's"—a refusal to testify before any Congressional committee about personal beliefs and a willingness to go to jail as a result.

—ERIC F. GOLDMAN, *The Crucial Decade*

The moment we begin scientific, unbiased RESEARCH into language we find, in people and cultures with the most unprepossessing exteriors, beautiful, effective, and scientific devices of expression unknown to western Indo-European tongues or mentalities. The Algonkian languages are spoken by very simple people, hunting and fishing Indians, but they are marvels of analysis and synthesis. One piece of grammatical finesse peculiar to them is called the obviative. This means that their pronouns have four persons instead of three, or from our standpoint two third persons. This aids in compact description of complicated situations, for which we should have to resort to cumbersome phraseology. Let us symbolize their third and fourth persons by attaching the numerals 3 and 4 to our written words. The Algonkians might tell the story of William Tell like this: "William Tell called his$_3$ son and told him$_4$ to bring him$_3$ his$_3$ bow and arrow, which$_4$ he$_4$ then brought to him$_3$. He$_3$ had him$_4$ stand still and placed an apple on his$_4$ head, then took his$_3$ bow and arrow and told him$_4$ not to fear. Then he$_3$ shot it$_4$ off his$_4$ head without hurting him$_4$." Such a device would greatly help in specifying our complex legal situations, getting rid of "the party of the first part" and "the aforesaid John Doe shall, on his part, etc."

—BENJAMIN LEE WHORF, *Language, Thought, and Reality*

A special kind of illustration is ANALOGY. An analogy draws a parallel between two things which have some resemblance, on the basis of which we infer other resemblances. When we draw comparisons, for example, between a large city and an ant hill, or between a college and a factory, or between the human nervous system and a telephone system, we are using analogy. Parallels of this sort, although they may be quite inexact in many respects, enable us to visualize ideas or relations and therefore to understand them better. Note that the first paragraph below uses analogy to explain, while the second uses it to argue.

By way of attempting to give the reader some general impression of the way people lived together in those days, and especially of the relations of the rich and poor to one another, perhaps I cannot do better than to compare society as it then was to a prodigious coach which the masses of humanity were harnessed to and dragged toilsomely along a very hilly and and sandy road. The driver was hunger, and permitted no lagging, though the pace was necessarily very slow. Despite the difficulty of drawing the coach at all along so hard a road, the top was covered with passengers who never got down, even at the steepest ascents. These seats on top were very breezy and comfortable. Well up out of the dust, their occupants could enjoy the scenery at their leisure, or critically discuss the merits of the straining team. Naturally such places were in great demand and the competition for them was keen, everyone seeking as the first end in life to secure a seat on the coach for himself and to leave it to his child after him. By the rule of the coach a man could leave his seat to whom he wished, but on the other hand there were many accidents by which it might at any time be wholly lost. For all that they were so easy, the seats were very insecure, and at every sudden jolt of the coach persons were slipping out of them and falling to the ground, where they were instantly compelled to take hold of the rope and help drag the coach on which they had before ridden so pleasantly. It was naturally regarded as a terrible misfortune to lose one's seat, and the apprehension that this might happen to them or their friends was a constant cloud upon the happiness of those who rode.

—EDWARD BELLAMY, *Looking Backward*

But the tendency of the time is much better illustrated by a group of professors of education who have just recently proposed that the list of "required reading" in schools should be based upon a study which they have just sponsored of the tastes of school children. . . . Would any pediatrician base the diet which he prescribed for the young submitted to his care simply on an effort to determine what eatables they remembered with greatest pleasure? If he knew that the vote would run heavily in favor of chocolate sodas, orange pop, hot dogs and bubble gum, would he conclude that these should obviously constitute the fundamental elements in a "modern" child's menu?

—JOSEPH WOOD KRUTCH, "Should We Bring Literature to Children, or Children to Literature?"

b. *Comparison and contrast.* The logic of a paragraph sometimes resides in a careful statement of the similarities or differences between two or more ideas or things. A writer may use this pattern to compare or contrast two things both of which he wishes to describe, as in the following:

The great leading distinction between writing and speaking is, that more time is allowed for the one than the other, and hence different faculties are required for, and different objects attained by each. He is properly the best speaker who can collect together the greatest number of apposite ideas at a moment's warning; he is properly the best writer who can give utterance to the greatest quantity of valuable knowledge in the course of his whole life. The chief requisite for the one, then, appears to be quickness and facility of perception—for the other, patience of soul and a power increasing with the difficulties it has to master. He cannot be denied to be an expert speaker, a lively companion, who is never at a loss for something to say on every occasion or subject that offers. He, by the same rule, will make a respectable writer who, by dint of study, can find out anything good to say upon any one point that has not been touched upon before, or who by asking for time, can give the most complete and comprehensive view of any question. The one must be done off-hand, at a single blow; the other can only be done by a repetition of blows, by having time to think and do better.

—WILLIAM HAZLITT, "On the Differences Between Speaking and Writing"

Roosevelt, as a public personality, was a spontaneous, optimistic, pleasure-loving ruler who dismayed his assistants by the gay and apparently heedless abandon with which he seemed to delight in pursuing two or more totally incompatible policies, and astonished them even more by the swiftness and ease with which he managed to throw off the cares of office during the darkest and most dangerous moments. Churchill too loves pleasure, and he too lacks neither gaiety nor a capacity for exuberant self-expression, together with the habit of blithely cutting Gordian knots in a manner which often upsets his experts; but he is not a frivolous man.

His nature possesses a dimension of depth—and a corresponding sense of tragic possibilities, which Roosevelt's lighthearted genius instinctively passed by.

Roosevelt played the game of politics with virtuosity, and both his successes and his failures were carried off in splendid style; his performance seemed to flow with effortless skill. Churchill is acquainted with darkness as well as light. Like all inhabitants and even transient visitors of inner worlds, he gives evidence of seasons of agonized brooding and slow recovery. Roosevelt might have spoken of sweat and blood, but when Churchill offered his people tears, he spoke a word which might have been uttered by Lincoln or Mazzini or Cromwell but not Roosevelt, greathearted, generous, and perceptive as he was.

—ISAIAH BERLIN, "Mr. Churchill"

The pattern may be used to clarify a principal topic by comparing and contrasting it with others. In the first paragraph below, Frederick Lewis Allen sharpens our sense of the "expectant good will" with which the Harding administration opened—by contrasting it with the austerity of the preceding Wilson administration. In the second paragraph, Van Doren defines the essay largely by contrasting it with other forms of writing.

Every new administration at Washington begins in an atmosphere of expectant good will, but in this case the airs which lapped the capital were particularly bland. The smile of the new President was as warming as a spring thaw after a winter of discontent. For four long years the gates of the White House had been locked and guarded with sentries. Harding's first official act was to throw them open, to permit a horde of sight-seers to roam the grounds and flatten their noses against the executive window-panes and photograph one another under the great north portico; to permit flivvers and trucks to detour from Pennsylvania Avenue up the driveway and chortle right past the presidential front door. The act seemed to symbolize the return of the government to the people. Wilson had been denounced as an autocrat, had proudly kept his own counsel; Harding modestly said he would rely on the "best minds" to advise him, and took his oath of office upon the verse from Micah which asks, "What doth the Lord require of thee but to do justly, and to love mercy, and to walk humbly with thy God?" Wilson had seemed to be everlastingly prying into the affairs of business and had distrusted most business men; Harding meant to give them as free a hand as possible "to resume their normal onward way." And finally, whereas Wilson had been an austere academic theorist, Harding was "just folks": he radiated an unaffected good nature, met reporters and White House visitors with a warm handclasp and a genial word, and touched the sentimental heart of America by establishing in the White House a dog named Laddie Boy. "The Washington atmosphere of today is like that of Old Home Week or a college class reunion," wrote Edward G. Lowry shortly after Harding took office. "The change is amazing. The populace is on a broad grin." An era of good will seemed to be beginning. —FREDERICK LEWIS ALLEN, *Only Yesterday*

The sonnet has a standard form very much as a man has. Leave off the sestet of your sonnet and you do about what a god does when he leaves the legs off a man. The drama has a standard form very much as a rendezvous has. Write a drama in which no spark is exchanged between the audience and the action, and you have done what fate does when it keeps lovers from their meeting. The novel has a standard form very much as a road has. You may set out anywhere you like and go wherever you please, at any gait, but you must go somewhere, or you have made what is no more a novel than some engineer's road would be a road if it had neither beginning, end, nor direction. *But the essay! It may be of any length, breadth, depth, weight, density, color, savor, odor, appearance, importance, value, or uselessness which you can or will give it.* The epigram bounds it on one side and the treatise on the other, but it has in its time encroached upon the territory of both of them, and it doubtless will do so again. Or, to look at the essay from another angle, it is bounded on one side by the hell-fire sermon and on the other by the geometrical demonstration; and yet it ranges easily between these extremes of heat and cold and occasionally steals from both of them. It differs from a letter by being written to more—happily a great many more—than one person. It differs from talk chiefly by being written at all. —CARL VAN DOREN, "A Note on the Essay"

c. *Repetition and restatement.* The logical development of a paragraph sometimes calls for a series of restatements of the topic. In such paragraphs, the topic thought is clarified and reinforced by being repeated in slightly different lights with slightly different emphasis. Obviously such repetition must be carefully planned if it is to avoid being merely tedious. The following paragraphs illustrate the skillful use of this kind of development.

We are at that point in our moral history as a people at which we have failed, for the first time in a moment of decision, to assert our moral purpose. We have not yet denied that purpose—the cock has not crowed for the second time—but we have failed to assert it. We have not yet changed the direction of our national life but we have lost our momentum, we have lost our initiative. We have not yet rejected our role as a revolutionary people moving with the great revolutionary current of history but we have ceased to move, we have begun to resist, to oppose. It does not require a prophet to see that we have come to a moment of critical decision—a decision which is none the less critical because it may be taken unaware. —ARCHIBALD MACLEISH, "The Conquest of America"

Obviously, science follows no plan. It develops at random. Its progress depends on fortuitous conditions, such as the birth of men of genius, the form of their mind, the direction taken by their curiosity. It is not at all actuated by a desire to improve the state of human beings. The discoveries responsible for industrial civilization were brought forth at the fancy of the scientists' intuitions and of the more or less casual circumstances of their careers. If Galileo, Newton, or Lavoisier had applied their intellectual powers to the study of body and consciousness, our world probably would be different today. Men of science do not know where they are going. They are guided by chance, by subtle reasoning, by a sort of clairvoyance. Each of them is a world apart, governed by his own laws. From time to time, things obscure to others become clear to him. In general, discoveries are developed without any prevision of their consequences. These consequences, however, have revolutionized the world and made our civilization what it is. —ALEXIS CARREL, *Man, the Unknown*

d. *Definition.* The logic of a paragraph sometimes requires that key objects or terms be defined. Definition is necessary to set the limits within which a topic or a term is used, especially when we are dealing with abstract matters. Full and exact paragraphs of definition are frequently important parts of papers, essays, and articles. Note that paragraphs of definition many times make use of details and examples, of comparison and contrast, and of restatement in order to insure clarity.

I have never seen Babbittry exactly defined, but I think what it means is fairly clear. It is not a matter of class or education. A king can be a Babbitt, and most of them are. I must take issue with Mr. Mencken, although he is supposed to be an authority on the subject. His definition, "A generic name designating the more stupid, sentimental, and credulous sort of business man," seems to me extremely inadequate. It implies the gross error, so many intellectuals fall into, of imagining that it requires no brains to be materially successful. To be successful in anything requires some sort of brains and character, despite the small amount of competition in cleverness. George F. Babbitt is not really a stupid man. He would not be worth bothering about if he was. Babbittry means more than stupidity, it connotes a certain kind of shrewdness, deliberate or otherwise. The real Babbitt is a man who uses valid human emotions and ideas for his own ends without a thought of ultimate truth. It is, for instance, not Babbittry to adore your mother if she happens to be adorable—many intelligent men do—it is only Babbittry when this affection is used for commercial and standardized purposes, as has been the case sometimes in this country. National Smile Week and National Day-dream Week are Babbittry at its worst, but it isn't Babbittry to smile or even, occasionally, to day-dream. Plain sentimentality is always folly, and to be sure it supports Babbittry and nourishes it, but until it is used for ulterior purposes it is not Babbittry itself. —STRUTHERS BURT, *The Other Side*

Induction is the kind of reasoning by which we examine a number of particulars or specific instances and on the basis of them arrive at a conclusion. The scientific method is inductive when the scientist observes a recurrent phenomenon and arrives at the conclusion or hypothesis that under certain conditions this phenomenon will always take place; if in the course of time further observation supports his hypothesis and if no exceptions are observed, his conclusion is generally accepted as truth and is sometimes called a law. In everyday living, too, we arrive at conclusions by induction. Every cat we encounter has claws; we conclude that all cats have claws. Every rose we smell is fragrant; we conclude that all roses are fragrant. An acquaintance has, on various occasions, paid back money he has borrowed; we conclude that he is frequently out of funds but that he pays his debts. Every Saturday morning for six weeks the new paper boy is late in delivering the paper; we conclude that he sleeps on Saturday mornings and we no longer look for the paper before nine o'clock. In each case we have reasoned inductively from a number of instances; we have moved from an observation of some things to a generalization about all things in the same category.

—NEWMAN and GENEVIEVE BIRK, *Understanding and Using English*

A sign is anything that announces the existence or the imminence of some event, the presence of a thing or a person, or a change in a state of affairs. There are signs of the weather, signs of danger, signs of future good or evil, signs of what the past has been. In every case a sign is closely bound up with something to be noted or expected in experience. It is always a part of the situation to which it refers, though the reference may be remote in space and time. In so far as we are led to note or expect the signified event we are making correct use of a sign. This is the essence of rational behavior, which animals show in varying degrees. It is entirely realistic, being closely bound up with the actual objective course of history— learned by experience, and cashed in or voided by further experience.

—SUSANNE K. LANGER, "The Lord of Creation"

e. *Explanation of causes and effects.* The logical development of a paragraph sometimes calls for a statement of the forces that produce a situation or the results produced by one.

Lake Erie, the last of the Great Lakes to be discovered, was the first to take form. In preglacial ages a mighty river flowed eastward through what is now the Lake Erie basin. When the ice sheet formed and moved south, it rammed one lobe along the axis of this stream. It gouged heavily into the soft Devonian shales to the east, and it carved deep grooves in the hard, resistant Devonian limestone at Sandusky Bay to the west. These grooves are conspicuous on the islands, especially on Kelleys Island, where one exposed section of this glacial sculpture has been made into a state park. The southwestern lobe of its basin, where the white pioneers found the Black Swamp, was first uncovered when the last of the ice sheets, known as the Wisconsin, began to melt back from the corner of present Ohio, Indiana and Michigan. The sun had beat upon the advancing front of this ice sheet, melting it down and releasing from its frozen grip the billions of tons of rock and gravel which were left piled up in terminal moraines 500 feet deep in places. The water filled in between the moraine and the receding ice sheet and discharged out of the Maumee lobe down the Wabash River. And when the water was extensive enough to be called a lake, Lake Erie had begun its metamorphosis to its present shore lines.

—HARLAN HATCHER, *Lake Erie*

The fading of ideals is sad evidence of the defeat of human endeavor. In the schools of antiquity philosophers aspired to impart wisdom, in modern colleges our humbler aim is to teach subjects. The drop from the divine wisdom, which was the goal of the ancients, to text-book knowledge of subjects, which is achieved by the moderns, marks an educational failure, sustained through the ages. I am not maintaining that in the practice of education the ancients were more successful than ourselves. You have only to read Lucian, and to note his satiric dramatizations of the pretentious claims of philosophers, to see that in this respect the ancients can boast over us no superiority. My point is that, at the dawn of our European civilization, men started with the full ideals which should inspire education, and that gradually our ideals have sunk to square with our practice.

—A. N. WHITEHEAD, *The Aims of Education*

f. *Elimination of alternatives.* The logical development of a paragraph sometimes requires that the central proposition be validated by the elimination of alternative propositions.

If the Moon had been separated from the Earth at a time when the latter was still completely molten, the liquid would have immediately covered the site of the rupture, and no more trace would have been left on the body of our planet than there is on the surface of a well from which a bucketful of water has been taken. But if at the time of rupture the Earth was already covered with solid crust, the newborn satellite must have carried away a large section of this rocky crust, leaving a clearly visible scar. A glance at the map of the Earth's surface discloses such a scar in the deep basin of the Pacific Ocean, which now covers about one-third of the total surface of the Earth. It would, of course, be rather unwise to draw such a far-reaching conclusion merely from the vast area and roughly circular form of the Pacific, but geologists have discovered an additional fact that lends strong support to the hypothesis that the Pacific basin is really the "hole" left in the Earth's crust by the separation of its satellite. We have already mentioned that the upper crust of the Earth is a layer of granite from 50 to 100 kilometres thick resting on a much thicker layer of heavier basalt. This is true of all the continents and also of parts of the Earth's crust that are submerged beneath the waters of the Atlantic, Indian, and Arctic oceans where, however, the granite layer is considerably thinner. But the vast expanse of the Pacific is a striking exception—*not a single piece of granite has ever been found on any of the numerous islands scattered through that ocean.* There is hardly any doubt that *the floor of the Pacific is formed exclusively of basaltic rocks, as if some cosmic hand had removed the entire granite layer from all this vast area.* Besides, in contrast to the other oceans, the basin of the Pacific is surrounded by a ring of high mountain chains (Cordilleras, Kamchatka, the islands of Japan, and New Zealand) of pronounced volcanic activity, known as the "ring of fire." This indicates that this roughly circular border line is much more closely connected with the structure of the entire crust than the shore lines of other oceans. It is, therefore, quite likely that the area now occupied by the Pacific is the very place where the huge bulk of matter now forming the Moon was torn away from the Earth.

—GEORGE GAMOW, *Biography of the Earth*

It is customary to regard the course of history as a great river, with its source in some small rivulet of the distant past, taking its rise on the plains of Asia, and flowing slowly down through the ages, gathering water from new tributaries on the way, until finally in our own days it broadens majestically over the whole world. Men have even personified this flow, made of it a being that develops of its own volition, following its own laws to the achievement of some preconceived goal. They have spoken of the "dialectic of ideas," and regarded men and whole civilizations as the passive instruments employed by this great Being in the working-out of its purposes. The observer not already committed to faith in such an interpretation finds it difficult to discern any such steady sweep in the course of human events, and above all he feels that to look upon humanity as a passive tool to which things are done and with which ends are accomplished, is a falsification of the cardinal fact that it is men who have made history and not history which has made men. Men have built up civilization, men have patiently and laboriously found out every way of doing things and toilingly worked out every idea that is today a part of our heritage from the past—men working at every turn, to be sure, under the influences of their environment and with the materials at hand, individual men and races and not even some such being as "humanity." The complex of beliefs and ideals by which the modern world lives and with which it works is not a gift from the gods, as ancient myth had it, but an achievement of a long succession of generations.

—J. H. RANDALL, *The Making of the Modern Mind*

EXERCISE 32g(1). Which of the methods of paragraph development discussed in Section 32g seems to be the most appropriate method of developing each of the following topic sentences into a paragraph? Why? After you have answered this question briefly, choose one of the topics and write a paragraph around it. Is your paragraph developed according to your original notion?

1. Attending a small college has disadvantages as well as advantages.
2. To watch a college "mixer" is to see every type of human being.

3. Wit and humor are not the same thing.
4. Athleticism focuses its attention on doing good for boys who least need it.
5. Contemporary society places too much emphasis on test scores.
6. The rapidly rising population of the world creates problems of future survival.
7. The civil rights issue is a continuum of the Civil War.
8. Good government begins at the local level.
9. Fraternities have to watch carefully the line between fellowship and snobbishness.
10. Some people come to college wanting to learn, but refusing, at the same time, to change a single idea they came with.
11. To know how to suggest is the great art of teaching.
12. The notion that women are poor automobile drivers is not supported by any real evidence.
13. A distinction should be drawn between liberty and license.
14. Campus slang is a puzzle to the uninitiated.
15. The differences in education and social conditioning for boys and girls in our society make for an enormous waste of female talent.
16. It is the dull man who is always sure, and the sure man who is always dull. —H. L. MENCKEN
17. A dormitory is not an ideal place for study.
18. A child who has learned to live and love in the movies will suffer when he enters a world in which there is odor as well as sight and sound.
19. We are too much inclined to measure progress by the number of television sets rather than by the quality of television programs.
20. The people you see at a patriotic rally are not very likely to be the ones that move you to love your country.

EXERCISE 32g(2). *You cannot do wrong without suffering wrong.* Write two separate paragraphs to develop this topic sentence. In the first paragraph, demonstrate by abstract argument or theory that the statement is either true or false. In the second, demonstrate the truth or falsity of the statement by giving examples.

EXERCISE 32g(3). *My reading tastes have changed since I came to college.* Write three separate paragraphs to develop this topic sentence. In the first paragraph, show why your tastes have changed. In the second, demonstrate how they have changed. In the third, contrast specifically your reading tastes in high school with your reading tastes in college.

Consistency in the Paragraph = ¶ CON

When we read effective writers we are often struck by the fact that what seems to hold their sentences together is more than mere adherence to an organizational principle. There is about their writing some inner consistency which unites everything they say into an authoritative whole. What we are responding to is a kind of consistency of TONE which pervades the whole of a passage of good writing.

Tone is one of those matters which is clear enough to us until we try to define it. We know well enough what we mean when, if our neighbor has complained about our barking beagle, we remark that we don't mind his complaining but we don't like his tone. But when we try to describe exactly what it is we don't like, we find it extremely difficult. For tone is produced by an interplay of many elements in speech and writing. Sentence structure, diction, the mode of organization and development we choose, the kinds of examples, illustrations, and details we draw on—these and many other factors are involved.

The best way to increase our awareness of tone in writing is to study carefully a variety of effective paragraphs, asking ourselves how we would describe their tone and then trying to determine how the writer has conveyed that tone to us. A writer's tone can be impersonal or personal, formal or informal, literal or ironic, sentimental or sarcastic, sincere or insincere, enthusiastic or indifferent, dogmatic or doubtful, hostile or friendly, condescending or respectful, modest or authoritative, serious or humorous, and the like. Obviously it can be a level in between any of these extreme pairs, or it can be a complex quality which can be adequately described only by a combination of several of these terms. Only by careful study of good writing can' we increase our awareness of the many factors that contribute to the control of tone.

32h **In your writing try particularly to choose an appropriate tone and to maintain it consistently, not only in individual paragraphs but throughout an entire paper.**

1. *Appropriate tone.*   An appropriate tone is one that reflects the writer's understanding of and respect for the needs and feelings of his audience. It is not easy to state what will make for such appropriateness in any particular paragraph or paper. But some things are generally to be avoided. Among them the most important are: talking down to your audience by repeating the obvious; talking over the heads of your audience, merely to impress them, by using words or allusions or examples they are unlikely to understand; being excessively dogmatic, or sarcastic; and being excessively or falsely enthusiastic.

This opening sentence of a student paper illustrates an extreme of inappropriate tone: *No one can tell me that people who vote for the characters on the Democratic ticket aren't putting their own selfish interests ahead of the true good of the country.* Whatever we may think of the thesis of the writer, his expression of it offends us. The language is emotional, his attitude dogmatic. We have the immediate feeling that there is no point in reading further, since we cannot hope, apparently, for any sort of balanced or reasoned discussion of the sort appropriate to the topic.

2. *Consistent tone.*   Consistency requires that once we have set a particular tone, we maintain it. A jarring shift in tone may ruin the effect of a paragraph even though it otherwise meets the tests of unity, coherence, and adequate development. The following paragraph from a student theme illustrates the point:

> Curiosity has developed ideas that have been vastly beneficial to mankind. We have seen mankind emerge from the age of great darkness into the age of great light. Today every hotrod artist profits from the ideas of past inventors and every housewife has a kitchen full of push-button gadgets that she couldn't have without ideas. Above all, modern scientific theory leads us to a clearer and deeper comprehension of the universe. So we see curiosity is really a helpful tool.

Except for poor transitions to the second and the last sentences, the principal fault of this paragraph is its jarring shifts of tone. The first two sentences and the next to last sentence set a serious, somewhat formal tone by such phrases as *vastly beneficial, we have seen mankind emerge,* the parallel phrases *great age of darkness* and *great age of light,* and *clearer and deeper comprehension of the universe.* But the language of both the third and the last sentences, and the examples cited in the third sentence depart completely from this tone of seriousness and formality. Having been prepared for comment about the great concepts of religion, politics, education, and science, or the like, we are offered *hotrod artists* and *push-button gadgets*. The effect is something like that of a cat meowing in a church service.

EXERCISE 32h(1).   Study the following paragraphs. Describe the tone of each and discuss the factors that contribute to it.

1. The motor car is, more than any other object, the expression of the nation's character and the nation's dream. In the free billowing fender, in the blinding chromium grilles, in the fluid control, in the ever-widening front seat, we see the flowering of the America that we know. It is of some interest to scholars and historians that the same autumn which saw the abandonment of the window crank and the adoption of the push button (removing the motorist's last necessity for physical exertion) saw also the registration of sixteen million young men of fighting age and symphonic styling. It is of deep interest to me that in the same week Japan joined the Axis, DeSoto moved its clutch pedal two inches to the left—and that the announcements caused equal flurries among the people.

   —E. B. WHITE, *One Man's Meat*

2. It is not easy to live in that continuous awareness of things which alone is true living. Even those who make a parade of their conviction that sunset, rain, and the growth of a seed are daily miracles are not usually so much impressed by them as they urge others to be. The faculty of wonder tires easily and a miracle which appears every day is a miracle no longer, no matter how many times one tells oneself that it ought to be. Life would seem a great deal longer and a great deal fuller than it does if it were not for the fact that the human being is, by nature, a creature to whom *"O altitudo"* is much less natural than "So what!" Really to see something once or twice a week is almost inevitably to have to try—though, alas, not necessarily with success—to make oneself a poet.

   —JOSEPH WOOD KRUTCH, *The Desert Year*

3. Outside of the three Rs—the razor, the rope, and the revolver—I know only one sure-fire method of coping with the simmering heat we may cheerfully expect in this meridian from now to Labor Day. Whenever the mercury starts inching up the column, I take to the horizontal plane with a glass graduate trimmed with ferns, place a pinch of digitalis or any good heart stimulant at my elbow, and flip open the advertising section of *Vogue*. Fifteen minutes of that paradisaical prose, those dizzying non sequiturs, and my lips are as blue as Lake Louise. If you want a mackerel iced or a sherbet frozen, just bring it up and let me read the advertising section of *Vogue* over it.

I can also take care of small picnic parties up to five. The next time you're hot and breathless, remember the name, folks: Little Labrador Chilling and Dismaying Corporation. —s. j. perelman, *Keep It Crisp*

4. Even though large tracts of Europe and many old and famous States have fallen or may fall into the grip of the Gestapo and all the odious apparatus of Nazi rule, we shall not flag or fail. We shall go on to the end. We shall fight in France, we shall fight in the seas and oceans, we shall fight with growing confidence and growing strength in the air; we shall defend our Island, whatever the cost may be. We shall fight on the beaches, we shall fight on the landing grounds, we shall fight in the fields and in the streets, we shall fight in the hills; we shall never surrender; and even if, which I do not for a moment believe, this Island or a large part of it were subjugated and starving, then our Empire beyond the seas, armed and guarded by the British Fleet, would carry on the struggle, until, in God's good time, the New World, with all its power and might, steps forth to the rescue and liberation of the Old. —winston churchill, Speech at Dunkerque

5. At first they had come in wagons: the guns, the bedding, the dogs, the food, the whiskey, the keen heart-lifting anticipation of hunting; the young men who could drive all night and all the following day in the cold rain and pitch a camp in the rain and sleep in the wet blankets and rise at daylight the next morning and hunt. There had been bear then. A man shot a doe or a fawn as quickly as he did a buck, and in the afternoons they shot wild turkey with pistols to test their stalking skill and marksmanship, feeding all but the breast to the dogs. But that time was gone now. Now they went in cars, driving faster and faster each year because the roads were better and they had farther and farther to drive, the territory in which game still existed drawing yearly inward as his life was drawing inward, until now he was the last of those who had once made the journey in wagons without feeling it and now those who accompanied him were the sons and even grandsons of the men who had ridden for twenty-four hours in the rain or sleet behind the steaming mules. They called him "Uncle Ike" now, and he no longer told anyone how near eighty he actually was because he knew as well as they did that he no longer had any business making such expeditions, even by car.

—william faulkner, *Delta Autumn*

Paragraphs for study.

We cannot learn to write well simply by following general prescriptions. The best way to develop skill in writing is to develop skill in observing how others write. Reading is an integral part of the process of learning to write, not something entirely separate from it. Test your understanding of the principles of good paragraphs by a close study of as many of the following paragraphs as possible. Analyze each to determine the main points, the topic sentence, the transitions from sentence to sentence, the method or methods of paragraph development and organization, and the tone.

1. By day it [the kitchen] was the scene of intense bustle. The kitchen-maid was down by five o'clock to light the fire; the laborers crept down in stockinged feet and drew on their heavy boots; they lit candles in their horn lanthorns and went out to the cattle. Breakfast was at seven, dinner at twelve, tea at five. Each morning of the week had its appropriate activity: Monday was washing day, Tuesday ironing, Wednesday and Saturday baking, Thursday "turning out" upstairs and churning, Friday "turning out" downstairs. Every day there was the milk to skim in the dairy—the dairy was to the left of the kitchen, and as big as any other room in the house. The milk was poured into large flat pans and allowed to settle; it was skimmed with horn scoops, like toothless combs.

—HERBERT READ, *The Eye of Memory*

2. The whole aim of good teaching is to turn the young learner, by nature a little copycat, into an independent, self-propelling creature, who cannot merely learn but study—that is, work as his own boss to the limit of his powers. This is to turn pupils into students, and it can be done on any rung of the ladder of learning. When I was a child, the multiplication table was taught from a printed sheet which had to be memorized one "square" at a time—the one's and the two's and so on up to nine. It never occurred to the teacher to show us how the answers could be arrived at also by addition, which we already knew. No one said, "Look: if four times four is sixteen, you ought to be able to figure out, without aid from memory, what five times four is, because that amounts to four more one's added to the sixteen." This would at first have been puzzling, *more* complicated and difficult than memory work, but once explained and grasped, it would have been an instrument for learning and checking the whole business of multiplication. We could temporarily have dispensed with the teacher and cut loose from the printed table.

—JACQUES BARZUN, *Teacher in America*

3. He [Wagner] was a monster of conceit. Never for one minute did he look at the world or at people, except in relation to himself. He was not only the most important person in the world, to himself; in his own eyes he was the only person who existed. He believed himself to be one of the greatest dramatists in the world, one of the greatest thinkers, and one of the greatest composers. To hear him talk, he was Shakespeare, and Beethoven, and Plato, rolled into one. And you would have had no difficulty in hearing him talk. He was one of the most exhausting conversationalists that ever lived. An evening with him was an evening spent in listening to a monologue. Sometimes he was brilliant; sometimes he was maddeningly tiresome. But whether he was being brilliant or dull, he had one sole topic of conversation: himself. What *he* thought and what *he* did.

—DEEMS TAYLOR, *Of Men and Music*

4. The words we choose to define or suggest what we believe to be important facts exert a very powerful influence upon civilization. A mere name can persuade us to approve or disapprove, as it does, for example, when we describe certain attitudes as "cynical" on the one hand or "realistic" on the other. No one wants to be "unrealistic" and no one wants to be "snarling." Therefore his attitude toward the thing described may very well depend upon which designation is current among his contemporaries; and the less critical his mind, the more influential the most commonly used vocabulary will be.

— JOSEPH WOOD KRUTCH, *Human Nature and the Human Condition*

5. If you work as a soda jerker you will, of course, not need much skill in expressing yourself to be effective. If you work on a machine your ability to express yourself will be of little importance. But as soon as you move one step up from the bottom, your effectiveness depends on your ability to reach others through the spoken or the written word. And the further away your job is from manual work, the larger the organization of which you are an employee, the more important it will be that you know how to convey your thoughts in writing or speaking. In the very large business organization, whether it is the government, the large corporation, or the Army, this ability to express oneself is perhaps the most important of all the skills a man can possess.

— PETER F. DRUCKER, "How to Be an Employee"

6. Lack of variety has often been urged in criticism of American place-names. Certain it is that not only do the European names *Berlin, Cambridge, Belmont, Burlington,* and their kind, appear in endless repetition, but words more distinctively American lose their distinctiveness through constant iteration. Not only do *Washingtons* and *Franklins* and *Jacksons* appear in wearisome numbers, but a name such as *Brooklyn* (a modification of Dutch *Breukelen*) is worn out by adoption in 21 states outside New York. The effectiveness of *Buffalo,* admirably American in quality, is spoiled by its application including compounds, in about 75 different places. Compounds with *Elk-, Bald-, Maple-, Beech-, Oak-, Red-,* and the like are open to similar objection. In many instances inventive power seems to have been entirely lacking. *Disputanta* is said to owe its name to lack of agreement on a name, and in a number of instances settlements have been named like streets by the use of numerals, as in the case of *Seven* (Tennessee), *Fourteen* (West Virginia), *Seventeen* (Ohio), *Seventy-six* (Kentucky and Maryland), *Ninety-six* (South Carolina).

— G. H. MC KNIGHT, *English Words and Their Background*

7. The pyramids were built with sheer muscle-power. Holes were bored in stone in the quarries of the Mokattam Mountains, wooden sticks were driven into them, and these, swelling when soaked with water, cracked apart the rock. On sledges and rollers the resulting blocks were dragged to the site. The pyramids rose layer by layer. Candidates for a doctorate in archaeology write these on the question of whether one construction plan was used or several. Lepsius and Petrie occupy diametri-

cally opposed positions on this controversy, but modern archaeology inclines to support the Lepsian point of view. Apparently there were several plans of construction, drastic changes being necessitated by suddenly conceived additions. The Egyptians, forty-seven hundred years ago, worked with such precision that mistakes in the lengths and angles of the great pyramids can, as Petrie says, "be covered with one's thumb." They fitted the stone blocks so neatly that "neither needle nor hair" can, to this day, be inserted at the joints. The Arab writer, Abd al Latif, remarked on this in wonder eight hundred years ago. Critics point out that the old Egyptian master builders misjudged their stresses and strains, as for example, when they made five hollow spaces over the burial-chamber ceiling to reduce the downward pressure, when one would have sufficed. But these fault-finders forget, in our own day of electronically analyzed T-beams, that it was not so long ago that we used to build with a safety factor of five, eight, or even twelve.   —C. W. CERAM, *Gods, Graves, and Scholars*

8. Science is not merely a collection of facts and formulas. It is preeminently a way of dealing with experience. The word may be appropriately used as a verb: one *sciences,* i.e., deals with experience according to certain assumptions and with certain techniques. Science is one of two basic ways of dealing with experience. The other is art. And this word, too, may appropriately be used as a verb; one may *art* as well as science. The purpose of science and art is one: to render experience intelligible, i.e., to assist man to adjust himself to his environment in order that he may live. But although working toward the same goal, science and art approach it from opposite directions. Science deals with particulars in terms of universals: Uncle Tom disappears in the mass of Negro slaves. Art deals with universals in terms of particulars: the whole gamut of Negro slavery confronts us in the person of Uncle Tom. Art and science thus grasp a common experience, or reality, by opposite but inseparable poles.
—LESLIE A. WHITE, *The Science of Culture*

9. What men, in their egoism, constantly mistake for a deficiency of intelligence in woman is merely an incapacity for mastering that mass of small intellectual tricks, that complex of petty knowledges, that collection of cerebral rubber-stamps, which constitute the chief mental equipment of the average male. A man thinks that he is more intelligent than his wife because he can add up a column of figures more accurately, or because he is able to distinguish between the ideas of rival politicians, or because he is privy to the minutiae of some sordid and degrading business or profession. But these empty talents, of course, are not really signs of intelligence; they are, in fact, merely a congeries of petty tricks and antics, and their acquirement puts little more strain on the mental powers than a chimpanzee suffers in learning how to catch a penny or scratch a match.
—H. L. MENCKEN, *In Defense of Women*

10. In his own person, man represents every aspect of the cosmos. Reduced to his lowest terms, he is a lump of carbon and a puddle of water mixed with a handful of equally common metals, minerals, and gases.

But man is likewise a unit of organic life; he is a member of the animal world, and of a special order of the animal world, the vertebrates, with capacity for free movements, for selective intercourse with the environment, for specially canalized responses through a highly developed nervous system. Still further, man belongs to the family of warm-blooded animals, the mammals, whose females give milk to their young and so form a close and tender partnership, often fiercely protective, for the nurture of their offspring; and through his own internal development, his whole life is suffused with emotions and erotic responses which have persisted, like so many other traits of domestication—the cow's milk or the hen's eggs—in exaggerated form. Starting as an animal among the animals, man has stretched and intensified certain special organic capacities in order to develop more fully what is specifically human. In a fashion that has no rivals in other species he thinks: he plays: he loves: he dreams.

—LEWIS MUMFORD, *The Conduct of Life*

11. It is now over a hundred years since the *Communist Manifesto,* and the course of history has not gone as Marx planned. It is true that the capitalist business cycle of prosperity and depression has gone on, and that possibly depressions have grown worse. There has certainly been a tendency toward the concentration of capital in giant industry, but it has not been uniform even in the German, British and American economies. The formula that the rich are growing richer and the poor are growing poorer has certainly not proved true. Government is intervening to regulate industry even in the United States, and in all industrial countries there has been a tendency to some degree of what is often called "state socialism." And, of course, there was in 1917 in industrially backward Russia—a country Marx himself disliked—the one major revolutionary movement to come to power under Marxist auspices. The Russians have established the dictatorship of the proletariat, but there are as yet not the slightest signs of the withering away of the Russian state. Marx, indeed, supposed that once the revolution was successful in a great nation— he apparently thought it would come first in the most advanced one of his day, Great Britain—it would spread at least to all the rest of Western society, and therefore throughout the world. Faithful Marxists can, of course, point out that until the revolution is world-wide, the state cannot possibly be expected to wither away in beleaguered Russia.

—CRANE BRINTON, *Ideas and Men: The Story of Western Thought*

12. It is difficult both to define slang and to indicate its relation to other linguistic phenomena. Popular impressions about it are often erroneous: there is no necessary connection, for example, between the slangy and the vulgar, or between the slangy and the ungrammatical; further, there is nothing new about the phenomenon of slang, nor is it anything peculiarly American. Some of these misconceptions we shall return to. In addition, it may be asserted that entirely competent treatments of slang sometimes take in too much territory. One such treatment, Krapp's discussion in *Modern English,* will serve as our point of departure.

Incidentally, it is striking testimony to the ephemeral character of a great deal of slang that Krapp's illustrations, brought together only forty-odd years ago, impress the reader as antiquarian specimens, for the most part. Truly, there is nothing so completely dead as last year's slang.

—STUART ROBERTSON and FREDERIC G. CASSIDY, *The Development of Modern English*, 2nd ed.

13. Only twice in literary history has there been a great period of tragedy, in the Athens of Pericles and in Elizabethan England. What these two periods had in common, two thousand years and more apart in time that they expressed themselves in the same fashion, may give us some hint of the nature of tragedy, for far from being periods of darkness and defeat, each was a time when life was seen exalted, a time of thrilling and unfathomable possibilities. They held their heads high, those men who conquered at Marathon and Salamis, and those who fought Spain and saw the Great Armada sink. The world was a place of wonder; mankind was beauteous; life was lived on the crest of the wave. More than all, the poignant joy of heroism had stirred men's hearts. Not stuff for tragedy, would you say? But on the crest of the wave one must feel either tragically or joyously; one cannot feel tamely. The temper of the mind that sees tragedy in life has not for its opposite the temper that sees joy. The opposite pole to the tragic view of life is the sordid view. When humanity is seen as devoid of dignity and significance, trivial, mean, and sunk in dreary hopelessness, then the spirit of tragedy departs. "Sometime let gorgeous tragedy in sceptred pall come sweeping by." At the opposite pole stands Gorki with *The Lower Depths*.

—EDITH HAMILTON, *The Great Age of Greek Literature*

14. We can now proceed to examine some more specific characteristics of productive thinking. In productive thinking the subject is not indifferent to his object but is affected by and concerned with it. The object is not experienced as something dead and divorced from oneself and one's life, as something about which one thinks only in a self-isolated fashion; on the contrary, the subject is intensely interested in his object, and the more intimate this relation is, the more fruitful is his thinking. It is this very relationship between him and his object which stimulates his thinking in the first place. To him a person or any phenomenon becomes an object of thought because it is an object of interest, relevant from the standpoint of his individual life or that of human existence. A beautiful illustration of this point is the story of Buddha's discovery of the "fourfold truth." Buddha saw a dead man, a sick man, and an old man. He, a young man, was deeply affected by the inescapable fate of man, and his reaction to his observation was the stimulus for thinking which resulted in his theory of the nature of life and the ways of man's salvation. His reaction was certainly not the only possible one. A modern physician in the same situation might react by starting to think of how to combat death, sickness, and age, but his thinking would also be determined by his total reaction to his object.

—ERICH FROMM, *Man for Himself*

15. One evening he and she went up the great sweeping shore of sands toward Theddlethorpe. The long breakers plunged and ran in a hiss of foam along the coast. It was a warm evening. There was not a figure but themselves on the far reaches of sand, no noise but the sound of the sea. Paul loved to see it clanging at the land. He loved to feel himself between the noise of it and the silence of the sandy shore. Miriam was with him. Everything grew very intense. It was quite dark when they turned again. The way home was through a gap in the sandhills, and then along a raised grass road between two dykes. The country was black and still. From behind the sandhills came the whisper of the sea. Paul and Miriam walked in silence. Suddenly he started. The whole of his blood seemed to burst into flame, and he could scarcely breathe. An enormous orange moon was staring at them from the rim of the sandhills. He stood still, looking at it.   —D. H. LAWRENCE, *Sons and Lovers*

16. At length as the craft was cast to one side, and ran ranging along with the White Whale's flank, he seemed strangely oblivious of its advance —as the whale sometimes will—and Ahab was fairly within the smoky mountain mist, which, thrown off from the whale's spout, curled round his great Monadnock hump; he was even thus close to him; when, with body arched back, and both arms lengthwise high-lifted to the poise, he darted his fierce iron, and his far fiercer curse into the hated whale. As both steel and curse sank to the socket, as if sucked into a morass, Moby Dick sideways writhed; spasmodically rolled his nigh flank against the bow, and, without staving a hole in it, so suddenly canted the boat over, that had it not been for the elevated part of the gunwale to which he then clung, Ahab would once more have been tossed into the sea. As it was, three of the oarsmen—who foreknew not the precise instant of the dart, and were therefore unprepared for its effects—these were flung out; but so fell, that, in an instant two of them clutched the gunwhale again, and rising to its level on a combining wave, hurled themselves bodily inboard again; the third man helplessly dropping astern, but still afloat and swimming.

—HERMAN MELVILLE, *Moby Dick*

17. At school, he was a desperate and hunted little animal. The herd, infallible in its banded instinct, knew at once that a stranger had been thrust into it, and it was merciless at the hunt. As the lunchtime recess came, Eugene, clutching his big grease-stained bag, would rush for the playground pursued by the yelping pack. The leaders, two or three big louts of advanced age and deficient mentality, pressed closely about him, calling out suppliantly, "You know me, 'Gene. You know me"; and still racing for the far end, he would open his bag and hurl to them one of his big sandwiches, which stayed them for a moment, as they fell upon its possessor and clawed it to fragments, but they were upon him in a moment more with the same yelping insistence, hunting him down into a corner of the fence, and pressing in with outstretched paws and wild entreaty. He would give them what he had, sometimes with a momentary gust of fury, tearing away from a greedy hand half of a sandwich and devouring it. When they saw he had no more to give, they went away.

—THOMAS WOLFE, *Look Homeward, Angel*

18. Nick laid the bottle full of jumping grasshoppers against a pine trunk. Rapidly he mixed some buckwheat flour with water and stirred it smooth, one cup of flour, one cup of water. He put a handful of coffee in the pot and dipped a lump of grease out of a can and spread it sputtering across the hot skillet. On the smoking skillet he poured smoothly the buckwheat batter. It spread like lava, the grease spitting sharply. Around the edges the buckwheat cake began to firm, then brown, then crisp. The surface was bubbling slowly to porousness. Nick pushed under the browned under surface with a fresh pine chip. He shook the skillet sideways and the cake was loose on the surface. I won't try to flop it, he thought. He slid the chip of clean wood all the way under the cake, and flopped it over onto its face. It sputtered in the pan.

—ERNEST HEMINGWAY, "Big Two-Hearted River"

19. He saw, facing him across the spring, a man of undersize, his hands in his coat pockets, a cigarette slanted from his chin. His suit was black, with a tight, high-waisted coat. His trousers were rolled once and caked with mud above mud-caked shoes. His face had a queer, bloodless color, as though seen by electric light; against the sunny silence, in his slanted straw hat and his slightly akimbo arms, he had that vicious depthless quality of stamped tin. —WILLIAM FAULKNER, *Sanctuary*

20. It was all over though. The big cat lay tangled in the willows: his head and shoulder raised against the red stems, his legs reaching and his back arched downward, in the caricature of a leap, but loose and motionless. The great, yellow eyes glared balefully up through the willows. The mouth was a little open, the tongue hanging down from it behind the fangs. The blood was still dripping from the tongue into the red stain it had already made in the snow. High behind the shoulder, the black pelt was wet too, and one place farther down, on the ribs. Standing there, looking at it, Harold felt compassion for the long, wicked beauty rendered motionless, and even a little shame that it should have passed so hard.

—WALTER V. T. CLARK, *The Track of the Cat*

''PARAGRAPH'' REVIEW EXERCISE. Discuss the papers on pages 234–237 in terms of their overall organization and their paragraph organization.

Specimen Paper 5

THE STUDENT'S ROLE IN THE UNIVERSITY

The university exists for, and because of, its students. From the students it receives the tuition which enables it to fulfill the function it was created for: to substitute for parents. If a person cannot make personal decisions for himself by the time he is eighteen, he has no place in college anyway.

It is clear, therefore, that there should be no such thing as dormitory regulations, except those which the students devise for themselves. Furthermore, since the university exists only in order to teach, it has not got the right to determine what the student is going to learn. The student should be free to learn what he wants to, and to take courses he wants to take not those that are required. Thus, all useless required courses should be abolished, and the courses students want should be chosen by them freely.

Finally, the students are the ones who actually go into the classrooms and listen to lectures. The shortcomings of various professors are noted by them. It is time that the administration recognized this essential fact. Students should have their opinions solicited before deciding questions of promotion or tenure.

Students across the country are now making their voices felt in protests and demonstrations of all kinds. They will not end until the administrations realize that the student's role in the university is the most important one, and that they have a right to be heard. Only then will education begin to improve, for we must have understanding.

Specimen Paper 6

LEARNING LIFE "ON THE JOB"

If you want to learn about life, work for a while as a clerk in a department store. I spent nine months as a clerk in one of the biggest department stores in Kansas City. I worked the "Notions" counter.

From my experience I would not want to state that people are all good or all bad. They are neither. Many times I was shocked to see young boys of ten years of age learning to shoplift some items which maybe an older sister could satisfactorily use but not them. Customers, just like people in other situations, can be nice. I particularly enjoyed saying "hello" to the "regulars."

This type of job can be an eye opener. It surely was for me. Some people became regular customers with happy and warm greetings. Others became regular shoplifters with a run to the phone to call a detective. I certainly did learn more about the world and more about its inhabitants.

But this job was very rewarding and a good builder in human relations. I truly believe that in order to really appreciate the people around you, you must have the experience of actually trying to understand people for what they are--people with hearts, feelings, minds, etc. It took one year practically of hard work and effort to build something inside me that I hope I never lose. I feel I have developed a love for mankind that has filled an empty place in my heart.

Specimen Paper 7

BLACK NATIONALISM

Most white people equate black nationalism with black militancy, but they are mistaken. Black nationalism means no more than it is, an effort by black people in this country to reestablish their identity.

The true black identity was lost during the centuries of slavery. Black people, unlike white immigrants, did not choose to come to America; they were forced to. Once here, they were treated as animals--valuable animals sometimes, but animals nonetheless. Families were broken, traditions were severed, and all semblance of racial identity or memory was lost.

Even after slavery was ended, black people were subjected to oppression of all kinds. Kept from good schools and good jobs, kept from any kind of social or economic advancement, the "ideal" black person became the one who was as "white" as possible. Taught to despise the remnants of heritage that remained to them, black people had no alternative but to think that the only way was to become "white"--so they straightened their hair, bleached their skin, adopted "white" aspirations, and looked down on their black brothers.

Today, the black man has learned to value himself for what he is. He is determined to help himself and his black brothers by reforging the cultural links that were broken over the centuries. He is beginning to learn about and understand his African heritage and, more important, to value it. He wants to learn more about black literature and music. He wants to see black people's destiny shaped by black people. In short, he wants to develop his identity and to be what he can become.

Specimen Paper 8

WOMEN DRIVERS

The other day as I was driving along Green Street I happened to get behind a woman driver. I followed her for a few blocks and since the traffic was heavy that day I could not pass her. There I was stuck behind her with the worst yet to come. Then I noticed that her turn signal was on for a right turn and her arm was out for a left turn. I didn't know what she was going to do. As I approached the corner, I waited to see what her next move would be; she went straight ahead. I guess she was drying her nail polish while conducting calisthenics for her turn signal.

Another incident, rather accident, that I happened to observe was when an aunt of a friend of mine was trying to back out of a parking space. She was parked with the front bumper against the curb rather than in the legal way for this town with the side of the car to the curb. The car had an automatic transmission, and when the lady pulled down the gearshift lever for reverse she was looking backwards and didn't notice that the lever stopped at low instead of at reverse. She then tramped on the accelerator, and the car went bounding up over the curb, knocking over a parking meter and smashing into the side of the adjoining bank building. What a way to rob a bank!

Now I realize that these are only two incidents to illustrate my thesis, but they are so typical and there are so many others that I could give, that I think they will suffice. A woman behind the wheel of an automobile is not to be trusted, not merely because she doesn't have the proper awareness of the mechanical monster she is sitting in, but also because she won't pay attention to what she's doing.

'' W H O L E   C O M P O S I T I O N ''   R E V I E W   E X E R C I S E
(Sections 31–32).

1. Study the tentative thesis statement and tentative outline below. Then
    write a more satisfactory thesis statement and make a complete (and
    formal) sentence outline.

    Tentative thesis statement: A large city is a better place to live than a
    small town.

    Tentative (rough) outline:

Bigger	Well known
Many more activities	Cultural services better
Location	Better library
Daily newspaper	More social activities
More stores and shops	Medical care better
Better schools	Organized athletics
Less prying by neighbors	More movie theaters
Better jobs available	Cleaner
Transportation to and from	Training available after high school
is better	More interesting people

2. Pick out one major section of the sentence outline you have just pre-
    pared and build at least one well-constructed paragraph around it.

Effective Sentences = EF

Every sentence is the result of a long probation [and] should read as if its author, had he held a plough instead of a pen, could have drawn a furrow deep and straight to the end.

—HENRY DAVID THOREAU

A sentence may be perfectly grammatical, logical, and clear and yet not be <u>effective</u>. Effective sentences do more than observe the requirements of grammar and the conventions of usage. They not only communicate simple facts and ideas; they also knit together a number of facts and ideas into more complex units of thought. They allow the writer who uses them skillfully to weave into the basic subject–verb–object pattern—the indispensable functional parts of the sentence—the modifiers that give interest, vitality, and fullness of meaning to his ideas. And the skillful use of sentences together, in carefully thought-out sequence, allows us to express even more exactly the meanings we have in mind.

Let us look at a sentence which Henry David Thoreau once wrote, explaining why he had left "civilized" life for two years:

> I went to the woods because I wished to live deliberately, to front only the essential facts of life, and see if I could not learn what it had to teach, and not, when I came to die, discover that I had not lived.

This is a well-written sentence; it is <u>clear</u>, <u>compact</u>, <u>effective</u>. Why?

<u>First</u>, the sentence expresses a single thought (*I went to the woods because I wished to live deliberately*), on which all the other statements impinge directly—*front the essential facts, learn what it had to teach,* and *not discover that I had not lived.* The main thought is clear and consistently held to; the contributing details never obscure it. In short, the sentence has UNITY.

<u>Second</u>, the sentence is <u>continuously</u> clear; we always know where we are. The pronoun *it* refers clearly to *life* and links up the second half of the sentence with the first. The phrases beginning *to live* and *to front* are connected by a parallel grammatical construction. The transition *and* introduces an expansion of the main idea; yet the two parts of the sentence are closely tied by the relationship of the words *live* and *die, front* and *learn.* Because all parts of the sentence are clearly related, the sentence has COHERENCE.

<u>Third</u>, the parts of the sentence are arranged effectively. The principal idea, *I wished to live deliberately,* gets an emphatic position near the beginning. The least emphatic part of the sentence, the middle, is devoted to supplementary statements. The repetition of the main idea, with its effective balance of *die* and *not lived,* gets the most strategic position of all, the end of the sentence. And the words *not lived,* playing upon the literal and figurative meanings of *live,* provide a stylistic as well as an actual conclusion to the sentence.

Because the major ideas of the sentence stand out clearly, the sentence has EMPHASIS.

Sentences do not have to be as long and complex as this one to be effective. Each of the following sentences has the qualities of unity, coherence, and emphasis which make for effectiveness.

> Nothing can come out of the artist that is not in the man. —H. L. MENCKEN
>
> The world is a fine place and worth fighting for. —ERNEST HEMINGWAY
>
> A wise man does not try to hurry history. —ADLAI STEVENSON
>
> Woman's virtue is man's greatest invention. —CORNELIA OTIS SKINNER

Unity, coherence, and emphasis are useful terms when we discuss sentence effectiveness. The "rules" of effective sentence-writing on the succeeding pages are based on these terms. These "rules" will often tell you where your sentences go wrong. But if you think of them only negatively, you will miss their most important purpose. They are not only guides to avoiding weak and ineffective sentences but also guides to constructing strong and effective ones. Only through controlling subordination and coordination, parallelism, and sentence variety can we construct mature sentences that are unified, coherent, and emphatic. Effectiveness is not merely a mechanical matter achieved by avoiding certain "errors." It is an active welding of our thought to the means we have for expressing it. There is no way of divorcing the sentence from the idea it expresses. The two go hand in hand. To revise a clumsy sentence means, first, to rethink it and, second, to use wisely the means the language offers for stating it clearly for the reader.

EXERCISE 33. Analyze the following sentences as the Thoreau sentence was analyzed above.

1. Humanity has but three great enemies: fever, famine, and war; of these by far the greatest, by far the most terrible, is fever.
   —SIR WILLIAM OSLER

2. Work consists of whatever a body is *obliged* to do, and Play consists of whatever a body is not obliged to do. —MARK TWAIN

3. Eternal truths will be neither true nor eternal unless they have fresh meaning for every new social situation.
   —FRANKLIN DELANO ROOSEVELT

4. The proper study of mankind is woman, and, by common consent since the time of Adam, it is the most complex and arduous.
   —HENRY ADAMS

5. A foolish consistency is the hobgoblin of little minds, adored by little statesmen and philosophers and divines. —RALPH WALDO EMERSON

6. He that hath wife and children hath given hostages to fortune; for they are impediments to great enterprises, either of virtue or mischief.
—FRANCIS BACON

7. Man is but a reed, the weakest in nature, but he is a thinking reed.
—BLAISE PASCAL

8. In the practical as in the theoretic life, the man whose acquisitions *stick* is the man who is always achieving and advancing, whilst his neighbors, spending most of their time relearning what they once · knew but have forgotten, simply hold their own. —WILLIAM JAMES

9. Farmers are interested in science, in modern methods, and in theory, but they are not easily thrown off balance and they maintain a healthy suspicion of book learning and of the shenanigans of biologists, chemists, geneticists, and other late-rising students of farm practice and management. —E. B. WHITE

10. Here, more than anywhere else in the world, the daily panorama of human existence—the unending procession of governmental extortions and chicaneries, of commercial brigandages and throat-slittings, of theological buffooneries, of aesthetic ribaldries, of legal swindles and harlotries—is so inordinately extravagant, so perfectly brought up to the highest conceivable amperage, that only the man who was born with a petrified diaphragm can fail to go to bed every night grinning from ear to ear, and awake every morning with the eager, unflagging expectation of a Sunday-school superintendent touring the Paris peepshows. —H. L. MENCKEN

33 Subordination = SUB

A mature sentence brings together several ideas, which it relates one to another through either COORDINATION or SUBORDINATION. Words and larger constructions joined by *and, but, or,* and other coordinating words are said to be <u>grammatically coordinate</u>. Words, phrases, and whole sentences which have the same construction are also coordinate. Constructions which are <u>gram</u>-

matically coordinate are usually felt by a reader to be coordinate in meaning as well, that is, of equal value or weight. Modifying words, phrases, and clauses, on the other hand, are grammatically subordinate. Constructions which are grammatically subordinate, though they are frequently vital to the full meaning of a sentence, are felt to be of lesser importance in the total meaning. The principle works both ways, for the reader expects ideas which seem logically of equal value in meaning to be placed in coordinate grammatical form, and ideas which seem to be of lesser importance to be placed in subordinate grammatical form.

Some sentences have two or more main ideas which are coordinate. Some have one dominant idea, combined with others of lesser significance. The majority combine one or more ideas of equal rank with a variety of lesser ideas. Mature writing requires all these forms. It therefore requires the proper use of coordination and subordination so that major and minor ideas can be marshaled into clear and coherent units of thought.

33a **Do not use coordinating conjunctions to join subordinate or unrelated ideas to the main clause.**

Coordinating conjunctions such as *and* should be used to join only words and ideas that are logically coordinate. If you use them to join a logically subordinate idea to a main clause, the resulting sentence will be inexact and poorly unified.

INEXACT	Sometimes violent storms arose and then the workers sought shelter in the huts.
REVISED	When violent storms arose, the workers sought shelter in the huts.
REVISED	Because violent storms sometimes arose, the workers sought shelter in the huts.
INEXACT	The treaty was signed at Panmunjon in 1953, and Korea was still not a united country.
REVISED	After the treaty was signed at Panmunjon in 1953, Korea was still not a united country.
REVISED	Although the treaty was signed at Panmunjon in 1953, Korea was still not a united country.
UNRELATED	My Uncle Bert was a golf instructor and moved here from New Mexico in 1959.
REVISED	My Uncle Bert, a golf instructor, moved here from New Mexico in 1959.
REVISED	My Uncle Bert, who moved here from New Mexico in 1959, was a golf instructor.

Notice that in each of the above examples, there is more than one possible revision. In the first two examples, the alternate revisions indicate different kinds of relations between the subordinate and the main clause. In the third, the alternate revisions subordinate different information. All the revisions bring what were two main clauses in the original sentences into more exact and unified relation to each other.

33b **Do not omit logical steps that seem evident to you but may not to the reader.**

UNRELATED   He was in the army, but he didn't have enough money to finish college.

REVISED   Although his service in the army entitled him to some schooling under the GI Bill, he didn't have enough money to finish college.

33c **Do not string out a series of miscellaneous facts as though they were all of equal importance.**

"Light-Horse Harry" Lee lived from 1756 to 1818 and was an officer in the Revolutionary War. His army was responsible for quelling the Whiskey Rebellion in Pennsylvania, and he also served his country as governor of Virginia and as a member of Congress. It was "Light-Horse Harry" who described Washington as "first in war, first in peace, and first in the hearts of his countrymen," and was the father of Robert E. Lee.

There is usually little reason for such a collection of ill-assorted facts except in a reference book. However, if you feel that they are necessary, be sure that you subordinate the less important to the more important ones.

The author of the description of Washington as "first in war, first in peace, and first in the hearts of his countrymen," was "Light-Horse Harry" Lee, father of Robert E. Lee. "Light-Horse Harry," having made a reputation as an officer in the Revolutionary War, later became governor of Virginia and led the army which quelled the Whiskey Rebellion.

33d **Do not use a coordinate conjunction to join items that are not logically of the same kind.**

Coordination implies logical equality. When items which are not logically of the same kind or class are joined, the result is confusing.

CONFUSING   Entered in the pet show were several dogs, a parrot, a monkey, and one rather mangy cocker spaniel. (The *mangy cocker spaniel* clearly belongs among the dogs, but the construction

of the sentence makes it appear that there are four classes
of things. There are only three classes: dogs, a parrot, and
a monkey.)

REVISED   Entered in the pet show were a parrot, a monkey, and
several dogs, one of which was a rather mangy cocker
spaniel.

EXERCISE 33a-d. Revise those sentences below that contain
faulty coordination.

1. The town was lax in its collection of taxes, and the sanitation department was unable to collect garbage frequently enough.
2. I was tired and the rain was increasing, but I did not seek shelter.
3. It began to snow, and we prepared our skis and ski poles.
4. Biologists are concerned with new sources of food for the ever-
   growing world population, and they are studying better methods of
   farming the ocean's fish and plant life.
5. The laser creates a powerful ray, and scientists find that it can accommodate twenty television channels or 20,000 telephone circuits.
6. We now have "eye banks" and "blood banks" and, with medical
   research's constant progress, we may someday have "kidney banks."
7. I enjoy any kind of spectator sport, whether it is baseball, football,
   or hockey.
8. The municipal business district of large cities is congested, and
   many stores open branches in suburban shopping centers that can
   be easily reached by automobile.
9. Fresh water is a worldwide problem and many countries are developing methods of converting salt water from the ocean and inland
   sources into fresh water.
10. Hitler would not listen to the advice of his generals and finally they
    conspired in a plot to assassinate him which failed.

33e Do not put the principal idea of a sentence in a subordinate construction.

In many sentences, determining which ideas to place in a main
clause and which to subordinate depends entirely on context. In
one context, we may wish to write, *While Lincoln was still President,
he was shot,* thus emphasizing the assassination itself. In another, we
may wish to write, *When he was shot, Lincoln was still in office,* thereby
making more prominent the fact that he was still in office. There is
no way of determining aside from context which of these versions
is the better sentence.

But in many sentences, the logic of normal expectation works on
the reader. A sentence such as *He happened to glance at the sidewalk,
noticing a large diamond at his feet,* contradicts our sense of the relative
importance of glancing at the sidewalk and noticing a diamond.
Except in a very unusual situation, we would normally take the

finding of a diamond to be the logically more important fact and would expect the sentence to read *Happening to glance at the sidewalk, he noticed a large diamond at his feet.* Sentences which subordinate what we would normally expect to be more important ideas to lesser ideas are said to have "upside-down" subordination.

INEFFECTIVE	The octopus momentarily released its grip, when the diver escaped.
REVISED	When the octopus momentarily released its grip, the diver escaped.
INEFFECTIVE	He was playing his first major league game, being a better first baseman than some who had been playing for years.
REVISED	Although he was playing his first major league game, he was a better first baseman than some who had been playing for years.
INEFFECTIVE	I visited my home town after being away twenty years, when I was astonished at the change in its appearance.
REVISED	When I visited my home town after being away twenty years, I was astonished at the change in its appearance.
REVISED	After being away twenty years, I visited my home town and was astonished at the change in its appearance.

EXERCISE 33e. Where necessary, improve the following sentences by putting principal ideas in main clauses and by subordinating lesser ideas.

1. Mr. James turned on the sprinkler when he noticed that the grass was brown.
2. She pulled the emergency cord, averting a train wreck.
3. He practiced the violin diligently, winning the national contest.
4. He had nearly arrived at his destination when he discovered he had forgotten his wallet and turned back.
5. In 1968, Senator Eugene McCarthy made a bid for the Democratic nomination, losing finally to Vice-President Hubert Humphrey.
6. After the publication of Ralph Nader's *Unsafe at Any Speed,* public pressure was brought to bear on car manufacturers.
7. Although she was trying to economize, she decided to take a taxi, being already late for her dental appointment.
8. According to the popular ballad, Casey Jones attempted to arrive on schedule, being prevented by a head-on collision with another train.
9. William H. Vanderbilt, who once said "The public be damned," indicated by that statement the attitude which characterized the maneuvers that had made his father Cornelius and himself rich.

10.   The World Health Organization is interested in preventing blindness and is working in particular on trachoma, a virus disease that causes blindness, since trachoma is prevalent in more than 90 percent of the rural population of some North African countries.

33f   **Avoid the "primer style" unless you want to achieve a specific effect.**

The primer style consists of a series of short, simple sentences of similar structure (e.g., subject is followed immediately by predicate, clauses are joined by *and*). (See "Variety," Section 34.) This style tends to give all actions and ideas equal weight and importance, and makes your writing seem monotonous and choppy. Although skilled narrative writers sometimes use the primer style deliberately and effectively, beginning writers will do well to avoid it.

CHOPPY   He stood on a street corner. The wind was blowing. He peered into the darkness. He was a stranger. He realized that he had no place to go.

REVISED   Standing on a windy street corner and peering into the darkness, the stranger realized that he had no place to go.

CHOPPY   A plane far off broke the sound barrier. Several windows on the avenue were shattered. The landlords were angry. They complained to the authorities.

REVISED   When several windows on the avenue were shattered by a distant plane breaking the sound barrier, the angry landlords complained to the authorities.

Joining a series of short clauses by *and* to make them into a longer sentence only compounds the error of the primer style.

And SENTENCE   We approached the river and we looked down from the bluff, and we could see the silvery stream and it wound below in the valley.

REVISED   When we approached the river and looked down from the bluff, we could see the silvery stream winding below in the valley.

EXERCISE 33f.   Which of the following groups of sentences are effective as they stand? Revise those that could be improved by subordination.

1.   It was dawn. The birds were singing. And suddenly it was good to be alive.
2.   I tried my best. I flunked the course. Now I'll have to take it over again.

3. The bookshelves were too expensive. I went to a lumber yard. I bought some shelves. I bought brackets for the shelves. I put them up myself.

4. They had him trapped in an alley. A shot rang out. The boy crumpled to the ground.

5. The traffic was heavy. We tried to turn off the highway. We thought we might move faster on one of the side roads.

6. They bought a trailer. The whole family liked to go camping. Any kind of travel would be cheaper with the trailer.

7. The new library was finished. But so was the money. There were no books to put on the shelves.

8. Some skindivers planned an outing and they went to an island off the Bahamas and some sharks attacked them, and one member of the group suffered severe lacerations of the right leg.

9. The professor was lecturing and he was talking too fast and so the students found it difficult to take notes.

10. He had served in the Peace Corps for two years and when he came back he decided to go back to school and qualify for a master's degree in social work.

33g Do not overload sentences with excessive subordination.

Unessential details in your sentences make your reader lose sight of the points you are trying to make.

EXCESSIVE
SUBORDINATION

My fishing equipment includes a casting rod *which Uncle Henry gave me many years ago* and which is nearly worn out, and an assortment of lines, hooks, and bass flies, which make good bait *when I can get time off from work to go bass fishing* at Hardwood Lake.

REVISED

My fishing equipment includes an old casting rod and an assortment of lines, hooks, and bass flies. The flies make good bait when I am bass fishing at Hardwood Lake.

In the particular ineffective kind of construction that is called the "house-that-Jack-built" sentence, one dependent clause is tacked on after another, each seeming to be an afterthought:

The heroine thought the hero was a gambler while he was really a government agent who was investigating the income tax frauds of gamblers who concealed the larger part of their winnings which they took in violation of laws of the state which would arrest them if they made their activity public, which is why she wouldn't marry him, which is why I was disgusted with the movie.

EXERCISE 33g. Revise the following sentences by eliminating excessive details and subordination.

1. Having little time and less energy, I decided that, for the time being at least, my desk would have to remain in its untidy state.

2. The master of ceremonies then introduced to the delegates, who were having their annual meeting at the Biltmore Hotel, which is located in New York City, Senator George Murphy, calling to their attention that Senator Murphy, before going into politics, had starred in many Hollywood musicals.

3. Prince Charles, who had studied in Scotland and Australia, was then enrolled in Cambridge University, from which he took a two-month leave of absence to study Welsh in Wales in preparation for his investiture as Prince of Wales.

4. The reporters, many of them wearing their presscards pinned to their lapels, flocked to the launch site, where the technicians were giving a last check to the spaceship that was to carry three astronauts, who were just then walking up the ramp, to the moon.

5. Muhammad Ali, who began his career under the name of Cassius Clay, said that he would resist induction into military service on the grounds that he was an ordained minister of the Muslims, a religious group he had joined shortly after he won the heavyweight championship of the world, which became his after his fight with Sonny Liston.

6. The students, angered by the reaction of the university administrators who, after having given several weeks to the consideration of the list of demands, had summarily rejected every item on the list, decided that, all other alternatives being exhausted, they would go on strike.

7. My sports car, which I bought from a friend of mine, a car enthusiast who buys old cars and then rebuilds them as a hobby, has developed a rumble in the engine which has begun to worry me for I know nothing about repairing cars and haven't the money to go to a mechanic.

8. Some psychiatrists, interested in the effects of mass media on social behavior, have discovered that television, with its overwhelming emphasis on violence, is harmful for young children, especially those between the ages of three and five, because it leads these children to equate violence with "good" men and acceptable behavior.

9. Gazing down the small-town street where I had played every afternoon in the days when I visited Grandmother during my summer vacations from school, I caught sight of a little boy, the son of an old playmate of mine, trotting along with a fishing rod I had given his father all those years ago.

10. My chief ambition, formed in my childhood years when, a passionate reader, I became acquainted with the novels of Pearl Buck, which enlivened many a rainy afternoon and quiet weekend, has been to visit China.

33h **Use all connectives (***but, as, while,* **etc.) accurately and clearly.**

Careless use of such conjunctions as *and, as, but, so,* and *while* conceals the exact relationship or shade of meaning that you intend to convey.

1. *Do not use the conjunction* as *in sentences where it could imply either time or cause.*

AMBIGUOUS | As the river rose to flood stage, many people fled to higher ground. (Time or cause intended?)
REVISED | *When* the river rose to flood stage, many people fled to higher ground. (Time intended.)
REVISED | *Because* the river rose to flood stage, many people fled to higher ground. (Cause intended.)

2. *Do not use the conjunction* as *in the sense of* whether *or* that.

FAULTY | I do not know *as* I want to go tomorrow.
REVISED | I do not know *whether* (or *that*) I want to go tomorrow.

3. *Use the conjunction* but *to connect contrasted statements.*

FAULTY | He was an All-American in college, *and* today he is in poor physical condition.
REVISED | He was an All-American in college, *but* today he is in poor physical condition.

The misuse (intended, of course) of *but, and though,* and *under it all* in the sentence below shows how baffling an illogical transition can be.

[Pittsburgh millionaires] are rough but uncivil in their manners, and though their ways are boisterous and unpolished, under it all they have a great deal of impoliteness and discourtesy. —O. HENRY

4. *Do not use the preposition* like *as a substitute for the conjunctions* as if *or* as though *in formal writing.*

FORMAL | He looks *as if* (or *as though*) he were exhausted.
INFORMAL | He looks *like* he is exhausted.

5. *Do not use the conjunction* while *in the sense of* and *or* but.

INEFFECTIVE	John is a doctor, *while* Ray is an engineer.
REVISED	John is a doctor *and* Ray is an engineer.
INEFFECTIVE	Monday was a cool day, *while* Tuesday was warmer.
REVISED	Monday was a cool day, *but* Tuesday was warmer.

6. *Do not use the conjunction* while *in cases where it is not clear whether time or concession is intended.*

AMBIGUOUS	*While* I was working at night in the library, I saw Jane often. (Time or concession intended?)
REVISED	*When* I was working at night in the library, I saw Jane often. (Time intended.)
REVISED	*Although* I was working at night in the library, I saw Jane often. (Concession intended.)

EXERCISE 33h. In the following sentences replace any connectives that are used weakly or inaccurately.

1. While I was at school, I worked in my father's office.
2. As the air conditioning broke down, the manager closed the theater.
3. She decided to take Route 91 to New York, as she had taken it once before.
4. President Nixon did not know in 1964 as he ever wanted to run for office again.
5. While my cousin lived in another city, we would meet at holiday time at my grandmother's house.
6. I bought a new car and my old one was still running.
7. I won a National Merit Scholarship but I was very proud.
8. I don't know if I could act, as I have never tried.
9. I really don't feel like I should take the risk of going out in this weather—not with the cold I have.
10. She was dead tired, but she lay down to rest.

34 **Variety** = VAR

Variety in length and structure of our sentences helps us avoid monotony. But a series of well-written sentences is more than a mere absence of monotony. It reflects the careful molding of sentence form to the writer's thought, and the careful choice of sentence structure and length to gain emphasis where the writer wants it (see Section 36). A long series of sentences identical in structure and similar in length, unless they are consciously planned for coherence and emphasis, is not only tiresome and ineffective, but also symptomatic of muddy thinking.

34a   **Avoid the overuse of short simple sentences** (see "Subordination," Section 33f).

> INEFFECTIVE   Jack aproached the mare warily. She saw the bridle in his hand. He stood still. The mare waited. Jack tried to toss the reins over her head. But she galloped away.
>
> REVISED   Jack warily approached the mare, who saw the bridle in his hand. He stood still and the mare waited. But when he tried to toss the reins over her head, she galloped away.

EXERCISE 34a.   Revise the following sentences to avoid the overuse of short simple statements.

1. She decided to take the subway. She didn't know the way. She asked directions. The train agent was very helpful.
2. He had never smoked marijuana before. He was invited to a pot party. He went. Someone offered him a "reefer." He took it. The effect was not quite what he had expected. He didn't finish it. He left the party.
3. Joe DiMaggio was a great baseball player. He could hit. He could field. He could run. Even more important, he had style.
4. She wanted to go on the stage. She took acting lessons. She took dancing lessons. She practiced long hours. She waited for her big opportunity. Finally it came.
5. Hemingway perfected a unique style. He wrote in short sentences. They were very short. They could almost be called "terse." This gave his stories a very intense quality.
6. Late-night TV talk shows are very popular. The host is usually very funny. The guests are from many walks of life. Some of them are politicians. Some are show-business celebrities. They talk about various things. The mixture makes for interesting conversation.
7. TV documentaries are very interesting. One showed the plight of the migrant workers. Another showed conditions in the ghetto. Still another showed the helplessness of our neglected senior citizens. The one I like best was entitled "Birth and Death."
8. The candidate smiled at the reporters. He smoothed his hair. He fumbled in his pockets. He adjusted his glasses. He was obviously stalling for time. Finally he cleared his throat. He began to speak.

9. He had served in Vietnam. He was tired. He was sad. He had seen the face of war. He had seen the nature of suffering. He hoped he would never have to see either again.

10. I studied hard. I read the textbook. I read outside sources. I wrote a 15-page paper. I bought the instructor a Christmas present. I flunked the course.

34b **Avoid the overuse of long compound sentences** (see "Subordination," Section 33g).

INEFFECTIVE — The stagecoach rounded a bend, but two masked horsemen blocked the road, and they covered the driver with their rifles, and then they ordered him to raise his hands.

REVISED — As the stagecoach rounded a bend, two masked horsemen blocked the road. Covering the driver with their rifles, they ordered him to raise his hands. (In this revision the first coordinate clause is reduced to a subordinate clause; the third coordinate clause is reduced to a phrase; the second and fourth coordinate clauses become the main clauses of separate sentences.)

INEFFECTIVE — He was chief of the volunteer fire company, and he was the town's grocer, but he was never too busy in his store to attend a fire.

REVISED — The chief of the volunteer fire company, who was also the town's grocer, was never too busy in his store to attend a fire. (The first coordinate clause becomes a noun phrase, the subject of the main clause in the revised sentence; the second coordinate clause becomes a subordinate clause; the third coordinate clause becomes the predicate of the main clause.)

INEFFECTIVE — She carefully powdered her nose, and then she applied her lipstick, and then she smiled at her reflection in the mirror.

REVISED — She carefully powdered her nose, applied her lipstick, and then smiled at her reflection in the mirror. (The compound sentence is revised to make a simple sentence with a compound predicate.)

EXERCISE 34b. Revise the following sentences to avoid excessive or false coordination.

1. Parents of college students are upset over the amount of time their children spend demonstrating and protesting and arguing among themselves when they should be studying.

2. *Funny Girl,* which had a long run on Broadway, breaking many box-office records, was made into a movie starring Barbra Streisand.

3. He had a great deal of difficulty in studying French because he was not good at languages but he worked extra hard, often long into the night, because he wanted to impress his teacher and also stay out of the army.

4. I have a very small collection of records and I can't buy anymore, at least for the present because I spent all my money, which I had gotten as a Christmas gift, on a new speaker for the stereo I bought last year at a sale.

5. Several universities are becoming increasingly concerned over the young mothers who could contribute so much to our society but have been out of their fields while raising children and they are providing grants for them to do postgraduate work to catch up.

6. I had schemed and schemed to meet him at school and I never could seem to manage it and I never ran into him at parties but then one day I saw him at the Laundromat and I hurried home to get some dirty clothes and when I got back he was gone yet I have to go on and find another way of meeting him.

7. The halfback was the star of the team because after running the kickoff back for a touchdown, he recovered a fumble and on the next play passed thirty yards for a second touchdown, after which he kicked the extra point and won the crowd's wild approval.

8. He was very interested in politics and he joined his campus chapter of the Young Republicans but he was almost certain that he preferred teaching as a career.

9. They had set off on their cross-country trip though they had only a few dollars among them but they planned to get jobs along the way and they weren't worried.

10. He had dropped out of high school but he decided to get a job and when he couldn't find one he decided to go back to school and later went on to college.

34c Use various sentence structures to avoid monotony and increase effectiveness.

It is easy to fall into monotonous and poorly controlled patterns of sentences. But effective variety can be achieved with relatively simple modifications of word order. Remember, however, that word order is closely associated with meaning and emphasis and that shifts in order will lend slightly different shades of meaning to the whole sentence. The decision about what if any variation to use in a particular context must depend upon the total meaning you wish to express and upon the relation of the individual sentence to the sentences that stand before and after (see Section 32 on "Paragraph Coherence"). The principal ways of varying sentences are outlined below.

1. *Vary the beginnings of sentences.** *

> *Deer* grazed peacefully in the valley and were unaware of the advancing hunter.

BEGINNING WITH A PREPOSITIONAL PHRASE
> *In the valley* the deer grazed peacefully and were unaware of the advancing hunter.

BEGINNING WITH A VERBAL PHRASE
> *Grazing peacefully,* the deer in the valley were unaware of the advancing hunter.

BEGINNING WITH AN EXPLETIVE
> *There* were deer grazing peacefully in the valley, unaware of the advancing hunter.

BEGINNING WITH A SUBORDINATE CLAUSE
> *As they grazed peacefully in the valley,* the deer were unaware of the advancing hunter.

BEGINNING WITH A COORDINATING CONJUNCTION
> *And* the deer, grazing peacefully in the valley, were unaware of the advancing hunter.

> *But* the deer, grazing peacefully in the valley, were unaware of the advancing hunter.

A sentence beginning with a coordinating conjunction usually depends for meaning on the preceding sentence.

2. *Vary the normal subject–verb–object pattern of sentences.* The subject–verb–object pattern of the English sentence is so strongly established that shifts in its order are likely to produce heavy emphasis. They must therefore be used with caution. Note the following:

SUBJECT–VERB	VERB–SUBJECT
Henry leaped over the hedge.	Over the hedge leaped Henry.
An empty bottle stood on the table.	On the table stood an empty bottle.

SUBJECT–VERB–OBJECT	OBJECT–SUBJECT–VERB
I never said that.	That I never said.
Helen adores Siamese cats.	Siamese cats Helen adores.

SUBJECT–VERB–COMPLEMENT	COMPLEMENT–SUBJECT–VERB
We shall never be wealthy.	Wealthy we shall never be.
Einstein was surely a genius.	A genius Einstein surely was.

* Note that slightly more than half the sentences in most good writing begin with the subject—a great deal more than any other structure. It is the exclusive or excessively heavy use of subject beginnings that should be avoided, not the frequent use.

3. *Vary the usual declarative statement by using interrogative or imperative sentences when it is effective to do so.*

INTERROGATIVE   What is a civilized man? By derivation of the word, he is one who lives and thinks in a city.

—BERNARD IDDINGS BELL

IMPERATIVE   Observations indicate that the different clusters of galaxies are constantly moving apart from each other. To illustrate by a homely analogy, think of a raisin cake baking in an oven.

EXERCISE 34c. Vary the beginning of each of the following sentences in three of the ways suggested above.

1. His head ached and his mouth felt dry and he knew his hangover had begun.
2. They wanted to dance and the record player was broken.
3. Nigeria seemed to be winning the war and Biafra found it difficult to gain recognition from other nations.
4. High school students read *Catcher in the Rye* and recognize in its hero a little of themselves.
5. He read history in his spare time and had become quite an expert on the eighteenth century.
6. They bought only old furniture which they refinished themselves, and were able to furnish their new home at relatively little cost.
7. He had heard that marijuana was not addictive and he longed to experiment with it himself.
8. The U.S. disapproved of the Communist regime and refused to recognize Red China.
9. Czechoslovakia had instituted some liberal reforms and it was invaded by Warsaw Pact countries.
10. The students promised that it would be an orderly demonstration, and the administration gave them permission to hold it.

EXERCISE 34(1). Revise the following paragraph by introducing greater variety in sentence structure.

Mark felt better as he slammed the front door. He did not even glance over his shoulder to see if his parents were watching him. He walked to a nearby park. He sat down on a bench. He knew why his parents had yelled at him. He didn't blame them. They had both worked hard at their restaurant to keep him in comfort. They wanted him to have the opportunities that they had missed. They wanted him to be a doctor. But he couldn't seem to concentrate at school. He wanted to sleep in class. He liked most of his teachers but he didn't really hear them. He brought home very poor marks. He wanted to work with automobiles. He didn't want to be a doctor. The smell of gasoline, the sound of the motor, the shine of the chrome all fascinated him. He would have to face them and tell them that he couldn't be something he didn't want to be. He delayed returning home to tell them and he did not look forward to the scene they would make and the lack of understanding they would show.

EXERCISE 34(2). Imitate the structures of the following sentences, preserving each grammatical part and keeping the emphasis the same, but substitute different ideas and different words for those given. You may, if you wish, use the prepositions, conjunctions, articles, and demonstratives used in the original sentence.

Example: The sentences immediately below are imitations of the sentences above that give instructions for this exercise. Look at the example sentences carefully and notice how they duplicate the patterns of verb forms, phrasing, punctuation, etc., of the originals. Then try writing similar imitations of the exercise sentences below.

Remember the days of your childhood, nursing each ancient wound and making old victories more glorious, but seek new wounds and new victories without hesitation. Memory can, when it chooses, deaden the spirit, the will, the intent, and the effectiveness needed for present action.

Pack the tobacco with your thumb, maintaining even pressure and making the surface flat, but avoid the tight pack or the loose one described in the last paragraph. A pipe will, when packed properly, give the taste, the even draw, the long smoke, and the contentment described by seasoned pipe-lovers.

Notice that you may supply or leave out modifying words when you need to. Your sentences need not be related to one another.

1. A sentence is a living thing. (*E.g.,* The heat wave was a withering experience.)
2. The good ones have neither too many nor too few parts.
3. And each part, like each organ of a living body, dies when cut off from the source of life.
4. A meaningless fragment shocks the reader as would a dissevered limb.
5. But that same fragment, performing its function in conjunction with the other organs of a good sentence, can be a thing of beauty.
6. Another quality which a sentence shares with an organism is flexibility.
7. With the energetic spurt of a strong verb, with the graceful gesture of an adjective or an adverb, with the persistence of a conjunction or the stubbornness of a noun, a sentence can adapt itself quickly to any demand.
8. Like any living thing, every sentence is a proud individual.

9. Although it is necessarily very much like its neighbors in all essentials, it has a life of its own to lead.
10. To conform mechanically to the structures of surrounding sentences would be an indignity to so capable an individual.
11. It might even be said that a sentence is not only a living organism but also a citizen in a community, its paragraph.
12. Two considerations, then, govern the way it is put together.
13. Its first duty is to do its job, as efficiently as possible, in the communicative work of the paragraph.
14. That every writer will make his sentences do this is taken for granted, but the good writer will, in addition, remember the second consideration.
15. He should be able to make each sentence live with harmony and distinction among the other citizens of the paragraph.

35 Parallelism = ‖

Parallel structure puts similar ideas into the same kinds of grammatical constructions. If one idea in a sentence is expressed by a phrase, other equal ideas should be expressed by phrases. If one idea is expressed by an infinitive, a gerund, or a clause, other equal ideas should be expressed by duplicate grammatical constructions. Parallelism helps make sentences grammatically clear by keeping elements of the same grammatical rank and function in the same kind of grammatical construction. But it is also an important device for organizing sentences, or groups of sentences, so as to emphasize their close relation in thought.

Suppose we are trying to get together our ideas about the things necessary for good writing, and that we have written the following in a first draft:

> Logical thinking is one of the things necessary for good writing. Good writers also have to organize their ideas coherently. And finally, anyone who wants to write well must express his ideas clearly.

If we look at this closely, we will see that *thinking, organizing,* and *expressing* are the main related processes we are talking about. Parallel structure can help us knit these together tightly and emphasize them clearly. Compare the following single sentence with our original three sentences:

Thinking logically,
organizing ideas coherently,
and are three requirements of good writing.
expressing ideas clearly

or:

Logical thought,
coherent organization,
and are the major ingredients of good writing.
clear expression

or:

Anyone who wishes to write well must learn
to think logically,
to organize ideas
  coherently,
and
to express them clearly.

Either of these three versions of our original first draft pulls our ideas together into a single economical unit and gives emphasis to the three major items we have in mind.

Notice how parallelism helps to keep the following sentences clear and to emphasize the relation between like ideas:

Strikes, though sometimes necessary, mean
loss of wages for workers,
interference with production
  for managers,
and
disruption of services
  for consumers.

Students can be successful if they
buy the assigned books,
do the required reading,
and
take careful notes.

Political language is designed
to make
lies sound truthful
and
murder respectable
and
to give an appearance of solidity to
  pure wind.

Note how parallelism can keep a complicated sentence from
getting out of hand, as in the following from Thomas Wolfe.

```
And always America is ‖ the place of deathless and enraptured
                          moments,
                        the eye   ‖ that    looked,
                        the mouth ‖ that ‖ smiled
                                         ‖ and
                                         ‖ vanished,

                        and
                        the word;
                        the stone,
                        the leaf,
                        the door   we  ‖ never found
                                       ‖ and
                                       ‖ never have forgotten.
```

Just as the judicious use of parallelism can be an aid to effective
sentences, violations of grammatically required parallelism can
throw the reader off and make for particularly ineffective sentences.
The following three sections call attention to three situations in
which we are most likely to violate required parallelism.

35a Use parallel structure for sentence elements joined by coordinating conjunctions.

For balance and smoothness in your writing let the structure
of the first of two or more coordinate elements set the pattern for
the structure of the remaining coordinate elements.

AWKWARD   She likes to sew and cooking.
PARALLEL   She likes to sew and cook.

AWKWARD   Sam is tall, with blue eyes, and has a congenial manner.
PARALLEL   Sam is tall, blue-eyed, and congenial.

NOTE: You may point up the parallel structure by repeating a
strategic word or words (see also "Emphasis," Section 36d).

AMBIGUOUS   He wants to write stories that describe the South and study
             the habits of the Creoles. (Stories that study the habit of the
             Creoles?)
REVISED   He wants *to* write stories that describe the South and *to*
             study the habits of the Creoles.

AMBIGUOUS   Mr. Gray helps his wife by cooking and ironing his own shirts.

REVISED   Mr. Gray helps his wife *by* cooking and *by* ironing his own shirts.

EXERCISE 35a. In the following sentences, express the coordinate ideas in parallel structure.

1. Smoking cigarettes may be almost as dangerous as to play Russian roulette.
2. The popularity of marijuana comes partly from the fact that it is forbidden and also because more young people want to escape reality.
3. We staggered out of the exam room and somehow the exam papers were turned in by us.
4. He bought a new automobile with automatic transmission and having power steering.
5. The student was told to obtain a transcript of his grades and that then he could appy for admission.
6. To be a good teacher, one must have patience, liking to help others, and to show an infinite capacity for learning.
7. The seminar room is 14 feet long and 10 feet in width.
8. The instructor insisted that everyone devise a paper topic, and that papers be completed within two weeks.
9. The play was powerful, shocking, and could not be easily understood.
10. The policeman told us to drive very slowly and that we should not put on our bright lights.

35b   **Avoid faulty parallelism with** *and who, and which.*

Do not use an *and who* or an *and which* clause in a sentence unless you have already used a parallel *who* or *which* clause.

FAULTY   We met Abner Fulton, a brilliant biologist and who is also an excellent pianist.

REVISED   We met Abner Fulton, who is a brilliant biologist and who is also an excellent pianist.

OR   We met Abner Fulton, who is both a brilliant biologist and an excellent pianist.

FAULTY   She likes a romantic novel with exciting action and which keeps her guessing.

REVISED   She likes a romantic novel which has exciting action and which keeps her guessing.

35c   **Use parallel constructions after correlatives.**

The correlatives are *either—or, neither—nor, not only—but also, both—and, whether—or.* When the correlatives *whether—or* are used, *or* is often followed by *not*. (I wondered *whether* he would come or *not*.) In such sentences of course a parallel construction is unnecessary.

FAULTY   You are either *late* or *I am early*. (An adjective made parallel with a clause.)

REVISED   Either *you are late* or *I am early*. (Two parallel clauses.)

FAULTY   Jim not only *has been* outstanding in athletics, but also *in* his studies. (A verb made parallel with a preposition.)

REVISED   Jim has been outstanding not only *in athletics*, but also *in his studies*. (Two parallel phrases.)

EXERCISE 35c.   Correct the faulty use of correlatives in the following sentences.

1. Not only does the press besiege the President, but also all members of Congress.
2. That's either his wife or I'm mistaken.
3. He was both taller and talked a lot more than I liked.
4. A good politician not only works well with people but also he does not compromise his ideals.
5. She had both long hair and was very charming.
6. But she was neither beautiful nor did I find her clothes very tasteful.
7. Not only was Martin Luther King, Jr., an effective leader of men, but also he spoke extremely well.
8. The instructor both spoke slowly and he also spoke a lot more loudly than was necessary.
9. The snowplow operator was uncertain whether he should plow during the storm or to wait until it was over.
10. This exam is either too difficult or I didn't study enough.

36 Emphasis = EMP

Effective sentences are sentences that keep important ideas uppermost in the mind of the reader. The careful use of subordination, variety, and parallelism, all contribute to this end, helping to emphasize major ideas in relation to minor ideas. But we can also control emphasis by the position of sentence elements and by repeated words and ideas.

36a **Place important words at the beginning or at the end of the sentence.**

Generally, the most emphatic place in a sentence is its ending; the next most emphatic its beginning; the least emphatic, its middle.

WEAK	Such matters as incorrect spelling and unconventional punctuation sometimes distract a reader from otherwise good writing.
MORE EMPHATIC	Incorrect spelling and unconventional punctuation sometimes distract a reader from otherwise good writing.
WEAK	The history of English vocabulary is the history of English civilization, in many ways.
MORE EMPHATIC	The history of English vocabulary is, in many ways, the history of English civilization.

EXERCISE 36a. Revise the following sentences by putting important words in an emphatic position.

1. He is an overbearing, egotistical bore, in my opinion.
2. The results of the flood were disastrous, by and large.
3. Women are more perceptive and far more sensitive than men are, as a rule.
4. Tolstoy had a profound understanding of people and of the passions that drive them, for the most part.
5. This university would be closed and its faculty fired, if I had my way.
6. Teddy Roosevelt was dynamic and full of life, I have read.
7. Test results prove that smoking seriously impairs the health, in most cases.
8. The lawyer shirked his responsibility and the judge was biased, it seems to me.
9. The day was clear, the sun was shining, and the snow was packed hard; it was a great day for skiing, in my opinion.
10. With its superior technology and its single-minded determination, the U.S. will definitely win the space race, if everything goes right.

36b **Use the periodic sentence for emphasis.**

A PERIODIC SENTENCE withholds its main idea until the end; a LOOSE SENTENCE begins with the main idea and ends with subordinate details. A skillful periodic sentence is therefore dramatic; it creates suspense.

The English poor, broken in every revolt, bullied by every fashion, long despoiled of property, and now being despoiled of liberty, entered history

> with a noise of trumpets, and turned themselves in two years into one of
> the iron armies of the world. —G. W. CHESTERTON

Similarly in the following sentence: the main idea—i.e., praise of
the English jury system—is carefully (perhaps too obviously so)
withheld until the end.

> In my mind, he was guilty of no error, he was chargeable with no exag-
> geration, he was betrayed by his fancy into no metaphor, who once said
> that all we see about us, kings, lords, and commons, the whole machinery
> of the State, all the apparatus of the system, and its varied workings, end
> in simply bringing twelve good men into a box. —HENRY PETER

Notice how much more effective the periodic sentence is here:

PERIODIC   After he had stood for five minutes with his arms hanging
limply at his sides, a look of beaten humility on his face, the
cowboy suddenly reached for his gun and began firing at the
two outlaws.

LOOSE   The cowboy suddenly reached for his gun and began firing at
the two outlaws after he had stood for five minutes with his
arms hanging limply at his sides, a look of beaten humility
on his face.

Be careful, however, not to use the periodic sentence too often. Too
much suspense is wearying. The periodic sentence is effective only
when used judiciously—when the subject matter warrants it.

PERIODIC AND   At the end of a dark valley, three flights down in a dark
INEFFECTIVE   basement full of grim and evil-looking sailors, I ate my
lunch.

Often, the periodic and loose constructions are equally effective.

LOOSE   Balboa reached the Pacific after a long, hazardous journey.

PERIODIC   After a long, hazardous journey, Balboa reached the Pacific.

LOOSE   He will be a good physician, if enthusiasm is a guarantee of
success.

PERIODIC   If enthusiasm is a guarantee of success, he will be a good
physician.

EXERCISE 36b. Change these loose sentences into periodic ones.

1. The radio operator collapsed after staying up all day and night at
the wireless.

2. I saw two cars crash head-on several years ago on a three-lane highway in Minnesota.
3. She began seeing a psychiatrist regularly after her marriage broke up.
4. I plan to join the Peace Corps because I want to work with people after I graduate from college.
5. He started a new business and made a million dollars after his first business failed.
6. The wine turned to vinegar, although we tried to keep it in a cool place.
7. You will be very uncomfortable if you go camping without the proper equipment.
8. Her doctor insisted that she take a vacation after she suffered a severe depression.
9. They decided it was time to start a family, because he had finally found a good job.
10. Your research paper will be accepted if, after you have finished typing it, the footnotes are in good order.

36c **Be sure that all items in a series are in logical order as well as in parallel form.**

LOGICAL ORDER means using a natural or chronological sequence for the events you want to relate. Thus, you might say, *He ate his dinner, went to a movie, and then retired to his room.*

Logical order may sometimes refer to climactic order—that is, building up ideas in rising order of importance. Making the strongest and most striking idea come last is good rhetorical strategy.

UNEMPHATIC   His life was tragic and brief.
EMPHATIC   His life was brief and tragic.

Violation of this principle may result in unintentionally humorous anticlimax.

Madame, your dinner was superbly cooked, beautifully served, and very good, too.

Intentional anticlimax is a good, but very limited, technique for humor.

If once a man indulges himself in murder, very soon he comes to think little of robbery; and from robbing he next comes to drinking and Sabbath-breaking, and from that to incivility and procrastination.

—THOMAS DE QUINCEY

EXERCISE 36c. Revise the following sentences by aranging ideas in more logical order.

1. John is an "A" student, a four-letter athlete, and a member of the glee club.
2. Michael goes to school at night and works at two different jobs.
3. Most students get bored with school after years of college, high school, and elementary school.
4. She inherited a million dollars, a house, and some jewelry.
5. Jason is a fine craftsman, a famous lawyer, and a chess player.
6. The play closed after the first week and received terrible reviews.
7. During his vacation David acquired some souvenirs, a wife, and a bad sunburn.
8. The earthquake caused 100 deaths and toppled several of the buildings in the area.
9. Laurence Olivier is one of the great Shakespearean actors of all time and a director and producer as well.
10. He finally graduated with honors after almost being expelled in his sophomore year and getting suspended in his junior year.

36d Use effective repetition of words and ideas to achieve emphasis.

For a discussion of how words may be repeated to heighten clarity, see Section 41d; for a discussion of ways in which the repetition of words and ideas serves to link sentences together in a paragraph, see Section 32d. Effective repetition is chiefly a matter of repeating key phrases or constructions—in many respects a matter of effective parallelism (see Section 35a). For example, note how Dr. Johnson's *I like their* is effectively repeated in the sentence below.

> I am very fond of the company of ladies. I like their beauty, I like their delicacy, I like their vivacity and I like their silence.   —SAMUEL JOHNSON

The repetition of key constructions in the passage below might strike some modern readers as overly eloquent, but the passage does illustrate how repetition may be used, not only to give continuity to what is being said, but also to bring the reader (or listener) to a rhetorical climax.

> I would rather have been a French peasant and worn wooden shoes. I would rather have lived in a hut with a vine growing over the door and the grapes growing purple in the kisses of the Autumn sun. I would rather have been that poor peasant with my loving wife by my side, knitting as the day died out of the sky, with my children upon my knee and their arms about me. I would rather have been that man and gone down to the tongueless silence of the dreamless dust than to have been that imperial impersonation of force and murder known as Napoleon the Great.
>
> —ROBERT INGERSOLL

The more recent paragraph below, with its repetition of *curiosity* and its use of a repeated sentence pattern, makes clear that even in more informal contemporary writing such repetition is an effective device.

The world does not much like curiosity. The world says that curiosity killed the cat. The world dismisses curiosity by calling it idle, or *mere* idle, curiosity—even though curious persons are seldom idle. Parents do their best to extinguish curiosity in their children, because it makes life difficult to be faced every day with a string of unanswerable questions about what makes fire hot or why grass grows, or to have to halt junior's investigations before they end in explosion and sudden death. Children whose curiosity survives parental discipline and who manage to grow up before they blow up are invited to join the Yale faculty. Within the university they go on asking their questions and trying to find the answers. In the eyes of a scholar, that is mainly what a university is for. It is a place where the world's hostility to curiosity can be defied.
—EDMUND S. MORGAN, "What Every Yale Freshman Should Know"

EXERCISE 36d. Discuss the effectiveness of the repetition of words and phrases in each of the sentences below. (Note how frequently effective repetition and effective parallelism reinforce each other.)

1. No one can be perfectly free till all are free; no one can be perfectly moral till all are moral; no one can be perfectly happy till all are happy. —HERBERT SPENCER
2. There is no mistake; there has been no mistake; and there shall be no mistake. —DUKE OF WELLINGTON
3. To know how to say what others only know how to think is what makes men poets or sages; and to dare to say what others only dare to think makes men martyrs or reformers or both. —ELIZABETH CHARLES
4. It is true that you may fool all the people some of the time; you can even fool some of the people all the time; but you can't fool all of the people all the time. —ABRAHAM LINCOLN
5. We are always doing something for Posterity, but I would fain see Posterity do something for us. —JOSEPH ADDISON

36e **In general, for greater emphasis use the active rather than the passive voice.**

Because the active voice of the verb is strong and emphatic, expressing direct action of the subject, it naturally imparts a stronger tone to your writing. The passive voice, stressing the importance of the receiver rather than the doer of the action, is much less emphatic.

In choosing which voice to use, be guided by whether you want to emphasize the doer or the receiver of the action:

PASSIVE He *was struck* on the head by a foul ball.
ACTIVE A foul ball *struck* him on the head.

The first sentence emphasizes *who* was struck; the second sentence *what* struck him. But do not think that the active voice is *always* the more effective. Even though less emphatic, the passive of course has legitimate uses. The principal situations in which it is most natural and useful are:

1. *When the subject is not known.* Consider the following:

Peter L. Little was attacked and badly beaten while walking through Eastern Park about 11:15 last night.

The play was first performed in 1591.

In the first of these, since the writer presumably does not know who attacked Peter L. Little, he is forced to use the passive or to resort to some much less economical alternative such as *Some person or persons unknown attacked and badly beat.* . . . The second sentence suggests that though there is a record of the play's performance, there is none of its performers.

2. *When the receiver of the action is more important than the actor.* Consider the following:

The new bridge was completed in April.

The experiment was finished on June 16; on June 17 the conclusions were reviewed by the advisory board and reported immediately to the Pentagon.

In such sentences as these, we have little interest in who completed the bridge, or who performed the experiment and reported the results; the important things are the bridge and the experiment.

The passive voice is perhaps most common in technical and scientific writing, where it both enables the writer to maintain the impersonal tone appropriate to science, and often makes for stylistic economy in reporting complex matters. As an example, examine the use of the passive in the following paragraph.

Two solid white cubes are suspended on wires that are painted black so as to be invisible against a black background. One cube is about 3 feet from the observer and the other about 12 feet. The observer's head is in a headrest so positioned that the cubes are almost in line with each other but he can see both, the nearer cube being slightly to the right. A tiny metal shield is then placed a few inches in front of the left eye. It is just big enough to cut off the view of the far cube from the left eye. The result is that the near cube is seen with both eyes and the far cube with just the right eye. Under these conditions the observer can fix the position of the near cube very well, because he has available all the cues that come from the use of the two eyes. But in the case of the far cube seen with only one eye, localization is much more difficult and uncertain.

—W. H. ITTELSON and F. P. KILPATRICK, "Experiments in Perception"

Except in such special situations, the passive tends to weaken writing, as in the following:

During the morning the equator *was crossed* by the ship.

A tree *was crashed into* by a car going ninety miles an hour.

If you use very many "weak passive" sentences like those above, your writing will sound monotonous and your ideas will appear dull and lifeless.

EXERCISE 36e. In the following sentences replace the passive voice with the active.

1. The administration building was taken over by students.
2. Police procedures were scrutinized by the press.
3. My Easter outfit was made by my mother.
4. The government scandal was investigated by the Senate.
5. The space ship was checked by the ground crew.
6. The returned astronauts were interviewed by reporters.
7. The deer was shot by my younger brother.
8. The menu was selected by the chairman of the refreshments committee.
9. Many major accidents are caused by drunken drivers.
10. Polio vaccine is distributed by the local Department of Health.

"EFFECTIVE SENTENCES" REVIEW EXERCISE (Sections 33 through 36). Indicate what strikes you as the principal error from the standpoint of effectiveness in each of the following sentences (faulty subordination, lack of emphasis, lack of parallelism, etc.) and then revise the sentence.

1. The necklace was a beautiful and priceless Egyptian treasure and it was in a glass display case that was heavily guarded.
2. The cat was jumping from window ledge to window ledge when he suddenly lost his hold and dived to his death.
3. While Chekhov was the principal support of his family, he attended medical school and wrote short stories.
4. To make concrete you need cement. It should be of good quality. You also need sand. You should use twice as much sand as concrete.

Gravel is the third thing needed. About three times as much gravel as cement goes into concrete. The gravel should be clean. Do not mix it with soil or dirt.

5. The substitute teacher was a married woman with a good sense of humor and who loved science ardently and conveyed this to her classes.

6. To a naughty child, a scolding parent seems like a giant standing seven feet tall with a large mouth, and having eyes that glared in the dark.

7. After consulting with the contractor, Mrs. Moore decided on cypress for the outside of the house and the house was finally done in redwood.

8. The perfume was very strong and its scent remained with us even after she had left the room.

9. Cockfighting ranks as a popular sport in Spain, Latin America, and part of the Orient and it takes place in a pit and spectators place bets on their favorite gamecocks, but the sport is illegal in the United States.

10. Our love of Colonial arts and crafts is reflected in our homes and in our home magazines but our love of modern technological skills is also reflected in our homes and magazines.

11. Arizona has the largest United States Indian population and the Hopi, Navajo, and Apache are the names of the Indian tribes there.

12. To become a responsible voter you should know the issues. You should listen to the candidates. You should become familiar with their views. You should also learn their weaknesses. You should also come to know their strengths. Then you can make a wise choice.

13. The Soviet Union has been having some trouble with its satellites in Eastern Europe, and Rumania and Czechoslovakia are only two examples.

14. Rachel Carson wrote a great deal about the problems that arise when insecticide is used and she was vigorously opposed by insecticide companies and some people who find insecticides helpful but what about the people who have been poisoned by them?

15. The average college student today regards the government as a cold, impersonal entity, and having little concern for the disadvantaged.

16. After consulting with his instructor, John was able to choose a topic for his paper after changing his mind several times.

17. Harlem is reached by walking up Fifth Avenue, the most glamorous street in the richest city in the world, and it is infested with rats and disease.

18. Terror gripped the city of Boston when the Boston Strangler roamed free, and later a movie was made that recalled those days.

19. She decided to work hard, finish school, and then she would get married.

20. The space trip was an unqualified success, and the astronauts had been kept in seclusion for weeks before it to guard them against infection.

Logic = LOG

In answering he states the question, and expoundeth the terms
thereof. Otherwise the disputants shall end, where they ought to
have begun, in differences about words, and be barbarians each
to the other, speaking in a language neither understand.

—THOMAS FULLER (1642)

I come from a state that raises corn and cotton and cockleburs and
democrats, and frothy eloquence neither convinces nor satisfies me.
I am from Missouri. You have got to show me.

—WILLARD DUNCAN VANDIVER

*C*orrect grammatical structure is not an end in itself but a vehicle for communicating thought clearly. Clear and purposeful writing is fundamentally a reflection of logical thinking. People who complain "My ideas are good, but I can't express them clearly in writing" are usually fooling themselves. Vague and undirected writing reflects vague and undirected thinking.

The treatment of logic that follows is brief and oversimplified. Space permits a discussion of only those matters that have an obvious relationship to the writing process. For more detailed treatments, see:

Altick, Richard. *A Preface to Critical Reading.* 4th ed. New York: Holt, Rinehart & Winston, Inc., 1962.

Beardsley, Monroe C. *Thinking Straight.* 3rd ed. Englewood Cliffs, N.J.: Prentice-Hall, Inc., 1966.

Bilsky, Manuel. *Patterns of Argument.* 2nd ed. New York: Holt, Rinehart & Winston, Inc., 1963.

Black, Max. *Critical Thinking.* 2nd ed. Englewood Cliffs, N. J.: Prentice-Hall, Inc., 1952.

Chase, Stuart. *The Tyranny of Words.* New York: Harcourt, Brace and Company, 1939.

Cohen, Morris, and Ernest Nagel. *An Introduction to Logic and Scientific Method.* New York: Harcourt, Brace and Company, 1934.

Fearnside, W. Ward, and William B. Holther. *Fallacy: The Counterfeit of Argument.* Englewood Cliffs, N. J.: Prentice-Hall, Inc., 1959.

Harris, Robert T., and James L. Jarrett. *Language and Informal Logic.* New York: Longmans, Green and Co., 1956.

Hayakawa, S. I. *Language in Thought and Action.* 2nd ed. New York: Harcourt, Brace & World, Inc., 1964.

Johnson, Wendell. *People in Quandaries.* New York: Harper & Brothers, 1946.

37a   **Define terms whose exact meaning is essential to clear and logical communication.**

Clear-cut definition is a key feature of logical thinking and writing. Your reader must know how you define your terms before he can comprehend your meaning. Much senseless argument, in fact, arises because people fail to agree on meanings. Your writing will gain in strength and clarity if you are always sure to define important terms that you use. To do so you will need to understand the requirements of sound definition.

1. *Definition by word substitution.* To define *education* as *learning,* or *freedom* as *liberty* serves little purpose. But many times concrete terms can be quite satisfactorily defined merely by offering a synonym which the reader is likely to know. This is particularly true with technical or other little-known terms. An appositive construction is often useful for such a definition:

> the *cardiac muscle,* or principal heart muscle
> the *meerkat,* or South African mongoose
> *cannikin,* an old New England word for a wooden bucket

2. *Formal, or logical, definition.* Logic is the basis of all careful and precise definition. The steps in constructing a sound formal definition are as follows:

a. *In defining a term, first put it into the class of objects* (genus) *to which it belongs.* This process is called CLASSIFICATION.

TERM		GENUS
A saw	is	a *cutting tool.*
A carpet	is	a *floor covering.*

In general, the narrower the classification, the clearer the eventual definition.

NOT	A rifle is a *weapon.*
BUT	A rifle is a *firearm.*

Though *weapon* is a legitimate classification for *rifle,* for purposes of definition it includes more than is necessary (*knives, spears, bows and arrows, clubs,* etc.).

b. *Next, distinguish it from other objects in its class.* This process is called DIFFERENTIATION.

TERM		GENUS	DIFFERENTIATION
A saw	is	a *cutting tool*	*with a thin, flat blade and a series of teeth on the edge.*
A carpet	is	a *floor covering*	*of woven or felted fabric, usually tacked to the floor.*

c. *Use parallel form in stating the term to be defined and its definition.* Do not use the phrases *is when* or *is where* in making definitions.

NOT   A debate *is when* two people or sides argue a given proposition in a regulated discussion.

BUT   A *debate is a regulated discussion* of a given proposition between two matched sides.

d. *Be sure that the definition itself does not contain the name of the thing defined or any derivative of it.*   Nothing is achieved when words are defined in terms of themselves.

NOT   A rifle is a firearm with *rifling* inside its barrel to impart rotary motion to its projectile.

BUT   A rifle is a firearm with *spiral grooves* inside its barrel to impart rotary motion to its projectile.

Whenever possible, define a term in words that are more familiar than the term itself. The complexity of Dr. Samuel Johnson's definition of the simple word *network* is notorious:

> *Network:* anything reticulated or decussated, at equal distances, with interstices between the intersections.

Ordinarily, of course, you will define terms without being aware of giving them a genus and a differentiation. But it is always possible to check the logic of a definition against the criteria given above. Consider the following example from a student paper:

> Finally, college is valuable to a person interested in success. By *success* I don't mean what is usually thought of when that word is used. I mean achieving one's goals. Everybody has his own goals to achieve, all of them very different. But whatever they are, college will give one the know-how and the contacts he needs to achieve them successfully.

This definition is obviously unsatisfactory; but the specifications for logical definition will help clarify why and how it breaks down. If the statement which this paragraph makes about *success* is isolated, it comes out like this: *Success is the successful achievement of goals which know-how and contacts gained at college help one achieve.* First, this statement violates one of the basic principles of definition because it defines the word in terms of itself—*success is the successful achievement. . . .* Next, the writer does not make it clear what he means by *goals,* and the qualifying clause *which know-how and contacts gained at college help one achieve* does nothing to help us grasp his intended meaning because we do not know what his definition would be for *know-how* and *contacts.* Hence he has failed in both aspects of good definition. He has neither put the terms into an understandable genus nor made a real differentiation. What he says is that success means being successful, which is not a definition. Very likely the writer had no very clear idea of what he was talking about and so could not hope to communicate it to his readers.

3. *Extended definition.* A good many words, particularly abstract words like *propaganda, democracy, virtue, religion, freedom,* and *justice,* require considerably more than a formal definition if their meaning is to be very clear. We may define a *representative democracy,* for instance, as a *form of government in which political power resides in the people and is given by them to elected representatives.* That is a sound logical definition. But clearly democracy as we understand it in the United States will not be contained in such a sentence. Nor is a person unacquainted with the United States likely to derive much understanding of our government from such a definition. If we are going to clarify the meaning of the term for ourselves and others, we shall need to provide illustrations, to make comparisons not only with other forms of government but perhaps also with "democracy" as it exists in other countries, or as it has been used in the past. Such an expansion, or extension, of our basic formal definition is what we mean by EXTENDED DEFINITION. Extended definitions may be one paragraph long, or may take an entire article or even a book. The following paragraph illustrates a simple extended definition. (For further examples see pages 218–219.)

> *Wit* originally meant knowledge, wisdom, intelligence, judgment, sense, meanings which are retained in such phrases as *at one's wit's end, to live by one's wits, dull witted,* and so on. As a form of humor (in the broadest sense of *humor* as something funny) *wit* is an intellectual matter. It is often spontaneous and consists in discovering analogies between things really unlike and expressing these connections in diverting and amusing ways. Wit startles us. We may smile at humor, but we will either laugh or be angry at a piece of wit. It was witty of Sir Boyle Roche when Curran boasted that he was the guardian of his own honor to congratulate him upon his sinecure. Wit is aggressive and often cruel. The common term *a stroke of wit* is usually justified. He that *maketh others afraid of his wit,* says Bacon, *had need be afraid of others' memory.* —BERGEN and CORNELIA EVANS, *A Dictionary of Contemporary American Usage*

EXERCISE 37a. Discuss the validity of the sentences below <u>as definitions</u>. What revisions would you suggest for greater accuracy?

1. Education is gaining knowledge or skill through school.
2. A home run is where the runner touches all the bases.
3. A pot party is where everyone is smoking marijuana.

4. Participatory democracy is the involvement of the people in the daily workings of government.

5. Disengagement means each of the belligerents withdrawing its forces.

6. Housemaid's knee is a swelling due to the enlargement of the bursa in front of the patella.

7. Analysis means to break something down into its parts.

8. *Boeuf bourguignon* is just a fancy beef stew.

9. Passive resistance is when people simply refuse to follow orders.

10. "Home is the place where, when you have to go there, they have to take you in."

37b Support or qualify all generalizations.

A generalization is an assertion that what is true of several particulars (objects, experiences, people) of the same class (genus) is true of most or all of the particulars of that class. For example, the statement *Drinking coffee in the evening always keeps me awake all night* is a generalization based on several particular experiences on separate evenings. Generalization is an essential process in thinking; without it, there could be no evaluation of experience—only the accumulation of isolated facts. Yet generalization has its dangers, as the following examples reveal.

1. *Base all generalizations on adequate evidence.* We all tend to generalize on the basis of a few striking examples, especially when they accord with what we want to believe.

The hasty generalization—leaping to conclusions on the basis of insufficient evidence—is especially dangerous because it can lead you to make absurd assertions. Test the soundness of this generalization:

PARTICULAR A	My sister Imogene dented the car's fenders yesterday.
PARTICULAR B	Mrs. Elliot has just driven her car through the rear end of the garage.
PARTICULAR C	Did you see that woman drive through that red light!
HASTY GENERALIZATION	Women can't drive.

To protect yourself, as well as to be fair to your readers, never advance a generalization unless you are prepared to support it with ample evidence. How much evidence you need depends on the purpose of your writing. Sometimes you will need to list only three or four examples; sometimes you will need to analyze the evidence itself in detail. Generalizations often take the form of topic sentences in paragraphs (see "Paragraphs," Section 32a).

2. *Be cautious in using such words as* always, never, all, none, right, wrong *in generalizations.* Broad generalizations are as pernicious as hasty generalizations. In fact, the two usually spring from the same desire—to reach a conclusion without going through the effort of collecting evidence. A valid generalization is often rendered invalid by the careless use of *never* instead of *seldom,* of *always* instead of *usually.*

OVERSTATED   People who are excessively radical in their youth always become conservative when they acquire power and property.

QUALIFIED   Even the most radical youths are likely to grow conservative when they acquire power and property.

EXERCISE 37b. Discuss the validity of the following sentences <u>as</u> generalizations. Restate those that seem exaggerated.

1. Any candidate who is honest cannot fail to win.
2. It is clearly impossible for any intelligent man to believe in religion in the twentieth century.
3. People who can't succeed in anything else go into teaching.
4. Women are more emotional than men.
5. A college degree increases one's earning power.
6. A good book is one that's easy to read.
7. A good teacher is one who gives easy exams.
8. A Communist is a person who's always finding fault with our government.
9. Anyone who gets to be head of a large corporation has to be ruthless and materialistic.
10. Any intelligent person realizes that birth control information should be disseminated by the government.

37c   **Base your arguments on honest evidence and present them fairly.**

Consciously or unconsciously, in our desire to be right, we tend to falsify, suppress evidence, call names, cheat, and hit below the belt in our arguments.

1. *Base your judgment on what you know, not on what you want to believe.* Prejudice (PREJUDGMENT, or judgment before the facts are examined) is the commonest type of unfairness. Notice in the examples below that a judgment is passed although no facts pertinent to that judgment have been stated.

I heard that he didn't get in until 3 A.M. last night, *and you can bet that he was spending his time in some cheap saloon.*

Did you hear what Peggy said about her? *It's our duty to ask her to resign from the club immediately.*

2. *Do not try to dismiss an argument or an opponent by appealing to general prejudice.*   If we are to argue soundly and fairly we must try to examine the issues in question, and to appeal to reason. Arguments which divert attention from the actual question by trying to appeal to the prejudices and emotions of the audience may succeed. But at best they do so at the expense of avoiding the real questions, and at worst by being irresponsible and dishonest.

Many appeals to emotion and prejudice make use of the connotations of words (see Section 40). Today, for example, words like *radical, fascist,* and *long-hair* can be counted on to bring an unfavorable response from many audiences. Words like *faith, democratic tradition, freedom,* and *efficiency* can be counted on to bring favorable responses from most audiences. The calculated—or careless—use of such words therefore tends to evoke an emotional rather than a reasonable response.

Much irresponsible argument consciously or unconsciously relies on such words. Candidate Jones is thus described as standing for "free, honest, and effective government," a description which leaves us with a pleasurable feeling that Jones is the right man for the job, but with no specific information about what programs he will or will not support. If, in contrast, Candidate Smith is described to us as "a radical with strong leftish ideas" we are likely to end up voting for Candidate Jones without ever having the faintest idea whether either Jones or Smith supports lower or higher taxes, slum clearance, or funds for new roads—all of which are questions we are vitally interested in.

a. *Do not sidestep an argument by trying to discredit the man who proposed it.*   This is known as ARGUMENT TO THE MAN (*argumentum ad hominem*). It fails to take into account that even though discredited for one thing, the man might be right about others.

> He has no business talking about the responsibilities of a democracy, *because he has just got out of jail.*
>
> Don't pay any attention to what Milton says about divorce. *He just couldn't get along with his wife.*

b. *Do not associate an idea with a great name or movement in the hope of imbuing your idea with borrowed prestige.*   This is the erroneous technique of TRANSFER (*argumentum ad verecundiam*). This method usually involves associating an idea with a great name or movement (or, particularly, with an attractive face or figure, as in advertising) in the hope that its prestige or glamour will be transferred to the proposal being argued. The transfer device also works in reverse: If a proposal or person can be associated with a movement or name in general disfavor (communism, economic-royalism, and so on), it or he has very little chance of being objectively and logically judged. The technique clouds the issue, for the associations made usually have no real bearing on the conclusions drawn.

> If Abraham Lincoln were alive today, I am sure he would devote his full energies to seeing our policy made the law of the land.
>
> She's lovely! She's engaged! She uses X!
>
> He believes in a high income tax, just as do the Marxists.

c. *Do not sidestep an argument by appealing to the instincts and ideas of the crowd.* This is known as ARGUMENT TO THE PEOPLE (*argumentum ad populum*) or the "bandwagon" approach. It assumes that what the crowd thinks or believes is right. Thus, to be right, one must go along with the crowd. Obviously this is not true, as many incidents of mob rule would bear out. Nonetheless it is a favorite approach among advertisers, who are masters of this appeal:

> Drink X! For 75 years *it has been the favorite drink of the man in the street. You'll like it too.*
>
> Decent, upright citizens will not be interested in anything he says.

EXERCISE 37c. Discuss the "fairness" of the statements below.

1. How can movie stars have happy marriages? They're too good-looking.
2. Just as an individual would be in trouble if he spent more than he earned, so must the government keep its expenditures in line with its revenue.
3. It says in the Bible that a woman taken in adultery must be stoned to death, and what was good enough for the Bible is good enough for us.
4. The reason that Congress doesn't investigate corruption is that the members of Congress are themselves corrupt.
5. How can Mr. Barry be a competent philosophy teacher? It is clear that he is a complete atheist.
6. What's wrong with our college students today is that they are pampered children.
7. He knew how to run the lathe, but I didn't hire him because he spent a year in reform school and once a criminal always a criminal.
8. The French take advantage of tourists; the Paris hotel I stayed at padded my bill.
9. Black people are born with a natural sense of rhythm.
10. Draft resisters are just afraid to die for their country.

37d **Be sure that statements involving cause-and-effect relationships are
logically sound.**

Some of the defects of thinking arise not from prejudice, unfairness, or ignorance of the facts, but from lack of training in logical
processes. The two major logical processes are induction and
deduction.

In the process of INDUCTION thinking proceeds from the particular to the general. This means, for example, that when particular facts are shown time after time to be true, or when a particular laboratory experiment time after time yields the same result,
or when a wide and varied sampling of people gives the same type
of answer to a given question, <u>then</u> a general conclusion based on
the facts in question may be drawn. Repeated experimentation and
testing led to the conclusion that the Salk vaccine would help
prevent polio. The scientist uses induction when he tests and retests
his hypothesis before stating it as a general truth. The whole "scientific method" proceeds by inductive processes.

In the process of DEDUCTION thinking proceeds from the general
to the particular. This means that from a general conclusion other
facts are deduced. Obviously, then, if deduction is to be valid, the
conclusion from which you operate must be true. Given sound and
valid conclusions from which to draw, deduction is a shrewd and
effective logical technique. Knowing that penicillin is an effective
weapon against infection, we wisely seek a doctor to administer it
to us if we have infections.

Notice that there is an induction–deduction cycle of reasoning.
The sound conclusions reached through induction may in turn
serve as the bases for deduction. For example, over many years the
National Safety Council has kept careful records of holiday highway accidents and has reached the valid conclusion that accidents
increase greatly on holiday week ends. From this conclusion, you
can deduce that it is safer not to travel on holiday week ends.

The intricacies of induction and deduction as systems of logic
would take many pages to explore. The foregoing is designed merely
to give a working definition of each, from which we can now proceed to examine a few of the most common errors in logic.

1. *Do not assume that there is a cause-and-effect relationship between
two facts merely because one follows the other in time.* This fallacy is
known as *post hoc, ergo propter hoc* ("after this, therefore because of
this").

Industrialism was not established until after the Protestant Revolution;
therefore Protestantism was the cause of industrialism.

I won't say she's to blame, but I do know that he didn't drink before he married her.

2. *Do not mistake a mere inference for a logically sound conclusion.* This fallacy is known as *non sequitur* ("it does not follow").

This is the best play I have seen this year and should win the Pulitzer Prize.

(Have you seen *all* the plays produced this year? Are you qualified to judge the qualities that make a Pultizer Prize play? Does it follow that just because a play is the best you have seen this year, it should therefore win the Pulitzer Prize?)

Steven will never get anywhere; he's got his head in the clouds.

3. *Do not assume the truth of something you are trying to prove.* This fallacy is known as BEGGING THE QUESTION.

His handwriting is hard to read because it is almost illegible.

I like Buicks because they are my favorite automobiles.

I don't care what he's done; if he's in jail he's done *something* wrong. Good people don't go to jail.

4. *Do not assume that because two circumstances or ideas are alike in some respects, they are alike in all other respects.* This is the fallacy of FALSE ANALOGY—and perhaps the principal cause of shoddy political thinking.

Of course he'll make a good Secretary of Agriculture—hasn't he lived on a farm all his life and hasn't he succeeded in making a profitable business of raising livestock!

(Undoubtedly, the Secretary of Agriculture should have experience with farmers' problems, and undoubtedly he should be a competent man. But a farming background and success in raising livestock are not in themselves proof that a man will be a good administrator or know what is best for all farmers.)

5. *Do not assume that there are only two alternatives when actually there are several.* Truth is sometimes an either/or sort of thing. Jones either went to New York or he didn't. You either passed the examination or you failed to pass it. Bill either voted Republican or he didn't. But most of the things about which we argue are not as clear-cut as this. Courses, or governments, are not simply "good" or "bad"; the in-between possibilities are many. Arguing as if there were only two possibilities when the facts justify a variety of possibilities is known as the ALL-OR-NOTHING FALLACY, or the FALSE DILEMMA.*

> Students come to college either to work or to loaf. You must admit that John hasn't been working very much. Clearly, therefore, he came to college for an easy four years.

> There's no sense talking further. Fords are either better than Chevrolets or they're not. All we have to do is get the facts and buy the better car.

6. *Avoid contradicting yourself.* This fallacy occurs when you are unwilling or unable to establish a clear conclusion or opinion—when you want to have your cake and eat it too.

> Democracy and communism are widely different political systems, although communism is really an economic system.

EXERCISE 37d. Discuss the validity of the reasoning in the following sentences. Point out which rules of logic are violated.

1. The government must cut spending because economy in government is essential.
2. World War I started during Wilson's term, World War II started during Roosevelt's term, and the Vietnam war escalated during Johnson's term; if we elect another Democratic president he'll start another war.
3. I knew Dwight Eisenhower would make a good president because he had led the Allied forces to victory in World War II.
4. Anyone who argues for increased contacts with the Soviet Union must be a Communist himself.
5. Students are like machines: they should be oiled regularly with recreation and given frequent rests or they'll wear out.
6. I'd make a good movie critic because I love going to the movies.
7. The Rockefellers make good governors because they're used to handling large sums of money.
8. He made very good grades in college so he's bound to do well in the business world.
9. That girl my brother's seeing is a very bad influence on him; he met her at Christmas time and within a year he had grown a beard and dropped out of college.
10. An old remedy for nosebleed is to tie a piece of red yarn around the person's throat. I didn't believe it would work until I tried it the other day when Johnny had a nosebleed. His nose stopped bleeding just a few minutes after. The old remedies are really wonderful.

---

* These two fallacies are frequently distinguished; but both involve ignoring alternative possibilities.

EXERCISE 37(1). Comment on the logic in the following conversation.

MR. JONES: Newspapers today coddle and spoon-feed the public by such devices as cheesecake, one-syllable words, clichés, jargon, etc. Don't you think it's about time that the public did something about this? It seems to me that our standards of literacy are getting lower and lower. Newspapers used to have a higher standard. They stood for something. Now they depend almost exclusively on cheap devices and sensationalism. All papers must follow this policy if they are to survive.

MR. SMITH: What you're saying is, "Let's go back to the covered wagon era." You don't want to progress. Don't you think automobiles are a sign of progress? I do. Similiarly, with newspapers. Today they reach many more people than they used to. Anyone can read and understand a newspaper today. That's more than they could do a hundred years ago. If that isn't progress, then nothing is.

EXERCISE 37(2). Comment in one or two paragraphs on the logic (generalization, fairness, reasoning, etc.) of the following selection.

SPORTS VERSUS THE SPORTSWRITER

The trouble with sports is the sportswriters. These tin-horn sports, these semiliterate dealers in clichés, cram the daily newspapers with misinformation and moronic opinions about athletes, coaches, and sports themselves. The day after a sports contest sees the poor sports lover once again a victim in another of the eternal successions of "mornings-after"—when sportswriters begin again their assault on the English language, good taste, and common sense.

One would think that people who pretend to know so much about the secret workings and inside strategy of sports would be able to report on a football or baseball game with some objectivity and penetration. But no! The sports writer goes to great pains to tell us what we already know: that Old Siwash won. He tells us further that it is his considered opinion that Old Siwash played the better game. He then proceeds to indulge in assorted bits of irrelevancy and viciousness, according to the state of his ulcers. He gives us the startling news that Old Siwash's supporters were eager to win the game; that Halfback Haggerty would not have fumbled the kickoff if he had caught it instead.

But a sportswriter in front of a typewriter is only an idiot; a sportswriter in front of a microphone is a jabbering idiot. The next time you listen to a radio broadcast of a football game, force yourself to listen to the half-time interviews. Listen to the sportswriters gather to tell one another, in their own substandard idiom, what marvelous jobs they have done in "bringing you the game." Listen to them inform you, in voices choked with emotion and borrowed Scotch, that the game isn't over until the final gun sounds—"that anything can happen." This is undoubtedly what sportswriters mean when they speak of "inside dope."

"LOGIC" REVIEW EXERCISE. The following problems are designed to direct your attention to some of the violations of logic that we encounter every day.

1. Analyze several automobile advertisements, several cosmetic or drug advertisements, and several cigarette advertisements in current magazines or on television on the basis of the following questions:
   a. What specific appeals are made? (E.g.: automobile advertising makes wide use of the "bandwagon" approach; cosmetic advertising often uses "transfer" methods.) How logical are these appeals?
   b. Are all terms clearly defined?
   c. What kinds of generalizations are used or assumed? Are these generalizations adequately supported?
   d. Is evidence honestly and fairly presented?
   e. Are cause-and-effect relationships clear and indisputable?

2. Look through copies of your daily newspaper and bring to class letters to the editor or excerpts from political speeches that contain examples of fallacious reasoning. Look for false analogies, unsupported generalizations, name-calling, and prejudices.

3. Read an opinion article in a popular magazine and write a report analyzing the logic underlying the opinions and conclusions stated.

Words = WDS

Dictionaries are like watches; the worst is better than none, and the best cannot be expected to go quite true.

—SAMUEL JOHNSON

38 The Dictionary

The study of words begins with the dictionary, the great storehouse of linguistic information. A good dictionary is a biography of words, recording spelling, pronunciation, part of speech, etymology, meaning, and, when necessary, principal parts, or plurals, or other forms. Very often it includes other information—lists of abbreviations, rules for punctuation and spelling, condensed biographical and geographical information, the pronunciation and source of many given names, and a vocabulary of rhymes. For writers and readers a dictionary is an indispensable tool.

Unabridged dictionaries.

For English the great standard work is the *New English Dictionary,* sometimes called the NED, a work issued in ten volumes and a supplement between 1888 and 1933 by the Clarendon Press, Oxford, England, and reissued in 1933 as the *Oxford English Dictionary* (OED). A historical work, this dictionary traces the progress of a word through the language, giving dated quotations to illustrate its meaning and spelling at particular times in history. Many pages may be devoted to a single word. *Set,* for example, receives twenty-three pages of closely printed type. Under one of the 150-odd definitions of *set*—"to fix or appoint (a time) for the transaction of an affair"—there are illustrative sentences taken from writings dated 1056, 1250, 1290, 1300, 1387, 1470–85, 1548–77, 1633, 1693, 1753, 1810, 1890, and 1893.

The unabridged dictionary most familiar to Americans is *Webster's New International Dictionary of the English Language,* first published in 1909, reissued in a second edition in 1934, and again thoroughly revised and published as *Webster's Third New International Dictionary* in 1961 by the G. & C. Merriam Company of Springfield, Massachusetts, the legal inheritor of Noah Webster's copyright. The Merriam-Webster entries are scholarly and exact, though by no means as exhaustive as the OED's. Other unabridged dictionaries are the *New Standard Dictionary of the English Language,* published by Funk and Wagnalls, and the *Random House Dictionary of the English Language,* published by Random House. The latter is the only entirely new unabridged dictionary of English to have been published in recent years. The wide resources of an unabridged dictionary are suggested by the following specimen entry.

¹**howl** \\'haůl, *esp before pause or consonant* -aůəl\ *vb* -ED/-ING/ -s [ME *houlen;* akin to MD *hūlen* to howl, MHG *hiulen, hiuweln* to howl, OHG *hūwila* owl, Gk *kōkyein* to shriek, wail, lament, Skt *kauti* he cries out] *vi* **1 :** to utter or emit a loud sustained doleful sound or outcry characteristic of dogs and wolves ⟨wolves ~*ing* in the arctic night⟩ ⟨the only sound is a melancholy wind ~*ing* —John Buchan⟩ **2 :** to cry out or exclaim with lack of restraint and prolonged loudness through strong impulse, feeling, or emotion ⟨the scalded men ~*ing* in agony⟩ ⟨the hungry mob ~*ed* about the Senate house, threatening fire and massacre —J.A.Froude⟩ ⟨proctors ~*ing* at the blunder⟩ **3 :** to go on a spree or rampage ⟨this is my night to ~⟩ ~ *vt* **1 :** to utter or announce noisily with unrestrained demonstrative outcry ⟨newsboys ~*ing* the news⟩ **2 :** to affect, effect, or drive by adverse outcry — used esp. with *down* ⟨supporters of the Administration ... ready to ~ down any suggestion of criticism —*Wall Street Jour.*⟩ **syn** see ROAR
²**howl** \\"\ *n* -s **1 :** a loud protracted mournful rising and falling cry characteristic of a dog or a wolf **2 a :** a prolonged cry of distress **:** WAIL **b :** a yell or outcry of disappointment, rage, or protest **3 :** PROTEST, COMPLAINT ⟨raise a ~ over high taxes⟩ ⟨set up a ~ that he was being cheated⟩ **4 :** something that provokes laughter ⟨his act was a ~⟩ **5 :** a noise produced in an electronic amplifier usu. by undesired regeneration of alternating currents of audio frequency **:** OSCILLATION — called also *squeal*

By permission. From *Webster's Third New International Dictionary*. © 1966 by G. & C. Merriam Co., Publishers of the Merriam-Webster Dictionaries.

Since dictionaries must say much in little space, they use a great number of abbreviations and seemingly cryptic entries. You will find these troublesome unless you take time to read the explanatory pages and acquaint yourself with the symbols used. It will be useful to follow through our sample entry.

In our specimen from *Webster's Third New International* we find two main boldface entries preceded with the superscripts [1] and [2]. The first we find labeled *vb* for *verb,* the second *n* for *noun.* The *-ed/-ing/-s* in the first entry and the *-s* in the second tell us that the endings of *howl* as verb and as noun are regular. The pronunciation is indicated between slant lines (called reverse virgules) as follows: \haůl or haůəl\. The note before the second tells us that this pronunciation occurs especially when the word is pronounced before a pause (as at the end of a sentence, for example) or before a word beginning with a consonant. If we refer to the inside front cover or to the prefatory material of the dictionary, we find that *aů* is pronounced like the *ow* in *now* or the *ou* in *loud,* and that ə is a symbol representing the sound of the first and last *a* in *banana.*

The material between the brackets shows us the origin or etymology of the word: *howl* comes from a word in Middle English

(ME) spelled *houlen,* and is related to Middle Dutch (MD) *hulen* and Middle High German (MHG) *hiulen* or *hiuweln,* all meaning *to howl;* to the Old High German (OHG) word *huwila* meaning *owl;* to the Greek (Gk) *kokyein* meaning *to wail* or *lament;* and to the Sanskrit (Skt) word *kauti* meaning *he cries out.*

The definitions that follow are divided into various senses by boldface numerals 1, 2, etc. The first group of these senses under ¹*howl* is preceded by the label *vi,* indicating that these are senses in which the verb is intransitive. The second group of two meanings is preceded by the label *vt,* indicating that these are senses in which the verb is transitive. For each sense we find enclosed in angle brackets ($<$ $>$) quotations typical of the contexts in which the word occurs in the meaning given. These verbal illustrations become a major part of the definition itself by showing us an actual context for the word. Those labeled by authors' names or by sources are actual quotations; those not so labeled are typical phrases offered by the dictionary editors. Under meaning 2 as a transitive verb, we are given a usage note telling us that in this meaning *howl* is used especially with *down* in the phrase *howl down.* A swung dash ($\sim$) replaces the word itself in all such verbal illustrations of the word. Finally we are referred to the word *roar* for a discussion of the synonyms of *howl.* (See pp. 306–307 for illustration and discussion.)

If we turn to the second boldface entry, ²*howl,* we find the pattern repeated for the senses in which *howl* occurs as a noun. Since there is no separate pronunciation or etymology given, we know that each of these is the same as for the verb. Under *a* and *b* of meaning 2, coordinate subsenses of that meaning are given. The words in small capitals (*wail* in meaning 2; *protest* and *complaint* in meaning 3, and *oscillation* in meaning 5) refer us to other boldface entries at the appropriate alphabetical point in the dictionary where further related definitions are given.

We may see something of the ways in which dictionaries must change if they are to be contemporary by comparing with the entry reproduced above the following entry for the noun *howl* from an earlier edition of the same dictionary, an edition first issued in 1934.

> **howl**, *n.* **1.** The loud, protracted, mournful cry of a dog or a wolf, or other like sound.
> **2.** A prolonged cry of distress; a wail; also, a wild yell of disappointment, rage, or the like; as, *howls* of derision.

As we see at a glance, the two meanings offered here are very close to those numbered 1 and 2 in the *Third New International*. But meanings 3, 4, and 5 listed in the *Third International* are all missing. They probably have developed since our earlier entry was compiled. As we might expect, neither would we find the intransitive verbal meaning of *to go on a spree* given in earlier editions.

Desk dictionaries.

Unabridged dictionaries are useful as reference works. For everyday purposes a good abridged or desk dictionary is more practical. Here is a list that may help you in selecting a good desk dictionary:

1. *Webster's Seventh New Collegiate Dictionary,* G. & C. Merriam Company, Springfield, Massachusetts. This is the successor to Webster's *New Collegiate Dictionary,* 1949. Based upon the *Third New International,* it profits from the extensive scholarship which marks the *Third.* Insofar as possible, the order of definitions under any one word is historical: The original meaning is given first, the second meaning next, and so on. It is characterized particularly by relatively full etymologies, a wide range of synonymies, and full prefatory material. Abbreviations, biographical names, and place names are listed separately at the end of the dictionary. Some users may find inconvenient the fact that the editors have followed the *Third New International* in not using the label *colloquial* or its approximate equivalent *informal,* and in using the label *slang* rather sparingly.

howl \'haù(ə)l\ *vb* [ME *houlen;* akin to MHG *hiulen* to howl, Gk *kōkyein* to shriek] *vi* **1 :** to emit a loud sustained doleful sound characteristic of dogs **2 :** to cry loudly and without restraint under strong impulse (as pain, grief) **3 :** to go on a spree ~ *vt* **1 :** to utter with unrestrained outcry **2 :** to affect, effect, or drive by adverse outcry — **howl** *n*

By permission. From *Webster's Seventh New Collegiate Dictionary.* © 1969 by G. & C. Merriam Co., Publishers of the Merriam-Webster Dictionaries.

2. *Funk & Wagnalls Standard College Dictionary,* Funk & Wagnalls, New York. This is a relatively recent addition to the list of excellent available desk dictionaries. Though without the illustrious background of the *Webster's Seventh,* its reliability is insured by an impressive advisory board, many members of which are among the leading linguists today. It is marked by a convenient type-size, by relatively simple and natural definitions, and by particular attention to usage labels for words judged to be *informal* (which replaces the term *colloquial*) and *slang.* Material on usage is incorporated in "some 260" notes, especially valuable for the student, though the bulk of the same material is in *Webster's Seventh* under the main entry for a word. Common meanings are placed first in each entry. The *Standard* runs biographical names and place names into the main body of the dictionary rather than listing them separately. Introductory material in the text edition includes valuable summaries of the history of the language, English grammar, and regional variations in American pronunciation.

> **howl** (houl) *v.i.* **1.** To utter the loud, mournful wail of a dog, wolf, or other animal. **2.** To utter such a cry in pain, grief, or rage. **3.** To make a sound similar to this: The storm *howled* all night. **4.** To laugh loudly: The audience *howled*. — *v.t.* **5.** To utter or express with howling: to *howl* one's disapproval. **6.** To condemn, suppress, or drive away by howling: often with *down*. — *n.* **1.** The wailing cry of a wolf, dog, or other animal. **2.** Any howling sound. [ME *houlen*. Cf. G *heulen*.]

3. *Webster's New World Dictionary,* The World Publishing Company, Cleveland. This dictionary emphasizes simplified definitions even of technical terms and includes a large number of words and phrases which are relatively informal. Common meanings are placed first in the definitions. Etymologies are quite full and thorough. All words are contained in the main alphabetical list.

> **howl** (houl), *v.i.* [ME. *houlen;* prob. echoic; cf. G. *heulen,* D. *hiulen,* etc.], **1.** to utter the long, loud, wailing cry of wolves, dogs, etc. **2.** to utter a similar cry of pain, anger, grief, etc. **3.** to make a sound like this: as, the wind *howled*. **4.** to shout or laugh in scorn, mirth, etc. *v.t.* **1.** to utter with a howl or howls. **2.** to drive or effect by howling. *n.* **1.** a long, loud, wailing cry of a wolf, dog, etc. **2.** any similar sound.
> **howl down,** to drown out the voice or words of with shouts of scorn, anger, etc.

4. *The American College Dictionary,* Random House, New York. This is convenient in format and type. Meanings of words are arranged so far as possible in order of frequency of occurrence. Synonym studies are particularly strong, and technical words tend to be treated rather fully. All words—general words, proper names, and abbreviations—are combined in the main alphabetical listing. Prefaces contain especially good discussions of synonyms and antonyms, and of usage levels, and a rather thorough guide to usage.

howl (houl) *v.i.* **1.** to utter a loud, prolonged, mournful cry, as that of a dog or wolf. **2.** to utter a similar cry in distress, pain, rage, etc.; wail. **3.** to make a sound like an animal howling: *the wind is howling.* —*v.t.* **4.** to utter with howls. **5.** to drive or force by howls. —*n.* **6.** the cry of a dog, wolf, etc. **7.** a cry or wail, as of pain or rage. **8.** a sound like wailing: *the howl of the wind.* **9.** a loud scornful laugh or yell. [ME *houle.* Cf. G *heulen;* imit.]

From *The American College Dictionary.* Copyright 1969 by Random House, Inc. Reprinted by permission.

5. *The Random House Dictionary of the English Language,* College Edition. Random House, New York. Based on the unabridged *Random House Dictionary of the English Language,* this is another recent addition to available desk dictionaries. It offers a great number of entries—155,000—yet maintains a pleasant type-size and format. Definitions are arranged with the most common given first. Synonymies are full, and recent technical words receive careful attention. A single alphabetical listing incorporates all biographical and geographical as well as other entries. Illustrations appear to be used at least somewhat more generously than in most of the other desk dictionaries. Among its prefaces, that by Raven I. McDavid, Jr. on usage, dialects, and functional varieties of English is a particularly valuable summary.

howl (houl), *v.i.* **1.** to utter a loud, prolonged, mournful cry, as that of a dog or wolf. **2.** to utter a similar cry in distress, pain, rage, etc.; wail. **3.** to make a sound like an animal howling: *The wind howls through the trees.* **4.** *Informal.* to laugh loudly. —*v.t.* **5.** to utter with howls. **6.** to drive or force by howls (often fol. by *down*): *to howl down the opposition.* —*n.* **7.** the cry of a dog, wolf, etc. **8.** a cry or wail, as of pain, rage, protest, etc. **9.** a sound like wailing: *the howl of the wind.* **10.** a loud, scornful laugh or yell. **11.** something that causes a laugh or a scornful yell, as a joke or funny or embarrassing situation. [ME *hul(en), houle;* c. D *huilen,* G *heulen,* LG *hülen,* Dan *hyle;* with loss of *h,* Icel *ȳla*]

From *The Random House Dictionary, College Edition.* Copyright 1968, 1969 by Random House, Inc. Reprinted by permission.

6. *The American Heritage Dictionary of the English Language.* American Heritage Publishing Company, Inc., New York, and Houghton Mifflin Company, Boston. This is the most recent of the desk dictionaries. Its most immediately distinguishing features are a large page (8 × 11 inches), great generosity of illustrations and drawings, and the incorporation of usage notes based upon a consensus of a panel of some 100 writers, editors, poets, and public speakers. The large page, with illustrations in wide margins, makes the book readable but bulky to handle. The number of entries compares with that in the *Random House Dictionary.* Definitions are arranged in what the editors believe is a logical order, with the initial definition being that which offers the central meaning and serves as the base for the most logical arrangement of other senses of the word. Synonymies seem generous; etymologies are made somewhat more readable by avoidance of all abbreviations. The single alphabetical listing incorporates abbreviations and biographical and geographical entries. Among the several special articles within the front matter, those on usage, on grammar and meaning, and on spelling and pronunciation are particularly clear and helpful summaries reflecting current scholarship. The inclusion of an appendix of Indo-European roots in the back of the dictionary is a special feature.

howl (houl) *v.* **howled, howling, howls.** —*intr.* **1.** To utter or emit a long, mournful, plaintive sound characteristic of wolves or dogs. **2.** To cry or wail loudly and uncontrollably in pain, sorrow, or anger. **3.** *Slang.* **a.** To laugh uproariously. **b.** To go on a carousal or spree. —*tr.* **1.** To express or utter with a howl or howls. **2.** To effect, drive, or force by or as if by howling. —*n.* **1.** The sound of one that howls. **2.** *Slang.* Something uproariously funny or absurd. [Middle English *houlen, howlen,* perhaps from Middle Dutch *hūlen.* See **ul-** in Appendix.*]

By permission from *The American Heritage Dictionary of the English Language.* Copyright 1969 by American Heritage Publishing Co., Inc.

The uses of a dictionary.

1. *Spelling.* The spelling entry of a word in the dictionary divides the word into syllables, showing how to separate it properly at the ends of lines (see "Syllabication," Section 18). It also gives the proper spelling of compound words—properness depending on whether the editors found them more often written as two single words (*half brother*), as a hyphenated compound (*quarter-hour*), or as one word (*drugstore*). Dictionaries also indicate foreign words that require italics (in manuscript, underlining). The *American Heritage,* the *Standard,* and the *American College* all label such words or phrases as Latin, German, etc.; *Webster's New World* uses a double dagger (‡). *The Random House Dictionary* indicates such words by printing the main entry word in boldface italic type. All dictionaries also indicate whether a word is always or usually capitalized in a particular meaning.

All good modern dictionaries list variant spellings of many words, though not all by any means list the same variants or give the same comments about them. Four recent desk dictionaries, *Webster's Seventh Collegiate,* the *Random House,* the *Standard,* and the *American Heritage,* for example, all list *centre* and *theatre* as well as the more common *center* and *theater.* But while the *Standard* indicates that *centre* is *"British"* and that *theatre* is "more commonly British," and the *Random House* cites both as "chiefly British," *Webster's* and the *American Heritage* cite *centre* as "chiefly British" and add no limiting label to *theatre.* All four cite *tendentious* and *tendencious* as possible spellings, and agree that the former is the more common. The *Standard,* the *American Heritage,* and the *Random House* list *adduceable* and *adducible,* indicating that they have equal standing; *Webster's* does not contain either form. Such variation among dictionaries is common, and we must be careful to examine the explanatory material at the front of a dictionary if we wish to know exactly what policy is followed. Frequently, though by no means always, if variant spellings are listed, the first will be somewhat more common; the most carefully edited dictionaries sometimes adopt some means of indicating that this is so. *Webster's Seventh Collegiate,* for example, indicates that two variants are equally common by joining them with *or* (*caddie* or *caddy*) but joins variants the second of which is less common by *also* (*woolly* also *wooly*). In general, if there is a question about spelling, choose the first listed variant unless there is a special reason for choosing the second.

EXERCISE 38(1). What is the preferred spelling of each of these words?

aeroplane	criticise	humour
aesthetic	daemon	medieval
canceled	enclose	Shakspere
cheque	judgement	theatre

EXERCISE 38(2). Rewrite the following compounds, showing which should be written as they are, which hyphenated, and which written as separate words.

bypass	illbred	supermarket
clearcut	onesided	uptodate
easygoing	selfgovernment	wellmarked
houseboat		

EXERCISE 38(3).   Copy the following foreign words, underlining those that require italics and supplying accents where needed.

bon voyage	dramatis personae	resume
coup d'etat	matinee	sine qua non
creche	nouveau riche	Weltschmertz
debutante		

2. *Pronunciation.* Dictionaries indicate the pronunciation of words by respelling them with special symbols and letters. Explanation of the symbols is given either at the bottom of the page on which the entry appears or in the prefatory pages or both.

Indicating pronunciations is the most difficult of all the tasks of dictionary editors. *Correct pronunciation* is a very flexible term. Generally speaking, it is the standard of pronunciation prevailing among educated people, but often correctness is a theory rather than a reality. Does a Southerner mispronounce *I* when he says *Ah?* Is a Bostonian incorrect in saying *pa'k* for *park?* Dictionaries do not even attempt to list all the variant pronunciations in use.

The pronunciation of words, moreover, is influenced by the situation. In formal speech, syllables are likely to be more deliberately sounded than in informal speech. Further, the pronunciation of a word is affected by its position in the sentence and by the meaning it carries. Yet dictionary editors have no choice but to deal with each word as an individual entity. They record its formal, or full, pronunciation—what may be referred to as "platform" pronunciation. Certainly, to pronounce every word in our conversation as deliberately as the dictionary recommends would make our speech stilted and pompous.

Dictionaries do, however, attempt to show frequently occurring variant pronunciations as they do variant spellings. We have seen, for example, in our sample entry from *Webster's Third New International* that an unabridged dictionary may even show variant pronunciations for such a simple word as *howl.* Again, as with variant spellings, though the first listed is sometimes said to be "preferred" the statements about pronunciation in most carefully edited modern dictionaries do not bear this out. Usually, unless there is a limiting label or comment attached to one or more variants, they are all equally "correct." In the last analysis, your preference will be determined by the pronunciation you hear in the cultivated conversation around you.

EXERCISE 38(4). What is the pronunciation of the following words? Check your dictionary and copy the pronunciations carefully.

alias	exquisite	heinous
bestial	forehead	hyperbole
clique	formidable	mischievous
deference	genuine	municipal
epitome	gondola	superfluous

EXERCISE 38(5). Is usage divided in the pronunciation of the following words? If so, which pronunciation seems more acceptable to you? Why?

adult	Don Quixote	interesting	precedence
apparatus	envelope	kilometer	program
cerebral	exit	lever	research
chassis	inquiry	margarine	route

3. *Etymology.* The etymology of a word—that is, its origin and derivation—often helps clarify its present meaning and spelling. Etymological information is sometimes interesting or amusing in its own right. Because the course of history changes or restricts or extends the meanings of words, however, many original meanings have been lost completely. *Presently,* for example, formerly meant *at once, immediately;* it now usually means *shortly, in a little while.*

EXERCISE 38(6). Trace the etymology of each of the following words.

assassin	egg	nay	shirt
bedlam	edge	neighbor	skirt
chapel	familiar	priest	slogan
draggle	incisive	screech	squelch

EXERCISE 38(7). From what specific names have the following words been derived?

ampere	gardenia	shrapnel
boycott	macadam	ulster
chauvinism	quisling	watt
dunce		

EXERCISE 38(8). From what language did each of the following words come?

almanac	dory	jute	mukluk	trek
cherub	goulash	kerosene	piano	tulip
cockatoo	huckster	moccasin	squadron	typhoon

4. *Meaning.*   Strictly speaking, dictionaries do not <u>define</u> words; they record the meaning or meanings that actual usage, past and present, has attached to words. When more than one meaning is recorded for a single word, the Merriam-Webster dictionaries list them in order of historical use. Most other dictionaries list the more general and present meaning first. Special and technical meanings are clearly labeled. Choosing the appropriate meaning out of the many that are offered is not difficult if you read them <u>all</u> and understand their order of arrangement as indicated in the prefatory pages of the dictionary.

EXERCISE 38(9).   How many different meanings can you find for each of the following words?

call	land	run
get	light	set
go	out	turn
high		

EXERCISE 38(10).   Trace the changes in meaning that have taken place in each of the following words:

bounty	gossip	machine
complexion	humor	manufacture
engine	intern	sincere
fond	knave	starve
generous	lozenge	virtue

EXERCISE 38(11).   Distinguish between the meanings of the words in each of the following groups.

ambitious, aspiring, enterprising	eminent, celebrated
apt, likely, liable	enormous, immense
common, mutual	equanimity, composure
deface, disfigure	restive, restless
diplomatic, politic, tactful	voracious, ravenous

5. *Synonyms and antonyms.*   A synonym is a word having the same or almost the same general meaning as the vocabulary entry. An antonym is a word having approximately the opposite meaning. In dictionaries, for practical reasons, not all entries show synonyms and antonyms. Well-edited desk dictionaries include paragraph-length discussions of groups of synonyms, defining the different shades of meaning associated with each member of the group. These discussions are located usually at the end of certain entries and cross-referenced at related entries. (For full illustration of synonym entries from various dictionaries, see pp. 306–307.)

6. *Grammar.* Grammatically, dictionaries are helpful in several ways. Good dictionaries indicate what part of speech each word is; or, if the word serves as more than one part of speech, the dictionaries will usually list each possibility and give illustrative sentences for each. Dictionaries also list the principal parts of verbs, the plurals of nouns, and the comparative and superlative degrees of adjectives and adverbs, but only when these forms are irregular or present spelling difficulties. Frequently, the past tense and present participle of a verb are not given when they are regularly formed by adding *-ed* and *-ing* (*walked, walking*). Similarly, plurals ending in *-s* or *-es* (*cats, dishes*) are often not given. And comparatives and superlatives formed by adding *more, most,* or *less, least,* or *-er, -est* are not given, unless the addition of the *-er, -est* endings presents a spelling difficulty (*heavy, heavier, heaviest*).

EXERCISE 38(12). What are the past tense and the present participle of each of these verbs?

broadcast	get	set
focus	lend	teach
dive	shrink	wake

EXERCISE 38(13). What is the plural (or plurals) of each of the following?

alumnus	crisis	index
bear	daisy	madame
court-martial	fish	stratum

EXERCISE 38(14). Write the comparative and superlative forms of each of the following:

bad	lengthy	red
ill	much	shyly
little	often	well

7. *Labels.* Dictionaries do not label words that belong to the general vocabulary. The absence of a label therefore means that the word is proper for formal and informal speaking and writing. Other words may have one of two kinds of label:

SUBJECT LABELS, indicating that the word belongs to a special field: law, medicine, baseball, finance, and so on.

USAGE or STATUS LABELS, indicating that a word is restricted in some special way in its occurrence, either in time, geographical range, or style. The following labels are in common use, but note that dictionaries vary both in their application of such labels and in the exact ways in which their editors define them. To be certain of the precise meaning of labels in your dictionary, be sure to read the explanatory material at the front of the dictionary.

The labels *obsolete* and *archaic* indicate that the word is restricted in <u>time</u>. *Obsolete* means that the word has passed out of use entirely, as *absume* and *enwheel,* which are not known to have occurred for some two hundred years. *Archaic* means that although the word has passed out of general use, it occurs occasionally or in special contexts, as *belike* and *eftsoons.*

Dialectal, and various labels such as *New England, Southern U.S., British, Australian,* and *Canadian,* all indicate restrictions in the geographical occurrence of the word. Dictionaries vary in the exact labels they apply, but as a general rule words that have a restrictive geographical label should not be used in writing unless a special purpose requires it. The term *dialectal* usually suggests a rather specialized local or provincial word, frequently rural or traditional. *Corn pone,* labeled *Southern U.S.* in the *American College Dictionary,* and *larrup* as a noun meaning a *blow,* labeled *dialect* by *Webster's Seventh Collegiate,* are examples.

Colloquial, informal, slang, illiterate, substandard and other similar labels are *level,* or *style,* labels. Dictionaries have their greatest variation both in the selection and the application of such labels.

Slang indicates that a word has not yet been dignified by inclusion in the general vocabulary; it frequently suggests that the word is used in a humorous way, often within a particular and limited group of people. *Hangup* (a fixation, an intense preoccupation) *shades* (sunglasses), and *snow* (cocaine or heroin) are typical examples. Of the dictionaries listed above, *Webster's Seventh Collegiate* is by far the most sparing in its use of this label, allowing many entries labeled slang by other dictionaries to pass without any label.

Colloquial and *informal* indicate that a word is more characteristic of cultivated speech or quite informal writing than of the more formal levels of writing. These terms are in much debate currently, particularly because *Webster's Third New International* applies no label of this kind to any word, nor does *Webster's Seventh Collegiate.* In the opinion of many, the failure of the latest Merriam-Webster dictionaries to use such labels limits their usefulness for students and others seeking guidance to determine the appropriateness of many words for particular writing contexts. The *Standard* substitutes the label *informal* for the more conventional label *colloquial,* used by both the *American College* and by *Webster's New World.* Thus the

Standard labels *fizzle* as *informal;* the *American College Dictionary* labels it *colloquial; Webster's Seventh* gives it no label.

Illiterate, substandard, and some other similar terms are labels indicating that a word is limited to uneducated speech, as *drownded* for the past tense of *drown.* Though dictionaries vary somewhat in the particular labels they use (the *Standard* uses *illiterate* to mean about the same thing as *Webster's substandard,* for example), their agreement in classifying a word as limited to uneducated speech is much greater than their agreement in labeling a word as slang, colloquial, and so on.

It will be clear from the comments above that if you are to use your dictionary wisely as a guide to usage, you will have to examine the explanatory notes in it carefully to determine exactly what labels are applied and how they are interpreted by the editors.

EXERCISE 38(15). Which of the following are standard English, which colloquial or informal, and which slang, according to your dictionary? If possible, check more than one dictionary to determine if they agree.

corny	goof	moll
cool	hipster	snollygoster
flap	jerk	wise-up
foul-up	kibitzer	yak

EXERCISE 38(16). In what areas of the world would you be likely to hear the following?

billabong	hoecake	potlatch
chuckwagon	laager	pukka
coulee	petrol	sharpie

EXERCISE 38(17). The following questions are designed to test your ability to use the whole dictionary—not only its vocabulary entries but also its various appendices. Any of the desk dictionaries discussed previously will help you find the answers.

1. What is the orthography of the word *embarrass?*
2. What is the preferred orthoepy of the noun *envelope?*
3. What is the etymology of the word *precise?*
4. What are two homonyms for the word *reign?*
5. What are some antonyms for the word *concise?*
6. What is the syllabication of the word *redundant?*
7. What are some synonyms for the adjective *correct?*
8. Give the meanings of these abbreviations: *syn., v. mus., R.C.Ch.*
9. What do the following phrases mean? *finem respice, ars longa vita brevis, de profundis, honi soit qui mal y pense.*

10. What is the population of Birmingham, Michigan?
11. What is the meaning of the symbol B/E?
12. How long is the Cumberland River?
13. Who was the oldest of the Brontë sisters?
14. From what language does the proper name *Nahum* come?
15. List six words that rhyme with *mince*.

Special dictionaries.

When you need specialized information about words, check one of the following dictionaries:*

Chambers's Technical Dictionary. Rev. ed. with supplement. New York: The Macmillan Company, 1949.

Abbrevs: (A Dictionary of Abbreviations). Compiled by H. J. Stephenson. New York: The Macmillan Company, 1943.

New Rhyming Dictionary and Poet's Handbook. Rev. ed. Ed. by Burgess Johnson. New York: Harper & Brothers, 1957.

A Dictionary of Slang and Unconventional English. 5th ed. Ed. by Eric Partridge. New York: The Macmillan Company, 1961.

The American Thesaurus of Slang. 2nd ed. Ed. by Lester V. Berrey and Melvin Van Den Bark. New York: Thomas Y. Crowell Company, 1953.

Webster's Dictionary of Synonyms. Springfield, Mass.: G. & C. Merriam Co., 1951.

A Pronouncing Dictionary of American English. Ed. by J. S. Kenyon and T. A. Knott. Springfield, Mass.: G. & C. Merriam Co., 1953.

The difference between the right word and the almost-right word is the difference between lightning and the lightning bug.

　　　　　　　　　　　　　—*Attributed to* MARK TWAIN

39 Vocabulary

The English language contains well over a million words. Of these, about two-fifths belong almost exclusively to special fields: e.g., zoology, electronics, psychiatry. Of the remaining, the large

---

* See also the list under *Reference Books* ("Dictionaries, Word Books") in "The Library," Section 45.

dictionaries list about 600,000, the desk dictionaries about 150,000. Such wealth is both a blessing and a curse. On the one hand, many English words are loosely synonymous, sometimes interchangeable, as in *buy* a book or *purchase* a book. On the other hand, the distinctions between synonyms are fully as important as their similarities. For example, a family may be said to be living in *poverty,* or in *penury,* or in *want,* or in *destitution.* All these words are loosely synonymous, but only one will describe the family exactly as you see it and wish your reader to see it. In short, as a writer of English you must use your words carefully.

Passive and active vocabulary.

In a sense, you have two vocabularies: a PASSIVE, or RECOGNI-TION, vocabulary, which is made up of the words you recognize in the context of reading matter but do not actually use yourself; and an ACTIVE vocabulary, which consists of "working" words—those you use daily in your own writing and speaking. In the passage below, the meaning of the italicized words is fairly clear (or at least can be guessed at) from the context. But how many belong in your active vocabulary?

Has it been duly marked by historians that the late William Jennings Bryan's last *secular* act on this globe of sin was to catch flies? A curious detail, and not without its *sardonic overtones.* He was the most *sedulous* fly-catcher in American history, and in many ways the most successful. His *quarry,* of course, was not *Musca domestica* but *Homo neandertalensis.* For forty years he tracked it with coo and bellow, up and down the *rustic* back-ways of the Republic. Wherever the *flambeau* of Chautauqua smoked and guttered, and the bilge of idealism ran in the veins, the Baptist pastors damned the brooks with the *sanctified,* and men gathered who were weary and heavy laden, and their wives who were full of Peruna and as *fecund* as the shad (*Alosa sapidissima*)—there the *indefatigable* Jennings set up his traps and spread his bait.   —H. L. MENCKEN, *Selected Prejudices*

Increasing your vocabulary.

There are no shortcuts to word power. A good vocabulary is the product of years of serious reading, of listening to intelligent talk, and of seeking to speak and write forcefully and clearly. All this does not mean that devices and methods for vocabulary-building are useless. But it does mean that acquiring a good vocabulary is inseparable from acquiring an education.

1. *Increasing your recognition vocabulary.* English has many words based on a common root form, to which different prefixes or suffixes have been added. The root form *spec-*, for example, from the Latin *specere* (to look) appears in *specter, inspection, perspective, aspect, introspection, circumspect, specimen, spectator.* Knowing the common prefixes and suffixes will help you detect the meaning of many words whose roots are familiar.

a. *Prefixes.*

PREFIX	MEANING	EXAMPLE
ab-	away from	absent
ad-*	to *or* for	adverb
com-*	with	combine
de-	down, away from, *or* undoing	degrade, depart, dehumanize
dis-*	separation *or* reversal	disparate, disappoint
ex-*	out of *or* former	extend, ex-president
in-*	in *or* on	input
in-*	not	inhuman
mis-	wrong	mistake
non-	not	non-Christian
ob-*	against	obtuse
pre-	before	prevent
pro-	for *or* forward	proceed
re-	back *or* again	repeat
sub-*	under	subcommittee
trans-	across	transcribe
un-	not	unclean

EXERCISE 39(1). Write words denoting negation from:

accuracy	conformity	mutable
adorned	distinctive	rational
agreeable	explicable	workable

EXERCISE 39(2). Write words denoting reversal from:

centralize	integrate	please
do	magnetize	qualify
inherit	persuade	ravel

b. *Suffixes.* These fall into three groups; noun suffixes, verb suffixes, adjectival suffixes.

---

* The spelling of these prefixes varies, usually to make pronunciation easier. *Ad* becomes *ac* in *accuse*, *ag* in *aggregate*, *at* in *attack*. Similarly, the final consonant in the other prefixes is assimilated by the initial letter of the root word: *colleague* (*com + league*); *illicit* (*in + licit*); *offend* (*ob + fend*); *succeed* (*sub + ceed*).

Noun suffixes denoting act of, state of, quality of.

SUFFIX	EXAMPLE	MEANING
-dom	freedom	*state of* being free
-hood	manhood	*state of* being a man
-ness	dimness	*state of* being dim
-ice	cowardice	*quality of* being a coward
-ation	flirtation	*act of* flirting
-ion	intercession	*act of* interceding
{ -sion	scansion	*act of* scanning
{ -tion	corruption	*state of* being corrupt
-ment	argument	*act of* arguing
-ship	friendship	*state of* being friends
⌠-ance	continuance	*act of* continuing
⎸-ence	precedence	*act of* preceding
⎸-ancy	flippancy	*state of* being flippant
⌡-ency	currency	*state of* being current
-ism	baptism	*act of* baptizing
-ery	bravery	*quality of* being brave

Noun suffixes denoting doer, one who.

SUFFIX	EXAMPLE	MEANING
{ -eer (general)	auctioneer	*one who* auctions
{ -ess (female)	poetess	*a woman who* writes poetry
-ist	fascist	*one who* believes in fascism
{ -or	debtor	*one who* is in debt
{ -er	worker	*one who* works

Verb suffixes denoting to make *or* to perform the act of.

SUFFIX	EXAMPLE	MEANING
-ate	perpetuate	*to make* perpetual
-en	soften	*to make* soft
-fy	dignify	*to make* dignified
-ize, -ise	sterilize	*to make* sterile

Adjectival suffixes.

SUFFIX	MEANING	EXAMPLE
-ful	full of	hateful
-ish	resembling	foolish
-ate	having	affectionate
-ic, -ical	resembling	angelic
-ive	having	prospective
-ous	full of	zealous
-ulent	full of	fraudulent

SUFFIX	MEANING	EXAMPLE
-less	without	fatherless
-able, -ible	capable of	peaceable
-ed	having	spirited
-ly	resembling	womanly
-like	resembling	childlike

EXERCISE 39(3). Write words indicating *act of, state of,* or *quality of* from the following words.

agree	judge	promote
contrive	locate	statesman
hopeless	pauper	thoughtful

EXERCISE 39(4). Write nouns indicating *doer* from the following.

advise	plan	sail
conserve	procrastinate	save
manipulate	profit	tend

EXERCISE 39(5). Write verbs indicating *to make* or *to perform the act of* from the following nouns and adjectives.

beauty	idol	moral
black	liquid	peace
captive	modern	victim

EXERCISE 39(6). Make adjectives of the following words by adding a suffix.

humor	rest	thwart
irony	speed	wasp
mule	talk	whimsey

c. *Combining forms.* Linguists refer to these as BOUND FORMS. They appear generally, but not always, as prefixes.

COMBINING FORM	MEANING	EXAMPLE
anthropo-	man	*anthropo*logy
arch-	rule	*arch*duke, mon*arch*
auto-	self	*auto*mobile
bene-	well	*bene*ficial
eu-	well	*eu*logy
graph-	writing	*graph*ic, bio*graphy*
log-, logue	word, speech	mono*logue*
magni-	great	*magni*ficent
mal-	bad	*mal*ady

mono-	one	*mono*tone
multi-	many	*multi*plication
neo-	new	*neo*-classic
omni-	all	*omni*bus
pan-, pant-	all	*pan*hellenic
phil-	loving	*phil*osophy
phono-	sound	*phono*graph
poly-	many	*poly*gamy
pseudo-	false	*pseudo*nym
semi-	half	*semi*formal

2. *Increasing your active vocabulary.*   Another way to increase word power is to keep transferring words from your <u>recognition</u> vocabulary to your <u>active</u> vocabulary. Make a conscious effort to introduce at least one new word a day into your active vocabulary. At the same time be alert to opportunities for increasing your recognition vocabulary. A good system is to enter each new word on a small card: Write the word on one side, the definition and a sentence illustrating its correct use on the other. Then you can quickly test yourself on the meaning of all the new words you collect.

EXERCISE 39(7).   Define each of the following words and use it correctly in a sentence.

extenuate	ostentatious	sensuous
inscrutable	fortuitous	calumny
homogeneous	ritual	finite
disparage	predatory	collate
intrinsic	officious	facetious
prodigious	taciturn	corpulent
palliate	malign	exacerbate

3. *Strengthening your active vocabulary.*   Are you sure that *enthusiast, fanatic, zealot,* and *bigot* mean what you think they mean? You know that *deadly, mortal,* and *fatal* are very much alike in meaning—but do you know the exact distinctions among them? All the desk dictionaries listed in Section 38 group synonyms and point out their differences. Unabridged dictionaries carry quite exhaustive discussions of synonyms. And the Merriam-Webster *Dictionary of Synonyms* is devoted exclusively to the grouping and differentiating of synonyms. The various editions of Roget's *Thesaurus* are valuable for the long lists of closely related words they provide, though they must be used cautiously because they give no discussion of distinctions in meaning and offer no guiding examples.

One of the most valuable ways to strengthen your vocabulary is to cultivate the habit of studying dictionary discussions of synonyms. The extent of dictionary resources for this purpose is illustrated by the following sample entries.

From *Webster's Third:*

syn HOWL, ULULATE, BELLOW, BAWL, BLUSTER, CLAMOR, VOCIFERATE: ROAR suggests the full loud reverberating sound made by lions or the booming sea or by persons in rage or boisterous merriment ⟨far away guns *roar* —Virginia Woolf⟩ ⟨the harsh north wind ... *roared* in the piazzas —Osbert Sitwell⟩ ⟨*roared* the blacksmith, his face black with rage —T.B.Costain⟩ HOWL indicates a higher, less reverberant sound often suggesting the doleful or agonized or the sounds of unrestrained laughter ⟨frequent *howling* of jackals and hyenas —James Stevenson-Hamilton⟩ ⟨how the wind does *howl* —J.C.Powys⟩ ⟨*roared* at his subject ... *howled* at ... inconsistencies —Martin Gardner⟩ ULULATE is a literary synonym for HOWL but may suggest mournful protraction and rhythmical delivery ⟨an *ululating* baritone mushy with pumped-up pity —E.B.White⟩ BELLOW suggests the loud, abrupt, hollow sound made typically by bulls or any similar loud, reverberating sound ⟨most of them were drunk. They went *bellowing* through the town —Kenneth Roberts⟩ BAWL suggests a somewhat lighter, less reverberant, unmodulated sound made typically by calves ⟨a woman *bawling* abuse from the door of an inn —C.E.Montague⟩ ⟨the old judge was in the hall *bawling* hasty orders —Sheridan Le Fanu⟩ BLUSTER suggests the turbulent noisiness of gusts of wind; it often suggests swaggering and noisy threats or protests ⟨expressed her opinion gently but firmly, while he *blustered* for a time and then gave in —Sherwood Anderson⟩ ⟨swagger and *bluster* and take the limelight —Margaret Mead⟩ CLAMOR suggests sustained, mixed and confused noisy outcry as from a number of agitated persons ⟨half-starved men and women *clamoring* for food —Kenneth Roberts⟩ ⟨easy ... for critics ... to *clamor* for action —Sir Winston Churchill⟩ VOCIFERATE suggests loud vehement insistence in speaking ⟨was not willing to break off his talk; so he continued to *vociferate* his remarks —James Boswell⟩

From the *American College:*

—**Syn. 3.** STOP, ARREST, CHECK, HALT imply causing a cessation of movement or progress (literal or figurative). STOP is the general term for the idea: *to stop a clock.* ARREST usually refers to stopping by imposing a sudden and complete restraint: *to arrest development.* CHECK implies bringing about an abrupt, partial, or temporary stop: *to check a trotting horse.* To HALT means to make a temporary stop, esp. one resulting from a command: *to halt a company of soldiers.* **17.** STOP, CEASE, PAUSE, QUIT imply bringing movement, action, progress, or conditions to an end. STOP is used in speaking of objects in motion or action: *the clock stopped.* CEASE, a more literary and formal word, suggests the coming to an end of that which has had considerable duration: *a storm ceases.* PAUSE implies the prospect of resumption after a short interval: *one pauses in speaking.* QUIT, in the sense of stop or cease, still very common in the U.S., is not used in England, though it survives in Scottish and Irish English (in England the term used is *leave off*): *make him quit.* —**Ant. 3, 17.** start, begin.

From *Webster's Seventh Collegiate:*

syn HUMOR, IRONY, SARCASM, SATIRE, REPARTEE: WIT suggests the power to evoke laughter by remarks showing verbal felicity or ingenuity and swift perception esp. of the incongruous; HUMOR implies an ability to perceive the ludicrous, the comical, and the absurd in human life and to express these usu. without bitterness; IRONY applies to a manner of expression in which the intended meaning is the opposite of what is seemingly expressed; SARCASM applies to expression frequently in the form of irony that is intended to cut or wound; SATIRE applies to writing that exposes or ridicules conduct, doctrines, or institutions either by direct criticism or more often through irony, parody, or caricature; REPARTEE implies the power of answering quickly, pointedly, wittily, and often humorously

By permission. From *Webster's Seventh New Collegiate Dictionary.* © 1969 by G. & C. Merriam Co., Publishers of the Merriam-Webster Dictionaries.

From the *Funk & Wagnalls:*

— Syn. 4. *Speech, address, talk, oration, harangue, lecture, discourse, sermon,* and *homily* denote something said to an audience. Any public speaking may be called a *speech.* An *address* is a formal *speech,* as on a ceremonial occasion. *Talk,* on the other hand, suggests informality. An *oration* is an eloquent *address* that appeals to the emotions, while a *harangue* is a vehement *speech,* appealing to the emotions and often intended to spur the audience to action of some sort. A *lecture* is directed to the listener's intellect; it gives information, explanation, or counsel. Any carefully prepared *speech* or writing is a *discourse. Sermon* and *homily* are concerned with religious instruction; a *sermon* is usually an interpretation of Scripture, and a *homily* gives ethical guidance.

By permission. From *Funk & Wagnalls Standard® College Dictionary.* Copyright 1969 by Funk & Wagnalls, a division of Reader's Digest Books, Inc.

From the *Random House:*

—Syn. 1. encourage, befriend; support, uphold, back, abet. HELP, AID, ASSIST, SUCCOR agree in the idea of furnishing another with something needed, esp. when the need comes at a particular time. HELP implies furnishing anything that furthers another's efforts or relieves his wants or necessities. AID and ASSIST, somewhat more formal, imply esp. a furthering or seconding of another's efforts. AID implies a more active helping; ASSIST implies less need and less help. To SUCCOR, still more formal and literary, is to give timely help and relief in difficulty or distress: *Succor him in his hour of need.* **4.** alleviate, cure, heal. **10.** support, backing. **—Ant. 4.** afflict. **8.** hinder.

From *The Random House Dictionary, College Edition.* Copyright 1968, 1969 by Random House, Inc. Reprinted by permission.

From the *American Heritage:*

Synonyms: *curious, inquisitive, snoopy, nosy, intrusive.* These adjectives apply to persons who show a marked desire for information or knowledge. *Curious* more often implies a legitimate desire to enlarge one's knowledge, but can suggest a less commendable urge to concern oneself in others' affairs. *Inquisitive* frequently suggests excessive curiosity and the asking of many questions. *Snoopy* implies an unworthy motive and underhandedness in implementing it. *Nosy* suggests excessive curiosity and impertinence in an adult; applied to a child, it may refer less unfavorably to habitual curiosity. *Intrusive* stresses unwarranted and unwelcome concern with another's affairs.

By permission from *The American Heritage Dictionary of the English Language.* Copyright 1969 by American Heritage Publishing Co., Inc.

EXERCISE 39(8). Indicate the distinctions in meaning among the words in each of the following groups.

1. anger, ire, rage, fury, indignation, wrath
2. conform, adjust, reconcile
3. correct, accurate, exact, precise
4. punish, chastise, castigate, chasten, discipline
5. obstruct, hinder, impede, bar, block, dam
6. ghastly, grim, grisly, gruesome, macabre
7. design, plan, scheme, plot
8. mock, mimic, copy, ape
9. obey, mind, heed, keep, observe, regard, comply
10. maudlin, mushy, sentimental
11. benevolent, humane, humanitarian, altruistic, charitable
12. neccessary, requisite, essential
13. fragrance, perfume, scent, incense, redolence, bouquet
14. grudge, spite, malice
15. perennial, perpetual, constant, incessant

Care should be taken, not that the reader may understand, but that he must understand.
　　　　　　　　　　　　　　　　　　　　　—QUINTILIAN

40　Exactness = EX

To write with precision, you must know both the denotation and the connotation of words. DENOTATION is the core of a word's meaning, sometimes called the "dictionary," or literal, meaning; for example, a *tree* is *a woody perennial plant having a single main axis or stem commonly exceeding ten feet in height.* CONNOTATION refers to the reader's emotional response to a word and to the associations the word carries with it. Thus, *tree* connotes *shade* or *coolness* or *shelter* or *stillness.* Obviously, the connotation of a word cannot be fixed, for individual responses differ. Some words have fairly standardized connotations (*flag* > *the emotion of patriotism; home* > *security, the sense of one's own place*). But even these words have other and less orthodox connotations. In fact, poets achieve many of their finest effects by avoiding standardized connotations. *Evening,* for example, connotes for most of us some quality of beauty, but T. S. Eliot jolts us out of our normal response by seeing

> . . . the evening . . . spread out against the sky
> Like a patient etherised upon a table.

If you ever decide to violate the generally accepted connotations of a word in your own writing, however, be very sure that you know exactly what you are doing. And always take pains to insure that the connotations of your words reinforce and are consistent with their denotative meanings. For example, one of the denotative meanings of *smack* is *to give a hearty kiss,* but no one (unless he were trying to be funny) would write

> He looked deep into her eyes, whispered endearing words, and *smacked* her on the ear.

Many words stand for abstractions: *democracy, truth, beauty,* and so on. Because the connotations of such words are both vague and numerous, state specifically what you mean when you use them, or make sure that the context makes their meaning clear. Otherwise, the reader will misunderstand your terms, or—what is worse—will think he understands them when he does not. (See Section 37a.)

40a **Carefully distinguish between words that are nearly synonymous.**

The meanings of many words are so similar that occasionally one may be substituted for another. But synonymous words cannot always be used interchangeably, and one of the characteristics of an exact writer is that he uses synonyms carefully, observing their shades of meaning. The careless use of synonyms distorts meaning.

> The man gained great *renown* as a gangster. (*Notoriety* would be more exact.)

Sometimes, unfortunately, a writer chooses the wrong word because he really does not know its meaning and fails to look it up.

> The minister *instigated* love and charity throughout the community. (The writer probably meant *inspired.*)

> We admired the speaker for his *sententious* appeal for funds. (*Eloquent* was probably intended.)

EXERCISE 40a(1). Replace the italicized words in the following sentences with more exact ones. Explain why each italicized word is inappropriate.

1. His characters are *garish* and alive; they are people you will remember as old friends.
2. His *obstinancy* in the face of danger saved us all.
3. The ambassador, being treated like a common tourist, sputtered in *intimidation.*
4. We can't blame Margaret for leaving him; certainly she had an ample *pretext.*
5. The school's most honored professor was without fault: a wise mentor to his students, and in addition a scholar recognized as *pedantic* and profound.

EXERCISE 40a(2). Explain the differences in meaning among the italicized words in each of the following groups.

1. an *ignorant,* an *illiterate,* an *unlettered,* an *uneducated* person
2. a *detached,* a *distinterested,* an *indifferent,* an *unconcerned* attitude
3. to *condone,* to *excuse,* to *forgive,* to *pardon* a person's actions
4. an *insurrection,* a *mutiny,* a *rebellion,* a *revolution*
5. a *barbarous,* a *cruel,* a *fierce,* a *ferocious,* an *inhuman,* a *savage* character

40b **Do not confuse words with similar sound or spelling but with different meanings.**

Most of these words are approximate HOMONYMS, that is, words that have the same pronunciation but different meanings (*idol, idle, idyll; aisle, isle*). You must treat these words as you would any other unfamiliar term: Learn the correct spelling and meaning of each as an individual word.

EXERCISE 40b. What are the differences in meaning in each of the following groups of words?

1. adapt, adept, adopt
2. alley, ally
3. allude, elude
4. anecdote, antidote
5. anesthetic, antiseptic
6. angel, angle
7. arraign, arrange
8. bloc, block
9. borne, born
10. Calvary, cavalry

11. cannon, canon
12. canvas, canvass
13. carton, cartoon
14. chord, cord
15. climactic, climatic
16. confidently, confidentially
17. costume, custom
18. elicit, illicit
19. epic, epoch
20. flaunt, flout

21. genteel, gentile	26. morality, mortality
22. historic, historical	27. prescribe, proscribe
23. human, humane	28. receipt, recipe
24. ingenious, ingenuous	29. statue, statute
25. marital, martial	30. waive, wave

40c Generally, avoid "invented" words.

A COINED word is a new and outright creation (like Gelett Burgess' *blurb*). A NEOLOGISM is either a new word or a new use of an old word or words (like Madison Avenue's *package plans*). A NONCE-WORD, literally ONCE-WORD, is a word made up to suit a special situation and generally not used more than once (*"My son,"* he said, *"suffers from an acute case of baseballitis"*). Though the great majority of neologisms and nonce-words are short lived, they are one of the ways by which new words and new functions for old words are constantly working their way into a changing language. Though as an inexperienced writer you need to devote most of your attention to learning the meanings of words already established by usage, you should not be afraid to try a new coinage if it seems to suit your purpose. As an experienced reader, your instructor will be able to judge whether the experiment is successful. Be careful, however, to avoid "unconscious" inventions—words that you "invent" because of spelling errors or an inexact knowledge of word forms (*understandment* for *understanding, multification* for *multiplication*).

EXERCISE 40c. In the following sentences correct the italicized words that seem to you to be "needless inventions."

1. His failure to fulfill that campaign promise is only one of his many *nonresponsible* acts since he was elected.
2. One glimpse of the activities of the police or the mobs in urban riots reveals the *savagism* that underlies human nature.
3. Teachers should be strictly *unpolitical;* they should not try to influence their students.
4. Even in our computer age, human behavior is largely *nonpredictable.*
5. Political activists in totalitarian regimes are subject to *disappearation* or some other kind of *silencement.*
6. The last candidate had a *Nixonesque* style and a *Trumanian* temper.
7. She was unable to confine her *schoolteacherish* attitude to the classroom.
8. He has a very *peculiaristic* mode of dressing.
9. *Disciplinist* methods are essential in raising well-behaved children.
10. He displayed *liberalistic* tendencies in economic affairs.

40d   **Avoid improprieties.**

An impropriety is a legitimate word wrongly used. In the sentence *He opinioned that Edwin was guilty* the word *opinion* is used as a verb, a grammatical function to which it is not accustomed.

IMPROPER	He was *biographing* President Truman.
PROPER	He was *writing a biography of* (or *working on a biography of*) President Truman.

Many words, of course, may function legitimately as more than one part of speech.

PROPER	That garage gives excellent *service*.
PROPER	That garage has agreed to *service* my car.

When in doubt about the grammatical function of a word, always turn to a good dictionary.

EXERCISE 40d.   In the sentences below correct the italicized words that are improprieties.

1. Senator Dirksen's slow delivery always *aggravated* me.
2. Are you trying to *infer* by that remark that I'm ignorant?
3. That highway is *stoplighted* all the way to town; let's take the turnpike.
4. He *implied* from what I had said that I wouldn't be there.
5. The cottage is nearly finished; we're going *to roof* it tomorrow.
6. Before we started building it, we had to *bulldoze* a clearing.
7. As each of the kids came out of the pool, I *toweled* him dry.
8. This year we're going to *holiday* in Bermuda.
9. Next summer we're going *to jeep* our way cross-country.
10. This book is really *learning* me good grammar.

40e   **Be alert to changes in meaning from one suffixal form of a word to another.**

A roommate whom you *like* is not necessarily a *likable* roommate, nor is a *matter of agreement* an *agreeable matter*. Many words have two, sometimes three, adjectival forms: e.g., a *changeable* personality, a *changing* personality, a *changed* personality. Be careful not to substitute one form for another.

FAULTY	The cook served our *favorable* dessert last night.
STANDARD	The cook served our *favorite* dessert last night.

FAULTY	He is a good student; he has a very *questionable* mind.
STANDARD	He is a good student; he has a very *questioning* mind.

EXERCISE 40e. Point out the differences in meaning between the italicized words in each of the following groups.

1. an *arguable* point
   an *argued* point

2. a *practical* solution
   a *practicable* solution

3. a *hated* person
   a *hateful* person

4. a *liberal* foreign minister
   a *liberated* foreign minister

5. a *single* effect
   a *singular* effect

6. an *intelligible* writer
   an *intelligent* writer

7. a *godly* man
   a *godlike* man

8. an *informed* teacher
   an *informative* teacher

9. a *peaceful* nation
   a *peaceable* nation

10. a *workable* arrangement
    a *working* arrangement

11. an *amicable* teacher
    an *amiable* teacher

12. a *yellow* piece of paper
    a *yellowed* piece of paper

40f   Avoid "elegant variation."

Often you will use a variety of synonyms and pronouns in order to avoid the awkward repetition of a word. And that is a perfectly legitimate stylistic device. But when your desire to avoid repetition is so overwhelming that you dig up a synonym or epithet for almost every word you have used previously, you are guilty of "elegant variation."

Pee Wee Pearce, the Chicago second-baseman, got three hits yesterday. The tiny infielder came up in the first frame and lashed a one-base blow to right field. In the third inning the diminutive keystone sacker knocked a single through the box. In the seventh the little ballhawk reached first safely on a screaming drive to the outer garden.

Here, in the short space of four sentences, we have well over a dozen examples of elegant variation:

Pee Wee	second-baseman	hits
tiny	infielder	one-base blow
diminutive	keystone sacker	single
little	ballhawk	reached first
lashed	right field	first frame
knocked	box	third inning
screaming drive	outer garden	seventh

313

In the first of the examples below, the use of the simple pronoun *he* would have made unnecessary the frantic search for synonyms for *king*. In the second, *visitor* could be omitted and *Two of the other people in attendance* changed to *Two others*.

The *King* appeared yesterday at the Navy Barracks. *His majesty* was in full dress and escorted by the Home Guards. After inspecting the cadets, the *royal guest* was entertained at the Officers' Club.

I saw many of my old classmates at your garden party. Two of your *guests* were my fraternity brothers. Another *visitor* played on the same football team with me. *Two of the other people in attendance* were brothers of my old girl friend.

EXERCISE 40f(1).   Find a specimen of elegant variation in a newspaper or popular magazine and rewrite it to show how the variation might be avoided.

EXERCISE 40f(2).   Comment in one or two paragraphs on the elegant variation in the following passage.

The outcome of the game was a personal victory for All-American Marty Jerome. The diminutive halfback scored ten times for the Mustangs, five of these coming in the final frame. In the first quarter the pint-sized wingback ran 10 yards for one score, scampered 45 for another, and actually bulled his way over for a third from the two-yard stripe In the second period the little fellow galloped half the length of the field for a marker after intercepting a Longhorn pass on his own fifty. In the third frame the mighty mite was held to one touchdown—that one coming on the last play of the period and featuring a series of fumbles. Lou Zamberg, Longhorn fullback, dropped the ball as he came through the line; Joe Harris, the Mustangs' giant tackle, picked it up, was hit from behind and fumbled. Like a streak of light the tiny Jerome grabbed it just before it hit the ground and dashed 85 long and magnificent yards to paydirt. The last frame was all Jerome's. In a display of ability seldom, if ever, seen, the little man ran for five tallies, one of them a 105-yard kickoff return. He scored again on an intercepted pass, then on a 20-yard rabbit-run through center, and twice more on bullet-like plunges from the 5-yard line to home base.

40g   Use words and phrases idiomatically.

Idiomatic writing means writing that strikes the reader as natural, smooth, unaffected. It means putting things in an English (or American) way. A Frenchman says *un cheval blanc* and *il fait froid*, but the literal translations, *a horse white* and *it makes cold,* are un-idiomatic to us; we say *a white horse* and *it is cold.* In English we use many idiomatic phrase-forms that are justified by custom rather than by logic or grammar, as *look up an old friend, strike a bargain, go down to the sea in ships.* Generally, native users of English uncon-sciously speak and write idiomatically, though all of us find it hard sometimes to hit upon the right idiomatic prepositions or infinitives or gerunds. Choosing just the right idiom is largely a matter of ex-perience—either our own or somebody else's. The most troublesome idioms in English are those which require a particular preposition after a given verb or adjective according to the meaning intended. The following list contains a number of such combinations which frequently cause trouble.

ABSOLVED BY, FROM	I was *absolved by* the dean *from* all blame.
ACCEDE TO	He *acceded to* his father's demands.
ACCOMPANY BY, WITH	I was *accompanied by* George. The terms were *accompanied with* a plea for immediate peace.
ACQUITTED OF	He was *acquitted of* the crime.
ADAPTED TO, FROM	This machine can be *adapted to* farm work. The design was *adapted from* a previous invention.
ADMIT TO, OF	He *admitted to* the error. The plan will *admit of* no alternative.
AGREE TO, WITH, IN	They *agreed to* the plan but *disagreed with* us. They *agreed* only *in* principle.
ANGRY WITH, AT	She was *angry with* me and *angry at* the treat-ment she had received.
CAPABLE OF	He is *capable of* every vice of the ignorant.
COMPARE TO, WITH	He *compared* the roundness of the baseball *to* that of the earth. He *compared* the economy of the Ford *with* that of the Plymouth.
CONCUR WITH, IN	I *concur with* you *in* your desire to use the re-vised edition.
CONFIDE IN, TO	He *confided in* me. He *confided to* me that he had stolen the car.
CONFORM TO, WITH CONFORMITY WITH	The specifications *conformed to* (or *with*) his original plans. You must act in *conformity with* our demands.
CONNECT BY, WITH	The rooms are *connected by* a corridor. He is officially *connected with* this university.

DIFFER ABOUT, FROM, WITH	We *differ about* our tastes in clothes. My clothes *differ from* yours. We *differ with* one another.
DIFFERENT FROM*	Our grading system is *different from* yours.
ENTER INTO, ON, UPON	He *entered into* a new agreement and thereby *entered on* (or *upon*†) a new career.
FREE FROM, OF	He was *freed from* his mother's domination and now he is *free of* her.
IDENTICAL WITH	Your reasons are *identical with* his.
JOIN IN, TO, WITH	He *joined in* the fun *with* the others. He *joined* the wire cables *to* each other.
LIVE AT, IN, ON	He *lives at* 14 Neil Avenue *in* a Dutch Colonial house. He *lives on* Neil Avenue.
NECESSITY FOR, OF NEED FOR, OF	There was no *necessity* (*need*) *for* you to lose your temper. There was no *necessity* (*need*) *of* your losing your temper.
OBJECT TO	I *object to* the statement in the third paragraph.
OBLIVIOUS OF	When he held her hand he was *oblivious of* the passing of time.
OVERCOME BY, WITH	I was *overcome by* the heat. I was *overcome with* grief.
PARALLEL BETWEEN, TO, WITH	There is a *parallel between* your attitude and his. This line is *parallel to* (or *with*) that one.
PREFERABLE TO	A leisurely walk is *preferable to* violent exercise.
REASON ABOUT, WITH	Why not *reason with* him *about* the matter?
VARIANCE WITH	This conclusion is at *variance with* your facts.
VARY FROM, IN, WITH	The houses *vary from* one another *in* size. People's tastes *vary with* their personalities.
WORTHY OF	That woman is not *worthy of* your trust.

EXERCISE 40g(1).   Provide the idiomatic prepositions needed in the following sentences.

1. Many students are oblivious _____ the criteria implicit _____ his criticisms.
2. He confided _____ me that he thought me different _____ what he had expected.

---

* *Different than* is colloquially idiomatic when the object of the prepositional phrase is a clause:

FORMAL	This town looks *different from* what I had remembered.
COLLOQUIAL	This town looks *different than* I had remembered it.

† In many phrases, *on* and *upon* are interchangeable: *depend on* or *depend upon; enter on* or *enter upon.*

3. I agreed _____ his proposal, which had been adapted _____ one I had made previously.
4. The jury absolved Robbins _____ all blame; hence he was acquitted _____ the charge.
5. Lois Bowers said she was angry _____ him because his actions did not conform _____ those of a gentleman.
6. The fence was built parallel _____ the street and connected _____ his neighbor's stone wall.
7. Having been freed _____ his parents' supervision, he saw no necessity _____ keep (*or* keeping) them informed of his whereabouts.
8. She is not capable _____ budget (*or* budgeting) her own income, for she is unable _____ add 4 and 4 and get 8.
9. We entered _____ a contract to buy the house after Mr. Jones agreed _____ our request for a twenty-year mortgage.
10. My father would admit _____ no disagreement _____ his wishes, and I had to accede _____ his demand that I leave the party at midnight.

EXERCISE 40g(2). Each of the following sentences violates a principle of exactness. Find and correct each error, giving reasons for your corrections.

1. I often wondered why I didn't exert more enthusiasm toward my studies.
2. Percival never got accustomed to one respect of college life—the calling of students by "Mr." or "Miss."
3. While in high school I was always challenged to learn by constant threats.
4. I have seen students regardlessly ignore the instructor's lecture and then wonder why they flunked the course.
5. He hadn't been in the army two days when he discovered that his sleeping habits were going to be much shorter.
6. A person has to earn a living in his chosen field if he is going to derive any satisfaction out of it.
7. The first impression I encountered from the neighbor's dog was one of enmity.
8. In spite of his round little face and twinkling eyes the preacher was a very serious and godlike man.
9. "The Charge of the Light Brigade" is a poem about a disasterfull calvary charge in the Crimean War.
10. He went to bed before all the election returns were in, but his confidential manner led us all into believing that he would be the winning candidate.

40h **Use specific words rather than general words.**

A general word stands for generalized qualities or characteristics, as *color, beast, vehicle.* A specific word singles out more definite and individual qualities, as *red, lion, tricycle.* The context determines whether a particular word is general or specific. For example, *man* is a general word in relation to *Leonard Chapman* and *Barney Rider*, but a specific word in relation to *mammal*. And *beast* is less specific than *lion* but more specific than *creature*.

No piece of writing can be vivid with generalized, abstract words. We can't always avoid using such words as *useful, democratic,* and *nice,* but we can submit them to a few down-to-earth questions: *useful* for what? *useful* how? *democratic* attitude as in a mob or *democratic* process as in an election for public office? *nice* as in prim? wealthy? fastidious? delicate? precise? agreeable? When we answer these questions, we are forced to be specific. And it is the writer's choice of particular, concrete words and phrases which arouses vivid responses in the reader's mind. When you use generalizations, be sure you illustrate or support them with concrete details: proper names, numbers, quotations, facts, and color words.

Try constantly to express your thoughts in concrete and unambiguous terms; search for the most specific words available.

GENERAL	A man walked down the street.
SPECIFIC	An old beggar shuffled along Main Street.
GENERAL	They had a picnic under a tree.
SPECIFIC	They ate pickles and drank lemonade under an old elm.
SPECIFIC	Mateo was a stocky man, with clear eyes and a deeply tanned face. His skill as a marksman was extraordinary, even in Corsica, where everyone is a good shot. He could kill a ram at one hundred and twenty paces, and his aim was as accurate at night as in the daytime.
MORE SPECIFIC	Picture a small, sturdy man, with jet-black, curly hair, a Roman nose, thin lips, large piercing eyes, and a weather-beaten complexion. His skill as a marksman was extraordinary, even in this country, where everyone is a good shot. For instance, Mateo would never fire on a wild ram with small shot, but at a hundred and twenty paces he would bring it down with a bullet in its head or shoulder, just as he fancied. He used his rifle at night as easily as in the daytime, and I was given the following illustration of his skill, which may seem incredible, perhaps, to those who have never travelled in Corsica. He placed a lighted candle behind a piece of transparent paper as big as a plate, and aimed at it from eighty paces away. He extinguished the candle, and a moment later, in utter darkness, fired and pierced the paper three times out of four. —PROSPER MÉRIMÉE, *Mateo Falcone*

The need for specific words is not limited to descriptive writing. Even in general exposition, a good writer leads into a generalization through images, illustrations, and examples. Note how concretely Bill Mauldin—no "literary" writer—deals with the abstraction *immigration.*

> But us champeens of the teeming shores aren't doing a new thing. The immigration battle has been going on in this country ever since the flag had thirteen stars. Every generation for 170 years has produced two schools of thought about immigration: One has been convinced that the country has reached its saturation point, that more material for the human melting pot that produces Americans will result only in lowering the standard of living, reducing wages, and producing a crop of "furrin ideas." The other group believes—rightly, I think—that when a country reaches the stage where it can't expand its population, add new blood, and realize fresh potentialities, it might as well fold its flag because it has reached the summit and can only go downhill until it expires.
>
> —BILL MAULDIN, *Back Home*

For further discussion and examples, see Section 32g.

40i **Avoid "omnibus" words.**

One of the chief impediments to exactness in writing is the overuse of words like *aspect, case, cute, factor, field, fine, important, nice, point, swell, thing, type, wonderful.* These are so general and inclusive in meaning that they are called OMNIBUS words. They have legitimate uses:

ACCURATE USE   The perfection of the assembly line was an *important factor* in the development of mass-production industries.

ACCURATE USE   One interesting *aspect* of Robbins' *case* was the fervor with which the defense attorney addressed the jury.

But be careful not to let omnibus words lure you from the search for the specific word you need. Overdependence on them will result in triteness, and in time may even rob you of the ability to see things with freshness and to describe them with vigor. (See "Triteness," 42c.)

LOOSE   My job has certain *aspects* which I dislike.
REVISED   My job has certain *responsibilities* which I dislike.

LOOSE   He has a *nice* home overlooking Lake Washington.
REVISED   He has a *large* (*comfortable, modern, rambling, expensive,* etc.) home overlooking Lake Washington.

EXERCISE 40i. Find at least four words that express more specifically the meaning of each of the following words.

Sample: walked—trudged, shuffled, sauntered, ambled

1. spoke (verb)
2. wrote
3. hit (verb)
4. cried
5. built

6. led
7. eat
8. correct (verb)
9. break
10. run

In composing, as a general rule, run your pen through every other word you have written; you have no idea what vigor it will give your style.
                                                    —SIDNEY SMITH

41 Directness = DIR

The challenge to <u>directness</u> comes from two fronts—wordiness and vagueness. A wordy writer uses more words than are necessary to convey his meaning.

WORDY   He attacks the pratice of making a profitable business out of college athletics from the standpoint that it has a detrimental and harmful influence on the college students, and, to a certain degree and extent, on the colleges and universities themselves.

IMPROVED   He attacks commercialization of college athletics as detrimental to the students, and even to the universities themselves.

A vague writer fails to convey his meaning sharply and clearly.

VAGUE   The report asserts the danger from unguarded machines which may lessen the usefulness of workers in later life as well as reducing their life expectancy.

IMPROVED   The report asserts that unguarded machines may severely injure or even kill workers.

Vagueness and wordiness are sometimes indistinguishable, as in the preceding examples. The weight of unnecessary words tends to obscure meaning. But very often wordiness is just awkwardness. The meaning is clear, but the expression is clumsy.

AWKWARD The notion that Communists are people who wear long black beards is a very common notion.

IMPROVED The notion is common that Communists are people who wear long black beards.

41a Eliminate deadwood by judiciously reducing clauses to phrases, phrases to single words.

DEADWOOD consists of words that add nothing to the meaning of a sentence. In *The football captain, who is an All-American player, played his last game today,* the words *who is* and *player* are deadwood. Sometimes you can prune a sentence by changing the position of important words. *Yesterday's snow is melting* is more concise than *The snow, which fell yesterday, is melting.* You can eliminate deadwood from your writing by careful proofreading. Remember that simple, direct expression is almost always best, and that all unnecessary words and phrases should be ruthlessly excised.

DEADWOOD When the time to go had arrived, Jay picked up his suitcase and went to the door.

REVISED When it was time to go, Jay picked up his suitcase and went to the door.

DEADWOOD After the close of the war, Phipps Ford entered the university as a special student.

REVISED After the war, Phipps Ford entered the university as a special student.

DEADWOOD She is attractive in appearance, but she is a rather selfish person.

REVISED She is attractive, but rather selfish.

DEADWOOD There were instances of aggression on the country's frontier in many cases.

REVISED There were many instances of aggression on the country's frontier.

One kind of deadwood is CIRCUMLOCUTION (literally, *talking around*)—the use of several words where a single exact one will do. *In this day and age* is a longer *today; call up on the telephone* a longer *telephone; destroyed by fire* a longer *burned; was made the recipient of* a longer *was given.*

EXERCISE 41a. Eliminate the deadwood from the following sentences.

1. The fastest type of automobile requires the best quality of gasoline.
2. I voted for him because he has an interesting-looking face and an impressive type of program.
3. Love and understanding of them are two of the most important things young children need.
4. This book is designed to transmit to you the basic fundamentals of good English.
5. Most congressmen spend a majority of the hours of each working day attending subcommittee meetings.
6. After several hours of shopping around to buy my mother a gift, I finally decided to give her a check to buy whatever she decided she preferred.
7. It's wrong to make unfair generalizations about acquaintances you don't know very well.
8. He is an expert in the field of atomic engineering.
9. After he finished his military service in the navy, he decided to go on and enroll again in school.
10. She had long blonde tresses on her head and long lashes on her eyes.

41b Use one exact word for two or more approximate words.

Deadwood and circumlocutions make sentences clumsy; a more serious violation of directness is the use of two or more loose synonyms for a single precise word.

LOOSE His *temperament* and *personality* are not very pleasant.

REVISED His *disposition* is not very pleasant.

LOOSE He spoke entertainingly of his *deeds* and *doings* as a foreign correspondent.

REVISED He spoke entertainingly of his *adventures* as a foreign correspondent.

EXERCISE 41b. Find a single synonym to express the meaning of the following pairs.

real and *true*	*amazed* and *surprised*
plays and *poems*	*severe* and *strict*
life and *times*	*flat* and *even*
love and *regard*	*proud* and *vain*
costly and *dear*	*conscientious* and *honest*

41c **Do not use words that needlessly repeat the meaning of other words.**

This clumsiness is known as REDUNDANCY or TAUTOLOGY—for example, *seen by the eyes* and *audible to the ears*.

NOT   He advanced *forward* and told the sergeant that he had captured four enemy spies.

BUT   He advanced (*or* came forward) and told the sergeant that he had captured four enemy spies.

NOT   Battalion A retreated *back* to the river bank.

BUT   Battalion A retreated to the river bank.

NOT   One of the first assignments in English was to write *my own* autobiography.

BUT   One of the first assignments in English was to write an autobiography.

Be careful to avoid unnecessarily long forms of words. *Irregardless* is merely a longer *regardless; preventative* a longer *preventive.* Even when the longer form does exist, as *truthfulness* and *virtuousness,* try substituting the shorter form (*truth, virtue*).

SUPERFLUOUS   He is a very *preeminent* man, having a reputation as the the country's greatest surgeon.

REVISED   He is an *eminent* man, reputed to be the country's greatest surgeon.

SUPERFLUOUS   In *summarization,* Lewis Doser spoke of the need for a larger library.

REVISED   In *summary,* Lewis Doser spoke of the need for a larger library.

EXERCISE 41c. Eliminate all redundancies or tautologies from the following sentences.

1. It was the consensus of opinion among the students that grades should be abandoned.
2. Teachers should provide several examples to illustrate the grammatical rules they are trying to teach.
3. So far as understanding his meaning is concerned, I would classify Joyce in the category of writers who are very difficult to read.
4. The Administration has promised to reduce taxes lower uncountless numbers of times, but to this day it hasn't done so yet.
5. The modern student of today is primarily interested in applying what he learns in the larger world outside the classroom.

6. I like rock and roll as well as the next person, but after listening to it for a whole afternoon I get tired of it and it becomes boring to me.

7. In good writing there is always a great deal of sincerity in the writer's use of words and phrases.

8. The instructor said firmly that the class would meet at nine A.M. in the morning.

9. We had planned to arrive back at the house before nightfall.

10. The car sped quickly down the highway for several miles before it finally skidded out of control.

41d   Avoid awkward repetition.

Awkward repetition makes a sentence wordy. Effective repetition is a legitimate way of securing emphasis.

EFFECTIVE   All *dullness* is in the mind; it comes out thence and diffuses itself over everything round the *dull* person, and then he terms everything *dull,* and thinks himself the victim of *dull* things.
—C. E. MONTAGUE

EFFECTIVE   Don't *join* too many gangs. *Join* few if any. *Join* the United States and *join* the family—but not much in between, unless a college.
—ROBERT FROST

EFFECTIVE   A *moderately* honest man with a *moderately* faithful wife, *moderate* drinkers both, in a *moderately* healthy house: that is the true middle class unit.
—G. B. SHAW

AWKWARD   Methods of using the harvesting equipment are being *improved* constantly to *improve* efficiency.

AWKWARD   The investigation revealed that the *average teacher teaching* industrial arts in California has an *average* working and *teaching* experience of five years.

AWKWARD   The *important subject* on which I am going to speak is the *subject* of fraternity affairs, a *subject* of great *importance* to college students.

EXERCISE 41d. Eliminate awkward repetition from the following sentences.

1. The instructor assigned *Tom Jones,* but most of the students read short, condensed digests of the novel.

2. Always check to see where the fire escape is located so you'll know where it is in case there's a fire and you need to escape.

3. Instead of working he was recounting a narrative of what had happened to him on the way to the office.

4. He is an industrial engineering student studying the principles of time-and-motion study.

5. As far as I'm concerned, government should keep out of intervening in private business, in my opinion.

6. A reckless driver is no better than a murderer who goes around killing people.
7. A student should investigate different fields of study before making a decision about what he wants to major in.
8. As the band struck up "Hail to the Chief," the President and the First Lady descended down the staircase.
9. Not long ago, it was difficult for people to believe that a spaceship could actually ascend up into space and land on the moon.
10. Last night we had to circle all around the block before finding a parking space in which to park the car.

41e Use simple, direct expressions in preference to needlessly complex ones.

This does not mean that all writing must be simple. Naturally, highly complex or technical subjects call at times for complex and technical language.

> One of the simplest ways of evolving a favorable environment concurrently with the development of the individual organism, is that the influence of each organism on the environment should be favorable to the *endurance* of other organisms of the same type. Further, if the organism also favors *development* of other organisms of the same type, you have then obtained a mechanism of evolution adapted to produce the observed state of large multitudes of analogous entities, with high powers of endurance. For the environment automatically develops with the species, and the species with the environment.
> —A. N. WHITEHEAD, *Science and the Modern World* [his italics]

But never be ashamed to express a simple idea in simple language. Remember that the use of complicated language is not in itself a sign of superior intelligence. (See "Appropriateness," Section 42d.)

NEEDLESSLY COMPLEX	Not a year passes without some evidence of the fundamental truth of the statement that the procedures and techniques of education are more complicated and complex than they were two decades ago.
MORE DIRECT	Each year shows that methods of education are more complex than they were twenty years ago.

Edgar Dale, in his "Art of Confusion," satirized the notion that language must be pompous and inflated in order to sound learned.

> Young Alvin H. Harrison hesitatingly entered the office of Dr. Maxim S. Kleeshay and timidly inquired about his master's thesis. "What did you think of it?" he asked.

325

"A worthy endeavor," replied the Doctor, "but it has one major defect. It is written at too elementary a level. I would like to offer somewhat tentatively the pertinent observation that graduate students, research workers, and professors will find it too easy and effortless to read—no disciplinary value. Remember that Chancellor Hutchins once said that good education is painful. Furthermore, you haven't stated any significant challenges in your introductory paragraphs."

"I didn't want to offer any challenges. I just wanted to make my ideas clear."

"That's a worthy primary objective, young man. But no educational writing today should fail to point out that the world is in peril, in flux, in conflict, changing, disordered, and disunited. It's either one world or two, you know.

"And another thing—it is interesting to note that you have a mistaken notion about communication on the scholarly level. It is obvious that you are unaware of the appropriate technical terminology in education. Your thesis is too sprightly, too simple."

"You mean that if I am dull enough and labored enough, I'll sound scholarly?"

"A very unfortunate and inaccurate way to put it, young man. I trust that it is not inappropriate to note some examples from your own thesis and to offer some suggestions (tentative, of course) as to how these examples might be shifted into more precise and scholarly language.

"You say on page 59, 'It will be hard to provide enough schools for the three million children entering in 1950.' It would have sounded much better if you had said, 'The phenomenon of fecundity has confronted American education with a challenge of Herculean proportions. An evaluation of the implication to the tax structure of state governments in providing adequate educational facilities is a difficult and complex task.'

"Let me make another point. A critical analysis of your thesis discloses that you are making little use of what is called the adjectival approach in education. You speak of 'thinking.' It would be much better to refer to 'critical thinking.' Change 'an approach to the problem' to 'a constructive approach to the problem.' Instead of 'world citizens' say 'functional world citizens.' At one point here, you say that the teacher is given 'help in working on her problems.' I would say that she had been given 'rather definite assistance in attacking specific difficulties.' You speak of 'reading practices.' Make it 'sound reading practices.' Utilize 'basic fundamentals' and 'desirable goals' a little more. Don't use the word 'function' alone. Say 'basic functions.' " *

EXERCISE 41e. Find a paragraph or two of "needlessly complex" writing in one of your textbooks. Explain in one or two paragraphs how you think the writing might be made more direct.

---

* Reprinted with permission from *The News Letter* (XIV, No. 3), a publication of the Bureau of Educational Research, The Ohio State University, Columbus, Ohio.

EXERCISE 41a-e. Each of the sentences below violates a principle of directness. Find and then correct the error.

1. We of the United States cannot expect to spread peace throughout other nations and countries until we can teach and educate our own people to respect each other as equal individuals.
2. His capacity for hard work makes him capable of working long hours each day.
3. The integration of public schools is a major step forward toward complete equality of all groups.
4. During the entirety of his whole college career, Peter continually went on thinking about his plan to work his way around the world.
5. It has just been in the past couple of years that black Americans have begun to make clear that they wish to develop their own racial identity by themselves without outside interference.
6. The reason for Nixon's choice of Agnew as a running-mate for Vice-President stemmed from the fact that he wanted a Southern candidate as nominee.
7. The first settlers in the West were prospectors who explored the new land as they prospected for gold.
8. The actress acted very badly, but the play was played through to the very end and conclusion.
9. He was the handsomest-looking man I had ever seen before in my life.
10. The increasing filth in our waterways through pollution has bothered and troubled scientists for a period of one and a half decades.

A speech is composed of three things: the speaker, the subject on which he speaks, and the audience he is addressing.

—ARISTOTLE, *Rhetoric*

42 Appropriateness = APPR

Because the English language is constantly growing, it continues to be a useful vehicle for conveying a thought accurately and effectively. Fortunately, words appear, disappear, or shift their meanings slowly so that there is always available a large core of stable, generally used words. Beyond this core are wide ranges of usage: slang, regional expressions, profanity, clichés, stilted diction, jargon. Words from these categories must be used sparingly if at all.

There are no words in the English language which cannot be used somewhere at some time. But when a piece of writing is overloaded with slang or clichés, the question of <u>appropriateness</u> must be raised. You may consider yourself such a casual, easy-going person that you think casual, easy-going language is appropriate to you. It may be—in a letter to a close friend about an exciting summer holiday. Even in letter-writing, however, you must also consider your audience and your subject: that letter to a friend would necessarily be different if you were expressing your sympathy for an illness in his family. But when you sit down to write essays for your courses, keep your eye on that core of stable, generally used and generally understood words. If you do depart from that area of general usage, you must have a good reason.

42a Ordinarily, avoid slang.

Webster's Seventh New Collegiate Dictionary defines SLANG as *an informal nonstandard vocabulary composed typically of coinages, arbitrarily changed words, and extravagant, forced or facetious figures of speech.* Sometimes slang results from an intentional mispronunciation (*hoss, dawg*) or sometimes from corrupting an ordinary word to cover a different range of meanings (*lousy, swell, tough, cool*). But usually a slang word is an exaggerated metaphor (*fishface, blockhead, highbrow, cash in your chips, ball and chain*).

It would be unrealistic to insist that all slang is vulgar or inappropriate. Slang, after all, is part of the current language; it contributes its share to the growth of the language. Some words move gradually from slang to general use (*rascal, parry*). Clipped forms (*auto, a-bomb, ad, gym, phone*) are entirely appropriate in certain kinds of informal writing. In fact, many skillful writers use slang effectively.

> All she would eat was the ice cream he had recklessly promised her for dessert, and his efforts to sell the yum-yum game to the little girl were disastrous and pitiable. He got himself full of whatever glop it was the child was supposed to eat, and his gorge set a new high as a result. The little girl was not only willing but delighted to let her father clean up the banana squush, or corn moisties, or whatever it was.
>
> —JAMES THURBER, *Alarms and Diversions*

But slang has two serious limitations: (1) a little of it goes a long way, and (2) it is not always appropriate. Even slang that is perfectly understandable becomes tiresome if it is used excessively. And if the particular slang applies to a restricted social or age group, communication is considerably reduced. Slang also tends to age quickly. We may know *crazy, goof balls, way out,* and *the most,* but how many of us know *lollapalooza, balloon juice, twenty-three skiddoo,* or *oh, you kid*—slang well known a few decades ago? The fact that *hep* became *hip* in a little more than ten years indicates how short-lived slang really is.

Then, too, since slang is inherently flippant and casual, it is usually inappropriate in formal writing. It is especially poor usage to mix slang and respectable words indiscriminately in the same sentence.

> Persuading Mrs. Ginnis to be seated, the chairman of the Committee on Indian Affairs asked her politely not to foul up the state's plans to hit pay dirt on Ishimago's claim.

EXERCISE 42a(1). Almost everyone has his favorite slang terms —*swell, lousy, groovy, awful,* and so on. Make a list of your own slang terms and compare the list with those of your classmates to see how "original" your own slang is.

EXERCISE 42a(2). Can you think of a situation or general context in which the following sentences might be appropriate? Explain.
1. We were invited to a party last night but we couldn't make the scene.
2. The trouble was that my boyfriend was all uptight about his car and I got hung up on a TV show I was watching.
3. I finally told him that he should do his thing and I'd do mine.
4. Anyway, I never got a chance to show off my crazy new hairdo and my really cool fur coat.
5. My boyfriend finally came when I was all decked out and he said I was a real ringading broad.
6. I asked him how he was making out with the car and he told me everything was coming up roses.
7. So we decided to blast off and go to a movie.
8. The movie was like dullsville so my boyfriend asked if I wanted to go and tie one on.

42b **Avoid substandard English.**

Substandard, or VULGATE, speech consists of PROFANITY, PROVINCIALISMS (sometimes called LOCALISMS or DIALECTICISMS), and VULGARISMS. Profanity may be fine for providing an emotional release, but it is inappropriate in formal communication. A PROVINCIALISM is a word whose use is generally restricted to a particular region, as *tote* for *carry; poke* for *bag; spider* for *frying pan; gumshoes* for *overshoes; draw* for *small valley.* A VULGARISM is an illiteracy: *ain't, could of, he done, we was.* Double negatives (*can't hardly, can't help but, not never*) are considered vulgarisms by many people, though *I cannot help but be confused* is hardly so objectionable an expression as *I can't never seem to get the point.* The vulgarisms that creep most frequently into writing are IMPROPRIETIES, good words incorrectly used (see "Exactness," Section 40d).

SUBSTANDARD	He *didn't ought to have* spent the money.
REVISED	He shouldn't have spent the money.
SUBSTANDARD	I wish Irving *had of drove more careful.*
REVISED	I wish Irving had driven more carefully.
SUBSTANDARD	*Let's don't* study tonight.
REVISED	Let's not study tonight.

Of all substandard English forms, the double negative (*can't hardly, scarcely none, don't want no,* and so on) is perhaps the most controversial. In the eighteenth century, Englishmen, applying the mathematical principle that two negatives make a positive, ruled out the double negative in grammar. The argument was that a person who says *I don't want nothing to do with you* is really saying *I want something to do with you.* Actually the double (or triple) negative is a means of being emphatic. But since its use is generally frowned upon, you do well to avoid it.

EXERCISE 42b(1). Find at least five examples of provincialisms (as *The cat wants in*) and describe the circumstances under which they could be used appropriately.

EXERCISE 42b(2). If you are a native of the region in which your college is located, ask a classmate from another region to give you a list of ten words or expressions that strike him as being provincialisms in your speech. If you come from another region yourself, make up your own list of provincialisms of the college area and compare it with your classmate's.

42c   Avoid trite expressions.

A trite expression, sometimes called a CLICHÉ, a STEREOTYPED, or a HACKNEYED phrase, is an expression that has been worn out by constant use, as *burning the midnight oil, Father Time, raving beauties, man about town.* Words in themselves are never trite—they are only used tritely. We cannot avoid trite expressions entirely, for they sometimes describe a situation accurately.* But the writer who burdens his language with clichés runs the risk of being regarded as a trite thinker. What would be your estimate of the person who wrote this?

A college education develops a *well-rounded personality* and gives the student an appreciation of *the finer things of life.*

Effectively used, triteness can be humorous. Note how the string of trite expressions in the example below explodes into absurdity when the writer transposes the words in the two clichés in the last clause.

A pair of pigeons were cooing gently directly beneath my window; two squirrels plighted their troth in a branch overhead; at the corner a handsome member of New York's finest twirled his night stick and cast roguish glances at the saucy-eyed flower vendor. The scene could have been staged only by a Lubitsch; in fact Lubitsch himself was seated on a bench across the street, smoking a cucumber and looking as cool as a cigar.
—S. J. PERELMAN, *Keep It Crisp*

Watch for trite words and phrases in your own writing. Whenever you discover any, replace them with new, original ways of expressing yourself. As you proofread your manuscripts, be as sensitive to clichés as you are to misspellings.

EXERCISE 42c(1). The selection below contains a number of trite expressions. List as many as you can identify.

The wily Indians, wishing to strike while the iron was hot, converged on the wagon train at the break of dawn. The hardy pioneers, firing in unison, presented the attacking force with a veritable hail of bullets. Dozens of the pesky redskins keeled over and bit the dust. The rugged frontiersmen continued to give a good account of themselves until broad daylight. Then the Indians broke through the ramparts. The defenders, their backs against the wall, were slaughtered mercilessly. When the dust had risen from the battlefield and when the smoke had cleared away, the carnage was frightful. Every single white man had gone to meet his Maker.

EXERCISE 42c(2). Copy the following passage. Circle all clichés and all expressions that are longer or more involved than they need be. Suggest more appropriate wordings for each.

The American Way is the only feasible route for educational personnel to tread in our educational institutions of learning. Despite its humble

* More fundamentally, of course, triteness is a disease of the personality. If people react to situations in stereotyped ways, their writing will reflect this fact.

origins, this child of adversity, born in a log cabin, has beyond a shadow of a doubt reached the summits in this fair country of ours.

There is too much of a tendency to view this great institution with alarm. But on the other hand people who live in glass houses, which is the type most inclined to cast aspersions and generally be wet blankets, are usually the ones by whom the criticisms are made.

Now I'm just an ordinary schoolteacher, and don't have any complicated ideas on how our schools should be run, but I know that Abe Lincoln, if he were alive, would disapprove of the newfangled techniques that are making a shambles of our educational system.

Foreigners are at the bottom of the attack on our American heritage and the American Way in education. These notorious radicals have wreaked havoc with our boys and girls.

42d Avoid jargon in writing for a general audience.

The term JARGON has several meanings. In a famous essay, "On Jargon," Sir Arthur Quiller-Couch defined the term as vague and "woolly" speech or writing that consists of abstract words, elegant variation, and "circumlocution rather than short straight speech." Linguists often define jargon as hybrid speech or dialect formed by a mixture of languages. An example would be the English-Chinese jargon known as pidgin-English.

To most people, however, jargon is the technical or specialized vocabulary of a particular trade or profession—for example, engineering jargon or educational jargon. Members of the profession, of course, can use their jargon when they are communicating with one another, for it is their language, so to speak. But the use of technical jargon is inappropriate when you are writing for a general audience.

Unfortunately, jargon impresses a great many people simply because it sounds involved and learned. We are all reluctant to admit that we do not understand what we are reading. What, for example, can you make of the following passage?

THE TURBO-ENCABULATOR IN INDUSTRY

. . . Work has been proceeding in order to bring to perfection the crudely conceived idea of a machine that would not only supply inverse reactive current for use in unilateral phase detractors, but would also be capable of automatically synchronizing cardinal grammeters. Such a machine is the Turbo-Encabulator. . . . The original machine had a base plate of prefabulated amulite surmounted by a malleable logarithmic casing in such a way that the two spurving bearings were in a direct line with the pentametric fan. . . . The main winding was of the normal lotus-o-delta type placed in a panendermic semiboloid slot in the stator, every seventh conductor being connected by a non-reversible tremie pipe to the differential girdlespring on the "up" end of the grammeters. . . .*

This new mechanical marvel was a joke, the linguistic creation of a research engineer who was tired of reading jargon.

EXERCISE 42 d . Make a list of twenty words, terms, or phrases that constitute the jargon in a field that you know. Define these terms in a way that a general reader could understand; then justify the use of the terms among the people in your field.

42e **Avoid artificial or stilted diction and "fine writing."**

Artificiality is not inherent in words themselves but in the use that is made of them. Simple facts and assertions should be stated simply and directly, or else you will run the risk of making your writing sound pompous and self-conscious, as in the following examples.

ARTIFICIAL   The edifice was consumed by fire.
NATURAL   The house burned down.

ARTIFICIAL   We were unable to commence our journey to your place of residence because of inclement weather conditions.
NATURAL   We could not come because it was snowing.

Many inexperienced writers believe, mistakenly, that an artificial diction makes for "good writing." They shift gears, so to speak, when they go from speaking to writing. They try to make their writing sound like the speech of a Hollywood version of a college professor, and once again the results sound stilted.

ARTIFICIAL   The athletic contest commenced at the stipulated time.
NATURAL   The game began on time.

ARTIFICIAL   I informed him that his advice was unsolicited.
NATURAL   I told him to mind his own business.

Your writing may become artificial simply because you are trying too hard to write effectively, because you have grown more concerned with <u>how</u> you write than with <u>what</u> you write. Writing marked by a continuously artificial diction is called "fine writing."

* Reprinted by permission of the publishers, Arthur D. Little, Inc., Cambridge, Mass.

FINE WRITING Whenever the press of daily events and duties relaxes its iron grip on me, whenever the turmoil of my private world subsides and leaves me in quiet and solitude, then it is that I feel my crying responsibility as one of God's creatures and recognize the need to speak out loudly and boldly against the greed and intolerance that carry humanity into the terrible destruction of armed conflict.

NATURAL I am a crusader for international peace.

EXERCISE 42e. Find an example of "fine writing" in a newspaper or magazine and explain in a short paper why you think it ineffective.

42f Avoid mixed and incongruous metaphors and other illogical comparisons.

One of the most effective means of reinforcing and enlivening communication is the use of comparison. An apt figure of speech can help make writing concrete and vivid, and by making one experience understandable in terms of another, it can help clarify an abstract idea.

The teacher shook her finger in my face as she might shake a clogged fountain pen.

When he tried to think of the future, he was like some blundering insect that tries again and again to climb up the smooth wall of a dish into which it has fallen.   —ROBERT PENN WARREN, *Night Rider*

Figurative language, however, has pitfalls for the unwary writer. The student who wrote *We are snowed by a bunch of baloney* was colorful but confused. Unless the figure of speech is clear, logical, and vigorous, it may well obscure rather than clarify your meaning. The following examples suggest the need for care in using figurative language.

Every field of study is pursued in the hope of finding a universal panacea.

Socialists are snakes in the grass, gnawing at the roots of the ship of state.

Unfortunately, the well-meaning search for fresh comparisons may betray a writer into using figures that are inappropriate to what he is trying to say.

The minister was not too proud to spend his days visiting the sick and the needy and those rejected by society. He was as little concerned with personal contamination as a pig in a mud puddle when the Lord's work was to be done.

The effective use of figures of speech in your writing is a real challenge. Nothing is more apt, more pointed, more expert than a good figure of speech. Nothing is flatter or more ludicrous than a poor one. Make a habit of reviewing the originality, congruity, logic, and appropriateness of every figure of speech you use.

EXERCISE 42f. Replace the mixed or incongruous figures of speech in the following sentences with fresher, more appropriate comparison.

1. We're skating on thin ice and if anybody upsets the applecart we'll all lose our bread and butter.
2. When our ship comes in we'll be sitting on top of the world.
3. It was a black day and although she had a green thumb she felt blue.
4. As the President said, university administrators should stiffen their spines and throw the book at disorderly students.
5. The Senate wanted to plug the loopholes in the tax bill but they couldn't because too many important people had their fingers in the pie.
6. He worked as busily as a beaver but one day he got as sick as a dog and decided to turn over a new leaf.
7. He jumped out of the frying pan and into the fire and got his fingers burned.
8. I'm as blind as a bat without my glasses, even in my apartment which I know like the back of my hand.
9. She was head over heels in love with him but she kept her feet firmly on the ground.
10. He had his back to the wall when he finally hit the nail on the head.

EXERCISE 42 a-f. First assume an "audience" (English teacher, classmates, group of businessmen, parents, etc.); then comment on the appropriateness of the language in the following selection in terms of that audience.

Like many other just plain "guys," I just graduated from high school. Being like most of these other guys, I naturally didn't really accomplish much during my previous school years. Yes, I got fair grades, met lots of swell kids, played football. I guess I'm just one of those guys who had the run of the school and never bothered to study.

No, I'm not bragging. I'm just telling you why high school was never like college.

A lot of people graduate from high school every year. A good percentage go to college and the rest go out and get a job. Four years later, the college student graduates. Does that mean he's going to get a better job than the fellow who went from high school directly to a job?

No. It doesn't mean a thing unless the guy in college really studied and hit the books. What I'm trying to bring out is that a person who goes to college and doesn't study is no better off than a guy who goes out and gets a job immediately after high school graduation.

So college for me is the "big jump." I fooled around in high school, and if I don't get right down and study now, I might as well quit school and start that $100.00 a week job.

Now, I don't have anything against a $100.00 a week job. It's just that twenty years from now, I'd probably still be there getting the same $100.00. This is it, so I guess it's time for me to bear down and study hard. I think this will be the "big jump."

"DICTION" REVIEW EXERCISE   (Sections 40 through 42). Revise each of the following sentences according to what you have learned in the sections on "Exactness," "Directness," and "Appropriateness."

1. He was trying to keep abreast of company developments when the tide turned against him and his reputation ebbed.
2. A college student has to invest most of his time with studying if he is going to be a successful student.
3. The joint was jumping as the manager came out and asked me to cool it.
4. Though I do very well in the field of philosophy, I have a striking incompetency in the field of mathematics.
5. The authorship of the novel has not been authenticated, but the evidence of the extant material that survives points to one Joshua Fiddings.
6. The sheriff suspicioned that the prisoners had hacksawed their way out of jail.
7. Compared to Johnson, who's as strong as a bear, Wilson is as slow as molasses and as weak as a kitten.
8. Mr. Smith's frequent forgetfulness of his wife's shopping instructions was the bane of her existence.
9. She was the apple of his eye but he took a dim view of her putting the cart before the horse and locking the stable door after the horse was stolen.
10. Professor Caitlin's life was poor in terms of meager remunerative values, but more students in the college remember him than any other teacher.
11. Coaches are paid for the type of teams they produce or for the number of winning games per season.
12. The principal censored the boy's actions in a meanly manner.
13. I thought I was doing the best thing when I signed up for the army.
14. Even though homemaking is an important occupation, only a small number of homemakers have thorough preparation for the task.
15. By reading *Yachting* I am able to keep abreast with the tide of affairs in the sailing world.

*"Awfully nice" is an expression than which few could be sillier:
but to have succeeded in going through life without saying it a
certain number of times is as bad as to have no redeeming vice.*

—H. W. FOWLER

43 Glossary of Usage = GLOS

This glossary discusses a number of words and phrases that present usage problems. The list is not complete; it includes only the most persistent trouble-makers.* A good desk dictionary or an unabridged dictionary will give detailed information on words and expressions that are not included here.

As far as possible the judgments noted in this glossary are consistent with the best available dictionaries and usage studies. Even so, many of the judgments and labels that appear here are tentative, for usage is sometimes vague and always changing. Moreover, usage is often a local or sectional matter; errors common in parts of the Middle West may be rare in the East, the South, or the Far West. In spite of this reservation, nearly all the words and phrases listed in the glossary will be inappropriate to the kind of writing expected of students in most college courses; those labeled ILLITERATE are, of course, inappropriate to the speaking of educated people as well as to their writing.

The following are the principal labels of usage in this glossary:

COLLOQUIAL means often used in informal conversation but generally avoided in all except quite informal writing. The great majority, if not all, of the words and phrases labeled colloquial in this glossary should be avoided in college writing unless used consciously for a special purpose.

* For further discussion of language levels and of usage labels see "The Standards of Modern English," pp. 11–16, and "The Dictionary," pp. 286–300.

INFORMAL means the language of familiar, everyday affairs. The label is used infrequently in this glossary and is applied only to a few words and phrases which occur frequently in less formal kinds of writing but are widely avoided in formal writing.

ILLITERATE means substandard, occurring only in the speech of uneducated speakers.

DIALECT means limited to a particular region and hence not generally used in writing.

SLANG means language comprising certain widely used current terms having a forced, fantastic, or grotesque meaning. Slang is generally unsuitable for formal writing and should be used in informal writing only with great care and then only for special purposes.

JARGON means the special language of a particular occupation or group. Jargon is not appropriate for most writing intended for general readers.

In addition to specifically labeled words, the glossary includes a number of words and phrases which, though standard, are so overused as to have become objectionable to many readers (*great, marvelous,* and *nice* as vague words of approval, for example) or are so closely associated with particular kinds of writing (law, business, journalism, for example) as to be avoided by most writers addressing general readers.

A, An. *A* is used before words beginning with a consonant sound even though the sound is spelled with a vowel (as in *universe*); *an* is used before words beginning with a vowel sound or with a silent *h*. Some speakers use *an* before words beginning with a pronounced *h*, as *an historian*, but *a* is preferred before such words.

a dog, a wagon, a habit, a union; an apple, an Indian, an hour, an uproar.

Above. The use of *above* to refer to something stated in an earlier section of a piece of writing—as in *the paragraph above, the above agreement*—is standard English and occurs frequently in legal and business writing. Except in such very formal contexts, many writers object to it as stilted and wooden.

Accept, Except. These verbs are sometimes confused because of their similarity in sound. *Accept* means "to receive." *Except* (as a verb) means "to exclude."

He *accepted* the gift with pleasure.

We *excepted* George from the list of candidates.

Ad. A shortened form of *advertisement* inappropriate in formal writing. Other clipped forms include *auto, exam, math, phone, photo.*

Affect, Effect. These words are sometimes confused because of their similarity in sound. As verbs, *affect* means "to influence," and *effect* means "to bring about." As a noun, *effect* means "result."

> His fame does not *affect* his personality.
> We *effected* a truce with our enemies.
> Her studying had a good *effect* on her grades.

Aggravate. In formal English *aggravate* means "to intensify" or "to make worse." Colloquially, it is often used as a substitute for *annoy* or *provoke.*

> FORMAL   The hot sun *aggravated* his suffering.
> COLLOQUIAL   His teasing *aggravated* her.

Agree to, With. *Agree to* means "consent"; *agree with* means "concur."

> I *agree to* the contract.
> I *agree with* John's opinion.

Ain't. An illiterate or dialect contraction of *am not* extended indiscriminately to *is not, are not, has not,* and *have not.* Though studies have shown *ain't* is used in speech by educated speakers in some parts of the U.S., it is strongly disapproved by the great majority of educated speakers and writers.

Alibi. In formal English, *alibi* has the technical legal meaning "a plea of having been elsewhere than at the alleged place where an act was committed." Colloquially, *alibi* means "an excuse."

All the farther. A dialect substitute for *as far as.*

> FORMAL   Lane Avenue is *as far as* this bus goes.
> DIALECTAL   Lane Avenue is *all the farther* this bus goes.

Allude, Refer. *Allude* means "to refer to indirectly." *Refer* means "to direct attention to."

> When he spoke of campus unrest, we knew that he was *alluding* to the recent student strike.
> The footnote *referred* the reader to another text.

Allusion, Illusion. *Allusion* means "an indirect reference." *Illusion* means "a misleading image" or "a false impression."

339

The speaker made an *allusion* to the President.

The heat waves from the road produced the *illusion* of a pool of water.

Already, All ready.   The adverb *already* means "previously." The adjective phrase *all ready* means "completely prepared."

When he reached the station, his train had *already* gone.

By eight o'clock we were *all ready* to start hiking.

All right.   *All right* is the only correct spelling. *Alright,* though occasionally used by writers of advertising and fiction, has not been generally accepted.

Alot.   Should be rendered as two words: *a lot.*

Also.   Not to be used as a substitute for *and.*

We packed a tent, our guns, *and* (not *also*) our fishing tackle.

Altogether, All together.   The adverb *altogether* means "wholly, completely." The adjective phrase *all together* means "in a group."

I am *altogether* pleased with my new piano.

We were *all together* for the family reunion.

Alumnus, Alumna.   An *alumnus* (plural *alumni*) is a male graduate. An *alumna* (plural *alumnae*) is a female graduate.

A.M., P.M.   Use these abbreviations only with figures.

Among, Between.   *Among* implies more than two persons or things; *between* implies only two. To express a reciprocal relationship, or the relationship of one thing to several other things, however, *between* is commonly used for more than two.

She divided the toys *among* the three children.

Jerry could choose *between* pie and cake for dessert.

An agreement was reached *between* the four companies.

The surveyors drove a stake at a point *between* three trees.

Amount, Number.   *Amount* refers to quantity or mass. *Number* refers to countable objects.

Irrigation requires a large *amount* of water.

The farmer raised a small *number* of beef cattle.

An, A.   See *A, An.*

And etc. Etc. (Latin *et cetera*) means "and so forth." The redundant *and etc.* means literally "and and so forth."

And/or. A legalism to which some readers object.

And which, But which. Do not insert *and* or *but* unnecessarily before a subordinate clause beginning with *which.* "Rising student enrollments present a problem *which* (not *and which*) is hard to solve."

Angle. Slang for *point of view* or *aspect.* In formal writing *angle* often seems inappropriate.

Newton had a new *angle* on the laws of physics.

Ante-, Anti-. *Ante-* means "before," as in *antedate. Anti-* means "against," as in *anti-American.* The hyphen is used after *anti-* before capital letters, and before *i,* as in *anti-intellectual.*

Any. Colloquial when used with the meaning "at all" in negative or interrogative sentences.

It hasn't rained *any.*
Did it hurt the dog *any?*

Anyone, Everyone, Someone. Not the same as *any one, every one, some one. Anyone* means "anybody," "any person"; *any one* means "any single person or thing." Similarly with *everyone* and *someone.*

He will talk to *anyone* who visits him.
He will talk to *any one* of the students but not to all of them.

Anyplace. Colloquial for *anywhere.*

Anyways, Anywheres. Dialect forms of *anyway, anywhere.*

Apt, Likely. In formal writing *apt* usually refers to a natural ability or habitual tendency. *Likely* refers to a probability. In informal English, *apt* is often used as a synonym for *likely.*

FORMAL   Grandma is *apt* at losing her glasses.
FORMAL   The hockey game is *likely* to be exciting.
INFORMAL   The hockey game is *apt* to be exciting.

Around. Colloquial when used to mean "about" or "near."

COLLOQUIAL   He left *around* midnight.
                       He liked to be *around* the beach.
FORMAL   He left *about* midnight.
                       He liked to be *near* the beach.

As.   In introducing clauses, *as* is somewhat less precise than *since* or *because*.

LOOSE	*As* we were late, we rode to the theater in a taxi.
MORE PRECISE	*Because* we were late, we rode to the theater in a taxi.

As a method of.   Overused and wordy when followed by a gerund.

WORDY	Swimming is useful *as a method of* developing coordination.
REVISED	Swimming is useful *for developing* coordination.

As . . . as, So . . . as.   In negative comparisons formal English prefers *so . . . as* to *as . . . as*. This distinction is not usually observed in informal English.

FORMAL	He is *as* tall *as* I am.
FORMAL	He is not *so* tall *as* I am.
INFORMAL	He is not *as* tall *as* I am.

As to.   An imprecise substitute for *about*.

INEXACT	He questioned me *as to* my plans.
IMPROVED	He questioned me *about* my plans.

At.   Redundant in such constructions as the following:

REDUNDANT	Where are you eating *at?*
	Where is he *at* now?
IMPROVED	Where are you eating?
	Where is he now?

At about, At around.   An unnecessary doubling of prepositions. Deadwood may be avoided by using *at, about,* or *around,* whichever is the most exact.

INEXACT	He arrived *at about* one o'clock.
EXACT	He arrived *at* (or *about*) one o'clock.

Auto.   See *Ad.*

Awful.   Colloquial when used to mean "ugly," "exceedingly bad," or "unpleasant." The use of *awful* and *terrible* in this sense, though common in some speech, is widely disapproved in writing.

COLLOQUIAL	The concert was *awful*.
IMPROVED	The concert was *very poor* (or *very bad*).

Badly.   Used informally in the sense of *very much* or *greatly* with the verbs *need* and *want*.

FORMAL   I *very much* need a new coat.

INFORMAL   I need a new coat *badly*.

Balance. Colloquial when used to mean "the rest," "remainder" (except when referring to a *bank balance*).

FORMAL   I stayed at home for the *rest* of the evening.

COLLOQUIAL   I stayed at home for the *balance* of the evening.

Bank on, Take stock in. Colloquial for *rely on, trust in.*

Being that, Being as how. Illiterate substitutes for the appropriate subordinating conjunctions *as, because, since.*

Beside, Besides. *Beside* is a preposition meaning "by the side of." *Besides,* generally used as an adverb, means "moreover," "in addition to."

He sat down *beside* her.

Besides, we have to wait here for John.

Between, Among. See *Among.*

Blame for, Blame on. Both expressions are standard, but the first is preferred by many in formal English.

ACCEPTABLE   He blamed the accident on the pedestrian.

PREFERRED   He blamed the pedestrian for the accident.

Bursted, Bust, Busted. The principal parts of the verb are *burst, burst, burst.* *Bursted* is an old form of the past and past participle which is no longer considered good usage. *Bust* and *busted* are illiterate.

But, Hardly, Scarcely. These words are negative in their implications. Avoid using them with other negatives.

WEAK   He *didn't have but* one more hour.

IMPROVED   He *had only* one more hour.

WEAK   He *hadn't scarcely* finished.

IMPROVED   He had *scarcely* finished.

WEAK   He *couldn't hardly* see.

IMPROVED   He *could hardly* see.

But that, But what. In formal usage *that* is preferable to *but what.*

FORMAL   I don't doubt *that* you are right.

COLLOQUIAL   I don't doubt *but what* you are right.

Calculate, Guess, Reckon.   The use of these terms to mean "think" or "expect" is colloquial.

Can, May.   In formal English *can* means "to be able"; *may* means "to have permission." Colloquially, *can* is commonly used to imply both ability and permission.

FORMAL   She *can* bake delicious pies.

FORMAL   *May* I go to the church supper with you?

COLLOQUIAL   *Can* I go to the church supper with you?

May is also used in the sense of possibility.

This problem *may* be solved as follows.

Can't hardly, Can't help but.   See *But, Hardly, Scarcely.*

Can't seem to.   Formal usage prefers *seem unable to.*

FORMAL   He *seems unable* to pass his history courses.

COLLOQUIAL   He *can't seem to* pass his history courses.

Case, Line.   Frequently used unnecessarily.

WORDY   *In the case of* Jones, he passed the exam.

BETTER   Jones passed the exam.

WORDY   *In the case of* Henry, the final paper was good.

BETTER   Henry's final paper was good.

WORDY   We need something *in the line of* a typewriter.

BETTER   We need a typewriter.

Compare to, Compare with.   *Compare to* is used to liken two things, to represent them as the same in some way; *compare with* is used to examine things in order to discover their likeness or unlikeness.

He *compared* the typewritten copy *with* the original to see if they were the same.

He *compared* a typewriter *to* a hand printing press.

Complected.   A dialect form occurring in such compounds as *light-complected, dark-complected.*

Considerable.   Standard as an adjective meaning "amount"; colloquial as a noun meaning "much"; illiterate as an adverb meaning "considerably" or "very."

STANDARD	They lost *considerable* property in the flood.
COLLOQUIAL	They lost *considerable* in the flood.
ILLITERATE	They were *considerable* (*very, considerably*) hurt by the flood.

Contact. There is some prejudice, which seems to be disappearing, against the verb *contact* meaning "to meet or talk with." The word is borrowed from commercial jargon. In formal and informal writing a more specific word, such as *meet, interview, consult, talk to,* or *write to,* is preferable.

Continual, Continuous. *Continual* means "frequently repeated." *Continuous* means "without interruption."

He was distracted by *continual* telephone calls.

We heard the *continuous* sound of the waves.

Convince, Persuade. Generally, you *convince* someone that something is so, but *persuade* him to do something. However, this distinction is becoming increasingly blurred.

He *convinced* me that I was wrong.

He *persuaded* me to go with him.

Could of. Illiterate form of *could have.*

Couple. *Couple* in the sense of *two or three* is colloquial, but in any case it should be followed by the preposition *of.*

Credible, Creditable, Credulous. These adjectives are sometimes confused. *Credible* means "believable." *Creditable* means "praiseworthy." *Credulous* means "inclined to believe on slight evidence."

His story seemed *credible* to the jury.

She gave a *creditable* piano recital.

The *credulous* child thought the moon was made of cheese.

Cute. Overused and trite as a vague word of approval.

Data, Phenomena. These nouns are the plural forms of *datum,* "a fact on which an inference is based," and *phenomenon,* "an observable fact or event." In informal usage *data* is frequently treated as a collective noun with a singular verb.

FORMAL	*This datum is* (or *these data are*) valuable.
INFORMAL	*This data is* valuable.

Deal. Colloquial in the sense of *bargain* or *transaction* (*the best deal in town*); of *secret arrangement* (*He made a deal with the gangsters*); and of *treatment* (*He had a rough deal fom the Dean*).

Definite, Definitely.   Often misspelled *definate, definately*, these words suggest fixed limits and are colloquial as vague intensifiers (*He is definitely handsome*).

Different than.   See "Exactness," Section 40g.

Don't.   A contraction for *do not*, not for *does not*.

He *doesn't* (not *don't*) want his dinner.

Doubt but what.   See *But that*.

Due to.   Since *due* is in origin an adjective, some writers object to the use of *due to* as a preposition introducing an adverbial phrase. It is interesting to note that *owing to,* which developed from a participle to a preposition in the same way, is accepted without question. The prepositional use of *due to* is increasingly widespread, and it is appropriate except in the most formal writing.

Due AS AN ADJECTIVE	His failure was *due to* laziness.
FORMAL	The festival was postponed *because of* (or *owing to*) rain.
INFORMAL	The festival was postponed *due to* rain.

Each and every.   Unnecessarily wordy.

Each other, One another.   Fastidious writers prefer *each other* when referring to two persons or things, and *one another* when referring to more than two, but the distinction is not widely observed.

Effect, Affect.   See *Affect, Effect*.

Emigrate, Immigrate.   *Emigrate* means "to move *from* a country." *Immigrate* means "to move *into* a country."

Erik *emigrated* from Sweden.
Erik *immigrated* to America.

Enthuse.   Colloquial for *become enthusiastic*.

FORMAL	We *were enthusiastic* about our vacation.
COLLOQUIAL	We *were enthused* about our vacation.

Equally as good.   The *as* is unnecessary. *Equally good* is more precise.

Etc.   Italics are correct but not necessary. This abbreviation for *and so forth* is appropriate in business usage and may be used in formal writing if its meaning is entirely clear. (See "Abbreviations," Section 17a(4).)

Everyplace. Colloquial when used as an adverb meaning "everywhere."

Everyone. Should be written as two words except when used as a synonym for *everybody*.

Every so often. This expression and *every bit as, every once in a while, every which way* are colloquial.

Everywheres. A dialect form of *everywhere*.

Exam. See *Ad*.

Except, Accept. See *Accept, Except*.

Except for the fact that. Wordy substitute for *except that*.

Expect. In colloquial English *expect* is sometimes used to mean "suppose."

FORMAL   I *suppose* I should mow the lawn.
COLLOQUIAL I *expect* I should mow the lawn.

Extra. There is some prejudice against the use of *extra* as an adverb meaning "unusually."

FORMAL   Monday was an *unusually* warm day.
COLLOQUIAL Monday was an *extra* warm day.

Farther, Further. In formal English some writers use *farther* when referring to distance and *further* when referring to degree or quantity. In informal English this distinction is not widely observed.

FORMAL   We walked two miles *farther*.
INFORMAL   We walked two miles *further*.

Faze. Colloquial for *disconcert, bother,* or *daunt*.

FORMAL   Ridicule did not *bother* him.
COLLOQUIAL Ridicule did not *faze* him.

Fellow. Colloquial when used to mean "person."

Fewer, Less. *Fewer* refers to number. In formal English *less* refers only to degree or quantity. In informal English *less* is sometimes used to refer to number.

FORMAL   He is *less* friendly than he used to be.
FORMAL   *Fewer* than half the students could solve the problem.
INFORMAL   *Less* than half the students could solve the problem.

347

Fiancé, Fiancée. These words, borrowed from the French, are sometimes confused. *Fiancé* (plural *fiancés*) refers to the betrothed man. *Fiancée* (plural *fiancées*) refers to the betrothed woman. In informal writing the accent marks are often dropped.

Fine. As an adjective to express approval (*a fine person*) fine is vague and overused. As an adverb meaning "well" (*works fine*) *fine* is colloquial.

First-rate. Standard in the meaning "of the finest class or quality." Colloquial when used as an adjective or adverb meaning "excellent" or "excellently."

STANDARD	As a student he is *first-rate;* as an athlete he is second-rate.
STANDARD	He is a *first-rate* student but a second-rate athlete.
COLLOQUIAL	That's a *first-rate* hat (*excellent, very good*).
COLLOQUIAL	He swims *first-rate* (*excellently, very well*).

Flunk. Colloquial for *fail*.

Folks. Colloquial when used to mean the members of one's family, or relatives, as in

My *folks* all got together for Thanksgiving.

Standard when used in the sense of people in general, or people of a specified group, as in *young folks.*

Former, Latter. *Former* refers to the first-named of two; *latter* refers to the last-named of two. *First* and *last* are used to refer to one of a group of more than two.

Function. Suggests elaborateness or formality when used to describe a social occasion. Pretentious or ironic when used loosely for *activity.*

Funny. Colloquial when used to mean "strange," "queer," or "odd."

Further, Farther. See *Farther, Further.*

Gentleman, Lady. *Man* and *woman* are preferable to the more pretentious *gentleman* and *lady* unless the speaker is intentionally making a distinction between refined and ill-bred persons. *Ladies and Gentlemen* is a conventional expression used in addressing an audience.

Get. The verb *get* is used in many colloquial and slang expressions that are inappropriate in formal writing. Among these are *get going, get to go, get at it, get wise to, get away with.*

Good. An adjective often used colloquially as an adverb in such sentences as *The motor runs good.* (Formal English would use the adverb *well* to modify the verb *runs.*)

Good and. Colloquial in such expressions as *good and hot, good and ready.*

Gotten. One form of the past participle of *get,* the principal parts of which are *get, got,* and *got* or *gotten.* Both forms are acceptable.

Grand, Great, Wonderful. Avoid the use of these inexact and overworked adjectives to mean "excellent."

Guess. Formal English prefers *think,* or *suppose,* to *guess* in such contexts as I *think* (not *guess*) your plan will work.

Guy. Colloquial in the sense of *boy, man, fellow.*

Had better, Had rather, Would rather. Standard idioms used to express advisability (with *better*) or preference (with *rather*). *Better* alone, however, is colloquial. The idiom *had better* is less formal than *ought* or *should.*

COLLOQUIAL   You *better* plan to be early.
STANDARD   You *had better* plan to be early.
You *ought* to plan to be early.
You *should* plan to be early.

Had of. An illiterate form.

I wish I *had* (not *had of*) seen the eclipse.

Had ought, Hadn't ought. Illiterate for *ought* and *ought not.*

He *ought* (not *had ought*) to treat his wife better.

Half a, A half, A half a. Both *half a* and *a half* are acceptable, but *a half a* ("a half a week") is redundant.

Hanged, Hung. The principal parts of *hang* when referring to death by hanging are *hang, hanged, hanged.* When *hang* is used to mean "suspend," the principal parts are *hang, hung, hung.* In informal English the distinction is not rigidly kept, *hang, hung, hung* being used in all senses.

FORMAL   The outlaw was *hanged* from a cottonwood tree.
INFORMAL   The outlaw was *hung* from a cottonwood tree.

Have got. Formal usage prefers *have.*

FORMAL   I *have* a headache.
COLLOQUIAL   I've *got* a headache.

Healthful, Healthy.   *Healthful* means "giving health." *Healthy* means "having health."

Himself, Myself, Yourself.   See *Myself, Yourself, Himself.*

Home.   Formal usage prefers *at home* after verbs which do not imply motion, as in *stay at home.* When the verb implies motion (*go home*), of course, no preposition is used.

Humans.   Most careful writers prefer *people* or *human beings.*

Idea.   Often vague for *belief, conjecture, intention, plan, theory,* and should be replaced whenever possible by a more specific noun.

If, Whether.   Formal English prefers *whether* to *if* after such verbs as *say, ask, know, doubt, wonder, understand.*

FORMAL   He did not say *whether* he would return.

COLLOQUIAL   He did not say *if* he would return.

Illusion, Allusion.   See *Allusion, Illusion.*

Immigrate, Emigrate.   See *Emigrate, Immigrate.*

Imply, Infer.   *Imply* means "to hint" or "to suggest." *Infer* means "to draw a conclusion."

He *implied* that I was ungrateful.

I *inferred* from his remark that he did not like me.

In, Into.   In formal usage *in* denotes location; *into* denotes direction. In colloquial English *in* is often used for *into.*

FORMAL   We were studying *in* the library.

FORMAL   I fell *into* the pool.

COLLOQUIAL   I fell *in* the pool.

In back of, In behind, In between.   Wordy for *back of, behind, between.*

Individual, Party, Person..   *Individual* refers to one particular person. *Person* refers to any human being as a distinct personality. *Party* refers to a group of people, except in legal language.

Jefferson defended the rights of the *individual.*

She is a *person* (not *an individual*) of strong character.

You are the *person* (not *party*) I am looking for.

Indulge. *Indulge* means "to be tolerant toward" or "to gratify one's desire"; it is not a synonym for *to take part.*

ACCURATE The old man *indulged* (*tolerated*) the noisy parrot.

INACCURATE The ladies *indulged in* (*took part in*) a quarrel.

BUT The ladies *indulged* themselves *in* quarreling (gratified their desires).

Infer, Imply. See *Imply, Infer.*

Ingenious, Ingenuous. *Ingenious* means "clever." *Ingenuous* means "frank" or "naïve."

Inventors are usually *ingenious* people.

He was too *ingenuous* to suspect that he was being tricked.

In my estimation. Like *in my opinion* and *in my judgment,* this phrase is often unnecessary, or is pretentious for *I think, I feel, I believe.*

In regards to. A confusion of the British idiom *as regards* with the American idiom *in regard to.*

Inside of. The *of* is unnecessary when *inside* is used as a preposition. *Inside of* is colloquial for *within* when used in reference to time.

FORMAL We stayed *inside* (not *inside of*) the house.

FORMAL He will arrive *within* an hour.

COLLOQUIAL He will arrive *inside of* an hour.

In the case of. See *Case, Line.*

In the line of. See *Case, Line.*

Into, In. See *In, Into.*

Irregardless. A nonstandard double negative resulting from the confusion of *irrespective* and *regardless.*

Is when, Is where. Noun clauses introduced by *when* or *where* and used to give a definition are avoided by careful writers. (See "Logic," Section 37a.)

LOOSE A first down *is when* the football is advanced ten yards in four plays or fewer.

PRECISE A first down *is made when* the football is advanced ten yards in four plays or fewer.

Its, It's. The possessive pronoun has no apostrophe. *It's* is a contraction of *it is.*

Just. Colloquial for *very, quite.*

> FORMAL   The customer was *very* indignant.
>
> COLLOQUIAL   The customer was *just* indignant.

Kind, Sort. These are frequently treated as plural in such constructions as *these kind of books* and *those sort of dogs.* Preferred usage in both speech and writing requires singular or plural throughout the construction, as in *this kind of book,* or *these kinds of books.*

Kind of, Sort of. Colloquial when used adverbially to mean "somewhat" or "rather."

> FORMAL   She is *rather* pleased.
>
> COLLOQUIAL   She is *kind of* pleased.

Kind of a, Sort of a. The *a* is omitted in formal usage.

> FORMAL   The child wanted some *kind of* toy.
>
> COLLOQUIAL   The child wanted some *kind of a* toy.

Lady, Gentleman. See *Gentleman, Lady.*

Latter, Former. See *Former, Latter.*

Lay, Lie. In colloquial usage, these verbs are often confused. (See "Tense and Mood," Section 3d.)

Lead. *Lead* is not the past tense of *to lead; led* is the correct form.

Learn, Teach. *Learn* means "to gain knowledge." *Teach* means "to impart knowledge."

We *learn* from experience.

Experience *teaches* us many things.

Leave, Let. *Leave* means "to depart." *Let* means "to permit."

I must *leave* now.

Will you *let* (not *leave*) me go with you?

Less, Fewer. See *Fewer, Less.*

Lie, Lay. See *Lay, Lie.*

Like, As, As if. *Like* is a preposition; *as* and *as if* are conjunctions. In informal English *like* is often used as a conjunction to introduce clauses. Formal English prefers *as* or *as if* in such constructions.

FORMAL   He looks *as if* (or *as though*) he might be tired.
INFORMAL   He looks *like* he might be tired.

Likely, Apt. See *Apt, Likely.*

Locate. Colloquial when used to mean "settle."

FORMAL   The immigrant *settled* in Iowa.
COLLOQUIAL   The immigrant *located* in Iowa.

Loose, Lose. *Loose* means "to free." *Lose* means "to be deprived of."

He *loosed* the dog from its leash.
Did you *lose* (not *loose*) your money?

Lots, Lots of. Colloquial for *much* or *a great deal.*

FORMAL   We had a *great deal* of time for recreation.
COLLOQUIAL   We had *a lot of* (or *lots of*) time for recreation.

Mad. Colloquial when used to mean "angry."

Manner. Often unnecessary in phrases like *in a precise manner,* where a single adverb (*precisely*) or a "with" phrase (*with precision*) would do.

Marvelous. Overused as a vague word of approval.

Math. See *Ad.*

May, Can. See *Can, May.*

May of. Illiterate for *may have.*

Mean. Colloquial for *ill-tempered* or *dangerous,* as in *a mean dog.*

Might of. Illiterate for *might have.*

Minus. Journalese for *lacking* or *without.*

Most. Colloquial when used in the sense of *almost.*

FORMAL   *Almost* everybody in the hall cheered the speaker.
COLLOQUIAL   *Most* everybody in the hall cheered the speaker.

Mr. In American usage *Mr.* is followed by a period and is never written out except humorously or ironically.

Must of. Illiterate for *must have.*

Myself, Yourself, Himself. In formal English these intensive pronouns are inappropriate as substitutes for the personal pronouns *I, you, him*.

FORMAL Jack and *I* trimmed the hedge.
COLLOQUIAL Jack and *myself* trimmed the hedge.

They are sometimes appropriate for emphasis.

The President *himself* will be there.
She *herself* said so.

Never-the-less. Should be written as a single word; *nevertheless*.

Nice. Overused as a vague word of approval.

No account, No good. Colloquial for *worthless, useless*.

Noplace. Colloquial for *nowhere*.

Nowhere near. Colloquial for *not nearly*.

Nowheres. A dialect form of *nowhere*.

O.K. Colloquial for *all right* or *correct*.

Off of. The *of* is unnecessary.

He jumped *off* (not *off of*) the wagon.

One and the same. Trite and tautological for *the same*.

One another, Each other. See *Each other, One another*.

On the average of. Trite for *about* or *almost*.

Ought to of. Illiterate for *ought to have*.

Out loud. Colloquial for *aloud*.

Outside of. Colloquial for *except, besides*.

FORMAL Nobody was there *except* me.
COLLOQUIAL Nobody was there *outside of* me.

Over with. Colloquial for *over, ended*.

FORMAL I am glad the cold weather is *over*.
COLLOQUIAL I am glad the cold weather is *over with*.

Party, Person, Individual.   See *Individual, Party, Person.*

Per.   Used mainly in commerical expressions, such as *forty hours per week, thirty cents per yard,* or in phrases of Latin origin, such as *per capita, per diem.* In ordinary writing, *per* is less appropriate than *a* or *an: twice a day, forty cents a dozen.*

Percent.   This abbreviation, meaning "by the hundred," is not followed by a period and may be written as one or as two words. In formal English, *percent* usually follows a numeral (*50 percent*) and is not used as a noun synonym for *portion* or *part. Percentage* is the correct noun for formal usage.

FORMAL   A small *part* of the class was absent.

FORMAL   A small *percentage* of the class was absent.

INFORMAL   A small *percent* of the class was absent.

Percentage.   Awkward in the sense of *number, part, portion.*

AWKWARD   The bay is rough a large *percentage* of the time.

BETTER   The bay is rough a large *part* of the time.

Person, Party, Individual.   *See Individual, Party, Person.*

Phenomena, Data.   See *Data, Phenomena.*

Phone.   See *Ad.*

Photo.   See *Ad.*

Plenty.   Now colloquial when used as an adverb meaning "very" or "amply."

FORMAL   He is a *very* big man.

COLLOQUIAL   He is a *plenty* big man.

Plus.   Journalese for *in addition to.*

Poorly.   Colloquial or provincial for *unwell, in poor health.*

FORMAL   Mother is in *poor health* this winter.

COLLOQUIAL   Mother is *poorly* this winter.

Practical, Practicable.   *Practical* means "useful, not theoretical." *Practicable* means "capable of being put into practice, feasible."

Franklin's *practical* mind made him a good statesman.

His political schemes were *practicable.*

Principal, Principle.   As an adjective *principal* means "chief, main"; as a noun it means "leader, chief officer," or, in finance, "a capital sum, as distinguished from interest or profit." The noun *principle* means "fundamental truth" or "basic law or doctrine."

What is his *principal* reason for being here?

He is the *principal* of the local elementary school.

That bank pays 5 percent interest on your *principal*.

He explained the underlying *principle*.

Prior to.   Usually pretentious for *before*.

Proposition.   Colloquial in the sense of a matter or person to be dealt with, as in *This course is a bad proposition.*

Proven.   A past participle of the verb *prove*, used less often than *proved*.

Put across, Put over, Put in.   *Put across* and *put over* are colloquialisms meaning "to accomplish something against opposition." *Put in* is colloquial for *spend*.

FORMAL   The club was successful in its membership drive.

COLLOQUIAL   The club *put across* its membership drive.

FORMAL   He *spent* a busy day at his office.

COLLOQUIAL   He *put in* a busy day at his office.

Quite a few, Quite a little, Quite a bit.   Colloquial for *many, more than a little, a considerable amount.*

Raise, Rise.   *Raise, raised, raised* is a transitive verb.

I *raise* flowers. I *raised* flowers. I *have raised* flowers.

Rise, rose, risen is an intransitive verb.

I *rise* at daybreak. I *rose* at daybreak. I *have risen* at daybreak.

Real.   Colloquial for *really* or *very*.

FORMAL   The sky was *very* cloudy.

COLLOQUIAL   The sky was *real* cloudy.

Reason is because.   A noun or noun clause should be used instead of *because* in this expression.

FORMAL   The *reason* for his absence *is his illness* (or *that he is ill*).

ILLOGICAL   The *reason* for his absence *is because he is ill.*

Reckon.   See *Calculate*.

Religion. *Religion* is not a synonym for *sect, cult, denomination,* or *faith.*

INACCURATE   He belongs to the Presbyterian *religion.*

ACCURATE   He belongs to the Presbyterian *denomination.*

Remember of. The *of* is unnecessary.

I *remember* (not *remember of*) seeing you before.

Reverend. The title *Reverend* is properly preceded by *the* and followed by *Mr.,* or followed by the first name or initials of the person referred to.

The Reverend Mr. Wells (not Reverend Wells)
Reverend John Wells, The Reverend John Wells
Reverend J. W. Wells, The Reverend J. W. Wells

Right, Right along, Right away. *Right* is colloquial or dialectal when used to mean "very" or "directly."

FORMAL   Being *very* tired, we went *directly* home.

COLLOQUIAL   Being *right* tired, we went *right* home.

Right along and *right away* are colloquial for *continuously* and *immediately.*

Rise, Raise. See *Raise, Rise.*

Said. The adjective *said* (*the said paragraph, the said person*) is a legal term and inappropriate in formal writing.

Seeing as how, Seeing that. Low colloquial for *since* or *because.*

Seldom ever, Seldom or ever. Unidiomatic for *seldom, seldom if ever, seldom or never, hardly ever.*

Set, Sit. See "Tense and Mood," Section 3d.

Shall, Will, Should, Would. There is a tendency to use *will* and *would* in all persons except when a condition or obligation is expressed. *Should* is used for all persons in conditions and obligations.

If he *should* come, call me immediately.
We *should* visit our new neighbors.

Would is used for all persons to express a wish or customary action.

Would that he had listened to my plea!
I *would* ride on the same bus every morning.

Shape. Colloquial for *condition.*

FORMAL   Wrestlers must keep themselves in good *condition.*
COLLOQUIAL Wrestlers must keep themselves in good *shape.*

Shape up. Colloquial for *proceed satisfactorily,* as in *our plans are shaping up.*

Should of. Illiterate for *should have.*

Show up. Colloquial in the meanings "appear" and "prove."

FORMAL   He did not *appear* at the office.
COLLOQUIAL He did not *show up* at the office.

FORMAL   John *proved* superior to Henry.
COLLOQUIAL John *showed up* better than Henry.

Sit, Set. See *Set, Sit.*

Size up. Colloquial for *estimate, judge.*

FORMAL   We *estimated* our financial needs.
COLLOQUIAL We *sized up* our financial needs.

So. In clauses of purposes, *so* instead of *so that* is colloquial.

FORMAL   We camped by a spring *so that* we would have fresh water.
COLLOQUIAL We camped by a spring *so* we would have fresh water.

So is colloquial or informal when used to introduce a main clause where formal usage would have a subordinating conjunction introducing a subordinate clause.

FORMAL   *Because* the rain began to fall, the swimmers left the beach.
COLLOQUIAL Rain began to fall, *so* the swimmers left the beach.

The "feminine" *so,* meaning "very," is colloquial and overused.

FORMAL   She is *very* happy.
COLLOQUIAL She is *so* happy.

Some. Colloquial when used as an adverb meaning "somewhat" or "a little."

FORMAL   He seems *somewhat* gayer.
COLLOQUIAL He seems *some* gayer.

Some is slang when used as an intensive.

He is *some* actor!

Someplace. Colloquial for *somewhere*.

Something, Somewhat. Colloquial for *slightly*.

COLLOQUIAL   He is *somewhat* of a liar.
COLLOQUIAL   He is *something* of a liar.

Somewheres. Dialect form of *somewhere*.

Sort of, Kind of. See Kind of, Sort of.

Sort of a, Kind of a. See *Kind of a, Sort of a.*

Stop. Colloquial when used as a substitute for *stay*.

FORMAL   I *stayed* overnight at a hotel.
INFORMAL   I *stopped* overnight at a hotel.

Such. As an intensive, *such* is colloquial.

FORMAL   He told a *very* interesting story.
COLLOQUIAL He told *such* an interesting story.

No such a is vulgate for *no such*.

FORMAL   There is *no such* place.
VULGATE   There is *no such a* place.

Suspicion. Dialectal when used in place of the verb *suspect*.

Swell. Slang as an adjective meaning "first-rate," "very good."

Sure. Colloquial for *certainly, surely*.

Take and. Illiterate in such expressions as *I'll take and swim across the lake.*

Teach, Learn. See *Learn, Teach.*

Terrible, Terribly. Colloquial for *very bad*.

That. Colloquial when used as an adverb. As a relative pronoun *that* may be used only to introduce restrictive clauses. (*Which* may be used for both restrictive and nonrestrictive clauses.)

FORMAL   Nobody can be *so* exhausted after such a short swim.
COLLOQUIAL Nobody can be *that* exhausted after such a short swim.

There, Their, They're. Don't confuse these. *There* is an adverb or an expletive (*he works there, there are six*). *Their* is a pronoun (*their rooms*). *They're* is a contraction for *they are*.

Than, Then. Don't confuse these. *Than* is a conjunction (*younger than John*). *Then* is an adverb indicating time (*then, not now*).

Thing. Whenever possible, *thing* should be replaced with a more specific word.

This here, That there, These here, Them there. Illiterate for *this, that, these, those*.

Through. Formal usage prefers *finished*.

FORMAL   I have *finished* working.
INFORMAL   I am *through* working.

Thusly. A pretentious form of *thus*.

Transpire. *Transpire* means "to become known." The use of *transpire* in the sense of *to come to pass, happen, occur* is still disapproved by some writers, though this meaning is fairly common in informal writing.

Try and, Sure and. Colloquial for *try to, sure to*.

FORMAL   *Try to* hold your head erect.
COLLOQUIAL   *Try and* hold your head erect.

FORMAL   *Be sure to* finish your work.
COLLOQUIAL   *Be sure and* finish your work.

Unique. Several adjectives such as *unique, perfect, round, straight,* and *complete* name qualities that do not vary in degree. Logically, therefore, they cannot be compared. Formal use requires *more nearly round, more nearly perfect* and the like. The comparative and superlative forms, however, are widely used colloquially in such phrases as *the most unique house, most complete examination, most perfect day*. Their occurrence even in formal English is exemplified by the phrase *more perfect union* in the Constitution.

FORMAL   His deeds are *unique* in history.
COLLOQUIAL   His deeds are *more unique* in history than people suspect.

Utilize. A waste of syllables. It is almost always a substitute for *use*. However, the word is now almost universally utilized.

Very. Careful writers tend to avoid using *very* to modify a past participle which has not been fully established as an adjective. They insert *much, well, greatly, deeply,* or some other appropriate adverb between *very* and the past participle. This distinction is commonly ignored in colloquial English.

FORMAL   He was *very much* overworked.

COLLOQUIAL   He was *very* overworked.

Wait on. Colloquial or provincial in the sense of *wait for. Wait on* means "to serve, attend."

FORMAL   I *waited for* a bus.

COLLOQUIAL   I *waited on* a bus.

Want in, Want out, Want off. Colloquial for *want to come in, want to go out, want to get off.*

Want to. Colloquial for *ought, should.*

FORMAL   You *should* be alert when crossing the street.

COLLOQUIAL   You *want to* be alert when crossing the street.

Way, Ways. *Way* is colloquial when used to mean "away" (*way across the mountains*). *Ways* is used provincially for *way* in such expressions as *a little ways up the hill.*

Where. Colloquial when used for *that.*

FORMAL   I read in the mayor's report *that* many local crimes are unsolved.

COLLOQUIAL   I read in the mayor's report *where* many local crimes are unsolved.

Where at. See *At.*

Whether, If. See *If, Whether.*

Wonderful. Overused as a vague word of approval.

Would of. Illiterate for *would have.*

Yourself, Myself, Himself. See *Myself, Yourself, Himself.*

*Spelling is no longer commonly regarded as a proper field for
individuality or experimentation.*   —STUART ROBERTSON

44 Spelling = SP

Language existed first as speech, and the alphabet is basically a
device to represent speech on paper. When letters of the alphabet
have definite values and are used consistently, as in Polish or Spanish, the spelling of a word is an accurate index to its pronunciation,
and vice versa. Not so with English. The alphabet does not represent English sounds consistently. The letter *a* may stand for the
sound of the vowel in *may, can, care,* or *car; c* for the initial consonant
of *carry* or *city; th* for the diphthong in *both* or in *bother.* Different combinations of letters are often sounded alike, as in *rec(ei)ve, l(ea)ve,* or
p(ee)ve. In many words, moreover, some letters appear to perform
no function at all, as in *i(s)land, de(b)t, of(t)en, recei(p)t.* Finally, the
relationship between the spelling and the pronunciation of some
words seems downright capricious, as in *through, enough, colonel, right.*
   Much of the inconsistency of English spelling may be explained
historically. English spelling has been a poor index to pronunciation
ever since the Norman Conquest, when French scribes gave written
English a French spelling. Subsequent tampering with English
spelling has made it even more complex. Early classical scholars
with a flair for etymology added the unvoiced *b* to early English
det and *dout* because they mistakenly traced these words directly
from the Latin *debitum* and *dubitum* when actually both the English
and the Latin had derived independently from a common Indo-
European origin. Dutch printers working in England were responsible for changing early English *gost* to *ghost.* More complications
arose when the spelling of many words changed less rapidly than
their pronunciation. The *gh* in *right* and *through,* and in similar

words, was once pronounced much like the German *ch* in *nicht*. Colonel was once pronounced *col-o-nel*. The final *e* in words like *wife* and *time* was long ago dropped from actual speech, but it still remains as a proper spelling form.

The English tendency to borrow words freely from Latin and French has given us groups like the native English *sight*, the French *site*, and the Latin *cite*. Our word *regal*, with its hard *g*, comes from the Norman French. Our word *regent*, with the *g* sounded as a *j*, comes from Parisian French. Words like *machine, burlesque*, and *suite* come directly from the French, with little change in spelling or pronunciation. *Envelope*, on the other hand, maintains its French spelling but is given an English pronunciation. From Spanish comes the proper noun *Don Quixote;* its Spanish pronunciation (dŏn kē·hō′tä) is still frequently heard, but the English adjective *quixotic* is pronounced kwĭks·ot′ĭk.

The complex history of the English language may help to explain why our spelling is illogical, but it does not justify misspelling. Society tends to equate bad spelling with incompetent writing. In fact, we tend to see only the misspellings and not the quality of the writing, and correct spellings may sometimes blind us to faulty constructions. That particularly American institution—the spelling bee—has for generations put a higher premium on the correct spelling of *phthisis* than on a clearly constructed sentence. To illustrate, we might experiment with our own attitude. Which of the two selections below seems better?

> Parants should teech children the importence of puntuallity.

> The condition of unpunctuality which exists in the character of a great many members of the younger generation should be eliminated by every means that lies at the disposal of parents who are responsible for them.

On first reading, the first sentence seems inferior to the second. Actually the former is the better sentence—more direct and succinct. But the misspellings make it difficult for us to take it seriously. Readers have been conditioned to treat misspellings as one of the greatest sins a writer can commit.

44a **Avoid secondary and British spellings.**

Many words have a secondary spelling, generally British. Though the secondary spelling is not incorrect, as an American writer you should avoid it. Here is a brief list of preferred and secondary spelling forms; consult a good dictionary for others.

1. AMERICAN *e*
   anemia
   anesthetic
   encyclopedia
   fetus

   BRITISH *ae, oe*
   anaemia
   anaesthetic
   encyclopaedia
   foetus

2. AMERICAN *im-, in-*
   impanel
   incase
   inquiry

   BRITISH *em-, en-*
   empanel
   encase
   enquiry

3. AMERICAN *-ize*
   apologize

   BRITISH *-ise*
   apologise

4. AMERICAN *-or*
   armor
   clamor
   flavor
   humor
   labor
   odor
   vigor

   BRITISH *-our*
   armour
   clamour
   flavour
   humour
   labour
   odour
   vigour

5. AMERICAN *-er*
   center
   fiber
   somber
   theater

   BRITISH *-re*
   centre
   fibre
   sombre
   theatre

6. AMERICAN *-o*
   mold
   plow
   smolder

   BRITISH *-ou*
   mould
   plough
   smoulder

7. AMERICAN *-ction*
   connection
   inflection

   BRITISH *-xion*
   connexion
   inflexion

8. AMERICAN *-l*
   leveled
   quarreled
   traveled

   BRITISH *-ll*
   levelled
   quarrelled
   travelled

9. AMERICAN -*e* omitted   BRITISH -*e*

    acknowledgment   acknowledgement
    judgment   judgement

44b   **Proofread your manuscripts carefully to eliminate misspelling.**

In writing a first draft, you are forming words into sentences faster than you can write them down. You are concentrating not on the words you are actually writing but on the words to come. A few mistakes in spelling may easily creep into a first draft. Always take five or ten minutes to proofread your final draft to make sure that you do not let them stand uncorrected.

The failure to proofread accounts for the fact that the words most often misspelled are not, for example, *baccalaureate* and *connoisseur,* but *too, its, lose, receive,* and *occurred.* Not trusting ourselves to spell hard words correctly, we consult a dictionary and take pains to get the correct spelling on paper. But most of us <u>think</u> we can spell a familiar word. Either we never bother to check the spelling, or we assume that a word pictured correctly in our minds must automatically spell itself correctly on the paper in front of us. This thinking accounts for such errors as omitting the final *o* in *too,* confusing the possessive *its* with the contraction *it's,* and spelling *loose* when *lose* is meant. You will never forget how to spell *receive* and *occurred* if you will devote just a few moments to memorizing their correct spelling.

On pages 373 to 375 is a list of 350 words often misspelled. Almost every one of them is a common word; to misspell any of them in a finished paper denotes carelessness.

44c   **Cultivate careful pronunciation as an aid to correct spelling.**

Some words are commonly misspelled because they are mispronounced. The following list of frequently mispronounced words will help you overcome this source of spelling error.

accident*a*lly	note the al
acc*u*rate	note the u
can*d*idate	note the first d
incident*a*lly	note the al
math*e*matics	note the e
prob*a*bly	note the ab
quan*t*ity	note the first t
represen*ta*tive	note the ta
soph*o*more	note the second o

surprise		note the first r
ath<u>le</u>tics	NOT	ath<u>e</u>letics
disast<u>r</u>ous	NOT	disaste<u>r</u>ous
heigh<u>t</u>	NOT	heigh<u>th</u>
gri<u>e</u>-vous	NOT	gre-vi-ous
ir-rel-e-<u>v</u>ant	NOT	ir-rev-e-lant
mis-chi<u>e</u>-vous	NOT	mis-che-vi-ous

However, pronunciation is not an infallible guide to correct spelling. Although, for example, you pronounce the last syllables of *adviser, beggar,* and *doctor* all as the same unstressed *ur,* you spell them differently. You must, therefore, proceed cautiously in using pronunciation as a spelling aid.

44d **Distinguish carefully between the spellings of words that are similar in sound.**

English abounds in words whose spelling or sound is similar to that of other words: for example, *rain, rein, reign.* The most troublesome of such words are listed below.

ascent: climbing, a way sloping up

assent: agreement, to agree

all ready: everyone is ready

already: by this time

all together: as a group

altogether: entirely, completely

altar: a structure used in worship

alter: to change

breath: air taken into the lungs

breathe: to exhale and inhale

capital: chief; leading or governing city; wealth, resources

capitol: a building that houses the state or national lawmakers

cite: to use as an example, to quote

site: location

clothes: wearing apparel

cloths: two or more pieces of cloth

complement: that which completes; to supply a lack

compliment: praise, flattering remark; to praise

corps: a military group or unit
corpse: a dead body

council: an assembly of lawmakers
counsel: advice; one who advises; to give advice

dairy: a factory or farm engaged in milk production
diary: a daily record of experiences or observations

descent: a way sloping down
dissent: disagreement; to disagree

dining: eating
dinning: making a continuing noise

dying: ceasing to live
dyeing: process of coloring fabrics

forth: forward in place or space, onward in time
fourth: the ordinal equivalent of the number 4

loose: free from bonds
lose: to suffer a loss

personal: pertaining to a particular person; individual
personnel: body of persons employed in same work or service

principal: chief, most important; a school official; a capital sum (as distinguished from interest or profit)
principle: a belief, rule of conduct or thought

respectfully: with respect
respectively: in order, in turn

stationery: writing paper
stationary: not moving

their: possessive form of *they*
they're: contraction of *they are*
there: adverb of place

whose: possessive form of *who*
who's: contraction of *who is*

your: possessive form of *you*
you're: contraction of *you are*

44e **Familiarize yourself with spelling rules as an aid to correct spelling.**

  1. *Carefully distinguish between* ie *and* ei. Remember this jingle:

> Write *i* before *e*
> Except after *c*
> Or when sounded like *a*
> As in *eighty* and *sleigh.*

i BEFORE *e*	*ei* AFTER *c*	*ei* WHEN SOUNDED LIKE *a*
thief	receive	weigh
believe	deceive	freight
wield	ceiling	vein

SOME EXCEPTIONS
leisure
financier
weird

  2. *Drop the final* e *before a suffix beginning with a vowel but not before a suffix beginning with a consonant.*
  a. *Suffix beginning with a vowel, final* e *dropped:*

please + ure	= *pleasure*
ride + ing	= *riding*
locate + ion	= *location*
guide + ance	= *guidance*

EXCEPTIONS:

In some words the final *e* is retained to prevent confusion with other words.

dyeing (to distinguish it from *dying*)

Final *e* is retained to keep *c* or *g* soft before *a* or *o.*

	notice + able	= *noticeable*
	change + able	= *changeable*
	singe + ing	= *singeing*
BUT	practice + able	= *practicable* (*c* has sound of *k*)

b. *Suffix beginning with a consonant, final* e *retained:*

sure + ly   = *surely*
arrange + ment = *arrangement*
like + ness   = *likeness*
entire + ly   = *entirely*
entire + ty   = *entirety*
hate + ful   = *hateful*

EXCEPTIONS:
Some words taking the suffix *-ful* or *-ly* drop final *e:*

awe + ful   = *awful*
due + ly   = *duly*
true + ly   = *truly*

Some words taking the suffix *-ment* drop final *e:*

judge + ment   = *judgment*
acknowledge + ment = *acknowledgment*

The ordinal numbers of *five, nine,* and *twelve,* formed with *-th,* drop the final *e. Five* and *twelve* change *v* to *f.*

fifth   ninth   twelfth

3. *Final* y *is usually changed to* i *except before a suffix beginning with* i.

defy + ance = *defiance*
forty + eth = *fortieth*
ninety + eth = *ninetieth*
rectify + er = *rectifier*
BUT cry + ing   = *crying* (suffix begins with *i*)

4. *A final single consonant is doubled before a suffix beginning with a vowel when* (a) *a single vowel precedes the consonant, and* (b) *the consonant ends an accented syllable or a one-syllable word. Unless both these conditions exist, the final consonant is not doubled.*

369

stop + ing = *stopping* (*o* is a single vowel before consonant *p* which ends word of one syllable.)

admit + ed = *admitted* (*i* is single vowel before consonant *t* which ends an accented syllable.)

stoop + ing = *stooping* (*p* ends a word of one syllable but is preceded by double vowel *oo*.)

benefit + ed = *benefited* (*t* is preceded by a single vowel *i* but does not end the accented syllable.)

EXERCISE 44e(1). Spell each of the following words correctly and explain what spelling rule applies. Note any exceptions to the rules.

argue + ment	=	?
beg + ar	=	?
bury + ed	=	?
conceive + able	=	?
eighty + eth	=	?
associate + ion	=	?
hop + ing	=	?
droop + ing	=	?

change + able	=	?
change + ing	=	?
awe + ful	=	?
precede + ence	=	?
shine + ing	=	?
busy + ness	=	?
defer + ed	=	?
peace + able	=	?

5. *Nouns ending in a sound that can be smoothly united with* -s *usually form their plurals by adding* -s. *Verbs ending in a sound that can be smoothly united with* -s *form their third person singular by adding* -s.

SINGULAR	PLURAL	SOME EXCEPTIONS		VERBS	
picture	pictures	buffalo	buffaloes	blacken	blackens
radio	radios	Negro	Negroes	criticize	criticizes
flower	flowers	zero	zeroes	radiate	radiates
chair	chairs				
ache	aches				
fan	fans				

6. *Nouns ending in a sound that cannot be smoothly united with* -s *form their plurals by adding* -es. *Verbs ending in a sound that cannot be smoothly united with* -s *form their third person singular by adding* -es.

SINGULAR	PLURAL
porch	porches
bush	bushes
pass	passes
tax	taxes

7. *Nouns ending in* y *preceded by a consonant form their plurals by changing* y *to* i *and adding* -es.

SINGULAR	PLURAL
army	armies
nursery	nurseries
sky	skies
mercy	mercies
body	bodies

EXCEPTIONS:

The plural of proper nouns ending in *y* is formed by adding *-s* (*There are three Marys in my history class*).

8. *Nouns ending in* y *preceded by* a, e, o, *or* u *form their plurals by adding* -s *only.*

SINGULAR	PLURAL
day	days
key	keys
boy	boys
guy	guys

9. *The spelling of plural nouns borrowed from French, Greek, and Latin frequently retains the plural of the original language.*

SINGULAR	PLURAL
alumna (feminine)	alumnae
alumnus (masculine)	alumni
analysis	analyses
basis	bases
datum	data
crisis	crises
hypothesis	hypotheses
phenomenon	phenomena

The tendency now, however, is to give many such words an anglicized plural. The result is that many words have two plural forms, one foreign, the other anglicized. Either is correct.

SINGULAR	PLURAL (*foreign*)	PLURAL (*anglicized*)
appendix	appendices	appendixes
beau	beaux	beaus
focus	foci	focuses
index	indices	indexes
memorandum	memoranda	memorandums
radius	radii	radiuses
stadium	stadia	stadiums

EXERCISE 44e(2). Spell the plural of each of the following words correctly and explain what spelling rule applies. Note any exceptions to the rules.

1.	frame	6.	branch	11.	echo	16.	Charles
2.	rose	7.	bass	12.	stratum	17.	no
3.	dash	8.	cameo	13.	church	18.	potato
4.	maze	9.	fly	14.	lady	19.	play
5.	table	10.	box	15.	mass	20.	pain

44f   Spell compound words in accordance with current usage.

Compound words usually progress by stages from being written as two words to being hyphenated to being written as one word. Since these stages often overlap, the correct spelling of a compound word may vary. For the spelling of a compound at any particular moment, take the advice of a good dictionary. (For the general use of the hyphen, see "Hyphen," Section 30. This section gives rules for the spelling of compounds.)

44g   Use drills to help cultivate the habit of correct spelling.

Spelling is primarily a habit. Once you learn to spell a word correctly, you no longer need to think about it. Its correct spelling becomes an automatic skill. But if you are a chronic misspeller you have the task not only of learning correct spellings but of unlearning the incorrect spellings you now employ. You must train your fingers to write the word correctly until they do so almost without your thinking about it. Here is a suggested drill that will aid you in learning correct spellings.

First, look carefully at a word whose spelling bothers you and say it to yourself. If it has more than one syllable, examine each syllable.

Second, look at the individual letters, dividing the word into syllables as you say the letters.

Third, try to visualize the correct spelling before you write the word. If you have trouble, begin again with the *first* step.

Fourth, write the word without looking at your book or list.

Fifth, look at your book or list and see whether you wrote the word correctly. If you did, cover the word and write it again. If you write the word correctly the third time, you have probably learned it and will not have to think about it again.

Sixth, if you spell the word incorrectly any one of the three times, look very carefully at the letters you missed. Then start over again and keep on until you have spelled it correctly three times.

Spelling lists.

The following lists contain most of the words whose spelling is troublesome. The words are arranged in alphabetized groups for easy reference and for drill.

Group 1

1. accidentally
2. accommodate
3. accompanied
4. achieved
5. address
6. aggravate
7. anxiety
8. barren
9. believe
10. ceiling
11. confident
12. course
13. disappear
14. disappoint
15. dissipate
16. efficiency
17. emphasize
18. exaggerate
19. exceed
20. fiery
21. finally
22. financial
23. forehead
24. foreign
25. forfeit
26. grief
27. handkerchief
28. hurriedly
29. hypocrisy
30. imminent
31. incidentally
32. innocence
33. intentionally
34. interest
35. legitimate
36. likely
37. manual
38. mattress
39. misspell
40. niece
41. parallel
42. psychiatrist
43. psychology
44. occasion
45. organization
46. piece
47. receive
48. religious
49. severely
50. villain

Group 2

1. arctic
2. auxiliary
3. business
4. candidate
5. characteristic
6. chauffeur
7. colonel
8. column
9. cylinder
10. environment
11. especially
12. exhaust
13. exhilaration
14. February
15. foremost
16. ghost
17. government
18. grievous
19. hygiene
20. intercede
21. leisure
22. library
23. lightning
24. literature
25. mathematics
26. medicine
27. mortgage
28. muscle
29. notoriety
30. optimistic
31. pamphlet
32. parliament
33. physically
34. physician
35. prairie
36. prejudice
37. pronunciation

38. recede
39. recognize
40. reign
41. rhetoric
42. rhythm
43. schedule
44. sentinel
45. soliloquy
46. sophomore
47. studying
48. surprise
49. twelfth
50. Wednesday

Group 3

1. apparent
2. appearance
3. attendance
4. beggar
5. brilliant
6. calendar
7. carriage
8. conqueror
9. contemptible
10. coolly
11. descent
12. desirable
13. dictionary
14. disastrous
15. eligible
16. equivalent
17. existence
18. familiar
19. grammar
20. guidance
21. hindrance
22. hoping
23. imaginary
24. incredible
25. indigestible
26. indispensable
27. inevitable
28. influential
29. irresistible
30. liable
31. marriage
32. momentous

33. naturally
34. nickel
35. noticeable
36. nucleus
37. obedience
38. outrageous
39. pageant
40. permissible
41. perseverance
42. persistent
43. pleasant
44. possible
45. prevalent
46. resistance
47. similar
48. strenuous
49. vengeance
50. vigilance

Group 4

1. allot
2. allotted
3. barbarian
4. barbarous
5. beneficial
6. benefited
7. changeable
8. changing
9. commit
10. committed
11. committee
12. comparative
13. comparatively
14. comparison
15. compel
16. compelled
17. competent
18. competition
19. compulsion
20. conceivable
21. conceive
22. conception
23. conscience
24. conscientious
25. conscious
26. courteous
27. courtesy

28. deceit
29. deceive
30. deception
31. decide
32. decision
33. defer
34. deference
35. deferred
36. describe
37. description
38. device
39. devise
40. discuss
41. discussion
42. dissatisfied
43. dissatisfy
44. equip
45. equipment
46. equipped
47. excel
48. excellent
49. explain
50. explanation

Group 5

1. hesitancy
2. hesitate
3. instance
4. instant
5. intellectual
6. intelligence
7. intelligent
8. intelligible
9. maintain
10. maintenance
11. miniature
12. minute
13. ninetieth
14. ninety
15. ninth
16. obligation
17. oblige
18. obliged
19. occur
20. occurred
21. occurrence
22. omission

23. omit
24. omitted
25. procedure
26. proceed
27. picnic
28. picnicking
29. possess
30. possession
31. precede
32. precedence
33. preceding
34. prefer
35. preference
36. preferred
37. realize
38. really
39. refer
40. reference
41. referred
42. repeat
43. repetition
44. transfer
45. transferred
46. tried
47. tries
48. try
49. writing
50. written

Group 6

1. obstacle
2. operate
3. opinion
4. pastime
5. persuade
6. piece
7. politician
8. practically
9. presence
10. professor
11. propeller
12. quantity
13. recommend
14. region

15. relieve
16. representative
17. reservoir
18. restaurant
19. ridiculous
20. sacrifice
21. sacrilegious
22. safety
23. salary
24. scarcely
25. science
26. secretary
27. seize
28. separate
29. shriek
30. siege
31. similar
32. suffrage
33. supersede
34. suppress
35. syllable
36. symmetry
37. temperament
38. temperature
39. tendency
40. tournament
41. tragedy
42. truly
43. tyranny
44. unanimous
45. unusual
46. usage
47. valuable
48. wholly
49. yoke
50. yolk

Group 7

1. accept
2. across
3. aisle
4. all right
5. amateur
6. annual

7. appropriate
8. argument
9. arrangement
10. association
11. awkward
12. bachelor
13. biscuit
14. cafeteria
15. career
16. cemetery
17. completely
18. convenient
19. cruelty
20. curiosity
21. definite
22. desperate
23. diphtheria
24. discipline
25. disease
26. distribute
27. dormitories
28. drudgery
29. eighth
30. eliminate
31. ecstasy
32. eminent
33. enemy
34. except
35. exercise
36. extraordinary
37. fascinate
38. fraternity
39. furniture
40. grandeur
41. height
42. hypocrisy
43. imitation
44. interest
45. livelihood
46. loneliness
47. magazine
48. material
49. messenger
50. mischievous

EXERCISE 44a-g. Following is a list of words chosen at random to illustrate some of the caprices of English spelling and pronunciation. You might like to try your skill at spelling them. Will any of the spelling rules apply here? How many of these words can you pronounce? How many can you define? Would a knowledge of pronunciations, definitions, or word origins be of help in spelling these words correctly?

1. aardvark	31. doughty	61. phthisis
2. abhorrence	32. dungeon	62. pituitary
3. alyssum	33. ecclesiastical	63. platypus
4. apocalypse	34. eerie	64. plebiscite
5. archipelago	35. eucalyptus	65. porpoise
6. arpeggio	36. flautist	66. psyche
7. baccalaureate	37. fortuitous	67. pyrrhic
8. bacchanalian	38. fugue	68. quay
9. balalaika	39. gargoyle	69. queue
10. baroque	40. gourmet	70. quixotic
11. bologna	41. gneiss	71. rheumy
12. bouillon	42. heterogeneous	72. rhinoceros
13. boutonniere	43. hieroglyphic	73. saccharin
14. catarrh	44. homogenous	74. salmon
15. catechism	45. hyperbole	75. scepter
16. charivari	46. icicle	76. schism
17. chlorophyll	47. idiosyncrasy	77. scythe
18. chrysalis	48. incarcerate	78. suave
19. cinnamon	49. jeopardy	79. svelte
20. clique	50. jodhpurs	80. tarpaulin
21. connoisseur	51. khaki	81. thyme
22. crescendo	52. knell	82. trauma
23. cryptic	53. larynx	83. tympany
24. cyanide	54. lymph	84. umlaut
25. cyclic	55. misogyny	85. vaccination
26. demagogue	56. moccasin	86. vacuum
27. delicatessen	57. myrrh	87. vitiate
28. diaphragm	58. niche	88. whey
29. discomfiture	59. nil	89. yacht
30. disparate	60. periphery	90. zephyr

The Library
and the
Research Paper

Knowledge is of two kinds: We know a subject ourselves, or we know where we can find information upon it.

A man will turn over half a library to make one book.

—SAMUEL JOHNSON

*T*he processes of RESEARCH range all the way from simple fact-digging to the most abstruse speculations; consequently, there is no one generally accepted definition of the word. *Webster's New Collegiate Dictionary* emphasizes the meaning of the first syllable, *re-*: "critical and exhaustive investigation . . . having for its aim the revision of accepted conclusions, in the light of newly discovered facts." The *New World Dictionary* stresses the meaning of the second syllable, *-search*: "systematic, patient study and investigation in some field of knowledge, undertaken to establish facts or principles." The second definition more closely describes what is expected of you in your first years in college. True, you will not often revise accepted conclusions or establish new principles. But you can learn to collect, sift, evaluate, and organize information or evidence, and to come to sound conclusions about its meaning. In doing so you will learn some of the basic methods of modern research, and the ethics and etiquette that govern the use the researcher makes of other men's facts and ideas.

When your instructor asks you to prepare a research paper, he is concerned less with the intrinsic value of your findings than with the value you derive from the experience. Writing a research paper demands a sense of responsibility, because you must account for all your facts and assertions. If your results are to be accepted—and that, after all, is a large part of your purpose—you must be prepared to show how you got those results.

It is the citing of sources that distinguishes the research paper from the expository essay in popular magazines. A good journalist undertakes research to assemble his materials, but his readers are primarily concerned with the <u>results</u> of his research. He expects to be accepted on faith. The researcher, however, writes for his peers— for readers who are able to <u>evaluate</u> his findings; for this reason he uses footnotes to help them check his evidence if they wish to do so.

In preparing a research paper, then, remember that your audience expects and demands that you indicate your sources. It expects you to be <u>thorough</u>—to find and sift all the relevant evidence; to be <u>critical</u> of your evidence—to test the reliability of your authorities; to be <u>accurate</u>—to present your facts and cite your sources with the utmost precision; to be <u>objective</u>—to distinguish clearly between your facts and the opinions or generalizations to which your facts lead you.

45 **The Library**

The library is one of the most valuable resources on the college campus, and every successful student draws constantly on its facilities. Learn how to use your college library efficiently—become familiar with the card catalog system, learn where and by what system books are shelved, get acquainted with periodical guides and special indexes. Once you have mastered these skills, you will be able to use your time on concentrated study and research rather than on aimless wandering about the library in search of fugitive items. This section is designed to help you familiarize yourself with your library and its functions.

The library catalogs.

The heart of the library is its card catalog. This is an alphabetical list of all the books and periodicals the library contains. Most libraries have a separate catalog that describes all periodical holdings in complete detail.

The CLASSIFICATION SYSTEM on which a card catalog is based serves as a kind of map of library holdings. In libraries where you have direct access to the shelves, familiarity with the classification system enables you to find classes of books in which you are interested without using the catalog. But the chief purpose of a classification system is to supply a CALL NUMBER for every item in the library. When you fill out a slip for a book, be sure to copy the call number precisely as it appears on the card.

American libraries generally follow either the Dewey decimal system or the Library of Congress system in classifying books. The system in use determines the call number of any book.

The Dewey system, used by most libraries, divides books into ten numbered classes:

001–099	General works	500–599	Pure science
100–199	Philosophy	600–699	Useful arts
200–299	Religion	700–799	Fine arts
300–399	Social sciences	800–899	Literature
400–499	Philology	900–999	History

Each of these divisions is further divided into ten parts, as:

800	General literature	850	Italian literature
810	American literature	860	Spanish literature
820	English literature	870	Latin literature
830	German literature	880	Greek literature
840	French literature	890	Minor literatures

Each of these divisions is further divided, as:

821	English poetry	826	English letters
822	English drama	827	English satire
823	English fiction	828	English miscellany
824	English essays	829	Anglo-Saxon
825	English oratory		

Further subdivisions are indicated by decimals. *The Romantic Rebels,* a book about Keats, Byron, and Shelley, is numbered 821.09 —indicating a subdivision of the 821 English poetry heading.

The Library of Congress classification system—used by large libraries—divides books into lettered classes:

A	General works
B	Philosophy—Religion
C	History—Auxiliary sciences
D	Foreign history and topography
E–F	American history
G	Geography—Anthropology
H	Social sciences
J	Political science
K	Law
L	Education
M	Music
N	Fine arts
P	Language and literature
Q	Science
R	Medicine
S	Agriculture
T	Technology
U	Military science
V	Naval science
Z	Bibliography—Library science

Each of these sections is further divided by letters and numbers which show the specific call number of a book. *English Composition in Theory and Practice* by Henry Seidel Canby and others is classified in this system as PE 1408.E5. (In the Dewey decimal system this same volume is numbered 808 C214.)

The catalog cards.

For most books (not periodicals) you will find at least three cards in the library catalog: an <u>author</u> card; a <u>title</u> card (no title card is used when the title begins with words as common as "A History of . . ."); and at least one <u>subject</u> card. Here is a specimen <u>author</u> card in the Dewey system; it is filed according to the surname of the author:

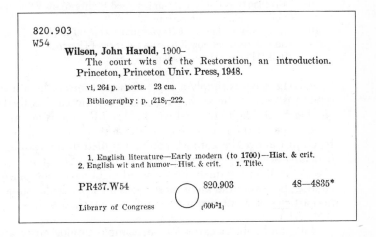

820.903
W54

Wilson, John Harold, 1900–
    The court wits of the Restoration, an introduction.
Princeton, Princeton Univ. Press, 1948.

    vi, 264 p. ports. 23 cm.

    Bibliography: p. [218]–222.

    1. English literature—Early modern (to 1700)—Hist. & crit.
    2. English wit and humor—Hist. & crit.   i. Title.

    PR437.W54   820.903   48—4835*

    Library of Congress   [60b²1]

1. $\dfrac{820.903}{W54}$ gives you the CALL NUMBER of the book.

2. "Wilson, John Harold, 1900–" gives you the name of the author and the date of his birth, and tells you that he was still living at the time this card was printed.

3. "The court wits . . . 1948" gives you the full title of the book, the place of publication, the name of the publisher, and the date of publication. (Note that library practice in capitalizing differs from general practice.)

4. "vi, 264 p. ports. 23 cm." tells you that the book contains 6 introductory pages numbered in Roman numerals and 264 pages numbered in Arabic numerals; that portraits appear in the book; and that the book is 23 centimeters high. (An inch is 2.54 centimeters.)

5. "Bibliography: p. [218]–222." tells you that the book contains a bibliography that begins on page 218 and ends on page 222. The brackets around 218 tell you that the page is not actually numbered but appears between numbered pages 217 and 219.

6. "1. English Literature . . . Title." tells you that the book is also listed in the card catalog under two subject headings—English Literature, and English Wit and Humor—and under one title heading, "Court wits of the Restoration. . . ." Notice that the subject heading "English Literature" has the subdivision "Early modern (to 1700)" and that this latter heading has the subdivision "Hist. & crit.," the heading under which you will find the first subject card. You will find the second subject card under a division of "English wit and humor" called "Hist. & crit." The Arabic numerals indicate subject headings; the Roman numeral ("I. Title.") indicates a title heading.
7. "PR437.W54" is the Library of Congress call number.
8. "820.903" is the class number under the Dewey system.
9. "48–4835*" is the order number used by librarians when they wish to order a copy of the card itself.
10. "Library of Congress" tells you that a copy of the book is housed in, and has been cataloged by, the Library of Congress.
11. "[60b^{2}1]" is a printer's key to the card.

A TITLE CARD is simply a copy of the author card, with the title typed just above the author's name. The title card is filed in the catalog according to the first word of the title that is not an article.

A SUBJECT CARD is also a copy of the author card, with the subject typed just above the author's name; it is filed in the catalog alphabetically according to the subject heading. (See item 6 above.) The subject cards, which are gathered together in one place in the catalog, help you find all or most books on a particular subject. (To find articles on a subject, use the reference tools described on pages 390–391.)

Title and subject cards for our sample catalog entry are illustrated at the top of page 383.

Except for the difference in the call number, catalog cards using the Library of Congress system are identical with those using the Dewey system. Note the example at the bottom of page 383.

Library holdings.

Libraries have three principal kinds of holdings: a general collection of books; a collection of reference works; and a collection of periodicals, bulletins, and pamphlets.

General collection of books.

The general collection includes most of the books in the library —all those that are available for general circulation. Small libraries usually place these books on open shelves and make them available to all who have library privileges. Most large university libraries,

820.903
W54
The court wits of the Restoration

Wilson, John Harold, 1900–
The court wits of the Restoration, an introduction.
Princeton, Princeton Univ. Press, 1948.

vi, 264 p. ports. 23 cm.

820.903
W54
ENGLISH WIT AND HUMOR

Wilson, John Harold, 1900–
The court wits of the Restoration, an introduction.
Princeton, Princeton Univ. Press, 1948.

vi, 264 p. ports. 23 cm.

Bibliography: p. ₁218₁–222.

1. English literature—Early modern (to 1700)—Hist. & crit.
2. English wit and humor—Hist. & crit. ɪ. Title.

PR437.W54   820.903   48—4835*

Library of Congress   ₁60b²1₁

PR
437
W54
Wilson, John Harold, 1900–
The court wits of the Restoration, an introduction.
Princeton, Princeton Univ. Press, 1948.

vi, 264 p. ports. 23 cm.

Bibliography: p. ₁218₁–222.

1. English literature—Early modern (to 1700)—Hist. & crit.
2. English wit and humor—Hist. & crit. ɪ. Title.

PR437.W54   820.903   48—4835*

Library of Congress   ₁60b²1₁

however, keep these books in stacks, which are closed to everyone except librarians, graduate students, faculty members, and persons holding special permits. If you want to borrow a book from such a library, you must first present a call slip bearing the call number of the book you want, the name of its author, and its title. This information you obtain from the CARD CATALOG.

Reference books.

Reference books include encyclopedias, dictionaries, indexes, directories, handbooks, yearbooks, atlases, and guides. Most libraries place these books on open shelves in the main reading room and do not allow their removal from the room. You should become familiar with the kinds of reference works available, and with the most important works of each kind. If you cannot find the book you want, or if you do not know what book will help you most, consult the reference librarian.

Following is a representative list of reference books available in most libraries.

Guides to Reference Books

Cook, M. G. *The New Library Key*. New York: H. W. Wilson Company, 1963.

Gates, Jean Key. *Guide to the Use of Books and Libraries*. New York: McGraw-Hill Book Company, 1962.

Murphey, Robert W. *How and Where to Look It Up: A Guide to Standard Sources of Information*. Consultant: Mabel S. Johnson. Foreword by Louis Shores. New York: McGraw-Hill Book Company, 1958.

Russell, H. G., R. H. Shove, and B. E. Moen. *The Use of Books and Libraries*. Minneapolis: University of Minnesota Press, 1958.

Shores, Louis. *Basic Reference Sources*. Chicago: American Library Association, 1954.

Winchell, C. M. *Guide to Reference Books*. 8th ed. Chicago: American Library Association, 1967.

General Encyclopedias

Columbia Encyclopedia. 3rd ed. Ed. by William Bridgewater and Elizabeth J. Sherwood. New York: Columbia University Press, 1963.

Encyclopedia Americana. New York: Americana Corporation. 30 vols. Revised annually.

Encyclopaedia Britannica. Chicago: Encyclopaedia Britannica, Inc. 24 vols. Revised annually.

New International Encyclopedia. 2nd ed. New York: Dodd, Mead and Company, 1914–16. 24 vols. Plate revision, 1922. Supplements, 1925, 1930.

The *Americana, Britannica,* and *New International* are all brought up to date by annual supplements, *The Americana Annual, The Britannica Book of the Year,* and the *New International Year Book.* (See section on Yearbooks below for bibliographical information.)

Dictionaries, Word Books

Dictionary of American English on Historical Principles. Ed. by Sir W. A. Craigie and J. R. Hulbert. Chicago: The University of Chicago Press, 1936–44. 4 vols.

Evans, Bergen and Cornelia. *A Dictionary of Contemporary American Usage.* New York: Random House, 1957.

Fowler, Henry W. *Dictionary of Modern English Usage.* 2nd ed. Rev. by Sir Ernest Gowers. New York: Oxford University Press, 1965.

New Standard Dictionary. New York: Funk & Wagnalls, 1959.

Oxford English Dictionary. Ed. by A. H. Murray et al. Oxford: The Clarendon Press, 1888–1933. 10 vols. and supplement. Reissued, corrected, 1933, 12 vols. and supplement. The original issue is known as *New English Dictionary.*

Perrin, Porter G. *Writer's Guide and Index to English.* 4th ed. Chicago: Scott, Foresman and Company, 1965.

Random House Dictionary of the English Language. New York: Random House, Inc., 1966.

Roget's International Thesaurus. 3rd ed. New York: Thomas Y. Crowell, 1962.

Webster's Dictionary of Synonyms. Springfield, Mass.: G. & C. Merriam Company, 1951.

Webster's New International Dictionary. 2nd ed. Unabridged. Springfield, Mass.: G. & C. Merriam Company, 1934. Revised through 1959.

Webster's Third New International Dictionary. Unabridged. Springfield, Mass.: G & C. Merriam Company, 1961, 1966. (See pp. 286–288.)

Yearbooks

Americana Annual, 1924 to date. New York: Americana Corporation, 1924–.

Britannica Book of the Year, 1938 to date. Chicago: Encyclopaedia Britannica, Inc., 1938–.

Facts on File. A weekly digest of world events. New York: Person's Index, Inc., 1940–.

New International Year Book, 1907 to date. New York: Dodd, Mead and Company, 1908–31; Funk & Wagnalls, 1932–.

Statesman's Year Book, 1864 to date. London: The Macmillan Company, 1864–.

United Nations Yearbook, 1946/47 to date. New York: Columbia University Press, 1947–.

United Nations Statistical Yearbook, 1945 to date. New York: Columbia University Press, 1945–.

45 LIBRARY

U. S. Bureau of the Census. *Statistical Abstract of the United States,* 1879 to date. Washington, D.C.: U. S. Government Printing Office, 1879–.

World Almanac and Books of Facts, 1868 to date. New York: The World-Telegram, 1868–1967; Newspaper Enterprise Association, 1968–.

Atlases and Gazetteers

Columbia-Lippincott Gazetteer of the World. New York: Columbia University Press, 1962.

Commercial Atlas. Chicago: Rand, McNally and Company. Issued annually.

Cosmopolitan World Atlas. Rev. ed. Chicago: Rand, McNally and Company, 1967.

Encyclopaedia Britannica World Atlas. New York: Encyclopaedia Britannica, Inc. Frequently revised.

National Geographic Atlas of the World. Enlarged 2nd ed. Washington, D.C.: National Geographic Society, 1966.

The Times Atlas of the World, Mid-century ed. London: The Times Publishing Company, Ltd., 1955–1959.

Webster's Geographical Dictionary. Springfield, Mass.: G. & C. Merriam Company, 1949. Frequently revised.

General Biography

American Men of Science. 11th ed. Ed. by Jaques Cattell. New York: R. R. Bowker Company, 1966. 6 vols.

Biography Index. New York: H. W. Wilson Company, 1946–. Quarterly. Cumulated annually, with permanent volumes every three years.

Current Biography: Who's News and Why. New York: H. W. Wilson Company, 1940–. Published monthly with semi-annual and annual cumulations.

Dictionary of American Biography. Ed. by Allen Johnson and Dumas Malone. New York: Charles Scribner's Sons, 1928–37. 20 vols. and index. Supplements, 1944, 1958.

Dictionary of National Biography. Ed. by Leslie Stephen and Sidney Lee. London: Oxford University Press, 1922. 22 vols. and supplements.

Directory of American Scholars. 5th ed. Ed. by Jaques Cattell. New York: R. R. Bowker Company, 1968–69. 4 vols.

International Who's Who, 1936 to date. London: Europa Publications, 1936–.

Webster's Biographical Dictionary. Springfield, Mass.: G. & C. Merriam Company, 1943. Frequently revised.

Who's Who, 1848 to date. London: A. & C. Black, 1849–.

Who's Who in America, 1899–1900 to date. Chicago: A. N. Marquis Company, 1899–.

Books of Quotations

Bartlett, John. *Familiar Quotations.* 14th ed. Ed. by Emily Morison Beck. Boston: Little, Brown and Company, 1968.

Mencken, H. L. *A New Dictionary of Quotations on Historical Principles from Ancient and Modern Sources.* New York: Alfred A. Knopf, 1942.

Stevenson, Burton. *The Home Book of Quotations.* 9th rev. ed. New York: Dodd, Mead and Company, 1964.

Mythology and Folklore

Cary, M., et al. *The Oxford Classical Dictionary.* Oxford: The Clarendon Press, 1949.

Frazer, Sir James G. *The Golden Bough.* 3rd ed. revised. New York: St. Martin's Press, Inc., 1911–1936. 13 vols.

Funk & Wagnalls Standard Dictionary of Folklore, Mythology, and Legend. New York: Funk & Wagnalls, 1949. 2 vols. Index volume forthcoming.

Hamilton, Edith. *Mythology.* Boston: Little, Brown and Company, 1942.

Sandys, John E. *Companion to Latin Studies.* 3rd ed. Cambridge: Cambridge University Press, 1938.

Whibley, Leonard. *Companion to Greek Studies.* 4th ed. Cambridge: Cambridge University Press, 1931.

Modern Literature

Cambridge Bibliography of English Literature. Ed. by F. W. Bateson. New York: The Macmillan Company, 1941–1957. 5 vols.

Cambridge History of English Literature. Ed. by A. W. Ward and A. R. Waller. Cambridge: Cambridge University Press, 1907–16. 14 vols. Index issued 1927. Reissued, without bibliographies, 1933. 15 vols. Reissued 1949.

Columbia Dictionary of Modern European Literature. Ed. by Horatio Smith. New York: Columbia University Press, 1947.

Hart, J. D. *Oxford Companion to American Literature.* 4th ed. New York: Oxford University Press, 1965.

Harvey, Sir Paul. *Oxford Companion to English Literature.* 4th ed. Oxford: The Clarendon Press, 1967.

Kunitz, S. J., and Howard Haycraft. *American Authors, 1600–1900.* New York: H. W. Wilson Company, 1938.

———. *British Authors of the Nineteenth Century.* New York: H. W. Wilson Company, 1936.

———. *Twentieth Century Authors.* New York: H. W. Wilson Company, 1942. Supplement, 1955.

Literary History of the United States. Ed. by R. E. Spiller et al. New York: The Macmillan Company, 1949. 3 vols. Vol. 3 is bibliography. Reissued, 1953, first two volumes in one. Supplementary volume brings bibliography to 1964.

Millett, Fred B. *Contemporary American Authors.* New York: Harcourt, Brace and Company, 1940.

Millett, Fred B., John M. Manly, and Edith Rickert. *Contemporary British Literature.* 3rd ed. New York: Harcourt, Brace and Company, 1935.

Parrington, V. L. *Main Currents in American Thought.* New York: Harcourt, Brace and Company, 1927–30. Reissued, 1939, 1 vol.

History

Cambridge Ancient History. Ed. by J. B. Bury et al. Cambridge: Cambridge University Press, 1923–39. 12 vols.

Cambridge Medieval History. Ed. by H. M. Gwatkin et al. Cambridge: Cambridge University Press, 1911–36. 8 vols.

Cambridge Modern History. Ed. by A. W. Ward et al. Cambridge: Cambridge University Press, 1902–26. 13 vols. and atlas.

Dictionary of American History. Ed. by J. T. Adams. New York: Charles Scribner's Sons, 1940. 5 vols. Vol. 6 (index), 1941.

Harvard Guide to American History. Cambridge: Harvard University Press, 1954.

Keller, Helen R. *The Dictionary of Dates.* New York: The Macmillan Company, 1934. 2 vols.

Langer, William L. *An Encyclopedia of World History.* Rev. ed. Boston: Houghton Mifflin Company, 1952.

Schlesinger, Arthur M., and D. R. Fox, eds. *A History of American Life.* New York: The Macmillian Company, 1927–48. 13 vols.

Music, Painting

Bryan, Michael. *Bryan's Dictionary of Painters and Engravers.* Rev. ed. London: George Bell and Sons, 1903–05. 5 vols.

Encyclopedia of Painting. Ed. by Bernard S. Myers. New York: Crown Publishers, Inc., 1955.

Encyclopedia of World Art. New York: McGraw-Hill Book Company, 1958–1968. 15 vols.

Grove's Dictionary of Music and Musicians. Ed. by Eric Blom. 5th ed. New York: St. Martin's Press, 1954. 9 vols. and supplement.

Reinach, Solomon. *Apollo: An Illustrated Manual of the History of Art Throughout the Ages.* Tr. by F. Simmonds. Rev. ed. New York: Charles Scribner's Sons, 1935.

Thompson, Oscar, and N. Slonimsky. *International Cyclopedia of Music and Musicians.* 9th ed. New York: Dodd, Mead and Company, 1964.

Philosophy, Religion

Catholic Encyclopedia. New York: Catholic Encyclopedia Press, 1907–1922. 17 vols. Supplements, 1950, 1954.

The Concise Encyclopedia of Western Philosophy and Philosophers. Ed. by J. O. Urmson. New York: Hawthorn Books, Inc., 1960.

Encyclopedia of Religion and Ethics. Ed. by James Hastings. New York: Charles Scribner's Sons, 1908–27. 12 vols. and index. Reissued, 1928. 7 vols. Reissued, 1951.

Ferm, Vergilius. *Encyclopedia of Religion.* New York: Philosophical Library, 1945.

Jewish Encyclopedia. New York: Funk & Wagnalls Company, 1901–06. 12 vols. Reissued, 1925.

New Schaff-Herzog Encyclopedia of Religious Knowledge. Ed. by S. M. Jackson. New York: Funk & Wagnalls Company, 1949–50. 12 vols. and index.

Science, Technology

Besserer, C. W. and Hazel. *Guide to the Space Age.* Englewood Cliffs, N. J.: Prentice-Hall, Inc., 1960.

Chamber's Technical Dictionary. Ed. by C. F. Tweney and L. E. C. Hughes. 3rd ed. revised with supplement. New York: The Macmillan Company, 1958.

Dictionary of Physics. Ed. by H. J. Gray. New York: Longmans, Green and Co., Inc., 1958.

Handbook of Chemistry and Physics. Cleveland: Chemical Rubber Publishing Company, 1914 to date.

Henderson, Isabella F. and W. D. *A Dictionary of Biological Terms.* 8th ed. by John H. Kenneth. New York: D. Van Nostrand Company, 1963.

Hutchinson's Technical and Scientific Encyclopedia. Ed. by C. F. Tweney and I. P. Shirshov. New York: The Macmillan Company, 1936. 4 vols.

McGraw-Hill Encyclopedia of Science and Technology. New York: McGraw-Hill Book Company, Inc., 1966. 15 vols.

Van Nostrand's Scientific Encyclopedia. 3rd ed. New York: D. Van Nostrand Company, 1958.

Social Sciences

Cyclopedia of Education. Ed. by Paul Monroe. New York: The Macmillan Company, 1925. 3 vols.

Encyclopedia of the Social Sciences. Ed. by E. R. A. Seligman and Alvin Johnson. New York: The Macmillan Company, 1930–35. 15 vols. Reissued, 1937.

Fairchild, Henry P. *Dictionary of Sociology.* New York: Philosophical Library, 1944.

Good, Carter V. *Dictionary of Education.* 2nd ed. New York: McGraw-Hill Book Company, Inc. 1959.

Monroe, Walter S. *Encyclopedia of Educational Research.* 3rd ed. New York: The Macmillan Company, 1960.

Munn, G. G. *Encyclopedia of Banking and Finance.* 5th ed. New York: Bankers Publishing Company, 1949. 2 vols. Supplement, 1956.

Warren, H. C. *Dictionary of Psychology.* Boston: Houghton Mifflin Company, 1934.

Periodicals, bulletins, pamphlets.

A PERIODICAL is a publication that appears at regular (periodic) intervals. BULLETINS and PAMPHLETS may or may not be periodicals, depending on whether they are issued as parts of a series of publications or as separate, single publications. They are usually kept in the stacks with the main collection of books. Recent issues of magazines and newspapers are usually kept in the open shelves of the reading room. Older issues are bound in volumes and shelved in the stacks.

A library's periodical catalog merely shows what periodicals are available. For guides to the contents of periodicals you must refer to periodical indexes, which are usually shelved in the reference room. A representative list of periodical indexes follows.

General indexes.

Readers' Guide to Periodical Literature, 1900 to date. Published semimonthly; cumulated every three months and annually. The *Readers' Guide* gives entries under author, title, and subject.

This is the most widely known and used of the general indexes. Because a great many periodical indexes use systems very similar to that of the *Readers' Guide,* it is worth examining some sample entries (p. 391).

The headings for 1 through 5 are SUBJECT ENTRIES; 6 and 7 are AUTHOR ENTRIES. Entry 8 indicates that an article indexed under the subject heading *Graffiti* was published in the June 1969 issue of *Science Digest,* Volume 65, pages 31 through 33. Titled "Walls Remember," it was illustrated and unsigned. (If we did not recognize the abbreviations, we could find them by looking at the first pages of the issue of the *Readers' Guide,* where all abbreviations and symbols used are explained.)

The second listing under entry 1 refers the user to a series of articles by D. Wolfle published in *Science* on the subject "Are Grades Necessary?" The first article appeared in the issue of November 15, 1968 (Volume 162, pages 745–746); the second and third appeared, respectively, in the issues for April 18 and June 6, 1969. Entry 2, under the subject heading *Graduate students,* indexes a review by D. Zinberg and P. Doty in the May 1969 issue of *Scientific American* of a book, *New Brahmins: Scientific Life in America,* by S. Klaw. The + that follows the page reference is an indication that the review is continued on a page or pages past 140. Entries 3, 4, and 7 are

1 **GRADING and marking (students)**
Answer to Sally; multiple-choice tests. W. R.
Link. Ed Digest 34:24-7 My '69
Are grades necessary? D. Wolfle; discussion. Science 162:745-6; 164:245, 1117-18 N
15 '68, Ap 18, Je 6 '69
ROTC: under fire but doing fine. il U S News
66:38 My 19 '69
2 **GRADUATE students**
New Brahmins: scientific life in America,
by S. Klaw. Review
Sci Am 220:139-40+ My '69. D. Zinberg
and P. Doty
3 **GRADUATION.** See Commencements
4 **GRADUATION addresses.** See Baccalaureate
addresses
5 **GRAEBNER, Clark**
Profiles. J. McPhee. por New Yorker 45:45-
8+ Je 7; 44-8+ Je 14 '69
6 **GRAEF, Hilda**
Why I remain a Catholic. Cath World 209:
77-80 My '69
7 **GRAF, Rudolf F.** See Whalen, G. J. jt. auth.
8 **GRAFFITI**
Walls remember. il Sci Digest 65:31-3 Je '69

From *Readers' Guide to Periodical Literature,* July 1969, p. 73. Reproduced
by permission of The H. W. Wilson Company.

cross references to the places in the *Guide* at which the user can find
the subject or author listed.

Two other general indexes are valuable supplements to the
Readers' Guide.

International Index to Periodicals, 1907 to date. This index deals with more
scholarly publications than does the *Readers' Guide.* Although most of
the periodicals it indexes are American, it also covers some foreign
publications.

Poole's Index to Periodical Literature, 1802–81, supplements through January
1, 1907. This is a subject index.

Special indexes.

These indexes list articles published in periodicals devoted to
special concerns or fields.

The Bibliographic Index. New York: H. W. Wilson Company, 1938–. Indexes current bibliographies by subject; includes both bibliographies
published *as* books and pamphlets and those that appear *in* books,
periodical articles, and pamphlets.

Book Review Digest. New York: H. W. Wilson Company, 1905–. Monthly,
cumulated annually. Lists books by author and quotes from several
reviews for each.

Essay and General Literature Index. New York: H. W. Wilson Company,
1934–. Indexes collections of essays, articles, and speeches.

New York Times Index. New York: The New York Times Company, 1913–. Semimonthly, with annual cumulation. Since this index provides dates on which important events, speeches, and the like occurred, it serves indirectly as an index to records of the same events in other newspapers.

Ulrich's International Periodicals Directory. New York: R. R. Bowker Company, 1968. 2 vols. Lists periodicals under the subjects they contain, with detailed cross references and index, thus indicating what periodicals are in the field we are interested in. Also indicates in what other guide or index each periodical is indexed, thus serving indirectly as a master index.

The titles of most of the following special indexes are self-explanatory.

Agricultural Index, 1916 to date. A subject index, appearing nine times a year and cumulated annually.

Applied Science and Technology Index, 1958 to date. (Formerly *Industrial Arts Index.*)

The Art Index, 1929 to date. An author and subject index.

Articles on American Literature, 1900–1950. Ed. by Lewis Leary.

Business Periodicals Index, 1958 to date. Monthly. (Formerly *Industrial Arts Index.*)

Catholic Periodical Index, 1930–1933, 1939–. An author and subject index.

Dramatic Index, 1909–1949. Continued in *Bulletin of Bibliography,* 1950 to date. Annual index to drama and theater.

The Education Index, 1929 to date. An author and subject index.

Engineering Index, 1884 to date. An author and subject index.

Industrial Arts Index, 1913–1957. An author and subject index, monthly, with annual cumulations. (In 1958 this index was split into *Applied Science and Technology Index* and *Business Periodicals Index.*)

Index to Legal Periodicals, 1908 to date. A quarterly author and subject index.

Public Affairs Information Service Bulletin, 1915 to date. Weekly, with bimonthly and annual cumulations. An index to materials on economics, politics, and sociology.

Quarterly Cumulative Index Medicus, 1927 to date. A continuation of the *Index Medicus,* 1899–1926. Indexes books as well as periodicals.

Indexes to Bulletins and Pamphlets

Boyd, Anne M. *United States Government Publications.* 3rd ed. New York: H. W. Wilson Company, 1949.

United States Government Publications: Monthly Catalog, 1895 to date. Washington, D.C.: U.S. Government Printing Office, 1895 to date.

Vertical File Service Catalog: An Annotated Subject Catalog of Pamphlets, 1932–34. New York: H. W. Wilson Company, 1935. Supplements, 1935 to date.

EXERCISE 45(1). Draw a diagram of the reference room of your library, indicating the position of the following reference books and indexes.

1. *Encyclopaedia Britannica*
2. *Encyclopedia Americana*
3. *Encyclopedia of the Social Sciences*
4. *Encyclopedia of Religion and Ethics*
5. *Jewish Encyclopedia*
6. *Dictionary of American History* (DAH)
7. *Dictionary of National Biography* (DNB)
8. *Dictionary of American Biography* (DAB)
9. *Current Biography*
10. *Twentieth Century Authors*
11. *British Authors of the Nineteenth Century*
12. *American Authors, 1600–1900*
13. *Who's Who*
14. *Facts on File*
15. *World Almanac*
16. *New English Dictionary* (NED), sometimes referred to as *Oxford English Dictionary* (OED)
17. *General Card Catalog*
18. *Readers' Guide to Periodical Literature*
19. *International Index*
20. *The New York Times Index*
21. *Agricultural Index*
22. *Education Index*
23. *Industrial Arts Index*
24. *The Art Index*
25. *Dramatic Index*

EXERCISE 45(2). Answer each of the following questions by consulting one of the standard reference guides listed in Exercise 45(1).

1. What occasions did the ancient Hebrews celebrate by dancing?
2. Among which tribe of American Indians is the highest development of shamanism found?
3. What was the minimum equipment of a typical "forty-niner"?
4. When and how did the expression *lime-juicer* originate?
5. How many articles on moving pictures in science education are listed in the *Education Index* for June, 1957–May, 1958?
6. Where can you find listed a scholarly article on the training of nuclear engineers, written in 1958?

7. Where can you find listed a 1945 article on the possibility of blending aralac (a synthetic fabric) with cotton?
8. Where can you find listed articles on French stained glass, printed in 1957 and 1958?
9. What was the first invention of Peter Cooper, American inventor, manufacturer, and philanthropist (*d.* 1883)?
10. What was the occupation of Frances Kyte, an Englishman (*b.* 1710)?

EXERCISE 45(3) . Write a brief paper on one of the following subjects. Be sure to answer all the questions raised. Read the prefaces or introductions to the reference works you are asked to describe, check to see how each work is organized, and make a special point of finding out how to use the works efficiently and effectively. If you have difficulty deciding what particular advantage each work has for research, consult Constance M. Winchell, *A Guide to Reference Books.*

1. Compare the *Dictionary of National Biography* and *Who's Who in America.* On what basis does each work include biographical data about an individual? Nationality? Contemporaneity? Prominence? What kinds of prominence? What kinds of information can you get about an individual in each work? Which work is more detailed? What particular research value does each have?
2. Compare the *World Almanac* and *Facts on File.* Both works are known as "yearbooks." How do they differ in methods of compilation of material? How does this difference affect the way in which they are organized? How does it determine the types of information included in each? How do you look up an item in each one? Under what circumstances would you consult the *World Almanac* rather than *Facts on File? Facts on File* rather than the *World Almanac?*
3. Compare the *Oxford English Dictionary* (OED) with the *American College Dictionary* or *Webster's Seventh New Collegiate Dictionary* or *Webster's New World Dictionary.* For illustrative purposes look up the word *kind* in each. What does each work tell you about the derivation of the word? About its history in the English language? How up-to-date is each dictionary? When would you use each one and for what purpose? What does each work tell you about the meaning of *devil* in the phrase *between the devil and the deep blue sea?* What does each work tell you about the sense in which Shakespeare meant the word *prevent?* What does each work tell you about *turbojet?* About *chemist?* About *fancy?*

46 The Research Paper

Choosing and limiting a subject.

Although your own interest in or curiosity about a topic is a good motivation in choosing a subject for your research paper, common sense requires that you choose a subject which is appropriate for research, and which you can limit in such a way that you can cope with it satisfactorily in the space and time at your disposal. It is clear that subjects developed largely from personal experience will not make satisfactory research topics since they do not require the acquaintance with library resources and the practice of note-taking which are part of the purpose of a research paper. It is clear also that topics such as "The History of Medicine," "The American Indian," or "Modern Warfare" are far too broad and general for, say, a 2,000-word paper. If they are to be made at all possible, they will have to be narrowed to such topics as "The Discovery of Anesthesia," "The Relation of the Mohicans to the Five Nations," "The Rival Claims of Types of Army Rifles in World War II," or similar relatively specific subjects.

Certain other kinds of topics will prove unsatisfactory for less obvious reasons. Some topics offer little practice because all necessary information can easily be found in a single authoritative source. Descriptions of technical or industrial processes ("The Production of Coffee"), narratives of a man's life ("Napoleon's Military Career"), or relatively simple narrative histories ("The History of Baseball") all usually fall in this group. Some topics are so controversial and complex that the time and space allowed for a student research paper are not sufficient to permit a careful weighing of evidence for both sides leading to a reasonably objective conclusion. Questions such as "Is the Supreme Court Too Powerful?" and "The Relative Merits of Federal and Local Support of Education" are of this kind.

The most satisfactory topics, then, are those which encourage you to explore the resources of the library and to develop habits of meaningful notetaking, and which give you practice in organizing and unifying information drawn from several sources. In your preliminary consideration of possible topics, you will do well to avoid topics which are too personal, too broad, too simple, or too highly complex to accomplish these aims.

Finally, it is wise to realize that choosing and limiting a topic requires more preliminary work than merely choosing a general topic you are interested in and arbitrarily narrowing it down to something you think you can manage. Unless you have already read widely about the topic you choose, you will need to begin your search for material, discover what material is in fact available in your library, and skim several articles or chapters of books before the direction you will wish to take becomes very clear to you. Even after you have made a preliminary outline and started taking notes you will still be engaged in more and more clearly limiting and defining your topic as you read. In fact, until you have made your preliminary survey of what is available about your topic, you may have only a very general sense of how you can limit it wisely.

The writer of the specimen paper which appears later in this chapter began with a rather vague idea and a hazy interest in what at the time he could describe only as "the getting into college problem." The topic took shape as he turned to the problem of finding and ordering material. In short, he had first to learn enough about his topic so that he could limit it intelligently.

EXERCISE 46(1).   If you do not have a topic which you are already interested in or curious about, and have not been assigned a specific topic, one good way to get started is to select a question and then to search out the most accurate possible answer to it. If you lack a topic, select one of the following questions and begin working on a research paper in which you will answer it—or another question to which it leads you. Use your ingenuity to discover exactly what the question means. Check the following parts of this section for guidance in finding material and getting it in order.

1. Was John Altgeld right in pardoning the Haymarket rioters?
2. Was Margaret O'Neill Eaton unjustly maligned?
3. What part did Theodore Roosevelt really play in the Spanish-American war?
4. Did Alfred really defeat the Danes?
5. How competent a general was Benedict Arnold?
6. Was Billy the Kid really a desperado?
7. Why was Joan of Arc burned at the stake?
8. Why did General Grant write his memoirs?
9. What caused the Reichstag fire?
10. How extensively did the early Algonquians engage in agriculture?
11. Was John Fitch cheated?

12. What differences are there between the poetic and historical accounts of Roland?
13. What was Theodore Roosevelt's attitude toward spelling?
14. Who was Martin Marprelate and what happened to him?
15. Was Samuel Tilden a victim of crooked politics?
16. Where did the American Indians come from?
17. How was Lincoln's "Gettysburg Address" received by his contemporaries?
18. Can a pitcher really curve a baseball?
19. What happened in the Scopes trial?
20. Why did Robert G. Ingersoll turn atheist?
21. What are the present theories on the migratory instincts of birds?
22. Was "Shoeless Joe" Jackson an unfortunate victim of circumstances?
23. Who won the Battle of Hampton Roads?
24. Was Stanton involved in Lincoln's death?
25. What happened to the settlers on Roanoke Island?
26. What was the Teapot Dome scandal?
27. What geographical knowledge did the man of 300 A.D. have?
28. Is the climate really growing warmer?
29. Was Lincoln really a good lawyer?
30. What are the plausible explanations for the statues on Easter Island?
31. Is the human race really growing taller?
32. Does the legend that Pocahontas saved John Smith's life square with the probable facts in the case?
33. Why did Thoreau go to jail?
34. Did Anne Boleyn deserve to have her head chopped off?
35. Did Fulton really invent the steamboat?
36. Did the Norsemen make voyages to America before Columbus?
37. Were Sacco and Vanzetti convicted on the basis of circumstantial evidence?
38. Who won the Battle of the Coral Sea?
39. Did Edgar Allan Poe die insane?
40. What are the reasons for the disappearance of the dinosaur?

Finding and ordering material.

1. *Bibliographical aids.*   Research begins, after your initial tentative choice of subject, with your preliminary search for material, and the preparation of a preliminary bibliography—that is, a list of articles, books, newspaper reports, or the like which you think are relevant to your subject. The sources for your preliminary bibliography are such reference works as the following:

Subject cards in the main card catalog.
Bibliographies at the end of pertinent articles in various encyclopedias.
Readers' Guide to Periodical Literature.

Appropriate special periodical indexes (*Engineering Index, Education Index,* etc.).
The New York Times Index.
Guides to reference books, such as those listed on page 384.

If you need help in selecting the most useful books from a long list, consult such aids as the following:

Book Review Digest. New York: H. W. Wilson Company. 1906 to date.
Technical Book Review Index. Pittsburgh: Carnegie Library, 1917–1929. Continued by Special Libraries Association, New York, 1935 to date.

The writer of our specimen paper (pp. 415 ff.) began to gather material with the most recent issue of *Readers' Guide* since his subject was a current one. He noted not only the articles listed under *College* but also those under likely headings to which there were cross references, such as *Attendance, Admissions,* and the like. It was not long before he discovered that there were enough articles to satisfy his needs. Resisting the temptation to rely exclusively on the *Readers' Guide,* he turned also to the *International Index* to see if anything on his subject had been published in more learned and specialized journals. Finding that there had been, he selected several other promising articles, made bibliography cards for them, and, armed with seven or eight of the most promising titles, sought out the periodicals themselves and started his preliminary reading. By the time he had skimmed through his fourth article, he had learned that American colleges were indeed facing serious problems, and that the major source of these problems was the population explosion. He learned, too, that there was much discussion of federal aid to education, of the teacher shortage, of expansion programs, and of entrance requirements.

He then went to the card catalog, looked up the subject heading *Education,* found several books listed under *Higher Education,* and took down the call numbers of several books and government pamphlets that seemed to be relevant to his research. He requested these, skimmed through the four that were available, found that two of them had material he thought he could use, prepared bibliography cards for them, withdrew them from the library, and took them home with him for more careful study. He was still not very clear about how he would work out his paper, but he knew now that there was ample material.

2. *Bibliography cards.* The writer of our specimen paper was careful throughout his preliminary search to make bibliography cards for each article, book, or pamphlet he thought he might use. Be careful to follow this procedure, even though it may seem unnecessary at the time. Failure to get all the necessary bibliographic information at the time you are consulting a book or article can cause frustrating delay and inconvenience later. Return trips to the library, time-consuming in themselves, sometimes result only in finding that a periodical is at the bindery or that a book is not available. At best, omission of a particularly useful piece of information may make it necessary to look through several books or periodicals to relocate an exact source.

The best method of keeping an accurate and useful record of your sources is to make out bibliography cards. The common sizes of cards are $3'' \times 5''$, $4'' \times 6''$, and $5'' \times 8''$. Most students prefer the $3'' \times 5''$ card for bibliographic entries and one of the larger sizes for note-taking.

Enter each bibliographic item on its own card and gradually build up a bibliographic card file on your subject. There are several different forms for such entries, and your instructor will give you complete directions if he wishes you to follow a form other than the one suggested here. The following is a common system:*

1. FOR A BOOK WITH ONE AUTHOR

> von Neumann, John. The Computer and the Brain. New Haven: Yale University Press, 1958.

2. FOR A BOOK WITH TWO OR MORE AUTHORS

> Graves, Harold F., and Lyne S. S. Hoffman. Report Writing. 3rd ed. Englewood Cliffs, N.J.: Prentice-Hall, Inc., 1965.

3. FOR AN EDITED BOOK

> Beal, Richard S., and Jacob Korg, eds. Thought in Prose. 3rd ed. Englewood Cliffs, N.J.: Prentice-Hall, Inc., 1966.

4. FOR A TRANSLATION

> Dostoyevsky, Fyodor. Notes from Underground. Trans. by Andrew R. McAndrew. New York: New American Library, 1961.

* Bibliographic forms suggested here, like footnote forms on pp. 407–409, are based on *The MLA Style Sheet.* Where MLA (the Modern Language Association) does not suggest a specific form, the form used here is based on Kate L. Turabian's *A Manual for Writers of Term Papers, Theses, and Dissertations,* 3rd ed. (Chicago: The University of Chicago Press, 1967).

5. FOR A BOOK WITH AN AUTHOR AND EDITOR

Swift, Jonathan. Gulliver's Travels. Ed. by Arthur E. Case. New York: The Ronald Press Company, 1938.

6. FOR A BOOK OF TWO OR MORE VOLUMES

Morison, S. E., and H. S. Commager. The Growth of the American Republic. 3rd ed. New York: Oxford University Press, 1942. 2 vols.

7. FOR AN ESSAY IN AN EDITED COLLECTION

Wescott, Glenway. "The Moral of Scott Fitzgerald," in The Great Gatsby: A Study, ed. Frederick J. Hoffman. New York: Charles Scribner's Sons, 1962.

8. FOR AN ARTICLE IN AN ENCYCLOPEDIA

"Universities," Encyclopaedia Britannica (Chicago, 1962), XXII, 852-879.

9. FOR A MAGAZINE ARTICLE, AUTHOR GIVEN

Peet, Creighton. "Effluent of the Affluent: Direct Legal Action Against Offenders," American Forests, LXXV (May 1969), 16-19.

10. FOR A MAGAZINE ARTICLE, NO AUTHOR GIVEN

"As School Term Ends, Campus Troubles Stay Alive," U.S. News and World Report, LXVI (May 19, 1969), 13.

11. FOR A NEWSPAPER ARTICLE

"Lum's Bid Approved on Caesar's Palace," The New York Times, August 22, 1969, p. 21.

12. FOR A BULLETIN

U.S. Government Printing Office. Style Manual. Rev. ed. Washington, D.C.: Government Printing Office, 1959.

13. FOR AN UN- PUBLISHED THESIS OR DISSERTATION	Rider, Maurice L. "Advanced Composition for Students in Engineering at The Ohio State University: Evaluation and Proposals." Unpublished doctoral dissertation. Columbus, Ohio: The Ohio State University, 1950.

EXERCISE 46(2). Select one or more of the following subjects and list all the likely sources in which you would look for (*a*) preliminary information and (*b*) periodical articles on the subject.

1. Jazz in the 1920's
2. The Early Plays of G. B. Shaw
3. The Scopes Trial
4. Hitler's Rise to Power
5. Religious Rites of the Navajo Indians
6. The Use of Hypnosis in Medicine
7. Hallucinogenic Drugs
8. The Development of Recording
9. Early Alphabets
10. The Care of Tropical Fish
11. Migratory Habits of Birds
12. Developments in Plastic Surgery
13. The Early History of the Teamster's Union
14. The Bessemer Process
15. Viking Exploration of America
16. Japanese Holidays
17. Foreign Students in the U.S.A.
18. Migratory Workers in the Southwest
19. The Development of the TVA
20. The Caste System in India

EXERCISE 46(3). Prepare a short bibliography (on cards) for one of the following topics.

1. Color Television
2. Socialized Medicine
3. The Erie Canal
4. Showboats
5. The Generalship of U. S. Grant
6. Disputed Points about the Life of Poe
7. The Assassination of Lincoln
8. The Early Career of General de Gaulle
9. Rockets and Interplanetary Travel
10. The Shakespeare–Bacon Controversy

EXERCISE 46(4).   Prepare a short working bibliography for one of the following persons and hand in a brief biographical sketch with it.

Charles Steinmetz	Louis Armstrong
Samuel Insull	Andrew Carnegie
Gamal Abdul Nasser	Frank Lloyd Wright
Tennessee Williams	David W. Griffith
James (Jim) Thorpe	George Herman Ruth
Sarah Bernhardt	Henry George
Charles Chaplin	Eugene Debs
George M. Cohan	Douglas Fairbanks, Sr.
Luther Burbank	Eudora Welty

3. *Preliminary organization.*   The processes of choosing and limiting a subject, making a preliminary search of materials available, and gathering bibliographic entries all help you bring your subject gradually into focus. As you begin to read sources, even at the preliminary stage of your research, your plan should slowly become more and more definite and clear. Try to crystallize it into some sort of outline for yourself.

Your early outlines may be quite general and will surely require considerable reworking. But they are useful as guides to let you review your own thinking about your topic, to suggest kinds of information you have and do not have, and to help you see possible patterns of final organization that you can work toward. At an early stage, the writer of our specimen paper at the end of this section had the following very general outline:

I. The problem
    A. Heavy enrollments
    B. Limited facilities
II. Solutions
    A. Building programs
    B. Federal aid to education
    C. Junior and community colleges
    D. Recruitment of teachers
    E. Televised instruction

Several days and a dozen articles and books later this preliminary outline had become the following:

I. The problem
    A. Current crisis
    B. Increase in enrollments
        1. In the 1960's
        2. In the future

II. Solutions
  A. Exploiting existing facilities
    1. At Hofstra (?)
    2. Co-op educational plans
    3. Others? (check)
  B. Building programs
    1. Costs (get figures)
    2. Federal aid
    3. Tuition
    4. Others? (check)
  C. Junior and community colleges
    1. Growth and development
    2. Present enrollment
    3. Future enrollment
  D. Recruiting teachers
    1. The teacher-salary problem
    2. Part-time teachers, retired teachers, etc.
  E. New methods of instruction
    1. Television
    2. Others (???)

Hardly a model outline and certainly far removed from a final plan. But it reflected a good deal of progress. He knew that he probably needed more information on new ways of using existing facilities. He had decided that the question of federal aid probably was best treated as a part of the problem of expanding building programs. He had discovered that teacher recruitment required discussion of at least two subdivisions. And he had realized that he had nothing on new methods of instruction except some material on the use of television. In short, a plan was beginning to emerge and he knew what more he must discover in order to determine whether the plan needed further changing and if so where.

4. *Note-taking.* Once you have finished your preliminary search to assure yourself that you have a workable subject, have established some sense of the directions you may take, and have jotted down some initial list of possible headings, you will begin to take notes on everything you read that seems at all pertinent to your topic. Do not be afraid of taking too many notes. It is much easier to lay aside notes that turn out to be superfluous than it is to return to the library to search out again sources you have already gone to the trouble of finding once.

Develop the habit of entering your reading notes on standard-size cards. They are easier to carry than a notebook, easier to refer to than full sheets of paper, and easier to rearrange as you experiment with different possible outlines. In taking notes, observe the same principles that you observed in writing out your bibliography cards: Make sure that all your notes are accurate and complete. Be particularly careful that you know the exact source from which you took each piece of information. Be <u>very</u> careful to distinguish between information which you are summarizing or paraphrasing and information which you are quoting. Place quotation marks around <u>all</u> material which you take word for word from any source. In general, force yourself to summarize, paraphrase, and record relevant facts rather than quote. Reserve exact quotation for particularly telling phrases, or for information that must be rendered precisely as you found it.

Be certain to use a separate card for each note. Do not include notes on two different subtopics in your outline on a single card. The usefulness of cards depends greatly on the convenience with which they can be shuffled and rearranged. Cards with separate notes can easily be combined when you are experimenting with arranging notes for your first draft. Cards that combine two or more notes on somewhat different items will prevent you from doing this.

The following note cards are representative of those prepared for the specimen paper included in this section. The first records exactly the quotation from which the writer draws in the first paragraph of his paper.

Harden, 430 - 431   A call to action

"Ladies and gentlemen, time is running out.
It's time that we in Michigan
develop a new sense of direction
in our thinking about education.
We have procrastinated too long."

The next card summarizes statistical information taken from a *Time* article, includes a specific quotation which the writer jotted down because it seemed potentially useful, and has a notation that the information in *Time* was based on an Office of Education announcement. The last fact not only insures that the figures are as authoritative as the writer would be likely to find, but also indicates another possible source for similar statistics which he can follow up if he wishes to or needs to.

Time, Dec. 13' 63, 76   *Enrollment Statistics*

    1963-64 record-breaking enrollment.
2140 colleges and universities - 4,529,000
students, up 7.7% over 1962-63.
    "By 1970 this population bulge
may well result in 7,000,000 collegians.
The 1980 enrollment may hit 9,000,000."
    (Information based on U.S. Office
of Education announcement.)

---

5. *Footnotes.* One of the purposes of making out accurate bibliography and note cards is to provide you with the information you will need for footnoting your research paper. Footnotes have three main uses:

a. To give information or commentary which, though related to the subject being discussed, would interrupt the flow of the narrative or argument. Some writers use this kind of note skillfully (for example, Van Wyck Brooks in *The Flowering of New England*), but there is a good deal of prejudice against it.

b. To give additional evidence or illustration in support of an assertion. For example, if you are arguing that Theodore Roosevelt was essentially a conservative, your footnote might cite one or more other writers who also think so. This device is known as the *See also* footnote, and is the vehicle for much pedantry and pretense. Readers rarely check on the "other writers."

c. To give the source of a fact or quotation.

The third use is by far the most important and most common. Though today, even in formal scholarship, there is a tendency away from the extremely heavy footnoting of earlier scholarship, accurate and honest documentation is one of the basic conventions of all research writing. Only careful and thorough footnoting can insure that you will not appear to represent someone else's work as your own, and that the interested reader can easily check the accuracy of your investigation and carry it further if he wishes.

Student research writers sometimes have difficulty determining what kinds of information require footnoting and what kinds do not. It is clear that direct quotations, charts, diagrams, tables, discussions which summarize ideas and opinions of others in your own words, and the like all require acknowledgment in footnotes. Difficulties arise principally in acknowledging opinion which the writer has paraphrased from others rather than reached independently, and in determining what is "common knowledge" and therefore does not require acknowledgment. With respect to the first, the student writer should be very careful to distinguish clearly between those opinions which he has actually arrived at independently in the course of his reading on his subject, and which therefore need no acknowledgment, and those which in fact he has paraphrased more or less wholly from a particular source and which therefore must be acknowledged. The writer should be careful to remember that ideas, interpretations, opinions, and conclusions reached by another writer are in many ways more important contributions on his part than bald facts, and therefore even more deserving of acknowledgment.

What constitutes "common knowledge" is really less difficult to determine than some students seem to feel. Any writer who reads in his subject to some depth will quickly come to see that certain kinds of facts are taken for granted by nearly all writers discussing the subject, while others are matters of dispute, or the result of special investigation. A student writing for the first time on Wordsworth may not have known when he started reading that the *Preface to the Lyrical Ballads* was first published in 1798, but he will quickly discover that everyone writing on the subject takes this as an established fact. On the other hand, the exact date at which a particular poem was written may be a matter of dispute, or at best may have been established only by someone's diligent research. Clearly, the first fact does not need a footnote; the second, equally clearly, does. In addition, common sense will tell us that specialized facts—such as the number of Polaroid cameras sold in 1963, the estimated population of Thailand in 1960, the highest recorded tide in San Francisco Bay, or the number of earthquakes in Peru in the nineteenth century—are unlikely to be "common knowledge." In contrast, the precise date of Lincoln's assassination, the birth and death dates of John F. Kennedy, or the longitude and latitude of New York are in the usual sense of the phrase "common knowledge," even though they may be far removed from the tip of your tongue at the moment. When common sense, fortified by the knowledge you have gained from your reading in a subject, still leaves you in doubt, footnote the information.

6. *Footnote form.* Footnote form, as used in professional scholarship and research, is complex and varied. Most of the forms have been evolved to meet the demands of formal scholarship designed to add to the fund of knowledge. Further, the conventions followed in reports of scientific research differ from those in the humanities and some of the social sciences. If, in your future study, you have occasion to publish research in your particular field, the vitally important thing to remember is that whatever the field, it will have its own established conventions which you will be expected to follow. You will have to consult the style of the publications in your field, study the conventions, and adhere to them exactly.

As a less experienced student, even though you are chiefly concerned with adding to your own knowledge, you are expected to adopt the habits of the professional scholar and follow an established set of conventions. The conventions described here are based on those established by the Modern Language Association, and set forth in *The MLA Style Sheet,* which has become the guide for some eighty professional journals in languages, humanities, and some areas of social science.

Unless your instructor directs otherwise, place footnotes at the bottom of the page on which the reference occurs and number them consecutively throughout the paper. In typewritten manuscript, single-space all footnotes and leave a double space between footnotes (see the specimen paper at the end of the section). Indicate the appearance of a footnote by placing a raised figure at the end of the statement to be documented. Then repeat the figure at the beginning of the footnote itself:

TEXT   of these about 100 were independent, over 10ő more were church-related, and more than 500 were public institutions.[1]

FOOTNOTE   [1] Paul Woodring, <u>The Higher Learning in America: A Re-assessment</u> (New York, 1968), p. 32.

Placing footnotes at the bottom of the page is only one of several ways of handling them. You can place all of them together on a separate page or pages at the end of your paper, or you can insert each in the text directly after the reference to it:

TEXT   "College teachers," writes Professor Seymour E. Harris, "do
not primarily seek high economic rewards, or they would not
have chosen teaching in the first place."[2] It becomes increas-

___

FOOTNOTE   [2] <u>Higher Education: Resources and Finance</u> (New York,
1962), p. 637.

___

TEXT   ingly apparent, however, that many who might otherwise have

Your instructor will tell you which of these methods he wants you
to use. In the absence of a final bibliography or list of "References
Consulted," some instructors prefer the form of the entry to include
the publisher, as below. Footnote 1 would then appear as

[1] Paul Woodring, <u>The Higher Learning in America: A Reassessment</u>
(New York: McGraw-Hill Book Company, 1968), p. 32.

The following list is based on footnote forms recommended by
the Modern Language Association. (Note that footnote and bibliography form differ.)

FOR A BOOK WITH ONE AUTHOR, FIRST EDITION

[1] Norman Lewis, <u>Comprehensive Word Guide</u> (New York,
1959), p. 129.

FOR A BOOK WITH ONE AUTHOR, LATER EDITION

[2] Ella V. Aldrich, <u>Using Books and Libraries</u>, 5th ed.
(Englewood Cliffs, N.J., 1966), p. 71.

FOR A BOOK WITH TWO OR MORE AUTHORS

[3] Harold F. Graves and Lyne S. S. Hoffman, <u>Report
Writing</u>, 4th ed. (Englewood Cliffs, N.J., 1965), p. 71.

FOR AN EDITED BOOK

[4] Charles McCurdy, ed., <u>Modern Art: A Pictorial
Anthology</u> (New York, 1959), p. 156.

FOR A BOOK WITH AN AUTHOR AND AN EDITOR

[5] William Shakespeare, "The Tragedy of King Lear," in
<u>The Complete Works of William Shakespeare</u>, ed. G. L.
Kittredge (Boston, 1936), pp. 1203-1204.

RESEARCH PAPER **46**

FOR A BOOK CONSISTING OF TWO OR MORE VOLUMES

⁶ Bernard Dorival, <u>Twentieth Century Painters</u> (New York, 1959), II, 80.

FOR A SIGNED ARTICLE IN A BOOK BY SEVERAL CONTRIBUTORS

⁷ Cleanth Brooks, "A Plea to the Protestant Churches," in <u>Who Owns America</u>?, ed Herbert Agar (Cambridge, Mass., 1936), p. 105.

FOR AN ARTICLE IN AN ENCYCLOPEDIA

⁸ "Universities," <u>Encyclopaedia Britannica</u> (Chicago, 1962), XXII, 852–879.

FOR A MAGAZINE ARTICLE, AUTHOR GIVEN

⁹ Creighton Peet, "Effluent of the Affluent: Direct Legal Action Against Offenders," <u>American Forests</u>, LXXV (May 1969), 16–19.

FOR A MAGAZINE ARTICLE, NO AUTHOR GIVEN

¹⁰ "As School Term Ends, Campus Troubles Stay Alive," <u>U.S. News and World Report</u>, LXVI (May 19, 1969), 13.

FOR A NEWSPAPER ARTICLE, AUTHOR GIVEN

¹¹ G. Milton Kelly, "Unfit Canadian Wheat Milled into U.S. Flour," <u>The Seattle Daily Times</u>, January 29, 1953, p. 1.

FOR A NEWSPAPER ARTICLE, NO AUTHOR GIVEN

¹² "Flying Saucers: Fact or Fancy," <u>Columbus Citizen</u>, August 10, 1952, p. 11.

FOR A BULLETIN

¹³ United Nations, <u>Economic Bulletin for Asia and the Far East</u>, X (June 1959), 2.

FOR AN UNPUBLISHED THESIS OR DISSERTATION

¹⁴ Maurice L. Rider, "Advanced Composition for Students in Engineering at The Ohio State University: Evaluation and Proposals" (unpublished Ohio State University doctoral dissertation, 1950), pp. 17–21.

Abbreviations. These abbreviations are customarily used in footnotes:

anon.   anonymous
art., arts.   article(s)

c., ca.	*circa* (about); used with approximate dates
cf.	*confer* (compare)
ch., chs. (*or* chap., chaps.)	chapter(s)
col., cols.	column(s)
diss.	dissertation
ed., edn.	edition
ed., eds.	editor(s)
e.g.	*exempli gratia* (for example)
et al.	*et alii* (and others)
f., ff.	and the following page(s)
ibid.	*ibidem* (in the same place)
i.e.	*id est* (that is)
introd.	introduction
l., ll.	line (s)
loc. cit.	*loco citato* (in the place cited)
MS, MSS	manuscript(s)
N.B.	*nota bene* (take notice, mark well)
n.d.	no date (of publication) given
n.p.	no place (of publication) given
numb.	numbered
op. cit.	*opere citato* (in the work cited)
p., pp.	page(s)
passim	throughout the work, here and there
rev.	revised
trans., tr.,	translator, translated, translation
v.	*vide* (see)
vol., vols.	volume(s)

Be particularly careful in your use of *ibid., loc. cit.,* and *op. cit.* Use *ibid.* to refer to the title cited in the note immediately preceding.

[1] Manly P. Hall, <u>Buddhism and Psychotherapy</u> (Los Angeles, 1967), p. 61.

[2] <u>Ibid.</u>, p. 110.

If the second note refers to exactly the same page as the first, use only *ibid.;* otherwise give the second page number. The use of the term *ibid.,* however, is rapidly disappearing. Modern practice permits the use of an abbreviated title or the author's name in a second or succeeding note.

[2] <u>Buddhism</u>, p. 110.

Similarly with *loc. cit.* and *op. cit.* It is generally easier and clearer to use the abbreviated title or the author's name. Technically *loc. cit.* means "in the same passage referred to in a recent note" and is never followed by a page number.

 [1] Manly P. Hall, <u>Buddhism and Psychotherapy</u> (Los Angeles, 1967), p. 61.

 [2] <u>Loc. cit.</u>

However, the second reference would be clearer this way:

 [2] Hall, p. 61.

The term *op. cit.* is properly used in citing a passage on a different page of a work recently noted.

 [1] Manly P. Hall, <u>Buddhism and Psychotherapy</u> (Los Angeles, 1967), p. 61.

 [2] <u>The New York Times</u>, February 5, 1970, p. 1.

 [3] Hall, <u>op. cit.</u>, p. 110.

But, as *The MLA Style Sheet* points out, you may again in such cases use the author's last name alone with the page number or the author's name and a shortened form of the title with the page number:

 [3] Hall, p. 110.

or:

 [3] Hall, <u>Buddhism</u>, p. 110.

7. *Quoted material.*

a. *The ethics of quotation.*　　Footnoting is in part a matter of manners and ethics. At best, a failure to acknowledge one's debt to others for words, facts, and ideas is a breach of manners; at worst, it is a form of theft known as plagiarism, an offense subject to legal action in the courts and to disciplinary action by a university. In the academic world acknowledgement of indebtedness is especially necessary because most researchers are rewarded for what they write not in money but in reputation.

　　Questions of what kinds of material must be footnoted have been discussed above. There remain some problems worth noting about the use of quoted material itself. The controlling principle guiding the use of all quoted material is that the original writer shall be represented as honestly and accurately as possible. Here are a few basic rules which will help you hold to this principle in handling quoted material.

1. When you quote material that is clearly not public property, acknowledge the source whether you quote it verbatim or in paraphrase.

2. Always acknowledge a direct quotation unless it can be classified as a "familiar quotation."

3. Transcribe direct quotations precisely and accurately. To omit even a comma may violate the meaning of a statement. <u>Check and recheck every quotation</u>.

4. Whenever you want to omit material from a quoted passage, indicate the omission (ellipsis) by using three spaced periods (. . .). If the omission is from the end of a quoted sentence, use four spaced periods (. . . .), the fourth indicating the period at the end of the sentence (see Section 19c). When you omit material from a quoted passage, be sure that what you retain is grammatically coherent.

5. When you wish to substitute in a quotation words of your own for the original, enclose your own words in square brackets (see Section 26f).

Even though you observe these rules, you may still be guilty of misrepresentation and deception in quoting if you are not careful to preserve the key words that indicate the <u>tone</u> of the original. Observe the following passage:

> Woodrow Wilson "was more than just an idealist," Herbert Hoover has written. "He was the personification of the heritage of idealism of the American people." He was also the twenty-eighth President of the United States, one of perhaps five or six in the nearly two hundred years of our country's history who can be, by anyone's reckoning, classified as truly great. Perceptive educator, courageous reformer, international leader, Wilson in his time was the spokesman of the future.*

The tone of the paragraph is one of praise which comes close to adulation. In quoting from the passage, you can alter the tone as well as the intent of the writer by making small changes in the original. For example, omission of the adjectives *perceptive, courageous,* and *international* in the last sentence would distort the writer's opinion of Wilson.

b. *The technique of quotation.*

1. Do not quote long, unbroken stretches of material. Such a practice puts the burden of discovering the purpose of your quotation upon the reader, or forces him to re-read the quotation in

---

*This and the examples given below are from *The New York Times,* December 13, 1959, Sec. 4, p. 10.

the light of your subsequent commentary. The <u>use</u> you make of a quotation, not the quotation itself, is your research contribution.

Make frequent use of paraphrase, or indirect quotation, whenever you do not need the precise words of the original, or when you can restate its point more briefly in your own words. Interpolate your own commentary and explanations whenever you feel they are needed.

2. When you work quoted material into a sentence of your own, be sure your words, grammar, and syntax are in logical relation to the quotation. Below are some examples of common errors in quoting material, followed by corrected versions.

INCORRECT — Woodrow Wilson was one of the five or six American Presidents who are "the personification of the history of idealism of the American people." (This confuses the statements of Hoover and the newspaper editor.)

CORRECT — Herbert Hoover describes Woodrow Wilson as "the personification of the heritage of idealism of the American people."

or — The editor describes Woodrow Wilson as one of five or six American Presidents "in the nearly two hundred years of our country's history who can be, by anyone's reckoning, classified as truly great."

INCORRECT — The newspaper declared that Woodrow Wilson was one of the five or six American Presidents that they could classify "as truly great."

CORRECT — The newspaper declared that Woodrow Wilson was one of the five or six American Presidents "who can be, by anyone's reckoning, classified as truly great."

SPECIMEN RESEARCH PAPER

The research paper presented in this section is a successful student paper. The assignment required that the student choose a topic interesting to himself, gather authoritative information about it from a number of sources, and organize the information clearly in a paper of about 2,000 words that would both report the information and make some evaluation of it. The student was also required to prepare a statement of purpose, a sentence outline, and a bibliography in proper form, and to document all evidence in appropriate footnote form. The paper reproduced here, although of course it is not an original contribution to knowledge, is a very able paper, clearly worth an honor grade in every respect. It will repay careful study. The accompanying commentary directs attention to some of the problems of writing and documentation which were faced and solved.

The format.

The title is centered near the top of the page, in capitals. The text is double-spaced, well-balanced. Two spaces (or, if your instructor prefers it, a ruled or typewritten line) separate the last line of the text from the first footnote. The footnotes are single-spaced, with a blank space between them to allow for the raised footnote numbers. Small Roman numerals are used to number the thesis and outline pages. Pages of the paper itself are numbered with arabic numerals consecutively throughout the entire paper, including the bibliography.

The title page, statement of thesis or purpose, and sentence outline.

The first three pages give a quick summary of this research paper. Notice that this prefatory material falls into three divisions: (1) *the title,* which is a very general statement; (2) *the statement of purpose,* which explains briefly what the paper attempts to do; and (3) *the outline,* which is a rather full statement of the contents of the paper. You will want to include these three divisions in your own papers.

This title page presents the necessary information in a simple, well-balanced format. Note that the information (sometimes called the "endorsement") answers five basic questions about the research paper:

1. *What* is it about?   (the title)
2. *Who* wrote it?   (the author)
3. *For what purpose* was it written?   (the course it was assigned in)
4. *For whom* was it written?   (the instructor assigning it)
5. *When* was it submitted?   (the date)

These items are not always arranged precisely as they are here; your instructor may give other directions. This title page simply presents an example of good standard practice.

The statement of purpose gives the reader an idea of what to expect in the rest of the outline. The sentence outline serves two purposes: (1) it is a kind of table of contents and (2) it is a summary, or abstract, of the paper. In a longer paper, a regular table of contents giving page references, or perhaps a formal summary, would be necessary. In a paper as short as this, the sentence outline alone serves well enough.

Note that this outline is not a *directive* outline; it is meant primarily as a guide to the reader, not to the writer. The major headings (indicated by Roman numerals) state the central ideas of the paragraphs appearing in the paper itself. The subdivisions are statements that either support or follow from the central ideas.

AMERICA'S COLLEGES FACE THE POPULATION EXPLOSION

By

Joseph B. O'Hare

English 101, Section F

Mr. Thomas Parker

June 18, 1969

Statement of Purpose:

The purpose of this paper is to show what American colleges and universities have done to meet the crisis of constantly increasing enrollments and how they are preparing for an even more critical future.

Outline:

I. The developing crisis in American education indicated a need for action.

   A. Enrollments have been steadily increasing since 1962.

   B. Applications for admission for 1964 were at an all-time high.

   C. The war-babies of the mid- and late 1940's began reaching college age in the early 1960's.

   D. It is estimated that by 1980 enrollments will have reached nine million.

II. Although special conditions sometimes make full use of facilities extremely difficult, many colleges have done a great deal with existing facilities to allow for the admission of many additional students.

   A. Hofstra College has shown that enrollments can be vastly increased through fuller use of plant and a year-round operation.

   B. The Co-operative Plan of Education makes it possible for colleges to double their enrollment.

   C. Other proposals suggest that much more can and will be done to make room for thousands of applicants--and without costly physical expansion.

ii

III. Physical expansion programs have cost billions of dollars and will cost billions more.

    A. Increased federal aid to education will help, but it must be supplemented by an increase in private support.

    B. Increased tuition rates cannot be avoided, but they will not significantly defray the costs of expansion.

IV. A significant proportion of the new college population will be absorbed by the new junior and community colleges.

    A. The number of junior and community colleges across the country is rapidly growing.

    B. Enrollment in these two-year institutions has increased significantly since the mid-1950's.

    C. It is estimated that enrollment in junior and community colleges will reach two million by 1971.

V. Much must be done to assure continued excellent instruction for college students.

    A. To attract people into the field of college teaching, faculty salaries must be made attractive.

    B. Salary increments will encourage qualified graduate students to become college teachers.

    C. Television, already in use in many colleges, can provide excellent instruction wherever there is a shortage of excellent instructors.

VI. In summary, America's colleges have done a great deal to make room for the many thousands who have sought higher education. Much remains to be done, but it is clear that America has responded to the call for action.

iii

Paragraph 1.

Text. Mr. O'Hare begins effectively by citing an authority who makes a general statement about the seriousness of the problem. In his note-taking Mr. O'Hare prepared this card:

Note that only the circled words are used in the text. Mr. O'Hare decided to omit the rest of the quotation for two reasons: first, because he wished to direct the attention of the reader to the <u>national</u> problem, not to the Michigan problem; second, because he wished to make a strong opening. Only after he has sounded <u>the call to action</u> does Mr. O'Hare indicate that Dr. Harden was addressing a Michigan audience (not to do so would be to distort the context of the statement), and then in a subordinate position that makes it possible for Mr. O'Hare to follow with the observation that Dr. Harden was also very much concerned with the national situation. Note, too, that Mr. O'Hare does not begin with *Edgar L. Harden said . . .;* he prefers, correctly, the more emphatic opening, *"Time," said Dr. Edgar L. Harden . . . .* Note, too, that he indicates ellipsis by using three spaced periods <u>after</u> the sentence period.

The second quotation is an important one. Although Mr. O'Hare is not involved here in a debate with those who would *educate the few,* he does, by implication, take his stand with Dr. Harden and those who would educate *the many.*

Documentation. Footnote 1 provides all the necessary information that does not already appear in the text. Since the name of the author and the date of the address are given in the text, Mr. O'Hare need supply only the title of the speech, the periodical in which it was published, the date of publication, and the page references. He could have used two footnotes (one for pages 430–431 and one for page 434), but decided, reasonably, that one entry could just as well satisfy the basic purpose of documentation, that of

AMERICA'S COLLEGES FACE THE POPULATION EXPLOSION

1   "Time," said Dr. Edgar L. Harden in March 1963, "is running out. . . . We have procrastinated too long." Dr. Harden
was at the time primarily concerned with the problems of
higher education in his own state of Michigan, but he made it
clear that the nation's colleges could not afford to sit still
and wait for the tidal wave that was sure to come. Nor did
he believe that the solution lay in mass rejection of "average"
applicants: "We are faced with the crucial question of who
shall go to college. The pressure of rising enrollments has
sharpened divergent views as to whether we should educate the
few or the many. It is my belief that the issue will be resolved in favor of the many."[1] Dr. Harden here defined suc-
cinctly the problem that was emerging and causing grave concern in the world of higher education. An understanding of
the process by which this crisis was recognized and defined
is essential to a proper evaluation of the approaches that
have been employed toward its resolution.

2   There was no crisis in the early 1950's, when the number
of students enrolling for degree credit had been 2,102,000.
But, although 1962-63 had been a lean year, with only a .3
percent increase in college enrollment, there was no question
that the many would very soon be knocking on the doors.[2]

[1] "It's Time . . . ," Vital Speeches, XXIX (May 1, 1963),
430-431, 434. Dr. Harden, President of Northern Michigan University, delivered this speech at the 24th Annual Citizens
Conference on Education, Lansing, Michigan.

[2] Garland G. Parker, "Statistics of Attendance in American Universities and Colleges, 1962-63," School and Society,
XCI (January 12, 1963), 5.

presenting one's sources fully and clearly. Note, however, that Mr. O'Hare does provide <u>additional</u>, <u>useful</u> information about Dr. Harden and the occasion of his address. Had he not, the reader might well have asked, "Who is this Dr. Harden, and why should we pay attention to him?"

Paragraph 2.

Text. Using the phrase *this crisis* as a transitional device, Mr. O'Hare now moves from the general to the particular, from a statement by an authority to specific evidence of the gravity of the problem. This paragraph illustrates the importance of paying close attention to the <u>date</u> of published material. Had Mr. O'Hare picked up the January 1963 *School and Society* article and stopped there, he probably would not have become aware (except through hearsay and personal experience) of important developments in the years that followed. Mr. O'Hare, however, continued looking, and succeeded in locating the <u>most recent</u> figures in the *Digest of Educational Statistics.* By gathering data for successive years, Mr. O'Hare was able to trace the developing crisis statistically and dramatically.

Documentation. Footnote 2 follows *MLA* form for first reference to an article in a periodical. Footnote 3 illustrates one of the special uses of footnotes—adding information which, had it been inserted in the text of the paper, would have interrupted the flow of the narrative. Mr. O'Hare felt, rightly, that he ought to move quickly from 1962 to succeeding years without interruption. In his first draft, the third sentence read: *The U.S. Office of Education reported that in September 1963* . . . . The revision, which relegated this information to the footnote, is more effective stylistically. Ideally, of course, Mr. O'Hare would have bypassed *Time* (a secondary source) and gone directly to the Office of Education report (the primary source). As it happened, Mr. O'Hare did look for it, but it was not available at the time, at least in his college library. A letter to the U.S. Office of Education would probably have resulted in receipt of the material, but time did not permit.

Footnote 4 reflects use of a primary source, a U.S. Office of Education report that <u>was</u> available and that brings up to date the statistics with which Mr. O'Hare is concerned. Footnote 5 is well handled. What is happening in England does not really concern us, but it is relevant and interesting information, and although it does not belong in the text, it is worthy of a few lines in a footnote.

Paragraph 3.

Text. Having presented the problem, Mr. O'Hare considers it worth while to comment briefly on a major contributing factor. The information about the G.I. Bill and the war-babies needs no documentation since it is general knowledge. Nor does it matter that many veterans did not go to college, that many never learned how to hold a baby in one hand and a book in the other, or that many war-babies did not go to college either. A research paper must be an honest and precise presentation of the best and

2

September 1963 saw 2,140 colleges and universities enrolling
4,529,000 students, a 7.7 percent increase over 1962.[3] By the
mid-Sixties the number of enrolled students had increased to
5,526,000, and a further increase to 6,300,000 was projected
for 1967.[4] It is not surprising that as early as 1964 it had
become evident that at least in some colleges the knocking
would have to be ignored. Applications for admission were up
44 percent at Ohio State, 41 percent at the University of
Massachusetts, 51 percent at Temple. American institutions
of higher learning, large and small, were filling up or full,
and there were still thousands waiting outside.[5]

3   What was happening was what had long been foretold.
There had been something of a crush when the soldiers and
sailors of World War II came home and began or resumed their
education under the G.I. Bill, learning quickly how to hold a
textbook in one hand and a baby in the other. But now the war-
babies were of college age, and behind them were their brothers
and sisters in high school, and there were only so many
teachers and so many dormitories. Where in 1948 Abilene Christian College had a student body of 1,783, in 1963 it had made

[3] "Next Year: 20% More Kids," _Time_, LXXXII (December 13,
1963), 76. _Time_'s figures were taken from a U.S. Office of
Education announcement.

[4] Kenneth A. Simon and W. Vance Grant, _Digest of Educa-
tional Statistics_, 1968, National Center for Educational
Statistics, U.S. Department of Health, Education, and Welfare,
Office of Education, Circular No. 1805 (Washington: U.S.
Government Printing Office, 1968), unpaged.

[5] "Knock on Any Door," _Newsweek_, LXIII (February 24,
1964), 85. The situation in England seemed to be no better.
"This year," reported Brian Jackson, "somewhere between 5,000
and 15,000 'qualified' candidates have failed to get a university place. Next year will be much the same." "Thousands in
the Wilderness," _New Statesman_, LXV (May 10, 1963), 700.

most authoritative information available, but it ought to be something more than a stringing together of quotes or a listing of statistics. Certainly it does not have to be uninteresting.

Note Mr. O'Hare's smooth transitions in this paragraph. In the third sentence, he brings us from the end of World War II to 1963; and in the fifth (with the emphatic *And the worst was yet to come*) he introduces the projected figures for 1980. This is good writing and good research technique. Note, too, how Mr. O'Hare establishes Paul Woodring as an authority before going on to quote him. The quotation, because it is relatively long, is quite properly indented and single-spaced, but *not* set off in quotation marks.

Documentation. Footnote 6 gave Mr. O'Hare some trouble, but he handled it well. To have used four footnotes (two for Abilene Christian College and two for the University of Maryland) would have been excessive. "The conventions of documentation," says *The MLA Style Sheet,* "are largely means to an end—enabling the reader to check you with ease—and any practice which ignores this end may result in pedantry." Note, too, the use of ellipsis (three spaced periods) to shorten the title of the 1964 almanac. Footnote 7 follows standard form for a footnote citing a published book with one author. Some instructors like to see the name of the publisher in the footnote, but probably just as many are satisfied with the inclusion of the publisher's name in the bibliography. Mr. O'Hare could have omitted the author's name in the footnote since he had cited it in the text: he has included it because he will refer to this work again later in the paper, and he will refer to it by author rather than by title. Thus the mention of the author's name in the footnote will avoid possible confusion later.

Paragraph 4.

Text. This brief transitional paragraph links the problem (presented in the first three paragraphs) and its solution. Note the use of numerals to establish clearly the four major areas of concern. It is now Mr. O'Hare's task to take them up one by one to show how each contributes to the solution of *the double problem of making room for the thousands seeking a college education and of preparing for the millions that would follow.*

3

room for 2,613 students; where in 1948 the University of Maryland had accommodated 14,000 students, in 1963 it had enrolled
25,000.[6] And the worst was yet to come. Paul Woodring, former teacher, administrator, and official of the Ford Founda-
tion's Fund for the Advancement of Education, observed:

> As we enter the last third of the twentieth century,
> some six million young Americans are enrolled . . .
> a higher number, and a larger proportion of the pop-
> ulation than at any other time in history. The num-
> ber is expected to rise to eight or nine million
> by 1980 . . . .[7]

4   The double problem of making room for the thousands then
seeking a college education and of preparing for the millions
that would follow remained a major concern of educators,
community leaders, and government officials for some time.
My research leads me to believe that the crisis in higher
education has been met in four ways: (1) through the more
efficient use of available facilities, (2) through the growth
of development and construction programs in both public and
private institutions, (3) through the addition to state systems of higher education of many new junior and community
colleges, and (4) through the recruitment of additional faculty,
the improvement of faculty status, and the introduction of
televised instruction.

5   In an effort to get optimal use of existing facilities,
several colleges radically changed the schedules of classroom occupancy. How much can be accomplished by this proce-

[6] The World Almanac and Book of Facts for 1949 (New York,
1949), pp. 384-393; The World Almanac . . . for 1964 (New
York, 1964), pp. 513-526.

[7] Paul Woodring, The Higher Learning in America: A
Reassessment (New York, 1968), p. 57.

Paragraph 5.

Text. Notice how Mr. O'Hare loses no time in getting to the first of the items he has defined for discussion: the more efficient use of available facilities. Notice, too, how he carefully supports the generalization in his topic sentence with a specific illustration, namely, the particular measures adopted at Hofstra College. Note, too, that he comments on the significance of the Hofstra report just before he introduces the author.

Documentation. Footnote 8 follows standard form for a signed article (here the author's name is given in the text) in a book by several contributors. Since Mr. O'Hare did not mention the publisher in footnote 8, he had to write *Cambridge, Mass.* to distinguish it from Cambridge, England.

Paragraph 6.

Text. Mr. O'Hare continues his discussion of item 1 by presenting another illustration of what is being done and by reporting on two proposals. He does not discuss either of the proposals at any great length because he is not writing a paper on experimental programs in American colleges. He is therefore justified in simply indicating the various kinds of proposals which have been submitted or adopted for more efficient use of college facilities.

Note how the last five words of the paragraph recall the first sentence of paragraph 5, with which Mr. O'Hare began his discussion of item 1. This is an effective device that not only ties the two paragraphs together but also indicates to the reader that discussion of item 1 is over and that we are ready to move on to item 2.

Documentation. Footnote 9 documents the direct quotation and gives further information about the cooperative plan, showing that it has been adopted by schools other than Northeastern. Footnote 10 is a reference to a source cited earlier in the paper (footnote 7); therefore Mr. O'Hare uses an abbreviated citation, mentioning only the author's surname and the pages on which the quoted material appears. The footnote could have read "Woodring, *op. cit.,* pp. 216–220" or "Woodring, *The Higher Learning,* pp. 216–220," but the form Mr. O'Hare used is that which most instructors would approve, because it is the most economical.

4

dure was revealed as early as 1960 in a report by the president of Hofstra College, John Cranford Adams:

> Hofstra is a place which has had to learn how to make efficient use of its plant. . . . Some 300 were enrolled when I went there fifteen years ago. We now enroll 8,000.
>
> We have been able to build up a campus worth about $10 million by operating with at least 65 per cent occupancy of classrooms and laboratories in an eighty-nine-hour week, when the national average is less than 40 per cent occupancy in a forty-four-hour week. Of course, Hofstra operates around the year.[8]

6   At Northeastern University, to cite another example, the "Co-operative Plan of Education" makes it possible for students to earn while they learn and for the university to double its enrollment. While one group of students is off campus, working for cooperating employers, another group is attending classes. As a result, writes James Cass, "the college can admit and graduate more students without expanding facilities."[9] An even more far-reaching solution has been proposed by Paul Woodring. Speaking of the pressures resulting from the high birthrate of the 1950's, he recommends that all professional specialization be removed from the undergraduate program, thus making it possible for colleges to grant the A.B. degree after three years of study instead of four, "and still provide twice as much time for the truly liberal studies as is now available in colleges requiring

[8] "The Hofstra Experiment for Commuters," in Higher Education in the United States: The Economic Problems, ed. Seymour E. Harris (Cambridge, Mass., 1960), p. 136.

[9] "While School Keeps," Saturday Review, XLVII (April 18, 1964), 69-70. Cass reports that some 30,000 students participate in cooperative plans at sixty colleges.

Paragraph 7.

Text. The first sentence smoothly and clearly introduces item 2. Mr. O'Hare's note cards containing the Office of Education data appear below. In his first draft, Mr. O'Hare passed on all these figures to the reader, but then decided that too many numbers all at once could very well tend to confuse rather than illuminate. Wisely, he added them all up and came out with a round seven billion, still a lot of money but a sum that can be easily understood. Then, having established the cost, he turned his attention to the critical question of where the money was to come from. He found that the Carnegie Commission on Higher Education had studied the problem and had recommended, not only more federal aid, but an increase in private support of colleges and universities.

Documentation. Footnote 11 follows standard form for a government publication bearing the name of an author (or, as in this case, two authors). Footnote 12 refers to a secondary source (*Newsweek*). Presumably Mr. O'Hare could have gone directly to the primary source (the Commission's report), but it was not available in his school library and time did not permit him to request a copy of the report by letter. Footnote 13 cites the publication referred to in the footnote immediately preceding it, and therefore the *ibid.* is justified. He could have used only one footnote, but since the two quotations are very different as well as being separated in the text, the cause of clarity is served by using a separate footnote for each.

Bokelman and Rork, p. 28
(U.S. Office of Education)
Cost of proposed campus improvement 1956-70

262 projects
Public - $85,029,000 - 48% for 1956-60
Private - $10,538,000 - 71% for 1956-60

Bokelman and Rork, p. 26
(U.S. Office of Education)
Estimated cost of buildings planned 1956-70

1956-1960: Public - $2,288,774,000
Private - 1,331,943,000
$3,620,717,000
67.4% of 1956-1970 cost

1961-1965: Public and Private - $1,313,942,000
1966-1970: " " " $318,253,000
Year not specified: " " " $121,247,000

5

highly specialized majors and offering professional training."[10] It is clear, therefore, that there are many different,
but effective, approaches to the problem of more fully
utilizing existing facilities.

7   There is no denying, however, that even with all our
colleges operating at total efficiency there is urgent need
for new facilities. The cost of new buildings and campus improvements has run into billions of dollars, and billions more
will be spent in years to come. The U.S. Office of Education
reported in 1960 that almost $7 billion would be spent during
the period 1956-70 on buildings and improvements.[11] Clearly,
some of those funds would have to come from the federal government. In December 1968, in an effort to help colleges and
universities meet the continually rising cost of education,
the Carnegie Commission on Higher Education sought more federal
funds for new school construction and student aid.

> "These institutions," the Commission said grimly,
> "now are being forced to choose among the alter-
> natives of limiting enrollments, raising tuition
> fees, postponing expansion and new programs, or
> allowing quality to deteriorate." . . . The Com-
> mission would boost Federal aid to colleges and
> universities from $3.5 billion last year to $7
> billion by 1970 and $13 billion by 1976.[12]

[10] Woodring, pp. 216-220.

[11] W. Bokelman and John B. Rork, College and University Facilities Survey; Part 2: Planning for College and
University Physical Plant Expansion, 1956-70, U. S. Department
of Health, Education, and Welfare, Office of Education, Circular No. 603 (Washington: U.S. Government Printing Office,
1960), pp. 26-28.

[12] "College for All," Newsweek, LXXII (December 23,
1968), 62.

Paragraph 8.

Text. Mr. O'Hare could have said a great deal more about tuition; his note cards are filled with all kinds of statistics and professional opinions. In a paper of this length, however, he could not possibly hope to make a full inventory; his task was to locate representative samples. Few research papers—few <u>good</u> research papers—make use of all the data collected. That much time and effort is "wasted" is not to be regretted; the search itself is valuable experience. Forcing material into a paper simply because it is there on a note card is almost as egregious a sin as distorting the material.

Documentation. Footnote 14, again, follows standard form for a government publication. Footnote 15 refers to the *Newsweek* article cited earlier, and quite correctly does so by the article title, since there is no author's name given.

6

Nathan M. Pusey and Dr. Clark Kerr of the Commission strongly
recommended that there must be, in addition to federal aid,
an increase in private support of higher education, "more than
doubling its current $9 billion a year to $21 billion by 1976,
if it is to supply just half of all college costs."[13]

8   The expectation that tuition and fees--even rising as they
have in the past decade--will contribute appreciably to the
funds available for expanding the university is shattered by
one look at the tables of revenues and expenditures released
by the National Center for Educational Statistics. Of the
total current funds revenue of the colleges and universities,
tuition and fees accounted for only 22 percent, or $2.8
billion. According to this report, "money spent for expansion
of plant assets is not generally from current funds," which
are made up largely of federal and state grants, tuition and
fees, and board and room charges.[14] At the same time that tuition and fees do not contribute to the expansion of the university facilities, their constant increase does operate to
the further detriment of the already economically disadvantaged
student. According to the Carnegie Commission report, "College
tuition, room and board, which escalate from about $1,500 a
year at a public school and approach $3,500 at a private
school, have priced out the poor."[15] Such considerations
underlay the Commission's proposal that federal aid grants be
substantially increased.

[13] Ibid.

[14] Paul F. Mertins, Financial Statistics of Institutions
of Higher Education, Current Funds Revenues and Expenditures,
1965-66, U.S. Department of Health, Education, and Welfare,
Office of Education, Circular No. 4169 (Washington: U.S.
Government Printing Office, 1968), p. 5.

[15] "College for All," p. 62.

Paragraph 9.

Text.   Mr. O'Hare now moves on to item 3 on his list: the growth of two-year institutions. Note how he provides a transition by introducing his subject as a "contrast" to the more "traditional" problems discussed in the preceding paragraphs. He supports his generalized statement by specific evidence of the rate of growth and by a breakdown of patterns of growth in particular areas of the country. He further supports his observations by quotations from Mr. Woodring, who has been established earlier in the paper as an authority, and from Mr. Gleazer, whose credentials are given in this passage.

Documentation.   Footnote 16 is a properly abbreviated reference to a work cited earlier in the paper. Footnote 17 illustrates another acceptable use of *ibid.* The page numbers must be given because they are different from the ones cited in the note immediately preceding. (Alternatively, Mr. O'Hare could have written "Woodring, pp. 32–33.") Footnote 18 is another example of a citation of an unsigned article in a periodical. Mr. O'Hare's explanation of the source for the quotation from Mr. Gleazer is quite properly included in the footnote, thereby eliminating the need for cumbersome explanations in the text.

7

9   In contrast to these traditional problems, one of the
most dramatic developments on the educational scene in the
past few decades has been the growth of junior and community
colleges. There were more than 700 two-year colleges in the
country in 1968; of these about 100 were independent, over
100 more were church-related, and more than 500 were public
institutions.[16] Speaking of these colleges, Paul Woodring
says:

> The greatest expansion of publicly supported two-
> year colleges has occurred since the end of World
> War II. California now leads the list with seventy-
> five, followed by New York with thirty-four and Texas
> with thirty-two. But these figures will soon be out-
> moded because new ones are being established at the
> rate of about fifty each year.[17]

Edmund J. Gleazer, Jr., Executive Director, American Association of Junior Colleges, speaking to a seminar of junior
college presidents and administrators, called the growth of
junior colleges "one of the great educational phenomena of
our day." He noted the 1966-67 enrollment in junior and community colleges of 1,500,000, an increase of 300,000 over
1965-66. The U.S. Office of Education predicts that some
2,000,000 students will be enrolled in these two-year colleges
by 1971.[18]

10   In spite of these encouraging developments, one of the
most difficult problems has been finding enough teachers to
staff the classrooms adequately, and finding funds to pay them
a just salary. "College teachers," writes Professor Seymour
E. Harris, "do not primarily seek high economic rewards, or

[16] Woodring, p. 32.

[17] Ibid., pp. 32-33.

[18] "Universal Community College Education," School and
Society, XCV (March 4, 1967), 139-146. Mr. Gleazer's remarks
are quoted in this article.

Paragraph 10.

Text.   Using *In spite of these encouraging developments* as a link, Mr. O'Hare now turns to consideration of item 4. The fourth sentence contains data derived from several cards (page 434). In a longer report, Mr. O'Hare would have written two or three sentences about each item; in a 2,000-word paper, however, he was wise to integrate the material into one well-structured sentence. Mr. O'Hare provides vivid emphasis for his statistics by citing Mr. Woodring's example of a typical professor's financial career.

Documentation.   Footnote 19 identifies the source by title rather than by author because the author has been mentioned in the discussion. Footnote 20 directs the reader to the seventeen pages from which Mr. O'Hare drew his information. Footnote 21 is a reference to an article in a periodical. Footnote 22 correctly documents an article for which no author's name is given. Footnote 23 is an abbreviated reference to a work cited earlier. Footnote 24 is a proper citation of a periodical article with no author.

8

they would not have chosen teaching in the first place."[19]
It becomes increasingly apparent, however, that many who might
otherwise have gone into teaching have chosen other fields
simply because teaching salaries are much lower than those in
other professions. During the next decade, American colleges
will have to make more efficient use of available faculty,
raise the student/faculty ratio, significantly add to the number of women, part-time, and retired teachers, and encourage
graduate students to remain in the profession,[20] but, most
important, colleges "will have to compete more successfully
than in the past with government, industry, and research institutes."[21] In a 1962-63 study conducted by the American
Association of University Professors, a special committee reported "continuing progress in faculty compensation levels,"
but noted that "the rate of increase . . . has declined,"
that "merit increases seem to have been fewer, and there seems
to be no immediate prospect of substantial improvement in the
unsatisfactory position of the upper ranks."[22] Here, obviously,
is an area in which much remains to be done. This is firmly
attested to by Paul Woodring, who charts the financial
progress through the years of the typical professor approaching
the end of his teaching career. Such a professor entered the
field of college teaching around 1930 at a salary not exceeding $2,000. Delayed by his return to the university to get

[19] Higher Education: Resources and Finance (New York,
1962), p. 637.

[20] Ibid., pp. 676-693.

[21] Christopher Jencks, "Will Congress Pay for Education?"
New Republic, CL (January 11, 1964), 11-14.

[22] "The Economic Status of the Profession, 1962-63:
Report on the Self-Grading Compensation Survey," AAUP Bulletin,
XLIX (June 1963), 153.

Higher Education: Employment of
Resources and Finance, p. 691 part-time teachers
"Part time teachers also offer a solution to the
shortage of college teachers" —
particularly in private urban colleges
with large
for about 2

Higher Education: Higher student/faculty
Resources and Finance, p. 677 ratio necessary.
Raising student/faculty ratio from 3 to 1
increases.

Higher Education: Employment of
Resources and Finance women teachers

Recent tren
needs to be

Higher Education: Retirement age and
Resources and Finance retired faculty

65) considered
w p. 681
be employed.

Higher Education: Inefficient use
Resources and Finance, p. 683 of faculty
Much faculty time is wasted on "non-profes-
sional tasks" such as filing, typing, etc..

Jencks, 13 Faculty salary
increases necessary
Salaries higher in other fields. Colleges
"will have to compete more successfully
than in the past with government, industry,
and research institutes. "

Paragraph 11.

Text. Mr. O'Hare links the question of present teachers and future teachers by discussing the programs designed to induce graduate students into the
field of college teaching. His generalization is supported by specific evidence
designed to show how efforts to recruit new teachers are intensifying.

9

his Ph.D., and by the Depression of the 1930's, it was not
until about 1940 that he reached the rank of assistant professor with a salary of approximately $3,000. During the
1940's, unless he was inducted into the Armed Forces, he became
an associate professor at a salary of about $4,000. In the
1950's, as a full professor, he began to earn $8,000 to $9,000.
Today he receives $13,000 to $14,000, and expects an increase
of about 6 percent a year until he retires.[23] Statistical
analysis verifies Woodring's assessment. Between the academic
years 1957-58 and 1965-66, salaries of full professors increased 60.5 percent, reaching a median of $12,953; instruc-
tors' salaries increased 48.2 percent, to a median of $6,761.[24]
The large rise in percentages does not represent large amounts
of money, however; rather it reflects the low base from which
the computations for later increases were made. Nevertheless,
the figures do represent improvement, even if they are somewhat less than competitive in an economy that bids high prices
for the well-trained and well-educated mind.

11   Programs to induce graduate students into college teaching are being worked out in several areas. Projections have
been made which indicate that there will be a need for 408,000
full-time teachers in 1973-74. This represents an increase of
61 percent over the number needed in 1963-64.[25] With these
future staffing needs in mind, the Cornell University Faculty
Committee on the Quality of Undergraduate Instruction recommended that graduate students be given "role orientation
and instruction" before they assume teaching assistant duties.

[23] Woodring, pp. 123-124.

[24] "Salaries," School and Society, XCV (October 28,
1967), 373-374.

[25] Joan Roos Egner and Douglas R. Pierce, "Inducting
Graduate Students into College Teaching," School and Society,
XCV (January 21, 1967), 55.

Documentation. Footnote 25 illustrates the citation of a periodical article with two authors, to which footnote 26 constitutes another reference. Footnote 27 is another example of the proper citation of a periodical article with no author.

Paragraph 12.

Text. Mr. O'Hare moves smoothly to the second part of item 4, the use of educational television to reach the ever increasing student population. His general introduction is followed by statistical evidence taken from a report of a U.S. Office of Education study. He makes effective use of direct quotation to summarize the importance of television for supplementing classroom teaching.

Documentation. Footnote 28 is a proper citation of a periodical article with no author. Footnote 29 gives only enough information to get the reader to the source of the quotation; the author's name and the title of the article are both mentioned in the text and so are not repeated in the note.

10

These recommendations were aimed at easing the burden of the
teaching assistant, thereby attracting more graduate students
into college teaching.[26]   Government help in the form of funds
for doctoral candidates "who show promise of developing into
good college and university teachers" has also been proffered.
The U.S. Office of Education announced that in the academic year of 1967-68 about $82 million would be set aside,
under the National Defense Education Act of 1958, to cover
the cost of 6,000 new graduate fellowships and some 9,000
awards continuing from previous years.[27]   Such efforts as
these, plus further increases in faculty salaries, should combine to make available the good minds, in sufficient numbers,
necessary to staff university and college classrooms.

12   Salary increments, however, will not alone solve the
problem of providing instruction for the millions. With the
unavoidable increase in the size of classes, many institutions
have turned to mechanical aids, particularly television, in
an effort to provide excellent instruction wherever there is
a shortage of excellent instructors. The U.S. Office of Education reported in 1967 that a larger number than ever of ETV
stations were supplementing classroom teaching in America.
There were 126 stations, among them ten new ones, capable of
reaching approximately 134,000,000 persons, including 36,000,000
of the 56,000,000 students enrolled in schools and colleges.[28]
In an article titled "Television's Role in Education," Henry
R. Cassirer said:

[26] Ibid., pp. 55-56.

[27] "Funds for Doctoral Study," School and Society, XCV
(April 1, 1967), 215.

[28] "Growth of Educational Television," School and Society,
XCV (January 21, 1967), 39.

Paragraph 13.

Text. This is a good closing paragraph. Although it does not specifically mention the four major areas of concern, it does effectively summarize all that has gone before. The first sentence recalls the first three paragraphs of this report; the second sentence brings to mind the work that has been done to solve the immediate problem; the third sentence leads to the expressed belief that the second half of the problem will also be solved. The Daniel Burnham quotation (Mr. O'Hare knew that he would use it in his conclusion the moment he saw it) echoes the call to action of the opening paragraph of this paper. In the final sentence, Mr. O'Hare looks forward to another generation, that of the grandchildren of the World War II veterans, and says, in essence, that his research has led him to believe that America's colleges are prepared to face the future.

Documentation. Footnote 30 illustrates proper citation for a secondary source. After documenting his own source, Mr. O'Hare furnishes us with Pollard's source, as given in Pollard. Since the Moore book will not appear in his bibliography, Mr. O'Hare provides a full description of the work, including publisher.

11

> When university auditoria are overcrowded, when there
> is a lack of outstanding specialists but a need that
> they be able to disseminate their teaching to a large
> body of day and evening students, television would
> seem to be the most suitable tool to adapt the scope
> and pace of university education to the urgent needs
> of the present.[29]

13   America's colleges have come to grips with the population
explosion. With the help of government, industry, and community leaders, our educators have managed to keep the doors
open. A great deal of money has been spent, and a great deal
more will be spent. There are still overwhelming problems,
but the best energies and brains of our nation have been
mobilized to solve them. America has heeded the advice of
Daniel Burnham:

> Make no little plans: they have no magic to
> stir men's blood and probably themselves will not
> be realized. Make big plans: aim high in hope and
> work, remembering that a noble, logical diagram
> once recorded will never die, but long after we are
> gone will be a living thing, asserting itself with
> ever-growing insistency. Remember that our sons
> and grandsons are going to do things that would
> stagger us. Let your watchword be order and your
> beacon beauty. Think big.[30]

In terms of higher education, America is thinking big. It is
a reasonably good bet that the children of those now knocking
on the doors will find that someone is there to let them in.

[29] School and Society, XCV (October 14, 1967), 345.

[30] Quoted by John A. Pollard in Fund-Raising for Higher
Education (New York, 1958), p. xiv. From Charles Moore, Daniel
H. Burnham, Architect, Planner of Cities (Boston: Houghton
Mifflin Company, 1921), II, 147.

Works cited.

Note first the heading, *Works Cited.* This is a more accurate heading here than *Bibliography* or *Selective Bibliography* would have been. The first would imply that Mr. O'Hare's list of books and articles was exhaustive, the second that he was listing only those sources he thought most important. The heading *Works Cited,* on the other hand, indicates that Mr. O'Hare has limited himself to listing the source material he actually used in writing his paper.

Note some special characteristics of bibliography form:

Items in the bibliography are arranged in alphabetical order by the surname of the author or, if no author is given, by the title of the work. When there is more than one author, the name of the first is reversed, with the surname given first, as usual; names of co-authors appear in normal form. If more than one work by the same author is listed, the author's name is replaced by a long dash after the first listing. (See the two works by Seymour Harris shown on page 441.) Note that the author's name is separated from the title of the work by a period rather than a comma.

Publication information for periodical articles follows the same form in the bibliography that it follows in footnotes, with commas or parentheses separating the items. Inclusive page numbers are given, even though only a single page of an article may be cited in the footnotes.

For books, the city of publication appears first, taken from the title page. (If more than one city is listed there, only the first one is used.) It is separated from the publisher's name (also taken from the title page) by a colon. The year of publication follows, separated from the publisher's name by a comma. The publication date is taken from the title page if it appears there, from the copyright page if it does not. If more than one date appears on the copyright page (as it does in revised editions), the latest one is used. Page numbers are not included in the entry.

12

WORKS CITED

Bokelman, W. Robert, and John B. Rork. <u>College and University Facilities Survey; Part 2: Planning for College and University Physical Plant Expansion, 1956-1970</u>. U.S. Department of Health, Education, and Welfare, Office of Education, Circular No. 603. Washington: U. S. Government Printing Office, 1960.

Cass, James. "While School Keeps," <u>Saturday Review</u>, XLVII (April 18, 1964), 69-70.

Cassirer, Henry R. "Television's Role in Education," <u>School and Society</u>, XCV (October 14, 1967), 345.

"College for All," <u>Newsweek</u>, LXXII (December 23, 1968), 62.

"The Economic Status of the Profession, 1962-63: Report on the Self-Grading Compensation Survey," <u>AAUP Bulletin</u>, XLIX (June 1963), 141-187.

Egner, Joan Roos, and Douglas R. Pierce. "Inducting Graduate Students into College Teaching." <u>School and Society</u>, XCV (January 21, 1967), 55-56.

"Funds for Doctoral Study," <u>School and Society</u>, XCV (April 1, 1967), 215.

"Growth of Educational Television," <u>School and Society</u>, XCV (January 21, 1967), 39.

Harden, Edgar L. "It's Time . . . ," <u>Vital Speeches</u>, XXIX (May 1, 1963), 430-434.

Harris, Seymour E. <u>Higher Education: Resources and Finance</u>. New York: McGraw-Hill Book Company, 1962.

_____, ed. <u>Higher Education in the United States: The Economic Problems</u>. Cambridge: Harvard University Press, 1960.

Jencks, Christopher. "Will Congress Pay for Education?" <u>New Republic</u>, CL (January 11, 1964), 11-14.

"Knock on Any Door," <u>Newsweek</u>, LXIII (February 24, 1964), 84-85.

13

Mertins, Paul F. <u>Financial Statistics of Institutions of Higher Education, Current Funds Revenues and Expenditures, 1965-66</u>. U.S. Department of Health, Education, and Welfare, Office of Education, Circular No. 4169. Washington: U.S. Government Printing Office, 1968.

"Next Year: 20% More Kids," <u>Time</u>, LXXXII (December 13, 1963), 76.

Parker, Garland G. "Statistics of Attendance in American Universities and Colleges, 1962-63," <u>School and Society</u>, XCI (January 12, 1963), 5-21.

Pollard, John A. <u>Fund-Raising for Higher Education</u>. New York: Harper and Brothers, 1958.

"Salaries," <u>School and Society</u>, XCV (October 28, 1967), 373-374.

Simon, Kenneth A., and W. Vance Grant. <u>Digest of Educational Statistics, 1968</u>. National Center for Educational Statistics, U.S. Department of Health, Education, and Welfare, Office of Education, Circular No. 1805. Washington: U.S. Government Printing Office, 1968.

"Universal Community College Education," <u>School and Society</u>, XCV (March 4, 1967), 139-140.

Woodring, Paul. <u>The Higher Learning in America: A Reassessment</u>. New York: McGraw-Hill Book Company, 1968.

<u>The World Almanac and Book of Facts for 1949</u>. New York: New York World-Telegram, 1949.

<u>The World Almanac and Book of Facts for 1964</u>. New York: New York World-Telegram and The Sun, 1964.

Writing

Summaries

*T*he formal summary, or précis (pronounced *pray-see*), has had a long history as a useful technique for condensing material. During the reign of Queen Anne (1702–1714) English diplomats began the practice of having their undersecretaries condense long documents in order to simplify the conduct of daily business. As a result précis-writing was established as a formal tradition in English diplomacy.

Naturally, we are not concerned here with training English diplomats, but over the years the effective summary has proved itself an extremely useful tool to many people—and particularly to college students. Often during your years in college you will need to reduce chapters of books to short, manageable statements for purposes of review and study.

Literally, the word *précis* means *cut down* or *trimmed;* making a précis is very much like trimming a bush down to its trunk and main branches: Beauty of style, illustration, and detailed explanation are all eliminated, leaving the gist of the material unadorned. Unlike a restatement or a paraphrase, a précis retains the original author's thought and approach, sometimes in his own words. The writer of a précis speaks in the author's voice—it is never necessary to say, "In this paragraph the author says. . . ." Rather you simply proceed with your condensation of his actual words.

Practice in preparing summaries will also help you to read with greater accuracy and to write with greater conciseness and directness. You cannot summarize effectively if you have not read carefully, discriminating between principal and subordinate ideas. Such discrimination, in turn, will help you to sharpen your own style and to avoid the prolixity that creeps into careless writing.

Procedure.

Before you try to summarize a passage, read it carefully to discover the author's purpose and his point of view. As you read, pick out his central ideas and notice how he arranges them. Be on the lookout for the author's own compact summaries, either at the beginning or end of a passage or at points of transition.

After studying the passage, you are ready to organize your summary. Ordinarily you will be able to reduce a paragraph—or sometimes a whole group of paragraphs—to a single sentence. Very complex paragraphs, however, may require more than one sentence.

Use a simple or complex sentence (Section 48) rather than a compound sentence to summarize a paragraph—unless the original paragraph itself is poorly organized. A compound sentence implies that there are two or more equally dominant ideas in the paragraph. If you find that you have written a compound summarizing sentence, recheck the paragraph to make sure that the author did not imply some subordinating relationship that you have missed. In determining the author's intent, be alert to such writing techniques as parallel clauses and phrases, which indicate ideas of equal weight, and transitional words and phrases, which show relationships among ideas.

Summarize the author's ideas in the order in which he has presented them, but avoid following his wording too closely. If you are overly scrupulous in trying to preserve the "flavor" of the original, you will find that your summary will be far too long. Do not hesitate, however, to pick up the author's key terms and phrases, for they are useful in binding the précis together. Discard any figures of speech, digressions, or discussions that are not essential to the "trunk and main branches." When you are all through, you should find that you have reduced the material to not over one-third of its original length.

Example.

We very rarely consider, however, the process by which we gained our convictions. If we did so, we could hardly fail to see that there was usually little ground for our confidence in them. Here and there, in this department of knowledge or that, some one of us might make a fair claim to have taken some trouble to get correct ideas of, let us say, the situation in Russia, the sources of our food supply, the origin of the Constitution, the revision of the tariff, the policy of the Holy Roman Apostolic Church, modern business organization, trade unions, birth control, socialism, the League of Nations, the excess-profits tax, preparedness, advertising in its social bearings; but only a very exceptional person would be entitled to opinions on all of even these few matters. And yet most of us have opinions on all these, and on many other questions of equal importance, of which we may know even less. We feel compelled, as self-respecting persons, to take sides when they come up for discussion. We even surprise ourselves by our omniscience. Without taking thought we see in a flash that it is most righteous and expedient to discourage birth control by legislative enactment, or that one who decries intervention in Mexico is clearly wrong, or that big advertising is essential to big business and that big business is the pride of the land. As godlike beings why should we not rejoice in our ominiscience?

—JAMES HARVEY ROBINSON, *The Mind in the Making*

Notice that this paragraph hinges on the sentence beginning *And yet most of us have opinions on all these. . . .* This sentence suggests the pattern that your summarizing sentence should probably take. The central idea of the paragraph is that we do not ordinarily take pains in forming our convictions on important matters, <u>but</u> we nevertheless express our opinions as a matter of right and even take delight in our apparent omniscience. The main clause of your summarizing sentence will express the second part of the central idea, retaining the author's ironic approach.

> We are godlike beings who delight in our ability to form and express convictions on birth control, on intervention in Mexico, or on the role of big business, without a moment's thought.

To preserve the author's qualification in the first part of the paragraph, however, you must precede the main clause with a subordinate clause.

> Although the few pains we take to understand such things as the situation in Russia, the sources of our food supply, the origin of the Constitution, the revision of the tariff, the policy of the Holy Roman Apostolic Church, modern business organization, trade unions, birth control, socialism, the League of Nations, the excess-profits tax, preparedness, and advertising in its social bearings give us little reason to have confidence in our opinions on these matters, we are godlike beings who delight in our ability to form and express convictions on birth control, on intervention in Mexico or on the role of big business, without a moment's thought.

But this "summary" is almost half as long as the original. To reduce it further, replace the specific examples with general terms.

> Although the few pains we take to understand such things as social, political, economic, religious, and medical issues give us little reason to have confidence in our convictions on these matters, we are godlike beings who delight in our ability to form and express such convictions without a moment's thought.

This summary, less than one-third the length of the original, would be acceptable for most purposes. But occasionally even a shorter summary is desirable.

> Although we have little reason to trust our convictions on the important issues of life, we delight in forming and expressing such opinions without a moment's thought.

Clearly this last sentence does not express everything in Robinson's paragraph, where the concreteness and the vigor of the short sentences are perhaps even more striking than its central thought. But a summary is concerned only with the central thought, not necessarily with retaining the author's style, and the central thought is preserved even in the shortest statement above.

EXERCISE 47(1). Write a two-sentence précis of the paragraph by Jacques Barzun, on page 227, beginning "The whole aim of good teaching."

EXERCISE 47(2). Write a one-sentence précis of the same paragraph.

EXERCISE 47(3). Try to write a one-sentence précis of the following paragraph. Does the effort tell you anything about the weakness of the paragraph itself?

Among the many interesting aspects of dietary training is the living together of the students. This allows each to get acquainted with people from all over the States and to exchange ideas and viewpoints from different sections of the country. By living in such a home, many girls grow into more mature individuals. It proves a good chance for girls who have always lived at home to become more independent. It also helps to establish feelings of self-sufficiency in those who have never before been on their own.

EXERCISE 47(4). Write the briefest précis you can of the following paragraph.

Great care and attention is given in the organization of pageants and other popular feasts, and of these a Russian crowd is particularly appreciative, throwing itself wholeheartedly into the enjoyment of every detail. The "crowd sense," which is just another expression of the corporate instinct, is peculiarly strong in Russia, and it is often curiously reminiscent of an English crowd, particularly in its broad and jolly sense of humor. But Russians of any class have a much stronger artistic sense than we have. This was so before the revolution, and it comes out in the organization of these festivals. They are all out to enjoy themselves, and anything particularly clever or pretty gets them at once. In Kiev, still as always a beautiful city on its lovely site, in the late summer of 1936, I saw a march past of all the wards in turn. They swung past with splendid vigor, squads of men or of women—one squad of women had in the middle of it a fine old man with a long beard who looked very pleased with his company. There were flowers and dancing everywhere; each ward was preceded by a dancing band of girl skirmishers in the picturesque Ukrainian costume, sometimes singing the charming Ukrainian folk songs. At one point various forms of recreation and amusement were represented: the fishermen carrying long fishing rods with colored paper fish hooped to them, the chess players carrying enormous cardboard knights, bishops, and castles. Interspersed between the detachments came curious and fanciful constructions, sometimes very ingenious; an effigy of Trotsky with long nose and black eyes and curls made an excellent Mephistopheles. It was a family feast of old and young, and we all exchanged our comments as each new surprise went past. With the usual courtesy to guests there was a chair set for me, and when I wanted to let a lady have it, I was genially told "that I had to submit to the will of the majority." At one time a torrent of rain came down, but the marchers swung past with all the more vigor and enjoyment. And so it was with the on-lookers. After several hours of it, I asked a neighboring policeman whether I couldn't go away: "No," he said very nicely, "you must stay and enjoy it." And enjoy it they certainly did, for in spite of more downpours of rain, from my room in my hotel I could hear them singing and dancing on the square outside till two in the morning. The one thing that fell below the level of all the rest was the exhausting reiteration of the portraits of Stalin and the other "big noises" of Communism. There must have been about forty of Stalin alone: one ten foot high, of the face alone. I noticed a sympathetic cheer when there came past a single portrait of Lenin.

—BERNARD PARES, *Russia: Its Past and Present*

An Index
to Grammatical
Terms

*T*his index gives brief definitions of common grammatical terms. Refer to specific sections of the handbook for fuller discussions.

Absolute.   An expression that is grammatically independent of the rest of the sentence. An absolute phrase, usually consisting of a noun followed by a participle, is often called the *nominative absolute.*

The hour being late, we hurried home.
The job finished, we put away our tools.

Active Voice.   See *Voice.*

Adjective.   A word used to describe or limit the meaning of a noun or pronoun. DESCRIPTIVE ADJECTIVES name some quality of an object: *white* house, *small* child, *leaking* faucet. LIMITING ADJECTIVES restrict the meaning of a noun to a particular object or indicate quantity or number. There are five kinds of limiting adjective:

POSSESSIVE	*my* suit, *their* yard
DEMONSTRATIVE	*this* carriage, *those* people
INTERROGATIVE	*whose* cat? *which* boy?
ARTICLES	*a* picture, *an* egg, *the* book
NUMERICAL	*one* day, *second* inning

(See also Section 4, "Adjectives and Adverbs.")

Adjective Clause.   A subordinate, or dependent, clause used as an adjective.

The man *who lives here* is an ichthyologist. (The adjective clause modifies the noun *man.*)
Dogs *that chase cars* seldom grow old. (The adjective clause modifies the noun *dogs.*)

Adverb.   A word used to describe or limit the meaning of a verb, an adjective, or another adverb. Classified by meaning, adverbs may indicate:

PLACE	Put the cat *outside.* (*Outside* modifies the verb *put.*)
TIME	He was *never* healthy. (*Never* modifies the adjective *healthy.*)
MANNER	She was *secretly* envious. (*Secretly* modifies the adjective *envious.*)
DEGREE	I was *quite* easily angered. (*Quite* modifies the adbverb *easily.*)

(See also Section 4, "Adjectives and Adverbs.")

Adverb Clause. A subordinate, or dependent, clause used as an adverb.

When you leave, please close the door. (The adverb clause, indicating time, modifies the verb *close.*)

The sheep grazed *where the grass was greenest.* (The adverb clause, indicating place, modifies the verb *grazed.* Adverb clauses also indicate manner, purpose, cause, result, condition, concession, and comparison.)

Adverbial Objective. A noun used adverbially.

While they walked *home,* I ran a *mile.*

Agreement. Correspondence in person and number between a subject and verb; in person, number, and gender between a pronoun and its antecedent; and in number between a demonstrative adjective and its noun. (See also Section 8, "Agreement.")

Antecedent. A word or group of words for which a pronoun stands.

She is a *woman who* seldom complains. (*Woman* is the antecedent of the pronoun *who.*)

Uncle Henry came for a brief visit, but *he* stayed all winter. (*Uncle Henry* is the antecedent of the pronoun *he.*)

Appositive. A substantive (a word or group of words used as a noun) placed beside another substantive and denoting the same person or thing.

John, my younger *brother,* is visiting in *Albany,* the state *capital.* (*Brother* is in apposition with *John,* and *capital* is in apposition with *Albany.*)

Most appositives are NONRESTRICTIVES (i.e., not essential to the basic meaning of the sentence) and so are set off with commas. RESTRICTIVE appositives limit the meaning of the sentence and are not set off with commas.

NONRESTRICTIVE   Tom Edison, *the inventor,* often worked sixteen hours a day.

RESTRICTIVE   The *inventor* Edison often worked sixteen hours a day.

Article. The articles *a, an,* and *the* are usually classed as adjectives. The definite article is *the.* The indefinite articles are *a* and *an.* They indicate that a noun follows.

Auxiliary. A "helping verb," used to make the form of another verb. The common auxiliaries are *be* (and its various forms), *have, shall, will, should, would, may, can, might, could, must, ought,* and *do.*

I *am* studying. He *may* return. You *must* leave.

Case.   The inflectional form of nouns and pronouns showing their relation to other words in the sentence. In English the three cases are nominative (*boy, I*), possessive (*boy's, my*), and objective (*boy, me*). Only personal pronouns have different forms for the objective case. (See also Section 2, "Case.")

Clause.   A grammatical unit containing a subject and verb. Clauses are of two kinds: main or independent, and subordinate or dependent. A MAIN CLAUSE makes an independent assertion.

When the moon shone, *the dog barked.*

A SUBORDINATE CLAUSE is used as a noun, adjective, or adverb and is dependent on some other element in the sentence.

When the moon shone, the dog barked. (The subordinate clause is adverbial.)

That he would survive was doubtful. (The subordinate clause is the subject of the verb *was.*)

(See also Section 1, "Sentence Sense.")

Collective Noun.   A noun naming a collection or aggregate of individuals by a singular form (as *assembly, army, jury*). Collective nouns are followed by a singular verb when the group is thought of as a unit, and a plural when the component individuals are in mind; as, the majority *decides;* the majority *were* slaves.

Common and Proper Nouns.   A COMMON NOUN names the general class to which a person, place, or thing belongs, as *man, country, state, river, ocean, dog, pencil, beauty.* A PROPER NOUN, on the other hand, distinguishes an individual person, place, or thing, as *Wallace, Europe, Massachusetts, Amazon, Atlantic, Rover, Parker, Beethoven's Fifth.*

Comparison.   A term used to describe the changes in the forms of adjectives or adverbs to show degrees of quality or quantity. The three degrees are positive, comparative, and superlative.

POSITIVE	COMPARATIVE	SUPERLATIVE
loud	louder	loudest
bad	worse	worst
slowly	more slowly	most slowly

Complement.   A term used to describe the word or words that complete the meaning of a verb. A complement may be a DIRECT OBJECT, as

The sexton rang the *bell.*

An INDIRECT OBJECT, as

Give *me* the dollar.

A PREDICATE NOUN (as SUBJECTIVE COMPLEMENT), as

Harry is a *baker*.

A PREDICATE NOUN (as OBJECTIVE COMPLEMENT), as

We made him our *secretary*.

A PREDICATE ADJECTIVE (as SUBJECTIVE COMPLEMENT), as

The man was *silent*.

A PREDICATE ADJECTIVE (as OBJECTIVE COMPLEMENT), as

Tom painted the fence *white*. (The adjective *white*, modifying the direct object *fence*, is also called the OBJECTIVE COMPLEMENT.)

An INFINITIVE, as

We had George *cook* pancakes.

Conjugation.   A term used to describe the changes in the inflectional forms of a verb to show tense, voice, mood, person, and number.

Conjunction.   A word used to connect words, phrases, and clauses. Conjunctions are of two kinds: coordinating and subordinating. COORDINATING CONJUNCTIONS (*and, but, or, nor, for*, etc.) join words, phrases, or clauses of equal grammatical rank. SUBORDINATING CONJUNCTIONS (*after, as, because, if, when*, etc.) join subordinate clauses with main clauses. (See also *Correlative Conjunctions* and Section 35, "Parallelism.")

Conjunctive Adverb.   An adverb used to join main clauses in a sentence. Common conjunctive adverbs are *also, besides, consequently, furthermore, however, likewise, moreover, nevertheless, then, thus*.

Coordinate.   Having equal rank, as two main clauses in a compound sentence.

Copula (Copulative Verb).   See *Linking Verb*.

Correlative Conjunctions.   Conjunctions used in pairs to join sentence elements of equal rank. Common correlatives are *either . . . or, neither . . . nor, not only . . . but also*.

Declension. See *Inflection* and *Case*.

Direct Address. A noun or pronoun used parenthetically to point out the person addressed, sometimes called NOMINATIVE OF ADDRESS or VOCATIVE.

> *George,* where are you going?
> I suppose, *gentlemen,* that you enjoyed the lecture.

Direct and Indirect Quotations. A direct quotation is an exact quotation of a speaker's or writer's words (sometimes called direct discourse). In indirect discourse the speaker's or writer's thought is summarized without direct quotation.

> DIRECT   He said, "I must leave on the eight o'clock shuttle."
> INDIRECT   He said that he had to leave on the eight o'clock shuttle.

Direct Object. See *Object* and *Complement*.

Elliptical Expression. An ellipsis is an omission of words necessary to the grammatical completeness of an expression but assumed in the context. The omitted words in elliptical expressions may be supplied by the reader or hearer.

> He is older than I (am).
> Our house is small, his (house is) large.

Expletive. The word *it* or *there* used to introduce a sentence in which the subject follows the verb.

> *It* is doubtful that he will arrive today. (The clause *that he will arrive today* is the subject of the verb *is.*)
> *There* are two ways of solving the problem. (The noun *ways* is the subject of *are.*)

Finite Verb. A verb form that makes an assertion about its subject. Verbals (infinitives, participles, gerunds) are not finite forms.

Gender. The classification of nouns and pronouns as masculine (*man, he*), feminine (*woman, she*), and neuter (*desk, it*). Some English nouns have special forms to indicate gender: *salesman, saleswoman; hero, heroine.*

Genitive Case. The possessive case. (See Section 2, "Case.")

Gerund. A verbal used as a noun. Gerunds, which end in *-ing,* have the functions of nouns, such as subject or object of a verb.

> *Fishing* is a bore, but I like *hiking.*

Idiom. An expression established by usage and peculiar to a particular language. Many idioms have unusual grammatical construction and make little sense if taken literally. Examples of English idioms are *by and large, catch a cold, have a try at, look up an old friend.*

Independent Clause. See *Clause.*

Independent Element. An expression that has no grammatical relation to other parts of the sentence. (See *Absolute.*)

Indirect Discourse. See *Direct and Indirect Quotations.*

Infinitive. A verbal usually preceded by *to* and used as a noun, adjective, or adverb.

NOUN	*To swim* is relaxing. (Subject.)
	We didn't dare (to) *leave.* (Object.)
	(*To* is usually omitted in infinitives after *dare, hear, make, see,* and some other verbs.)
ADJECTIVE	I have nothing *to say.* (*To say* modifies the noun *nothing.*)
	There is no time *to waste.*
ADVERB	We were ready *to begin.* (*To begin* modifies the adjective *ready.*)
	He came *to inspect* the house. (*To inspect* modifies the verb *came.*)

Inflection. Variation in the form of words to show changes in meaning or to indicate case (*he, him*), gender (*aviator aviatrix*), number (*man, men*), tense (*walk, walked*), etc. DECLENSION is the inflection of nouns and pronouns; CONJUGATION the inflection of verbs; and COMPARISON the inflection of adjectives and adverbs.

Interjection. A word used to express emotion. An interjection is grammatically independent of other words in the sentence.

Oh, you startled me.
Ouch! You are stepping on my foot.

Intransive Verb. See *Verb.*

Irregular Verb. See *Strong Verb.*

Linking Verb. A verb that shows the relation between the subject of a sentence and an adjective or a noun in the nominative case. The chief linking verbs are *be, become, appear, seem,* and the verbs pertaining to the senses (*look, smell, taste, sound, feel*).

He *seems* timid.   The cake *tastes* sweet.   He *is* a thief.

Modification.   Describing or limiting the meaning of a word or group of words. Adjectives and adjective phrases or clauses modify nouns; adverbs and adverb phrases or clauses modify verbs, adjectives, or adverbs. (See also Section 4, "Adjectives and Adverbs.")

Mood.   The form of the verb used to show how the action is viewed by the writer or speaker. English has three moods: indicative, imperative, and subjunctive.

The INDICATIVE MOOD states a fact or asks a question.

> The wheat *is* ripe. *Is* breakfast ready?

The IMPERATIVE MOOD expresses a command or request.

> *Report* to the office at once. Please *give* me your attention.

The SUBJUNCTIVE MOOD expresses doubt, supposition, concession, probability, a condition contrary to fact, a regret, or wish.

> The grass looks as if it *were* dying.
> I wish that he *were* more congenial.

(See also Section 3, "Tense and Mood.")

Nonrestrictive Modifier.   A modifying phrase or clause that is not essential to pointing out or identifying the person or thing modified. Nonrestrictive modifiers are set off with commas.

> Mr. Smith, *who was watching from the window,* saw the boys stealing the apples.
> The *Prentice-Hall Handbook for Writers,* which is in its fifth edition, was first published in 1951.

Noun.   A word used to name a person, place, or thing. A COMMON NOUN names any one of a class of persons, places, or things.

> *man, table, valley, carrot*

A PROPER NOUN names a specific person, place, or thing.

> *Stephen, Kansas, Canada, Labor Day, Last Supper*

A COLLECTIVE NOUN names a group by using a singular form.

> *committee, herd, jury*

A CONCRETE NOUN names something that can be perceived by the senses.

house, lake, flower

An ABSTRACT NOUN names an idea or quality.

hope, tragedy, kindness

Noun Clause. A subordinate clause used as a noun.

What I saw was humiliating. (Subject.)
I shall accept *whatever he offers.* (Object of the verb.)
We will be ready for *whatever happens.* (Object of the preposition *for.*)

Number. The form of a noun, pronoun, verb, or demonstrative adjective to indicate one (*singular*) or more than one (*plural*).

Object. A word, phrase, or clause that is affected by the action of a transitive verb. A DIRECT OBJECT receives directly the action of a transitive verb.

I followed *him.*
You may keep *whatever you find.*

An INDIRECT OBJECT receives indirectly the action of a transitive verb.

Give *me* the money. (*Money* is the direct object of *give; me* is the indirect object.)

The OBJECT OF A PREPOSITION is a substantive that follows the preposition.

We sat on the *porch.* (*Porch* is the object of *on.*)
The horse galloped across the *meadow.* (*Meadow* is the object of *across.*)

Objective Complement. See *Complement.*

Parenthetical Expression. An inserted expression that interrupts the thought of a sentence. Parenthetical items are set off by commas, dashes, or parentheses.

His failure, *I suppose,* was his own fault.
I shall arrive—*this will surprise you*—on Monday.
The old seaman (*actually he was only forty*) loved children.

Parse. To analyze the function of a word or group of words in a sentence.

Participle. A verbal used as an adjective. Though a participle cannot make an assertion, it is derived from a verb and can take an object and be modified by an adverb. As an adjective, a participle can modify a noun or pronoun. The present participle ends in *-ing: running, seeing, trying.* The past participle ends in *-d, -ed, -t, -n, -en,* or changes the vowel: *walked, lost, seen, rung.*

Parts of Speech. The classification of words on the basis of their function in the sentence. The eight parts of speech are: noun, pronoun, adjective, verb, adverb, preposition, conjunction, and interjection. Each of these is discussed in this "Index to Grammatical Terms."

Passive Voice. See *Voice.*

Person. The form of a pronoun and verb used to indicate the speaker (first person—*I am*); the person spoken to (second person—*you are*); or the person spoken about (third person—*he is*).

Phrase. A group of related words lacking both subject and predicate and used as a noun, adjective, adverb, or verb. On the basis of their form, phrases are classified as PREPOSITIONAL, PARTICIPIAL, GERUND, INFINITIVE, and VERB phrases.

PREPOSITIONAL	We walked *across the street.* (Adverb)
PARTICIPIAL	The man *entering the room* is my father. (Adjective)
GERUND	*Washing windows* is tiresome work. (Noun)
INFINITIVE	*To see the sunset* was a pleasure. (Noun)
VERB	He *has been educated* in Europe. (Verb)

Predicate. The part of a sentence or clause that makes a statement about the subject. The predicate consists of the verb and its complements and modifiers.

Preposition. A word used to relate a noun or pronoun to some other word in the sentence. A preposition and its object form a prepositional phrase.

The sheep are *in* the meadow.

He dodged *through* the traffic.

Principal Clause. A main or independent clause. See *Clause.*

Principal Parts. The three forms of a verb from which the various tenses are derived.

PRESENT INFINITIVE	PAST TENSE	PAST PARTICIPLE
join	joined	joined
go	went	gone

(See also Section 3, "Tense and Mood.")

Progressive. The form of the verb used to describe an action occurring, but not completed, at the time referred to.

I *am studying.* (Present progressive.)
I *was studying.* (Past progressive.)

Pronoun. A word used in place of a noun. The noun for which a pronoun stands is called its ANTECEDENT. (For a discussion of the relation of pronouns and antecedents, see Section 8, "Agreement.") Pronouns are classified as follows:

PERSONAL	*I, you, he, she, it,* etc. (See the declension in Section 2, "Case.")
RELATIVE	*who, which, that* I am the man *who* lives here. We saw a barn *that* was burning.
INTERROGATIVE	*who, which, what* *Who* are you? *Which* is your book?
DEMONSTRATIVE	*this, that, these, those*
INDEFINITE	*one, any, each, anyone, somebody, all,* etc.
RECIPROCAL	*each other, one another*
INTENSIVE	*myself, yourself, himself,* etc. I *myself* was afraid. You *yourself* must decide.
REFLEXIVE	*myself, yourself, himself,* etc. I burned *myself.* You are deceiving *yourself.*

Regular Verb. See *Weak Verb.*

Relative Clause. A clause introduced by a relative pronoun.

Restrictive Modifier. A modifying phrase or clause that is essential to pointing out or identifying the person or thing modified. Restrictive modifiers are not set off with punctuation marks.

People *who live in glass houses* shouldn't throw stones.
The horse *that won the race* is a bay mare.

(See also *Nonrestrictive Modifier.*)

Sentence. A group of words expressing a unit of thought and normally containing a subject and predicate. Sentences are classified on the basis of their form as simple, compound, complex, or compound–complex. A SIMPLE SENTENCE has one main clause. Either the subject or the verb may be compound.

The students demonstrated. The boys and girls played tag.

A COMPOUND SENTENCE has two or more main clauses.

He flew to Aspen, but I drove to Stowe.

A COMPLEX SENTENCE has one main clause and one or more subordinate clauses.

The burglars ran when they heard the police coming.

A COMPOUND–COMPLEX SENTENCE has two or more main clauses and one or more subordinate clauses.

He seized the reins, and the horses reared because they were frightened.

Sentences are classified on the basis of their meaning as declarative, interrogative, imperative, and exclamatory. A DECLARATIVE SENTENCE states or asserts something.

John smiled. The crowd cheered.

An INTERROGATIVE SENTENCE asks a question.

Where are you going? Why are you going there?

An IMPERATIVE SENTENCE expresses a request or command.

Please pass the bread. Don't eat those grapes.

An EXCLAMATORY SENTENCE expresses strong emotion and is followed by an exclamation point.

What a temper he has! I will not go!

Strong Verb.   A verb that forms its past and past participle by a vowel change or by other individual spelling changes. (See Sections 3 and 3d.)

begin, began, begun; spring, sprang, sprung.

Subject.   The person or thing about which the predicate of a sentence or clause makes an assertion.

Subjective Complement.   See *Complement.*

Substantive.   A word or group of words used as a noun. Substantives include pronouns, infinitives, gerunds, and noun clauses.

Substantive Clause.   A subordinate clause used as a noun. See *Noun Clause.*

Syntax.   The relationship between words in a sentence.

Tense.   The time or the state of the action expressed by a verb. (For a discussion of verb tenses, see Section 3, "Tense and Mood.")

Verb.   A word or phrase used to assert an action or state of being. A TRANSITIVE VERB is one that takes an object.

Jack *whistled* a gavotte.

An INTRANSITIVE VERB is one that does not require an object.

The wind *whistled.*

Some verbs may be either transitive or intransitive.

The whistle *blew.* (Intransitive.)
The referee *blew* the whistle. (Transitive.)

(See also *Finite Verb; Strong Verb; Weak Verb; Verbal.*)

Verbal.   A word derived from a verb but used as a noun or adjective (or sometimes as an adverb). See separate entries from the three verbals: *Gerund, Infinitive,* and *Participle.*

Vocative.   See *Direct Address.*

Voice.   The property of a verb that shows whether the subject acts (ACTIVE VOICE) or is acted upon (PASSIVE VOICE).

ACTIVE   Ed *is taking* a walk.
PASSIVE   A walk *is being taken* by Ed.
ACTIVE   Grace *bought* some flowers.
PASSIVE   Some flowers *were* bought by Grace.

Weak Verb.   Also called a REGULAR VERB. A verb that forms its past and past participle by adding *-d, -ed,* or *-t* to the infinitive: *move, moved, moved; kneel, knelt, knelt.*

Index

A

a, an, 338
Abbreviations, 102–103
  of countries, states, 103
  with dates, 102
  of firm names, 103
  in footnotes, 409–410
  in formal writing, 102
  Latin, 103
  of months, days, 103
  with numerals, 102–103
  of personal names, 103
  of *street,* 103
  of titles, with proper names, 102
  of *volume, chapter, page,* 103
above, 338
Absolute, defined, 450
absolve by, from, 320
Abstract noun, defined, 457
accede to, 315
accept, except, 338
accompany by, with, 315
Accusative case (see *Objective case*)
acquitted of, 315
Active voice, 40–41
  for emphasis, 267–268
  paradigm, 40
  (see also *Voice*)
ad, for *advertisement,* 339
adapted to, from, 315
Adjective clauses:
  defined, 450
  diagramed, 53
  as modifiers, 31
  position of, 81
  restrictive and nonrestrictive,
    punctuation of, 123–124
Adjective phrases, 29
  diagramed, 53
Adjectives:
  distinguished from adverbs, 46–
    49

Adjectives (*cont.*)
  articles as (see *Articles*)
  comparative form of, 27–28, 48–
    49
  demonstrative, 450
  descriptive, 450
  function of, 27–28
  logically incomparable, 48
  interrogative, 450
  limiting, 450
  after linking verbs, 28
  numerical, 450
  possessive, 450
  predicate, 28
  proper, capitalization of, 148
  in series, punctuation with, 128–
    129
  superlative form of, 48–49
admit to, of, 315
Adverb clauses:
  defined, 451
  diagramed, 54
  function of, 31
  punctuation of, 116–117
Adverb phrases, 29–30
  diagramed, 53
Adverbial objective, defined, 451
Adverbs:
  distinguished from adjectives,
    45–49
  comparative forms of, 48–49
  conjunctive, 116–117
  defined, 450
  function of, 27–28
  position of, 79
  misplacement of, 79
  superlative forms of, 48–49
affect, effect, 339
aggravate, 339
agree to, with, in, 315, 339
Agreement, 64–69
  defined, 451
  (see also *Agreement of pronoun and
    antecedent; Agreement of subject
    and verb*)

Cause and effect:
  explanation of, in paragraph development, 203, 212, 219–220
  relationships, 280–282
cf., 410
ch., chs., 410
Chronological order in paragraphs, 210–211
Circumlocution, 321–322
cite, site, 366
Clauses:
  adjective, 31 (see also *Adjective clauses*)
  adverb, 31 (see also *Adverb clauses*)
  defined, 452
  dependent (see *Subordinate clauses*)
  diagramed, 52–55
  independent (see *Main clauses*)
  main, 32 (see also *Main clauses*)
  misplacement of, 79–80
  noun, 31, 457 (see also *Noun clauses*)
  principal (see *Main clauses*)
  relative, 459
  substantive (see *Noun clauses*)
Clichés, 330–331
Clipped forms (see *ad*)
clothes, cloths, 366
Coherence in paragraphs, 196–205
  through logical order of sentences, 197–198
  through consistent point of view, 200
  through parallel grammatical structure, 200–201
  through repetition of key words and phrases, 201–202
  through use of transitional markers, 203–205
Coined words, 311
col., cols., 410
Collective nouns:
  choice of pronoun with, 68
  choice of verb with, 66
  defined, 452, 456
Colloquial usage, 14–15, 298–299
  defined, 15, 337

Colons:
  after *as follows* or *the following,* 131
  before appositive or summary, 131
  capitalization with, 117
  position outside quotation marks, 139
  before long quotations, 140
  to separate main clauses, 117
Comma splice, 62–63
Commas:
  to set off appositives, 124–125
  to set off contrasted elements, 120–121
  with coordinate adjectives, 128–129
  with dates, addresses, geographical names, 129
  to set off mild interjections, 125
  after introductory clauses and phrases, 119–120
  with items in a series, 127–129
  to separate main clauses, 115–116
  to prevent misreading, 132
  to set off nonrestrictive elements, 123–125
  overuse, 132–134
  to set off parenthetical expressions, 126
  position outside quotation marks, 140
  superfluous, 132–134 (see also *Superfluous commas*)
  to set off transitions, 126
  to set off words in direct address, 125
Common noun, defined, 452, 456
Comparative form:
  of adjectives, 27–28, 48–49, 452
  of adverbs, 48–49, 452
Comparison:
  and contrast in paragraph development, 215–217
  defined, 452
  illogical, 92
  incomplete, 92–93

D

O

1 SENTENCE SENSE = SS	**2 CASE = CA**
1a Sentence recognition 1b Parts of speech 1c Phrases 1d Clauses	2a Nominative 2b Possessive 2c Objective

6 SENTENCE FRAGMENT = FRAG	**8 FAULTY AGREEMENT =**
7 COMMA SPLICE = CS or CF, **FUSED SENTENCE = FS** 7a Comma splice 7b Fused sentence	8a Subject, verb in number 8b Pronoun, antecedent 8c Demonstrative adjective, nou

11 MISPLACED PARTS = MIS PT	**12 DANGLING** **CONSTRUCTIONS = DG**
11a Adverbs (almost, only, etc.) 11d "Squinting" modifiers 11b Modifying phrases 11e Split infinitives 11c Modifying clauses 11f Awkward separation	12a Participles 12b Gerunds 12c Infinitives 12d Elliptical clauses

15 MANUSCRIPT FORM = MS	**16 NUMBERS = NOS**
15a Materials 15d Proofreading 15b Legibility 15e Corrections 15c Arrangement	16a Spelled out 16b Dates 16c Street numbers, decimals, et
 16d In ()'s 16e At beginning of sentence

19 END PUNCTUATION = END P	**20 MAIN CLAUSES**
19a Assertions, commands 19e Use of (?) 19b After abbreviations 19f Indirect question 19c Ellipsis 19g Emotional statement 19d The question mark 19h Overuse of !	20a With coordinating conjunctic 20b Without coordinating conjun
 20c With conjunctive adverb 20d With amplifying clause

23 ITEMS IN A SERIES	**24 FINAL APPOSITIVES** **AND SUMMARIES**
23a Coordinate series 23b Coordinate adjectives 23c Dates, addresses, etc. 23d Use of semicolon	24a Short final summary 24b Long or formal summary

27 ITALICS	**28 CAPITALS**
27a Titles 27d Foreign words 27b Names of ships, etc. 27e Special stress 27c Letters, words, numbers 27f Overuse	28a First word of sentence 28b I and O 28c Proper nouns and derivatives 28d Unnecessary

31 WHOLE COMPOSITION = PLAN	**PARAGRAPH UNITY = ¶ UN**
31a Selecting subject 31f Beginning 31b Limiting subject 31g Rough draft 31c Preliminary notes 31h Ending 31d Thesis statement 31i Second draft 31e Complete outline 31j Final revisions	32a Topic sentence 32b Keeping to subject

33 SUBORDINATION = SUB	**34 VARIETY = VAR**

33a And sentences 33e Upside-down
33b Omission of logical   subordination
    steps 33f Primer style
33c Miscellaneous facts 33g Excessive subordination
33d Coordination of 33h Misuse of conjunctions
    logical unequals
	34a Short simple sentences
	34b Long compound sentences
	34c Varied sentence structure

37a Defining terms	37b Support for generalizations

40 EXACTNESS = EX	**41 DIRECTNESS = DIR**
40a Near synonyms 40f Elegant variation 40b Near homonyms 40g Idiomatic usage 40c Invented words 40h Specific vs. general 40d Improprieties words 40e Meaning of suffixal 40i Omnibus words forms	41a Eliminating deadwood 41b Inexact words 41c Redundancy 41d Awkward repetition 41e Needless complexity